AF290962

Imperial Rule in India

Imperial Rule in India

Paternal Governance and Conquest under the Lawrences and Montgomery

Jonathan Orr

First published in Great Britain in 2026 by
Pen & Sword History
An imprint of Pen & Sword Books Limited
Yorkshire – Philadelphia

ISBN 978 1 03614 224 7

A CIP catalogue record for this book is
available from the British Library.

Typeset by Mac Style
Printed in the UK by CPI Group (UK) Ltd, Croydon, CR0 4YY.

The Publisher's authorised representative in the EU for product
safety is Authorised Rep Compliance Ltd., Ground Floor,
71 Lower Baggot Street, Dublin D02 P593, Ireland.
www.arccompliance.com

For a complete list of Pen & Sword titles please contact

PEN & SWORD BOOKS LIMITED
47 Church Street, Barnsley, South Yorkshire, S70 2AS, England
E-mail: enquiries@pen-and-sword.co.uk
Website: www.pen-and-sword.co.uk
or
PEN AND SWORD BOOKS
1950 Lawrence Road, Havertown, PA 19083, USA
E-mail: uspen-and-sword@casematepublishers.com
Website: www.penandswordbooks.com

For Shruti and Jude

We cannot expect to hold India forever. Let us so conduct ourselves in our civil and military relations as when the connexion ceases, it may do so, not with convulsions, but with mutual esteem and affection; and that England may then have in India a noble ally, enlightened, and brought into the scale of nations under her guidance and fostering care.*

Henry Montgomery Lawrence

---

* H. M. Lawrence, Military Defence of our Empire in the East, *The Calcutta Review*, Vol. 2, Oct–Dec 1844, p. 72.

Contents

Acknowledgements ix
List of Images xi
Glossary of Indian and Anglo-Indian terms xiii
Maps xvii
Prologue: 'Will you be governed by the Pen or the Sword?' xix

Introduction: 'The Titans of the Punjab'? 1

Imperial Connections 9

Education and Training 17

First Impressions: Calcutta in Regency Times 28

Part I: Life in the Mofussil: The Origins of Paternal Governance 39

The 'confounded zeal' of Henry Lawrence, Revenue Surveyor 1833–38 41

'Cutcherry on Horseback': John Lawrence and the Making of a Sahib-Zillah 1831–46 61

'The active and judicious measures' of Robert Montgomery, Collector and Magistrate 1829–49 94

Part II: Conquest and Loss – George and Henry Lawrence's Afghan War 127

The Great Game 129

The Army of the Indus 136

Political Agent at Ferozepur 145

The Rising 152

Retreat from Kabul   169

Captivity and Deliverance   176

Nepalese Sojourn   189

Epilogue   210
Notes   215
Abbreviations   244
Bibliography   245
Index   254

Acknowledgements

The origins of this book can be traced back to my early travels in India and Pakistan where I first discovered the vestiges of Lawrencian and Montgomery rule. They range from memorials in Lucknow and Kolkata, street names in Amritsar and Delhi, municipal buildings and residences in Lahore, Kanpur and Kasauli, to the establishment of schools in both countries.[1] One of the most enduring legacies is the Lawrence School, Sanawar. Founded in the 1840s and situated some three hundred miles north of Delhi amongst the deodars and pine trees of the Shivalak Himalayan range, the school was the brainchild of Henry Lawrence and his wife Honoria. Originally established for under-privileged children of British soldiers, it is today one of India's most prestigious schools where the names of 'Sir Henry' and 'Lady Honoria' are still spoken of in hushed, reverential tones.

I am indebted to various people who have helped me in the research and publication of this book. The late Kanwar Ratanjit Singh (Reggie) of the historic Chapslee, Shimla kindly put me in touch with contacts from the Lawrence School, Sanawar. Harbir Singh Romana (Estate Manager of the Lawrence School, Sanawar) generously gave me an in-depth guided tour of the school while Prabhsharan Singh Kang (past president of the old Sanawarians) shared his research into his alma mater and his links to the other Lawrence schools at Lovedale in South India and at Ghora Gali in Pakistan. Anu Mongia of the London branch of the Old Sanawarians introduced me to various former pupils including a direct descendant of Sir Henry Lawrence. A highlight of a visit to the city of Kanpur was exploring Robert Montgomery's official residence of the 1840s. Many thanks must go to Surendra Singh (IAS), then Collector & District Magistrate of Kanpur, for graciously showing me around.

At Foyle College a debt of gratitude goes to William Lynn of the Former Pupils Association, as well as to Jim Goodman and Mildred Deans for facilitating a visit to the Foyle Archives and to my former history teacher, Jim Heasley. Thanks are also due to Ian Bartlett who drew my attention to local references regarding Robert Montgomery. As the bibliography and notes section of this book indicate, much time was spent in the Asian and African Reading Room of the British Library where the ever-obliging staff assisted me with numerous requests. I would also like to thank Professor Rory Miller (Georgetown University, Qatar), an old friend from my Trinity days, for reading an early draft of the work and to Professor T.G. Fraser (former Provost of Magee College, University of Ulster) for his Indian insights. Special credit must go to Professor Francis Robinson (Royal Holloway, University of London) for casting a critical eye over the text and suggesting Pen and Sword as a potential publisher. At Pen and Sword, it has been a pleasure to work with commissioning editor Lester Crook whose guidance has been invaluable.

On a personal note, I would like to thank my Indian in-laws who have made visiting India such a pleasure: Dr. Vinod and Priti Garg in Bathinda, Sanjeev (District and Sessions Judge rtd.) and Rani Garg in Chandigarh, Dr. Vijay and Sushma Mohan in Pune, and of course my mother-in-law, Amita, in Chennai. Sadly, both my father-in-law, G.M. Gupta ("Guptaji") and my father, the Very Reverend Cecil Orr, are no longer with us, but both their spirits live on. I would also like to thank my brothers, Richard and David, and my sister Melissa as well as my sister-in-law, Swati Gupta, and brother-in-law, Ritesh Shukla, for their interest in the project. The deepest debt, of course, is due to my wife Shruti and son Jude who have had to share their lives with the Lawrences and Montgomery for quite some time. I hope this book provides some recompense. Finally, I wish to express my deep gratitude to my mother and father for all their support. On my travels they would often reach for The Times Atlas of the World, open the relevant section, and plot my whereabouts. The atlas is now in my possession and their marks bear testimony to some of my happiest memories.

London

February 2026

List of Images

1. Statue of John Lawrence, Waterloo Place, London. (*Author's photograph)*
2. Statue of John Lawrence, Foyle College, Londonderry. (*Author's photograph*)
3. Robert Montgomery by William Carpenter, Lahore (1854). (*Foyle College, Londonderry*)
4. Lieutenant Henry Lawrence, oil on canvas, attributed to James Heath Millington (1828). (*National Army Museum (NAM) Accession number: 2000-04-129-1*)
5. Captain George St. Patrick Lawrence, cavalry officer and military secretary to Sir William Hay Macnaghten. Image taken from M. Diver, *Honoria Lawrence: A Fragment of Indian History*. (London: John Murray, 1936)
6. John Lawrence by T.W. Knight. Image taken from Edward Henry Nolan, *The illustrated history of the British Empire in India and the East*. (London: James S. Virtue, 1878)
7. Foyle College, Londonderry, early 19th Century. (*Foyle College, Londonderry*)
8. The East India College at Haileybury by Thomas Medland (1810). (*From the British Library Collection: Maps_K_Top_15_74*)
9. Addiscombe Military Seminary. Image taken from H.M. Vibart, *Addiscombe – Its Heroes and Men of Note* (London: Archibald Constable & Co., 1894)
10. Ludlow Castle (the British Residency from 1832 to 1857) – 'The Delhie Book – Reminiscences of Imperial Delhi, a collection of 120 Company-style paintings commissioned by Sir Thomas Metcalfe in 1844.' (*From the British Library Collection:Shelfmark_Add Or 5475_ff60v_61r*)
11. James Thomason, Lieutenant-Governor of the North-Western Provinces. (*National Gallery of Scotland Accession number: EP V 649.1*)
12. Honoria Marshall (Lawrence). Image taken from M. Diver, *Honoria Lawrence: A Fragment of Indian History* (London: John Murray, 1936)
13. Henry Lawrence painted by Delhi artist Ghulam Husain Khan (c. 1847). (*From the British Library Collection: Add.Or.2409*)
14. The District Magistrate's residence at Allahabad by Sita Ram (1814–15). (*From the British Library Collection: Add.Or.4733*)
15. The Collector and District Magistrate's residence at Kanpur (Cawnpore). (*Author's photograph*)

16. Dost Muhammad, the Amir of Kabul by an East India Company artist (c. 1835). (*NAM Accession number: 1964-08-44-1*)
17. Akbar Khan, son of Dost Muhammad, by an East India Company artist (c.1840). (*NAM Accession number: 1964-08-44-2*)
18. Shah Shuja ul-Mulk, head of the Sadozai clan, by Louis and Charles Haghe after Jas Atkinson (1842). (*NAM Accession number: 1951-01-42-26*)
19. George Lawrence in Afghan dress by Lieutenant Vincent Eyre (1842). (*NAM Accession number: 1950-11-55-16*)
20. The Fort of Shewaki, near Kabul, where George Lawrence and his fellow British hostages were held by Akbar Khan. Drawn by W.L. Walton, published by J. Hogarth, H. Graves and Company, Pall Mall, (c) 1846. (*NAM Accession number: 1971-02-33-561-3*)
21. Watercolour of the British Residency in Kathmandu, Nepal by an anonymous artist, dated 1843–6. An original Palladian bungalow, with a two-storey Gothic extension. (*From the British Library Collection:Shelfmark_Add Or 5233*)

Maps

Map of Central Asia   xvii
Map of Northern India (Julie Witmer Custom Map Design)   xviii

Glossary of Indian and Anglo-Indian terms

Amin	Indian assistant revenue surveyor or field measurer
Amil	revenue and police administrative officer in pre-British period
Ayah	Indian nanny
Babu	Indian clerk (lit. meaning father)
Bheesti	water carrier
Bania	Hindu merchant caste
Bhaiachara	Village brotherhood; a form of joint landholding in which land is held by co-sharers on an equal basis
Biswa	a twentieth share of a village or estate
Biswadar	a coparcener
Burdasht khana	Storehouse, supply depot
Burkundaz	armed guard, rank and file policeman
Canoongo	(also spelt kanungo/qanungo) revenue accountant at pargana level
Cantonment	military station
Caravanserai	inn for travellers
Chaprassi	messenger/government orderly
Charpai	bed consisting of a wooden frame strung with rope
Chaudhari	minor chieftain of a pargana
Chowki	police post
Chowkidar	watchman
Chummery	a building or bungalow shared by unmarried army officers
Collector	British revenue officer within a district
Crore	ten million
Cutcherry	office or courthouse
Coss	a measure of distance, varying from one and a quarter to two and a half English miles
Cotwal	chief police officer of a town or city
Dacoit	armed robber, bandit
Dak	post
Dak-wallah	postman
Dhoti	Loin cloth worn tucked between the legs and fastened at the waist

District	the main administrative unit of British India
Doab	the area between two rivers
Dogra	Hindu Rajput
Dooley	a litter or palanquin borne on men's shoulders
Durbar	royal court, gathering of a ruler's attendants
Durkhast	land revenue engagement or agreement signed by zamindars
Fakir	religion mendicant
Firangi	foreigner, usually a European
Furlough	leave
Ghats	riverfront usually constructed with steps
Ghazi	holy warrior
Ghilzai	prominent Pashtun tribe traditionally located in the Ghazni and Qalat regions of Afghanistan
Griffin	newcomer in his first year in India
Gorait	messenger
Havildar	Indian non-commissioned officer
Haveli	traditional townhouse or mansion usually built around a courtyard
Hindustani	the language of the Muslim conquerors of Hindustan. Also known as Urdu. Derived from Hindi and including Persian and Arabic words.
Istumrardar	revenue farmer or holder of land leased on a perpetual rent
Izzat	honour, reputation
Jagir	land of which the revenue was made over to an individual as payment for special services.
Jagirdar	holder of a jagir
Jat	agricultural ethnic group mostly located in the Punjab
Jama	(also spelt Juma/Jumma) total revenue demand
Jamabandi	Detailed rent-roll or revenue statement of a village or estate
Jamadar	junior Indian officer
Kajahwah	a large baskets or cradle hung on the side of a camel
Khansama	cook
Khalsa	the Sikh brotherhood or community
Khewat	revenue document recording the shares and revenue responsibility of each landholder
Khidmutgar	male waiter
Khillat	dress of honour usually given as part of investiture into public office
Khusrah	measurement register of an estate containing dimensions and description of every field created by Indian revenue surveying team

Lambardar	village headman; one who pays land revenue on behalf of several small proprietors
Lakh	one hundred thousand
Maafee	land held free of revenue
Maafeedar	holder of land held free of revenue
Mahal	revenue paying unit – usually a village; Palace
Ma-bap	benevolent overseer. Lit. father and mother
Mahalwari	land revenue system in North-Western Provinces and Punjab in which the demand is levied on the mahal or estate
Maidan	open space, parade ground
Malik	village headman
Malikana	allowance paid to a proprietor excluded from the revenue engagement
Mohurrir	clerk
Mofussil	provincial India – 'up country'
Mootsuddy	native writer or clerk
Munshi	teacher or secretary
Muqaddam	village headman; In revenue terms the manager of an estate
Mouzah	village
Nawab	provincial ruler (Muslim)
Palanquin	oblong box carried on two horizontal poles by four bearers used to transport a person
Palki	palanquin or litter
Panchayat	council of elders usually numbering five
Pargana	sub-division of a district varying in size between 50,000 to 150,000 acres
Patta	deed of lease
Pattidar	one of the sharers in the proprietary right of an estate
Pattidari	a form of joint landholding in which sharers hold land according to their ancestral share
Peshkar	assistant in revenue affairs
Punkah	fan suspended from ceiling and pulled to create a current of air
Patwari	village accountant
Raj	government
Raja	ruler
Rani	wife of a raja
Rajput	Hindu warrior caste
Risaldar	Indian commander of a troop of horse
Ryot	cultivating tenant or peasant proprietor

Sahib–Zillah	district officer
Sati	widow burning
Seer	land under owner cultivation
Sepoy	Indian soldier
Shajra	field map created by Indian revenue team
Sirdar	chieftain (Punjabi)
Sowar	Indian mounted soldier or cavalryman
Sudder/Sadr	chief, central. i.e., Sudder/Sadr Board of Revenue
Subedar	provincial governor; senior Indian officer
Syce	groom
Tahsil	sub-division of a district usually larger than a pargana
Tahsildar	Indian revenue officer in charge of a tahsil
Talukdar	holder of an estate
Tappa	area of land smaller than a pargana
Thana	a police station or area under the jurisdiction of a police station
Thanadar	local police chief
Thug	secret cult of professional highway robbers and murderers
Thuggee	the practice of the thugs
Vakil	agent or representative
Vizier (Wazir)	chief minister
Zamindar	a person having a proprietary right in the land
Zillah	district

Note on transliteration: readers of Indian colonial texts will find numerous inconsistencies in the spelling of place names. To avoid confusion, I have retained the names used by contemporary British officials albeit with some exceptions. For example, I have used Cawnpore for the modern city of Kanpur, Benares for Varanasi, and Allahabad for Prayagraj. For other places, however, I have made some compromises such as using the modern spelling of Azamgarh rather than Azimgurh/Azimghar, and Gorakhpur for Gorruckpore or Gorruckpur. I have also used the name Ferozepur rather than Ferozepore or Firozpur, and Bamian for Bamean or Bamiyan.

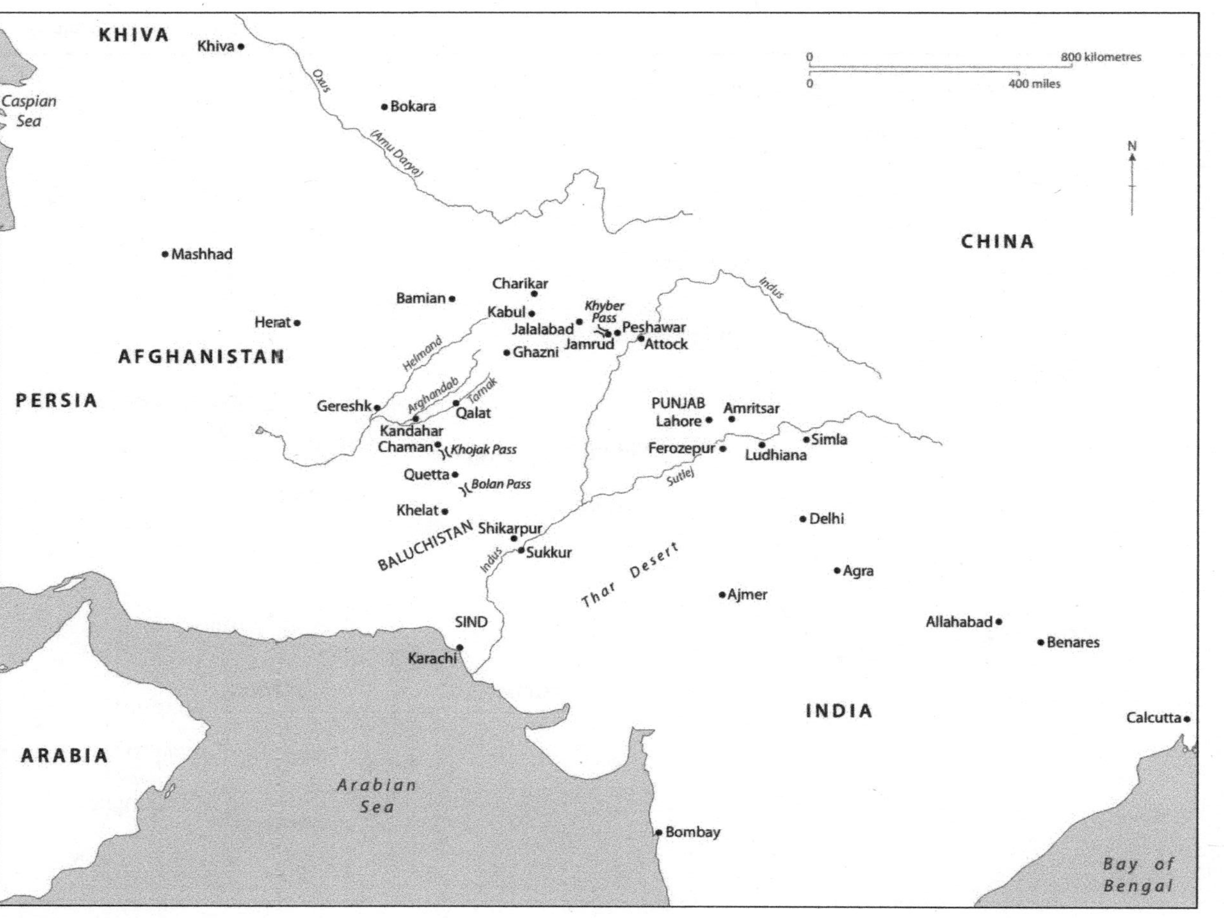

Central Asia

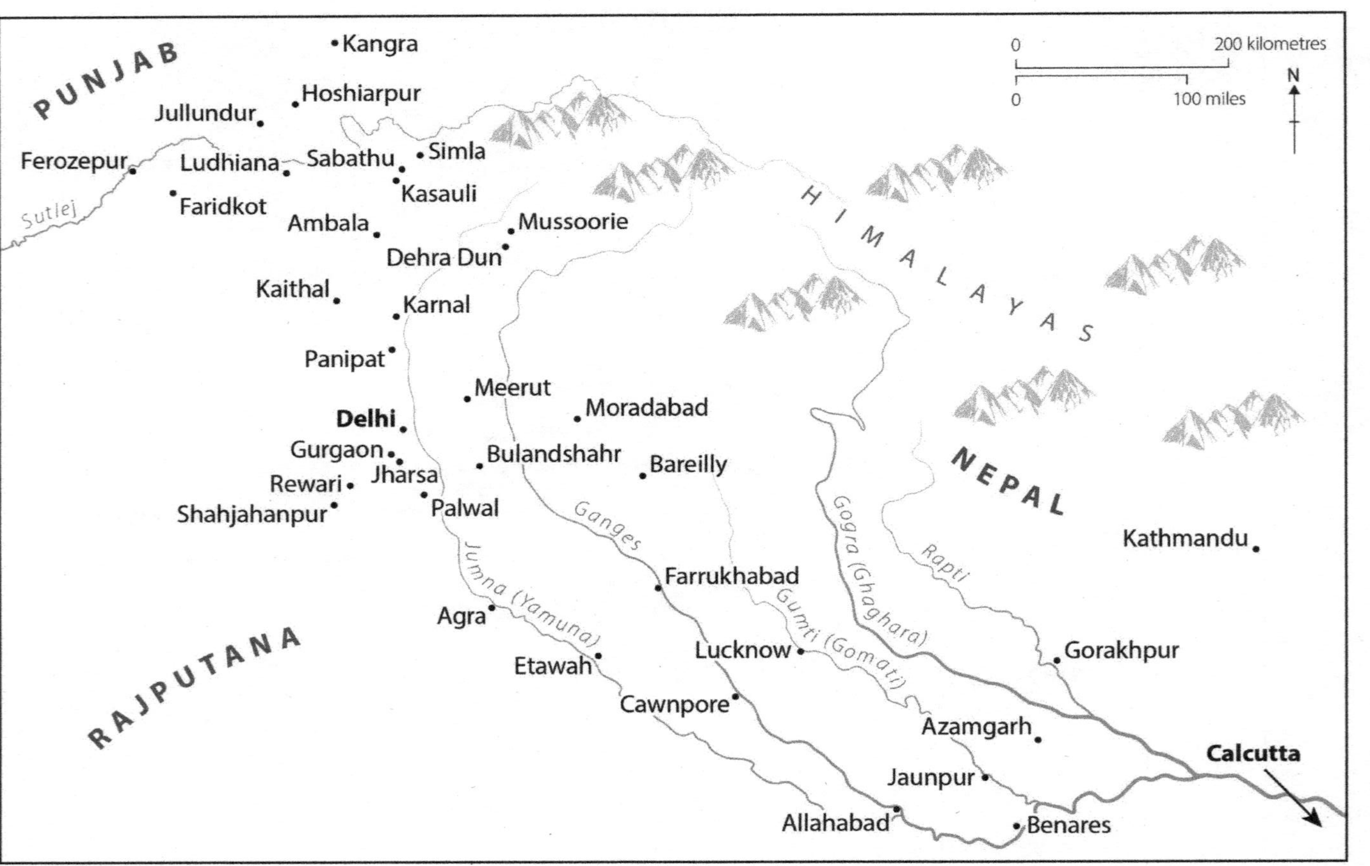

Northern India

Prologue

'Will you be governed by the Pen or the Sword?'

In the grounds of Foyle College, Londonderry stands an imposing bronze statue of John Laird Mair Lawrence, Viceroy of India (1864–69) and one of the school's most famous alumni. Measuring eight feet and six inches high upon a sturdy granite plinth, the statue projects an aura of unbounded confidence. With legs astride, his substantial frame leans backwards, accentuating a broad chest. His rugged face casts a determined gaze across the River Foyle towards the Donegal mountains. Reflecting a well-known distaste for ostentation, his clothes are a mixture of the informal: open neck shirt, casual overcoat, and high-rise breeches. Spurs are attached to a pair of plain leather boots. In the sculptor J. E. Boehm's portrayal, Lawrence is depicted not as a regal viceroy responsible for the destiny of millions but as a down-to-earth district officer as if addressing a gathering of Punjabi village elders. Of prime, symbolic importance is what Lawrence is holding. In his right hand he extends forth a quill pen, while in his left, and slightly less prominent, is clasped a sheathed sword. The implication is clear: Lawrence urges the assembled to accept his civil administration 'by the pen'. But make no mistake. If refused, the sword is ready to be unsheathed.

Today the statue serves as a mute reminder of an almost forgotten imperial past. But it was not always so. Over the years it has evoked strong emotions and has attracted a good deal of criticism. Originally intended to proudly commemorate one man's significant contribution to the British Empire, it has at times been a source of irritation rather than inspiration. Indeed, no sooner was the statue unveiled in the southeast corner of Waterloo Place, London in 1882 than it drew widespread censure on purely aesthetic grounds. The sculptor had miscalculated the public mood. An illustrious imperial figure clothed in casual attire and assuming a provocative stance was not, it seemed, an appropriate image to gain the public's affections. *The Builder*, an architectural journal, noted with restrained disapproval that the model was 'characteristic and forcible in manner and not cut out on the regulation type of our public statues'.[1] Other commentators were more forthright. The *Athenaeum's* fine arts critic described Boehm's Lawrence as 'a big and swaggering figure, course and demonstrative; a man like this would have driven the East into rebellion'.[2] Beatrix Potter, the

Victorian children's author, was outraged: 'Considering Mr Boehm's reputation, his sculpture is shocking'.[3]

In response to this stinging criticism, Boehm took the unprecedented step of replacing the statue, at his own expense, with an entirely new version espousing a 'less truculent attitude'.[4] In this second reincarnation, John Lawrence's legs are now placed closer together while his arms are firmly by his side. Instead of a quill pen, he clasps a piece of folded parchment. His left hand now rests gently on the hilt of his sword in an equally unobtrusive manner. The statue's clothes are also more formal. The shirt is now fully buttoned, a waistcoat has been added, and over a more refined coat is draped a quasi-regal inspired cape complete with tassels. The inscription on the plinth reads: 'John, First Lord Lawrence, Ruler of the Punjaub during the Sepoy Mutiny of 1857, Viceroy of India from 1864 to 1869. Erected by his fellow subjects British and Indian.'

As for the original statue, far from being discarded, it took on a new lease of life many miles from the imperial metropole. In 1887, as part of the Queen's Jubilee, the sculptor presented it as a gift to the municipality of Lahore, where it was re-erected in front of the city's high court. Over the next few decades, the statue's presence excited little attention beyond those of an antiquarian persuasion. But by the 1920s it once again attracted controversy. This time the statue became a focal point for protest by Indian nationalists, and even aroused the ire of Mahatma Gandhi when he visited Lahore in November 1921. In a speech to supporters, he linked the call for the statue's removal to the wider campaign against British rule, exhorting his audience to action 'even at the risk of imprisonment or death'.[5] What particularly riled protestors was the inscription on its plinth: 'Will you be governed by the pen or the sword?'[6] Although the quotation was not John's, but that of his assistant, R.N. Cust (used in an appeal to village headmen of the Hoshiarpur district during the 2nd Anglo-Sikh War), Boehm had found its aptness irresistible.[7] Such artistic licence, of course, mattered little to those who saw both the inscription and the statue as unmistakable totems of imperial oppression. The statue was vandalized, and the wording defaced. For a time, it was placed under police protection. Eventually, though, a compromise of sorts was reached by the middle of 1926. Although the statue remained *in situ*, the inscription was altered to become less antagonistic. Henceforth it would read: 'With Pen and Sword, I served you.'[8] While this gesture placated more moderate elements, it continued to be a focus for sporadic protest into 1930s.[9]

By the mid-twentieth century the Indian independence movement spearheaded by Mahatma Gandhi, Jawaharlal Nehru and Mohammed Ali Jinnah had finally succeeded in forcing Britain to relinquish its hold on a country once considered to be 'the Jewel in the Crown' of the British Empire. Victorian statues of imperial soldiers and administrators occupying prominent positions within Indian cities were no longer in vogue. Many, though not all, were removed, and relegated to museum grounds or municipal storage yards where they were left to slowly decay.[10] The case of the Lawrence statue was no different. At midnight on 25th August 1951, it was removed, transported by bullock cart, and left to languish in a disused corner of Lahore Fort.

That may well have been the end of the matter, but for the prospect of Indian commemorations to mark the centenary of the 1857 Indian Revolt as well as the tenth anniversary of Indian independence. Concern that Raj-era statues would become the unwelcome focus for attack during these celebrations now re-ignited interest in their welfare and led to calls for their repatriation.[11] It was the removal of another statue – that of fellow Ulsterman John Nicholson (originally placed at Delhi's Kashmir Gate) – to his alma mater of the Royal School, Dungannon, which prompted Foyle College to salvage John Lawrence's statue.[12] Overcoming the rival claims of Haileybury College (formerly the East India Company's civil service college), Foyle's board of governors regarded 'the acquisition of the statue of this famous Ulsterman and Old Boy of Foyle College as important in preserving in a visible form a valuable school tradition.'[13]

Understandably, the Government of Pakistan, within whose jurisdiction the statue now lay, did not share the same enthusiasm for this effigy of British imperialism. Yet there was no vindictive action on their part, either to refuse granting its repatriation or, more radically, to have the statue destroyed or even melted down and recast in the form of an indigenous freedom fighter. Instead, the Minister of the Interior, Lt. Gen K.N. Sheikh, simply alluded to the popular resentment the statue had evinced and expressed the wish that their sensitivities on the matter be respected. 'As you know,' he told Sir Olaf Caroe, one of the last British governors of the Northwest Frontier Province who acted as intermediary,

> there has been a certain amount of feeling against this statue….the sword in one of its hands has been broken, the pen which used to be in the other hand is missing and the inscription underneath has been struck off… I hope you will not restore the inscription after the statue is taken away.[14]

Transported back from Lahore, and restored in London, it was re-erected, without the controversial inscription, at the then school site of Lawrence Hill.[15] At its unveiling on 1st March 1963, it was left to the deputy chairman of the Board of Governors, Professor J.L. McCracken, an historian, to provide some post-colonial comment:

It is not fashionable to say so nowadays, but Lord Lawrence undoubtedly advanced the cause of civilizations in India. Perhaps the logical outcome of this was the removal of this statue. In a very real sense, it is a measure of his achievements that we have his statue here today. May it serve as an inspiration to future generations of Foyle boys and as a further strengthening of the continuity of the traditions of the school.[16]

Introduction

'The Titans of the Punjab'?

This book explores the remarkable careers of four men of Irish extraction – George, Henry and John Lawrence and Robert Montgomery who, during the second and third quarters of the nineteenth century, were at the very forefront of the colonial enterprise in India. They came from modest backgrounds in Ulster, the most northern province of Ireland, where they attended Foyle College, Londonderry. After receiving initial training in England, they made the arduous voyage to India. Further language tuition was provided in Calcutta before they began their careers as soldiers and administrators in the Delhi Territory and the North-Western Provinces. George and Henry would later take part in the ill-fated 1st Anglo-Afghan War, before all four Ulstermen gained pivotal roles in the administration of the frontier province of Punjab following the 1st Anglo-Sikh War. Henry was appointed British Agent and later Resident at Lahore (1846–49), and, with the assistance of his brother John, governed the province in partnership with the Sikh aristocracy. After the 2nd Anglo-Sikh War, however, this collaborative approach was shelved in favour of outright control.

The annexation of the province in 1849 saw full administrative responsibility handed over to a Board of Administration whose composition eventually assumed a distinctly Irish tincture: Henry Lawrence as President, John Lawrence as Financial Commissioner and Robert Montgomery serving as Judicial Commissioner. Administering the Punjab, however, would in time reveal irreconcilable differences between Henry and John on how their notions of paternal governance should be exercised. Henry's deep-rooted sympathy for the traditional power and privileges of the Sikh aristocracy in Punjab brought him into conflict with John who saw little worth in pandering to their anachronistic needs, preferring instead to elevate the position of the Punjab peasantry. In this increasingly fractious fraternal relationship, it was their old school friend Robert Montgomery who would act as mediator – a role he later described as that of a 'regular buffer between two high-pressure engines'.[1] Eventually matters came to a head. In 1853 Lord Dalhousie decided to dissolve the Board and appoint John as Chief Commissioner, after Henry felt obliged, albeit reluctantly, to leave his beloved province. Although he was appointed the Governor-General's

Agent in Rajputana, it did little to salve his disappointment. Four years later all three Lawrence brothers and Montgomery would face a desperate battle for survival during the 1857 Indian Revolt or Mutiny; a cataclysmic event that would claim the life of Henry who had only recently assumed the role of Chief Commissioner of Oudh based at Lucknow. John and Robert, on the other hand, would not only survive the uprising; they would also be instrumental in defeating it. Both men were duly rewarded for their efforts. In 1859 Robert was appointed Lieutenant-Governor of the Punjab, while five years later John attained the highest position within the civil administration as Viceroy of India.

Once Henry and John Lawrence had departed from the scene of their triumphs, it was only a matter of time before their exploits became the stuff of legend. From the late 1860s onwards, Victorian biographers began publishing their admiring accounts of the two great men 'in letters all of gold'.[2] Their aim was to elevate their subject matter from lowly origins to mythical hero status. Character traits such as courage, honour, self-belief, compassion, and selfless devotion to duty were duly emphasised in works which sought to capture the public imagination. Arguably the most panegyric of all the accounts of the two brothers was Reginald Bosworth Smith's official *Life of Lord Lawrence* (1883). For the Harrovian schoolmaster turned biographer, John was depicted in grand heroic terms – a man whose great physical, moral, and intellectual powers plainly set him apart from his peers:

> No Samson, no Hercules, no Milo, no Arthur, can have had more stories of personal prowess, of grim humour, of the relief of the distressed, to tell than he. Physically he was a Hercules himself…And when these physical characteristics are combined with others, moral and intellectual, which are conspicuously wanting in most Indian races – with absolute truthfulness in word and deed, with active benevolence, with a sagacity which is the result not of mere shrewdness, but of untiring honesty of purpose, with boundless devotion to duty and hard work – their possessor becomes a power indeed in the land.[3]

Bosworth Smith was one of several biographers who drew parallels with Oliver Cromwell in both John's appearance and conduct.[4] He was portrayed as the Puritan warhorse with unpretentious habits of shirtsleeves rolled up, cigar in mouth, dictating orders to his Indian clerks. 'Like Cromwell, John Lawrence was rough and downright in all he said and did,' Bosworth Smith wrote, 'like Cromwell, he cared naught for appearances, spoke his mind freely, swept all cobwebs out of his path, worked like a horse himself, and insisted on hard work in others.'[5]

The author was keen to make use of the reminiscences of fellow administrators. Hercules Scott offered an admiring vignette of the man whom he initially regarded with a high degree of trepidation. Based on John's reputation as a very strict overseer, it was intensified by his brusque manner and craggy features. Scott admitted that his work at first must have 'bristled with irregularities and blunders' but in time he was able to earn the confidence of his superior. He duly acknowledged John's expertise of fiscal, revenue, police, and judicial matters and was in awe of his work ethic: 'There were, as it appeared to me, certain guiding principles which ran through his whole texture, and were constantly impressed on us: duty to Government, consideration for the natives, order and promptitude in work, personal self-sacrifice, and justice between man and man.'[6] Likewise, in his memoir *Pictures of Indian Life* (1881), R.N. Cust warmly recollected John's paternalistic approach earlier in his career. Sent as an assistant to Hoshiarpur, the main town of the Jullundur district, he first found John amid a large group of Sikh and Muslim landholders arranging the new land revenue settlement in March 1846. 'He was full of energy,' wrote Cust,

> and was impressing upon his subjects his principles of a just state-demand, and their first elementary ideas of natural equity, for, as each man touched the pen, the unlettered token of agreement to their lease, 'he made them repeat aloud the new trilogue of the English Government: "Thou shall not burn thy widow; thou shall not kill thy daughters; thou shall not bury alive thy lepers;" and old greybeards, in the family of some of whom there was not a single female blood relative, went away chanting the dogma of this new Moses, which next year were sternly enforced. Here I learnt my first idea of the energetic order, and the rapid execution, which make up the sum total of good administration. Here I first knew the man, who was my model, my friend, and my master.[7]

Henry Lawrence, too, was spoken of in fulsome terms with contemporaries often emphasising his compassionate and magnanimous nature. For James Abbott, Deputy Commissioner of Hazara, Henry's spirit 'inspired every act of the local government, which touched the heart of all his subordinates with ardour... All caught from him the sacred fire; his presence seemed all pervading, for the interests of the meanest were as dear to him as those of the most powerful.'[8] Similarly, in his two-volume *Lives of Indian Officers* (1867), the historian, J.W. Kaye, asked whether there was anyone within the Anglo-Indian Empire who had 'so lustrous a combination of ennobling and endearing qualities'.[9] Henry, Kaye wrote, had 'a rare union of determined purpose, of moral as well as physical courage, with a singular frankness and courtesy of demeanour....shown equally to Europeans and to natives'.[10] This empathy for all races was also noted by Siege of Lucknow veteran, Lieutenant General J.J. McLeod Innes V.C. In his biography *Sir Henry Lawrence – The Pacificator* (1898), Innes saw Henry's most important contribution as the 'leader of a school of Indian administrators…which gave special consideration to the feelings, traditions and modes of thought of the native community'.[11] For officers such as Herbert Edwardes, who penned the first volume of *Life of Sir Henry Lawrence* (1872), it was Henry's faith in his subordinates which left a lasting impression: 'What those days were! How Henry Lawrence would send us off to great distances: Edwardes to Bunnoo, Nicholson to Peshawur, Abbott to Hazara, Lumsden to somewhere else, etc., giving us no more helpful directions than these, "Settle the country; make the people happy; and take care there are no rows!"'[12]

Biographers also highlighted the differing character traits of the two Lawrence brothers. Sir Richard Temple, who was John's secretary during the 1850s, contrasted John's formidable administrative ability with Henry's 'unsystematic almost unmethodical' approach to business. The elder Lawrence 'was not sufficiently alive to financial considerations.'[13] Bosworth Smith went further in categorising the different personalities of both brothers through the prism of racial stereotyping. The 'sturdy mixture' of the Scottish and Irish character found in Ulster was seen as particularly suitable for meeting the rigorous demands of imperial duty: 'Nowhere within the circuit of the British Islands is a more interesting, a more vigorous, or more strongly marked type of character to be found than among the inhabitants of the North and the North-east of Ireland.'[14] In this attempt at ethnic profiling, it was Henry, the author believed, who personified more of the impulsive, romantic Irishman – adventurous, honourable and sensitive, while John epitomised the doughty Scot who encapsulated the values of simplicity, caution and strength of mind. The difference was pithily summed up by the Victorian writer, J.L. Trotter: 'Sir Henry represented the poetry of Indian statesmanship; John its hard direct prose.'[15]

The purpose of these biographies, however, was not simply to commemorate, inform and entertain a growing Victorian readership; they also served a crucial didactic, moralizing function. For as long as the British empire remained a living entity, the Lawrences' example could inspire the next generation of soldiers and administrators. Here the emphasis was on self-reliance and a strong work ethic. When, for example, Henry made the crucial switch from military to civil employment as an Assistant Revenue Surveyor, Herbert Edwardes argued that the achievement was based on his own endeavour:

> The young lad who has been fired with the deeds and fame of Havelock, and Outram, and John Nicholson, and Henry Lawrence, and has chosen to

go to India too; that fair-haired, blue-eyed one, whose face bespeaks much imagination but not much of will; had better believe it here on English ground that it is not "big brothers" that make great men. With the help of God they make themselves.[16]

Sir Richard Temple was more emphatic in his 1889 biography, *Lord Lawrence*, part of a series entitled 'English Men of Action'. For Temple, John's chief accolade was nothing less than the 'saviour of the Indian Empire' whose prompt actions proved crucial in defeating the Indian Revolt of 1857.[17] He too was at pains to portray his superior as 'a self-made and self-taught man' whose distinguished career had been accomplished by sheer dint of hard work and whose character was one of 'massive vigour, simplicity and single-mindedness'. Despite lacking 'the advantages of high education, of family connection, of contact with political life, of guidance from the lights of the age,' John, Temple argued, had raised himself by 'his own up-heaving force,' and propelled himself 'by his own motive power'. His example, he told his readers, 'should have a spirit-stirring effect on the middle class from which he sprung…With virtue, energy and resolution like his, British youths of scanty means, winning their places by competition, may carry with them to the Eastern empire the possibilities of national usefulness and the resources for conquering fortune in her noble sphere.'[18] It was no coincidence that the school prize for mathematical studies and map-making given to Rudyard Kipling's eponymous hero Kim was none other than Reginald Bosworth Smith's *Life of Lord Lawrence*.[19]

The veneration of the Lawrences has had an enduring lifespan, continuing well beyond both the Victorian and Edwardian eras. J.L. Morison, in his admiring 1930s biography of the elder Lawrence, wrote 'he had more fresh and sound ideas about India than any of his Indian contemporaries. His benevolent statesmanship has still to find an equal in the East'.[20] Similarly, in Philip Woodruff's (aka Philip Mason) *The Men who Ruled India*, published a few years after Indian Independence, the author presented an image of self-less, hardworking, duty-bound administrators who could be justly proud of their achievements: 'They were men who by the middle of the nineteenth century had brought peace to the country instead of anarchy, had mapped the fields and made lists of every man's rights and had made a beginning of the task of building roads, bridges and railways, of harnessing the rivers to irrigation.'[21] Standing tall in this pantheon of empire builders were of course the Lawrences whom Mason dubbed 'the Titans of the Punjab':

No doubt they were hard men to live with, sometimes a torture to themselves and to those near them. But they were dynamic; there is a size and force to them we lack. Without their taut strung emotions, they would not have achieved what they did. What that was can perhaps never wholly be understood because there was something about it miraculous.[22]

Such were the brothers' towering reputations that even post-independent Indian historians have tended to follow the same largely sympathetic interpretation. N.M. Khilnani believed that 'if there was any man in India who could have carried out the plan for establishing a friendly and stable Sikh Government, it was Henry Lawrence…he could analyse the elements of Sikh thought and sentiment and his discernment of the temper of Sikh chiefs and the Court was unfailing'.[23] Although John, he argued, had 'none of that indefinable genius for personal influence which distinguished his brother', he was nonetheless 'a civil administrator of high calibre'. He 'had unbounded capacity for work and aptitude for detail' and 'his powers of organization were almost unrivalled.'[24] Similarly, B.J. Hasrat regarded Henry Lawrence as, 'by far, the best man that could have been selected' to reestablish a Sikh government: 'A sense of moderation guided him in his dealings with the Sikhs, whose national traits he understood so well.'[25]

More recently, Henry Lawrence's great-grandson, Sir John Lawrence, felt obliged to write his own biography of his forebear (*Lawrence of Lucknow*, 1990), arguing that Herman Merivale in the original *Life of Sir Henry Lawrence* had done little more than 'stitch together the material left by Edwardes' and that his second volume was 'incomplete'. Despite the later offerings of Innes and Morison, Sir John believed that there remained 'from the outset a need for a new biography'.[26] His book, though, proved something of a disappointment. For although we have him to thank for placing the Henry Lawrence Papers on permanent loan to the British Library, his own efforts added little to our understanding.[27]

One study to make greater use of archival sources is *Brothers in the Raj – The Lives of John and Henry Lawrence* (2000) by the American academic Harold Lee. His aim, he told his readers, was firstly to provide 'a convenient and more up-to-date single-volume biography of both brothers'. Although this had already been attempted in F.P. Gibbon's *The Lawrences of the Punjab* (1908), Lee's main reason for writing the book was his belief that biographers such as Edwardes & Merivale had not adequately addressed the personal and professional relationships of Henry and John. The central theme of his work, he explained, was to explore 'their tensions as siblings and differences in personality on the one hand and their differing views of how the Punjab and indeed India should be ruled on the other'.[28] Although applying modern scholarship to his subject, Lee nevertheless remained curiously non-committal in his evaluation of the intertwined strands of the brothers' careers, content, it seems, to let the reader 'draw his or her own conclusions'.[29]

As this brief historiographical review has suggested, Victorian and Edwardian accounts of Henry and John Lawrence have invariably presented an image of larger-than-life imperial figures whose colonial endeavours have been heavily glorified. Even more recent studies have maintained largely uncontested interpretations of their Indian careers. There is a sense that myth has tended to obscure reality. Hence the need for a modern reappraisal based on a critical examination of the primary historical sources and the use of previously unpublished material. Furthermore, the scope of such research must include those close associates who have hitherto received scant attention but deserve rightful recognition. Elder brother, George Lawrence, for example, has for too long occupied a mere footnote in Anglo-Indian history. Indeed, as one biographer of Henry Lawrence has pointed out, 'George Lawrence never found a Homer, or even a Horace, to sing his praises'.[30] Up to now, readers have had to make do with his somewhat uneven autobiography, *Reminiscences of Forty-Three Years in India* (1874).[31]

George rose to prominence during the 1st Anglo-Afghan War when he was appointed military secretary to the Envoy to Kabul, Sir William Hay Macnaghten. When Macnaghten was killed in the Kabul uprising in December 1841, George only narrowly escaped a similar fate. Taken hostage, he also managed to survive the doomed retreat from Kabul and was only released after an eight-month long captivity. After the Treaty of Bhyrowal (December 1846), he assumed an important role as Henry's political agent based at Peshawar. Later, during the 2nd Anglo-Sikh War, he found himself again being taking hostage, this time at the hands of the Sikh chieftain Chattar Singh. Good fortune, though, once more prevailed and he was ultimately released. He would eventually succeed Henry as Resident to the Rajputana States. Unlike Henry, George had no literary ambitions, nor was he an administrator of the calibre of John. Nevertheless, he was universally regarded as a practical, highly dependable officer of 'indomitable energy and pluck'.[32] Robert Montgomery described him as 'a little, burly fellow' who carried the nickname 'Cocky Lawrence', while the redoubtable Lady Sale, in her famous *Journal of the Disasters in Afghanistan, 1841–2*, admiringly labelled him 'a very spunky, active man'.[33]

Robert Montgomery, grandfather of Viscount Montgomery of Alamein, likewise, has received insufficient recognition despite his achievements in the North-Western Provinces and in the Punjab. A slim biography written by his grandson, Brian Montgomery, supplies only a skeletal account of his career. Those few published reminiscences by former colleagues tend to emphasis his affable, unassuming, and cheerful nature (he was nicknamed Mr Pickwick after the eponymous Dickens character); traits which seem at first curiously at odds with other aspects of his character – namely a man of steely determination, a prodigious worker, and a proponent of swift coercive measures.[34] His close colleague Richard Temple, however, saw all these attributes combine during the 1857 Revolt: 'he would rise to the level of emergencies with alacrity, yet with calmness, and confront the most critical danger with a smiling face.'[35]

By revealing Robert Montgomery's and George Lawrence's significant involvement in Anglo-Indian affairs during the 1830s and 1840s, this book aims to place these lesser-known agents of empire within their proper historical setting. For the first time, an almost day-to-day account of the extraordinary role played by George in the 1st Anglo-Afghan War is offered, while Robert's administrative functions as Collector and Magistrate in Azamgarh, Allahabad and Cawnpore can now be fully appreciated. The latter's efforts in combatting female infanticide and thuggee are particularly illuminating. The book also provides a comprehensive re-appraisal of Henry and John Lawrence's early career in the Delhi Territory and the North-Western Provinces. Previous accounts have not given sufficient weight to this period. Yet these years are crucially important to our understanding of their subsequent careers in the Punjab and beyond. For it was during this time that their philosophy of paternal governance took shape. My research sheds fresh light on their key roles in the formation and implementation of land revenue policy under the influential figures of R.M. Bird and James Thomason. A final chapter focuses on Henry's time as British Resident at the Court of Nepal, where he was able to devote himself to literary pursuits on Anglo-Indian themes. Although he was to find Nepal 'shut out from civilization', the period was nonetheless vital in distilling his administrative philosophy and in establishing himself as a leading authority on Punjab affairs.[36] In short, the book will argue that the Lawrences and Montgomery's apprenticeship years formed the essential bedrock upon which their subsequent careers in the Punjab and beyond rested.

Imperial Connections

The first few years of the nineteenth century witnessed a vast extension of the East India Company's rule across much of northern India. Driven by what C.A. Bayly has described as 'insecurity on its extended frontiers and the desire to seize new revenues,' it was achieved through a combination of political pressure and outright military might and came largely at the expense of two regional powers: the Nawab of Oudh (Awadh) and the Maratha Confederacy.[1] In 1801, under the expansionist Governor-Generalship of Richard Wellesley, the former was forced to cede half of his entire lands – the end result of a gradual erosion of autonomy which could be traced back to the Treaty of Allahabad (1765) and the introduction of the Subsidiary Alliance system. Officially Wellesley justified cession in moral terms on the grounds of Oudh's inept government, yet the financial rewards for doing so were all too apparent. The acquisition of new districts that included Bareilly, Moradabad, Farrukhabad, Etawah, Cawnpore, Allahabad, Azamgarh, and Gorakhpur yielded a gross annual revenue of Rs 13,523,475.[2] Soon afterwards the power of the Maratha Confederacy was also overturned. In 1803 large tracts of land within the Ganga-Jumna *doab* together with those in the Delhi-Agra region, the traditional centre of Mughal rule, were handed over when the French trained army of Daulat Rao Sindia, the Maharaja of Gwalior, was defeated by forces under Generals Gerard Lake and Arthur Wellesley during the Second Anglo-Maratha War.[3] In the same year, under a supplemental agreement to the Treaty of Bassein, the Marathi *Peshwa* also surrendered control of the Bundelkhand districts of Banda and Hamirpur – a territory which yielded an estimated annual revenue of Rs 3,616,000.[4]

Occupying much of the modern Indian state of Uttar Pradesh, the British initially named this vast crescent shaped collection of territories as the Ceded and Conquered Provinces. In November 1834 it was briefly retitled the Agra Presidency (when the Delhi Territory was integrated) before becoming the North-Western Provinces in June 1836.[5] Covering a landmass of nearly 72,000 square miles, it was roughly equal to the size of England and Scotland combined. Within its thirty-two districts under six divisions (Delhi, Rohilkhand, Meerut, Agra, Allahabad, and Benares), it contained a population of over twenty-three million.[6] Central to the nascent British administration in what was the heartland of Hindustan was the land revenue. By the late 1830s it amounted to approximately 40 million rupees annually, the equivalent of some 80% of the total revenue for the North-Western Provinces (the other taxes included customs, stamp duties, salt tax, Abkarry [liquor]). Deductions were made for the cost of tax collection, meeting the civil, judicial and police charges as well as paying for buildings, roads, and other public works. This left what seemed to be a very healthy revenue surplus of around 30 million rupees.[7] But this excluded the substantial cost of naval and military expenditure and the 'home' charges (i.e. the salaries and pensions of Company employees in Britain as well as dividends paid to proprietors of East India stock). Moreover, any remaining surplus was required to offset deficits occurring within the presidencies of Bengal, Madras and Bombay.[8] For most of the 1830s and 1840s, however, the N.W.P. surplus proved insufficient to offset the total Indian deficit. Although a surplus of one and a half a million pounds sterling was achieved in 1836 (thanks to Governor-General Bentinck's administrative cost-cutting), by the end of the decade Indian central coffers recorded a deficit of £2 million largely due to the costs of the 1st Anglo-Afghan War.[9]

Despite the Company's increased responsibilities, European manpower in India remained a modest affair when compared to the indigenous contribution. In 1800 the number of European soldiers serving in both the British Army in India and the East India Company's army amounted to 22,832 compared to 115,300 Indian soldiers. By 1830 the expatriate figure had risen to 36,409 compared to 187,067 indigenous recruits.[10] In percentage terms, the European military contribution thus amounted to little more than 16% of the overall total. In the civil service, the European element formed an even smaller proportion of the overall administrative machinery. During the period 1802 to 1833 the number of writers sent to the three presidencies of India (Bengal, Madras and Bombay) amounted to only 1190.[11] Again this figure was dwarfed by the many thousands of Indian support staff working at district, *pargana* and village level.

Modest though it may have been in absolute terms, the demand for imperial manpower was nonetheless significant, and was met not only by a rising population in Britain, but also in Ireland. In the 1750s Ireland had a population of 2.5 million. By the 1830s the figure had reached 7.8 million and accounted for just under a third of the entire UK population. Burdened by an increasingly surplus population, large numbers of Irish looked to the British Empire for their livelihood. Both the British Army and the East India Company's own army would prove attractive options, facilitated by recruitment depots based in Ireland. For those willing to take the King's or the Queen's shilling as rank and file soldiers, India offered an escape from poverty at home and an opportunity to better oneself abroad.[12] By 1830, 42 per cent of men serving in the British Army were Irish, while in the Company's Bengal Army the figure reached 48 per cent of all European recruits for the period 1825–50.[13] Little wonder that one historian has concluded that 'without Irishmen, the rampant growth of Britain's empire at this stage would scarcely have been possible'.[14]

Although there were few obstacles for Irishmen to become soldiers in the East India Company during the first half of the nineteenth century, entrance to the officer class or the civil administration was much more stringent. For the young men who hailed from the lesser branches of the gentry or the rising professional middle classes an opening to such careers crucially depended on patronage. In this respect the East India Company was no different to any other professional field – be it government, the law, the church, or banking. Patronage pervaded all areas of public life. Yet, in contrast to those other fields of gentlemanly employment, once the all-important Company nomination had been obtained, opportunities for career progression were based largely on talent rather than influence. Although the vast fortunes made by officials in the previous century were no longer possible, Company service in India remained an attractive career choice, offering both a steady income and kudos. By contrast, the law, the church, and medicine required the funding of an expensive university education, while obtaining a commission in the regular British army often involved great expense with little financial reward. Careers in the East India Company, on the other hand, provided one of the few options for men of limited financial means to rise both socially and economically.

The conferring of Company posts rested with the governing body of the East India Company based in London known as the Court of Directors. This was a remarkably tight-knit group of some twenty-four members, the majority of whom had already held official positions in India.[15] Although each year six directors were appointed by the Company's stockholders for a four-year term, it was customary for a director to be re-elected after an out of office gap of one year. With its self-perpetuating membership, it was unsurprising that the makeup of civil servants became increasingly drawn from a relatively small network of extended families and old friendships.[16] On an annual basis each director had the right to nominate a small number of civil officers or writers with a more generous quota given for military cadet nominations within the Company's Indian armies. The total number of appointments varied year to year; in 1814 only seven civil appointments were made, while in 1828 the figure reached sixty-nine.[17] From 1809 onwards, trainee civil officers were given places at the East India College, Haileybury, while artillery and engineering cadets proceeded to the Company's military seminary based at Addiscombe, Croydon.

Cavalry and infantry cadets were often sent directly to India without the need for prior training in England.

Given their prominent contribution as common soldiers to the British Empire in India, it was reasonable to expect that Irishmen serving as military officers would form an equally significant proportion. But this was far from the case. One study investigating the birthplace of officer cadets to the East India Company's Army in the period 1796–1854 revealed a geographic breakdown dominated by Greater London (20.7%), the rest of England (29.5%), and those born in India (19%). Ireland accounted for only 8.3%, while Scotland, despite a population of less than 3 million in 1851, accounted for 14.1%.[18] The geographic split for civil appointments was, if anything, even more disappointing from an Irish perspective. Research into the birthplace or place of residence of parents whose sons attended Haileybury in the period 1809–1850 once more showed that those from families based in London (27.2%), from other parts of England (27%) and those who were on active service in India (23.2%) formed an overwhelming part of all civil recruits. The Irish contribution in this sphere was a paltry 4.7%, less than half of those supplied by Scotland (12.7%).[19]

Why were Irishmen under-represented in the officer class and civil administration in the first half of the nineteenth century? One answer may lie in the long running historic divisions within Ireland itself. While most of the regular Irish soldiers were Catholic, the officer class was overwhelming Protestant. The colonisation of Ireland during the seventeenth century had impoverished the Catholic gentry, the social group from which potential officer recruits could be drawn. Furthermore, the Glorious Revolution of 1688 had specifically prohibited Irish Catholics from serving in the army, and it was not until the 1790s that they were openly admitted (although a blind eye was turned towards rank-and-file Irish Catholic recruitment from 1750s onwards). Conversely, Irish Protestant landed families and those on its periphery were able to maintain a strong tradition of military and public service into the nineteenth century. They remained, however, a relatively small social group within Irish society and were geographically disadvantaged when it came to building the necessary connections to the Company's London based elite.

Scotland's overproportionate contribution, on the other hand, may well have been the result of a deliberate, conciliatory policy adopted by successive Westminster governments following the Anglo-Scottish Union of 1704.[20] Those north of the border may also have been more adept at working the patronage system. At any rate, a distinct Scottish presence within the EIC Court of Directors had been established by the late eighteenth century. According to one study, these Scottish directors displayed a clear tendency to promote the careers of their own countrymen.[21] No doubt those few directors of Irish affiliation acted similarly, but as they held less prominent positions within the Company hierarchy proportionally fewer opportunities were available for Irish candidates. Only after a competitive entrance exam was instituted in 1853 did the proportion of Irish recruits to the civil service reach expected levels. Between 1855 and 1863 twenty-four percent of the total intake came from Irish universities.[22] A rebalancing of military officer recruitment also seems to have occurred after the end of Company rule in 1858 when the Crown assumed responsibility. One historian has posited that the Anglo-Irish officer class may well have accounted for 'as many as 30 per cent of those serving in India' during the second half of the century.[23]

Given that Company positions were at a premium during the first half of the nineteenth century, the Lawrence family was undoubtedly fortunate in benefiting from the patronage of John Hudleston MP, an East India Company director and former civil servant in the Madras Presidency. Here family connections proved crucial: Hudleston's wife was a cousin of Mrs Lawrence senior. His standing within the Court of Directors ensured that a total of five Lawrences were able to receive Company nominations. Except for John, all were Addiscombe cadetships. Alexander, the eldest, entered Addiscombe in 1818, while in the following year it was George's turn. Both were given cavalry appointments, the most coveted of military commissions: Alexander in the Madras Presidency and George in the Bengal Presidency. Henry's nomination proved to be slightly more complicated. Although Hudleston had initially nominated Henry for a cadetship, Henry's father had magnanimously transferred it to another needful recipient. Fortunately, Hudleston's friend and fellow director, Mr John Morris, was able to appoint Henry to an Addiscombe cadetship in August 1820. Although Hudleston had ceased to be a director by the time John Lawrence was deciding his future, it was Morris who once more bestowed his patronage. This time, though, it was a civil nomination to Haileybury. John initially regarded this decision as a bitter disappointment as he had set his sights on a military career in emulation of his older siblings and father. Yet advice from his much-loved sister Letitia, it seems, finally persuaded John to accept the opportunity to train as a civil appointee. The last of the Lawrences reverted to tradition, however. Richard Lawrence attended Addiscombe in the years 1832–34.

For Robert Montgomery, it was figure of Josias Dupre Alexander MP (1771–1839) from Boom Hall, Derry who provided the all-important Addiscombe nomination. Josias' uncle, James Alexander, (1730–1802, 1st earl of Caledon) had pursued a highly lucrative career in revenue administration within the Bengal Civil Service. When he left Bengal in 1772, he had amassed a personal fortune estimated at £534,468.[24] A family history attributed such riches to his 'fortunate speculations in wheat'.[25] A quintessential 'nabob' who bought both a large estate in Ulster and political influence, James laid the foundation for other members of his family to establish fruitful careers in India. His nephew, Josias, joined the East India Company in 1796 and served in several official positions before eventually becoming a director. Similarly, his patronage of Robert Montgomery was based on kinship ties. A relative of Robert's mother's first husband, the Revd Mounsey Alexander, Josias was also instrumental in conferring a commission to Robert's younger brother James who joined the 60th Bengal Native Infantry.[26]

The Lawrences and Montgomery's imperial connections were notable but not unique. Other examples in Ulster could be found of whole families benefiting from a single sub-continental contact. John Nicholson, whose family hailed from Lisburn, and who would later serve with the Lawrences in Punjab, forged an Indian career courtesy of his uncle, James Weir Hogg. Following a successful legal career in Calcutta, Hogg returned home to become a MP and a director of the East India Company. The connection led to John and his four brothers (Alexander, James, Charles and William) all receiving cadetships in the Company's army.[27] Similarly, the Indian career of Belfast-born Henry Pottinger, Political Agent of Sindh and later the first Governor of Hong Kong, was launched through the patronage of fellow Ulsterman, Lord Castlereagh.[28] Four of Pottinger's brothers took up careers in the Company's army, while his nephew, Eldred, served alongside George Lawrence in Afghanistan. Another Lisburn family, the Grahams, had five members serving in India at the time of the 1857 Rebellion. In 1820 Dr James Graham senior was appointed an assistant surgeon in the East India Company, which ultimately paved the way for three of his sons and a nephew to pursue Indian military postings.[29]

For the Pottinger, Nicholson and Graham families, there may well have been career ambitions, a taste for adventure, and a sense of duty behind their pursuit of an Indian career, but the main impetus undoubtedly stemmed from limited employment opportunities and financial constraints at home. Pottinger came from impoverished gentry stock while Nicholson was the son of a physician who had died prematurely leaving a wife and seven children. The Lawrence family faced similar pecuniary challenges with the military career of Alexander Lawrence senior exemplifying, like many others, the personal cost of empire. The son of a Coleraine mill owner in the north of Ireland, Alexander had been orphaned at the age of ten and left in the charge of his two elder sisters. He departed Ulster for India as an unpaid volunteer officer in 1783, aged seventeen years old. On two occasions he won commissions only to see them fall through due to paperwork errors, forcing him to eventually purchase one. During his Indian service, he was badly injured leading the final assault on Tipu Sultan's fortress of Seringapatam in May 1799 and later found himself shipwrecked off the coast of Malabar. Despite re-joining his regiment in Ceylon, recurrent liver and fever problems forced him to return to England in 1808. Still only a captain, Alexander had little to show beyond his battle injuries for his twenty-five years' service. Eventually, he was promoted to major after already being passed over once. Thereafter he held posts in Yorkshire and in Guernsey, before taking to the field once more in the Waterloo campaign alongside fellow Seringapatam veteran, the Duke of Wellington. His military service finally ended when an abscess in his liver burst in 1816 as he was making his way back to Ireland. Forced to retire on a meagre army pension (it was eventually increased after much wrangling with the government and the East India Company), Alexander received little recompense for his years of dedicated service. The experience left both him and his wife Letitia determined to seek more certain prospects for their sons through direct employment in the East India Company rather than the British Army.

Robert Montgomery's immediate family background was not based on any long-standing military service to the empire. Instead, Robert, born on 2nd December 1809, was a son of the rectory. His father was Samuel Law Montgomery, the Rector of Moville, County Donegal where the family had established a small estate during the seventeenth century Plantation of Ulster, some 20 miles northeast of Derry. Later they branched into business with Robert's grandfather running a successful wine and spirits business in Derry before it was sold when his son (Robert's father) became a clergyman. Robert's mother was Susan Maria McClintock from Trentagh near Letterkenny. Her first marriage had been to the Reverend Mounsey Alexander, himself a former Rector of Moville. Unfortunately, Alexander died young leaving Susan a widow. Thirteen years later, though, she married Samuel Law Montgomery, Robert's father. Robert Montgomery choice of an imperial career was dictated in part by the familial pecking order. His elder brother, Samuel, followed his father into the church and was in line to inherit the small family estate at Moville. Robert, and his younger brother James, were thus obliged to seek alternative sources of employment, which led his mother Susan, despite her remarriage, to exploit the Alexander Indian connection.

It is also noteworthy that both the Lawrence and Montgomery families resided within a small geographic area of northwest Ireland: Derry and its hinterland of County Donegal, specifically the Inishowen peninsula. They formed a noticeably tight knit community where kinship ties were strengthened through marriage particularly amongst clerical families. On 5th May 1798 Alexander Lawrence senior married Letitia Catherine Knox, the daughter of the Revd George Knox of Lifford, Co. Donegal. In an age of pre-birth control when large middle-class families were not unusual, the union produced a total of twelve children. George was born in Trincomalee, Ceylon on 17th March 1804, Henry in Matura, Ceylon on 28th June 1806, and John in Richmond, Yorkshire on 4th March 1811.[30] Henry and John Lawrence continued the tradition by marrying daughters of the rectory. Henry married Honoria, daughter of the Revd George Marshall, Rector of Carndonagh, while John married Harriette, daughter of the Revd Richard Hamilton, Rector of Culdaff. The extent of these clerical connections was further exemplified by the Lawrences' maternal uncle, the Revd James Knox, who was headmaster of Foyle College. It was here, in January 1815, where George and Henry began their formative education as boarders, lasting a period of four years. They were later joined by Robert Montgomery who entered Foyle in April 1819, while John Lawrence attended in the years 1823 to 1825 having previously spent the years 1819–23 at Mr Gough's school, College Green, Bristol.[31]

Education and Training

Foyle College

Foyle College's foundation was inextricably linked to the Londonderry Plantation of the early seventeenth century – the state backed colonisation scheme involving London's livery companies. Mathias Springham, a member of the Merchant Taylors Company, had established a small 'Free Grammar School' within the city's historic walls in 1617. By the time of the Lawrences' arrival, and reflecting the city's expansion, the school had moved to a larger site half a mile north of the city overlooking the River Foyle. Now renamed Foyle College, the new building was, according to one contemporary writer, 'a large substantial house…evidently designed to possess the requisites of durability, more than architectural variety or grandeur'.[1] This simple, classically proportioned edifice reflected a similarly robust, classics-led curriculum catering largely to the sons of the local gentry and Derry's mercantile class. In 1818 pupils numbered one hundred and ten, half of whom were boarders.[2] Provision was made for Hebrew, Greek and Latin as well as for 'commercial education', arithmetic, algebra, trigonometry, English, and book-keeping. Although a Royal Commission concluded in 1825 that Foyle was 'one of the most useful and best conducted schools in Ireland,' most biographers of the Lawrences were less enamoured.[3] Sir Richard Temple's remark that the school 'tended rather to form and strengthen the character than to enlighten the intellect' was perhaps the most charitable.[4] One modern writer, however, believed Foyle College to be 'a tough, no-nonsense, God-fearing institution that produced boys ideally matched to the East India Company's needs'.[5] School annals appear to support this view. Apart the Lawrences and Montgomery, some seventeen pupils were recorded as finding Indian employment in a twenty-year period between 1814–1834.[6]

In recounting these formative years, few contemporaries could point to any notable characteristics or achievements that set the Lawrences or Montgomery apart from their peers. In Herbert Edwardes' biography of Henry, one school friend recollected that 'Henry's intellectual attainments then gave little promise of his future'.[7] Introverted by nature, and caring little for games, only his involvement in impromptu amateur dramatics during the summer holidays appeared to fire his imagination. Similarly, in his life of Lord Lawrence, Bosworth

Smith unearthed little evidence on which to predict future success: 'I cannot find by careful inquiry among the few schoolfellows of John Lawrence who have survived him that, even now, looking back in the light of all that he has done, they saw, or think that they saw, any promise of his future eminence. He cast no shadow before him.'[8] In contrast to Henry's diffidence, John appeared to exhibit a more pugnacious side to his personality during his days at Foyle. Fellow pupil Robert Montgomery noted that his 'determined and quick tempered' character would find an outlet in mock battles between boarders and day pupils in the school's surroundings as well as some bruising encounters with the nearby rival Academical Institute.[9] By his own admission, though, John later expressed regret that he 'did not work regularly and continuously' at school, nor did he avail of the opportunities 'for securing a good education'. It was a sentiment shared by Henry. Robert Montgomery, on the other hand, attributed his successful career to the 'vigorous training' he had received at Foyle College.[10] When the time came for George and Henry to leave Foyle in July 1819, their headmaster uncle, in a letter to the boys' father, acknowledged that they had 'not yet attained to the highest branches of literature,' but trusted that they had 'not passed their years unprofitably'.[11]

If Foyle College's academic legacy was unremarkable, the forging of personal relationships and memories nonetheless proved enduring. During the Lawrences' stay at Foyle College, a spinster aunt, affectionately known as 'Aunt Angel', fulfilled the role of a surrogate mother. A woman of intense piety, she regularly conducted religious instruction for the students with the Lawrence boys receiving special attention. Herbert Edwardes believed that the more sensitive Henry 'got Aunt Angel's teachings well by heart, and remembered them gratefully through life'.[12] John, by contrast, was less receptive. Montgomery recalled how they would often try in vain to slink past their aunt's room only for the door to suddenly burst open and for her to usher the boys in for further instruction.[13] According to Richard Temple, Aunt Angel's pious instruction had a detrimental effect on John: 'the religious training, to which he was subjected, appears to have been somewhat too severely strict the recollection of it, however, rendered him adverse to formalism of any kind.'[14]

The Lawrences' time in Derry was also seen as crucial in forming their cultural identity. Despite being born outside Ireland, most biographers agreed that the Lawrences' Ulster roots left an indelible mark. For J.L. Morison, 'Foyle College definitely fixed their Irish nationality for them. Sons of an Irish father and Irish mother, but homeless so far as locality was concerned, these years in Ulster elicited the latent Irish qualities in them, and confirmed them.'[15] Similarly, Temple noted that John's school days in Derry were 'of great importance in the forming of his mind and disposition, as he breathed the air, imbibed the ideas, and gathered the associations of Ulster'.[16] For Robert Montgomery, Irish born and bred, the experience of growing up in Co. Donegal was equally significant. According to his grandson Brian Montgomery, Robert's personality was 'conditioned by the strictly religious atmosphere of a small parish in the Protestant Church of Ireland….a minority living in the midst of a predominantly Roman Catholic community'.[17] It was an experience that may well have mentally equipped Robert for the life of an isolated district officer in rural India.

Both the Lawrences and Montgomery families shared the same Ulster planter heritage originating from the Crown's sponsorship of the colonisation of the province by Protestant English and Scottish settlers in the early seventeenth century. Central to Ulster planter ideology was the Siege of Derry (1689–90). As part of the Williamite Wars waged between the Protestant William of Orange and the Catholic King James II, the accounts of the besieged inhabitants' dogged resistance and ultimate deliverance were part of the collective consciousness of subsequent generations of Ulstermen. As their Indian careers unfolded, historical parallels would be drawn between this Ulster planter ideology and the Lawrences and Montgomery's experiences in India during the 1840s and 1850s. With its tropes of courage, steadfastness and ultimate deliverance, the example of Derry's siege would be invoked as a stoical response to the challenges of imperial rule, most notably in attempting to defeat the 1857 Revolt. Richard Temple noted John Lawrence's recourse to the historical associations of his youth: 'His heart was with Ulster, and in his hardest times he would recur to the defence of Derry.'[18] For J.W. Kaye, the Lawrence brothers 'heard the grand historical traditions of the famous city by which they dwelt, and went forth into the world with the old watchword of Derry, "No SURRENDER," engraved on their hearts'.[19] More pertinently, John Lawrence, after his appointment as Viceroy of India, referred to Derry's siege at an assembly of Punjabi chieftains held in his honour by Robert Montgomery (Lieutenant-Governor of the Punjab) at Lawrence Hall, Lahore in October 1864:

It is quite true that we were at school together forty years ago at a place very famous in history, Londonderry, celebrated for defending itself against great odds. Perhaps some of the old North Irish blood flowed in our veins, for we came from that part. And when the time came in India we found ourselves fighting against still greater odds, the blood of the old defenders of Derry warmed within us and like old war horses we buckled to our work.[20]

For Henry, though, this historic parallel would reach both its most apposite and tragic during the Siege of Lucknow. 'No surrender! Let every man die at his post; but never make terms,' were among the final words he reportedly told the embattled garrison in early July 1857.[21]

The East India Company Military Seminary, Addiscombe

The East India Company Military Seminary, where Alexander (1818–19), George (1819–21) and Henry Lawrence (1820–22) as well as Robert Montgomery (1826–28) received their military training, first opened its doors in 1809. Based around an imposing eighteenth century country mansion near the then small town of Croydon in Surrey, Addiscombe offered a two-year course with the purpose of training young cadets to serve in the East India Company's army as engineers, artillery, and cavalry officers.[22] Infantry officers were later admitted, but it was more usual for them to go to India directly without prior training. Entrance to each branch depended on examination results except for cavalry appointments which were at the discretion of the Company's Court of Directors.

The main objectives of Addiscombe were to provide technical military training, scientific knowledge, and languages within a disciplined environment. The long fifty-four-hour academic week was dominated by mathematics, which accounted for almost half the timetable. Lessons on fortification, which focused on methods of defensive building construction, were also given due prominence, as well as some rudimentary tuition in military drawing and surveying. Provision was also made for the study of Hindustani, while the addition of a few hours per week for French and Latin gave a cultured gloss to the syllabus.

Life at Addiscombe, however, offered little in the way of creature comforts. The standard of accommodation was undeniably spartan. Wooden partitions in the dormitories divided each cadet's small sleeping compartment. Measuring only nine feet by six feet, they contained an iron bed that could be raised during the day, a table, chair, drawer and 'washing apparatus'. In Addiscombe parlance, the cadets mockingly described their cubicles as 'kennels'. The diet was equally frugal with little variation. Breakfast consisted only of tea and bread and butter. Lunch was again bread but with cheese and table beer, while beef, mutton, veal, or occasionally pork was served for dinner.[23] The founding editor of *The Calcutta Review*, J.W. Kaye, himself a former Addiscombe cadet, painted an austere picture of the college's daily routine in the early 1830s which consisted of long periods of study punctuated by intervals of drill. Only a small amount of time was given over for the cadets' recreation.[24] Kaye argued that such a rigorous regime had a dispiriting and detrimental effect on the young cadets. Barred from going beyond the seminary's grounds without permission, there were limited options for the boys to enjoy their leisure time. Punishment for flouting the rules was extra drill or solitary confinement in the infamous "Black

Hole" – a small, darkened room where the only piece of furniture was a high stool.[25] Kaye, who wrote a novel about an Addiscombe cadet called Peregrine Pultuney, expressed frustration with a system that seemed to encourage immoral behaviour: "What wonder is it then, that we should stroll into a public-house and enjoy a comfortable bowl of punch, a good fire, and what is perhaps still better, an hour or two of privacy, which we cannot get within the walls of the institution, packed together as we are like so many dogs in a kennel?"[26]

Although little is known of the time spend by Alexander, George and Robert Montgomery, some details do emerge of Henry's spell at the college. After a further year attending Mr Gough's school, College Green, Bristol and passing the obligatory entrance examination, Henry began his studies at Addiscombe in August 1820. As one of one hundred and fourteen cadets, he was helped to settle in by his elder brother, George. 'You may depend my dearest mother,' wrote the elder Lawrence, 'that while I am able Henry shall want neither a friend or a brother, and that it shall be my study to render Addiscombe as comfortable and agreeable an abode for him as I am able.'[27] It did not take long for Henry to form new friendships. One fellow cadet called Tindal offered the full use of his study to Henry, while George described his brother's friendship with another boy called Lewin as 'very thick'. During his time at Addiscombe, Henry continued to espouse a strong Irish identity.[28] One contemporary remembered him as 'a very rough Irish lad, hard-bodied, iron-constitutioned, who could, when necessary, take or give a licking with a good grace'. Pat, as Henry was then nicknamed, was seen as proud of his Irish roots and was quick to react to any perceived slight. Another fellow cadet noted: 'He had a fiery temper, off in an instant at any reflection on Ireland, but full of good humour, and easily made to laugh; always ready to side with the losing party or the weak.'[29] For J.H. Macdonald, Henry's college record was 'one of steady application and good conduct'. He did not remember him 'ever being sent to the black hole, or getting into any serious scrape'.[30] Despite the tendency to be riled at times, the picture that emerges of Henry is that of a serious minded young man who usually preferred solitary pursuits such as country walks or reading the works of Walter Scott rather than participating in team games or more boyish activities.[31] Such earnestness also extended to what he saw as frivolous entertainment. After a ball one evening, he wrote disappointingly to his sister Letitia: 'What a wretched unprofitably evening! Not a Christian to speak to. All the women decked out with flowers on their heads, and their bodies half naked.'[32]

During his time at Addiscombe, Henry did not stand out in academic terms and, like his time at Foyle, there was no inkling from contemporaries that a dazzling career awaited. One fellow cadet recalled: 'I am satisfied that had our Addiscombe Professors been asked to name the cadet of all the 120 youths present at the academy whom they deemed most likely to distinguish himself in after life, Henry Lawrence's name would have occurred to none.'[33] Indeed contemporaries regarded him as being 'backward for his age in scholarship, and slow in acquisition'. The curriculum and the standard of teaching, however, did little to inspire students. One example was in the provision of Hindustani. The practical benefits of learning the language were obvious to all, but its provision left most cadets at the end of their course with only a cursory understanding, not to mention a deep dislike. From the very beginning, it was reported that there was a 'general disinclination and inattention of the cadets to the study of Hindustani', prompting the college authorities to employ an external examiner.[34] The appointment of assistant lecturer, Munshi Hasan Ali, a native speaker, in 1810 was a measure designed to raise standards. But after six years he returned home to India on account of the climate and was not replaced. In the 1820s a Mr Bowles, who had never been to India, headed the department. According to Addiscombe's chronicler, he had 'an unfortunately pronounced way of rendering the language'. Nicknamed "Chaw" on account of his pronunciation of the Hindustani word for the number four, his idiosyncrasies regularly invited ridicule from the cadets who were only too keen to encourage digression from their lessons.[35] Indicative of the students' linguistic aversion was the periodic outbreaks of 'Hindustani fever' during examination times. Many cadets did their best to avoid being examined on the subject by feigning illness and seeking refuge in the college's hospital.[36]

More fundamental criticisms were levelled against Addiscombe. J.W. Kaye argued that the college placed undue emphasis on theoretical learning that ill-equipped the engineer or the artillery officer when facing real-life challenges in India. In his opinion there needed to be more surveying, sketching and hands-on experience: 'There should be a soul of practicality pervading the whole educational course; and the advancement of the cadet should not be tested so much by what he can do in the study-hall, as by what he can do in the field.'[37] Henry Lawrence no doubt shared Kaye's criticism on the curriculum's imbalance. In a later article on army reform, he stressed 'military science, rather than mathematics' as 'the desideratum'.[38] Significantly, given his future career as a revenue surveyor, Henry's favoured pursuit at Addiscombe was making military surveys of the surrounding country largely on his own initiative. The subject of his education would continue to irk him in later years and reflect poorly on the purpose of institutions like Addiscombe in preparing young men for their Indian career. 'For my part,' he later told one colleague, 'my education consisted of kicks. I was never taught anything – no not even at Addiscombe.'[39] In contrast to Alexander and George, who both joined the cavalry courtesy of John Hudleston's patronage, Henry took the more difficult path by opting for the artillery. Having achieved the necessary marks, he left Addiscombe in May 1822 to become a Bengal artillery officer.

Still only 15 years old when he left Foyle College in October 1824, Robert Montgomery would spend, alongside John Lawrence, a further two years at Wraxall Hall School, 'a large rambling Elizabethan house' six miles from Bath which was best remembered for its frozen water basins and draughty dormitories during winter.[40] Attending Addiscombe in the years 1826–28, Robert seemed destined for a career as an officer in the Bengal Engineers. However, the poor performance of William Alexander (nephew of Robert's patron Josias Alexander) at Haileybury changed matters. Rather than leave his nephew bereft of a future in colonial service, Josias engineered a swap of his nominations that set Robert firmly on the path of civil employment.

The East India College, Haileybury

Like the military seminary at Addiscombe, the East India College at Haileybury, Hertfordshire, which John Lawrence attended after Wraxall Hall (1825–27), was founded in response to the growing demands of empire and the need to train a new breed of the Company's civil servants on a professional basis. Previously, administrators such as Mountstuart Elphinstone had simply gone directly to India, learned the basics on the job and, through their own extensive reading and personal experience, had gradually achieved proficiency in the skills of administration and diplomacy. Some like John Shore received perfunctory private training at a commercial school in Hoxton studying 'bookkeeping and merchants' accounts' before joining the Bengal Civil Service.[41] Others, such as David Ochterlony and Thomas Munro, began their career in the military before progressing to civil appointments. This ill-defined, unstructured approach, which relied on individual initiative, personal connections, and available opportunities, was now replaced by a more systematic arrangement. The East India College initially opened at Hertford Castle in 1806 but moved to a purpose-built location at Haileybury in 1809 for the express purpose of educating young men as administrators for service in India. The course duration was the same as Addiscombe (two years), although some allowance was made during John Lawrence's time (1827–29) due to the shortage of qualified civilians when it was cut to one year or two terms provided students were eighteen years old and had passed the necessary examinations with distinction.[42] Although John had fulfilled the second requirement, the first compelled him to complete a second year.

Considering the tender age of some of the students, the breadth of Haileybury's curriculum was ambitious. Spanning a wide spectrum, it included mathematics, natural history, chemistry, law, political economy, history, classical literature, Sanskrit, Persian, Arabic, Hindustani, Bengali and Telegu. Much, too, was said of the quality of the teaching staff. Thomas Robert Malthus, who was Professor of History and Political Economy for thirty years until his death in 1834, was perhaps the most celebrated. William Empson, Professor of Law (1824–52), was another influential figure actively involved in the intellectual debates of the age. According to one Haileyburian, Sir George Campbell, Empson was 'a good deal of a Benthamite' who instilled in him 'a very sound belief in the greatest happiness of the greatest number'.[43]

First time visitors to Haileybury were much impressed by its classically inspired front edifice as well as its physical setting. The handsome Grecian porticos and ionic columns gave the college 'considerable architectural pretensions'; a grandeur which was enhanced by its elevated position within parkland overlooking the Lee Valley and Hertford Heath. Designed by the architect, William Wilkins, it was favourably compared to his more famous work, the National Gallery. Yet behind this façade, its aesthetic qualities swiftly diminished for those with more intimate knowledge. A scholastic quadrangle was written off by Professor Monier-Williams, as 'three sides of a square of dingy common looking brick buildings…which would scarcely have been tolerable in a barrack, a prison or a workhouse'.[44] Student accommodation was modest. It consisted of a small bedsitting room measuring twelve feet by eight, plus a recess for the bed and a large cupboard, which included a chest of drawers and washing facilities.[45]

In contrast to the strict, ordered, and sombre atmosphere of its sister college at Addiscombe, discipline at Haileybury was decidedly lax. Rules tended not to be rigorously enforced, and the threat of expulsion was rarely invoked for more serious transgressions. College authorities generally refrained from imposing harsh punishments that would risk conflict with Company directors who were loath to ruin the career prospects of their nominations. After all it was directors who paid their stipends and who could (and did) intervene to overrule unpopular decisions.

No account appears to exist of the daily routine in the early years of the college, but John Beames' candid and often humorous account of Haileybury in the 1850s may not be too wide of the mark.[46] The day would begin at seven when the elderly housekeeper or bedmaker arrived to light the fire. The 'scout' or waiter would soon afterwards turn up to fill the bath, make the table for breakfast, clean the boots and in general make enough noise to wake the student from his slumber. Once up, they would wrap a long overcoat over their pyjamas and hastily make their way to chapel at eight o'clock where any absenteeism was reported to the Dean. Breakfast could be as simple as bread, butter and jam with tea or coffee. On some occasions grander affairs were organised when groups of students would descend on someone's room to enjoy the delights of curried soles and considerable qualities of wine. Such high-spirited 'breakfast parties' were, for the most part, overlooked by the college authorities.[47]

Haileybury thus reflected a very different culture compared to Addiscombe and one where the intellectual demands placed on the students, given the distinguished teaching staff, were remarkably light. Lectures would last only two to three hours in the morning, and unlike Oxbridge there was no tutorial system. For most students there was little incentive to exert themselves intellectually as they knew that their appointments to India were secure so long as they scraped a pass in their examinations. Afternoons were therefore leisurely affairs with students free to do as they pleased. Some played cricket or rowed or even hunted. Others took the opportunity to roam the surrounding countryside or visit surreptitiously the nearby towns of Hertford, Ware and Hoddesdon. Only the dedicated few would spend their time writing up lecture notes. Dinner was served at six and there was a return to chapel at eight. Thereafter the studious students would read into the night, while most would socialise in their rooms. On some nights a 'tavern' or party was hosted in one of the student's rooms where drinking, smoking, and singing would go on until the early hours of the morning.[48] Again, strict curfews were never stringently enforced. Little wonder that most students held fond memories of their college days.

It was into this milieu that John Lawrence entered in the summer of 1827 after successfully passing the entrance examination. Aged sixteen years old, he was one of forty-four students in that year's intake with the overall number attending the college hovering around the one hundred mark.[49] Contemporaries included Martin Gubbins, future Commissioner of Oudh, James Cumine, future Magistrate and Collector of Etawah, and Donald McLeod who would be one of his closest colleagues in the Punjab. In his two-year spell at Haileybury, Bosworth Smith concluded that John was 'neither very idle nor very industrious'.[50] Although not among the most intellectually distinguished of his year, John was no slouch either. As his term exam results showed, he managed to achieve prizes in history, Bengali as well as a gold medal for law.[51] At the end of the course in May 1829, John achieved a respectable third place for his presidency of Bengal.

During his time at Haileybury John struck up a firm friendship with John Hallett Batten, the son of its principal. Batten painted an unassuming portrait of the future viceroy whose quiet demeanour was reflected in his tendency to exist on the periphery of the college's social life rather than at its centre. His natural instincts often led him to roam the extensive woodlands, meadows, and open heath of the surrounding countryside. Sometimes, like others, he would go on unsanctioned jaunts to the nearby towns, and there were periodic visits to the local hostelries to play skittles, bowls or quoits. But there was no mention of his involvement in the college's notorious breakfast clubs or evening parties. Mostly, it seems, his gaunt figure could be found hanging around the college quadrangle or in the reading-room with Batten; a fact that disappointed Batten's father who was sorry to see him 'loafing about with that tall Irishman instead of sticking to the more regular students'.[52] John's 'rugged and uncouth' appearance may have been off-putting to those of passing acquaintance, but it was, according to Batten, 'sufficiently set off by an intelligent face and by his high good humour'. Like Henry, John's Ulster roots appeared to be never far from the surface, and he was keen to initiate his fellow students into 'the mysteries sacred to St. Patrick's Day, Hallowe'en, the glorious, pious and immortal memory of King William, the 'prentice boys of Derry, etc.'[53] On one occasion John sought to enact the Orange tradition of lighting a celebratory bonfire on college grounds. It was, it seems, the only recorded instance of him incurring the censure of the college authorities.[54]

What then did students like John Lawrence gain from their two years at Haileybury? In truth, the benefits for most students were modest. Haileybury's teaching methods tended to concentrate on the academic rather than the practical, and in this respect it had more in common with a university rather than a dedicated training college. In the study of Indian languages, for example, a knowledge of Sanskrit might well give the student a linguistic and cultural appreciation as well as honing his mental acumen, but it did little to increase his fluency of the living vernacular. George Campbell, writing in 1852, found its study to be as useful to an Indian magistrate as 'a knowledge of the tongue of the ancient Germans' to an English commissioner of police 'who might now and then discover a slang term to be of orthodox Saxon origin'.[55] For Hindustani or Bengali there was little emphasis on the colloquial spoken word. Those in the field saw its shortcomings. Brigadier-General John Jacob criticised a system which encouraged a young officer 'to read a native book, or to converse with his moonshee in elegant phraseology,' but which left him 'quite incapable of understanding the expressions of a peasant, or of making the peasant understand him'.[56]

The cultural environment of Haileybury also seemed to contradict its very *raison d'être* by promoting an almost detached, abstract view of India. John Beames noted wryly that 'it was considered "bad form" to talk about India'.[57] Why this was considered almost taboo is unclear. It was true that most of the professors themselves had never set foot in India. Yet there may well have been a feeling that it was sufficient to teach the theoretical and leave the practical for when its graduates took up their first civil appointments in a *mofussil* district. In any case an increasing number of students came from families with long associations with India so the dissemination of practical knowledge may well have been viewed as superfluous. Ultimately, though, these drawbacks mattered little for most of its alumni. Haileybury's strength, they argued, lay in fostering an *esprit de corps* that would be cherished by them throughout their Indian careers and beyond.[58]

First Impressions: Calcutta in Regency Times

In the 1820s the only viable means of reaching India was by sailing ship. Operating under charter to the East India Company, fully rigged vessels would leave from several designated English ports, navigate southwards through the Atlantic via St Helena, round the Cape of Good Hope and across the Indian ocean to reach Madras and then finally Calcutta. Covering some 15,000 nautical miles, the voyage usually took around five months to complete depending on weather conditions. The timings for the maiden voyages of the Lawrence brothers and Robert Montgomery were largely similar. Henry Lawrence first sailed from Deal in Kent in September 1822 and reached Calcutta on 21st February 1823, while Robert Montgomery sailed from Liverpool in the first week of June 1828 and docked at Calcutta on 13th November. John Lawrence, who was accompanied by Henry on his return to India, embarked at Portsmouth onboard the *Thalia* on 2nd September 1829 and landed in Calcutta on 9th February 1830. George Lawrence's voyage, by contrast, made more rapid progress, leaving England on 5th of May 1821 and arriving in Calcutta on the 10th September – a journey time of four months and five days. At the time of departure, Henry was only sixteen years old, his brother George a year older, while Robert Montgomery and John Lawrence were both nineteen.

Completion of these long, arduous journeys was no small achievement. Passengers were forced to live in cramped conditions, without the possibility of fresh food and water for weeks. Violent storms and in some cases severe bouts of seasickness were not uncommon while frequent periods of boredom were inescapable.[1] For those fortunate to procure a cabin, the allowance of such private space was meagre. The noted travel writer, Fanny Parkes, whose voyage on the Marchioness of Ely took place in 1822, had a stern cabin measuring only twelve feet by ten feet which she shared with her husband.[2] Henry Lawrence's long friendship with James Thomason, Lieutenant-Governor of the North-Western Provinces, began when they shared a cabin in the same year.[3] Robert Montgomery, on the other hand, did not have the luxury of a cabin on his maiden voyage. The young cadet was on board the *Abberton*, a three-mast 431-ton ship which like many EIC ships was built more for cargo and less for the comfort of passengers. Robert's situation would improve significantly some years later, though, when he made the voyage home on an East Indiaman vessel called the *Southampton*: 'I believe I am reckoned the burra sahib on board. What a change a few years makes. After a lapse of 14 years, I have the best cabin in the ship.'[4]

Reaching the Bay of Bengal and navigating the eighty or so miles up the Hooghly River marked the final part of the voyage. An air of expectation and impatience grew amongst the passengers. For much of this section the banks were lined with dense jungle inhabited by tigers and other wild animals. There was little at this stage to suggest that a large, expanding metropolis was imminent. Robert Montgomery's initial feelings may well have been ones of disappointment and irritation. At night, when his ship, the *Abberton*, was moored along the Hooghly's banks, he tried unsuccessfully to sleep on deck. Attacked by numerous mosquitoes, he was also unnerved on hearing the unusual cries of nearby jackals and hyenas.[5] Travelling further, though, the vegetation thinned to reveal an impressive scene. In this final stretch, newcomers could admire the large, handsome Palladian mansions of Garden Reach with its groves of lofty trees and substantial lawns stretching down to the waters' edge. To William Huggins, a former Indigo planter writing in 1824, it was like 'a fairy isle, in the midst of a desert' that allowed wealthy British merchants the opportunity to 'breathe an air unpolluted by the smoke and effluvia of Calcutta'.[6] Becoming one of the most fashionable addresses amongst European settlers, it gave an impressive foretaste of Calcutta's claim to being called the 'City of Palaces'.[7]

Extending six miles from Kidderpore in the south to Cossipore in the north, Calcutta had, by the 1830s, a population approaching 230,000 people. The overwhelming number were composed of Bengali Muslims and Hindus, the latter forming a majority on a scale of two to one. The British population, by contrast, was minuscule and amounted to little more than three thousand persons according to one estimate.[8] Other nationalities included Armenians, French, Portuguese, Chinese, Danish and Dutch. The city had become the commercial heart of the East India Company whose interests covered a wide array of industries that included jute, tea, rice, textiles, and timber. Business was booming and this was reflected in the great number of ships docked on the Hooghly, forming what one observer described as 'forests of masts and sails'.[9] Its opulence was also confirmed when long haul passengers disembarked at Chandpal Ghat. These broad riverfront steps, which thronged with a wide variety of different nationalities, led to Esplanade Row where newcomers could gaze in wonder at the stately buildings bathed in the tropical sunlight.[10]

Alongside several substantial private dwellings ornamented by spacious verandas, the Esplanade was home to the Supreme Court of Calcutta, the Doric styled town hall and the colossal, neo-classical Government House – the residence of the Governor-General and the centre of British power in India.

William Huggins was overwhelmed by its splendour and declared: 'I have seen the Thuilleries and palace of Versailles, and think neither of them equals the government house in uniformity and majesty of design.'[11] 'Government house is the most remarkable public edifice in Calcutta', gushed the writer Walter Hamilton.[12] The Esplanade was impressive enough to remind Bishop Heber of St Petersburg, though his enthusiasm dimmed somewhat over the Governor-General's residence, which he felt 'narrowly missed being a noble structure'.[13]

To the south of the esplanade, lay the vast, expansive *Maidan*. Popular for morning and evening canters, it was also the place to be seen. In the relative cool of the evening, the great and the good of Calcutta society would take their evening drive along the broad, well-tended road known as "the Course". Overlooking the *Maidan* was the fashionable Chowringhee district where many grand buildings were located.[14] These large, stucco-fronted houses, set within their own gardens and positioned along a generously proportioned thoroughfare, greatly impressed observers. 'Chowringhee, an entire village of palaces…altogether forms the finest view I ever beheld in my life,' remarked Lord Valentia in 1803.[15] Similarly, Honoria Marshall noted its exclusive reputation: 'Most of the upper class of Europeans in the Presidency have houses out of town, especially about Chowringhee, a post on the river and very [pretty]; Every house is detached and surrounded by a compound (or enclosure) laid out in garden and shrubberies. The houses are upper roomed and have generally flat roofs surrounded by a balustrade and open porticos in front.'[16] The travel writer Fanny Parkes, who rented one such property for the costly sum of 325 rupees per month, particularly admired their generously proportioned pillared verandas, which gave 'an air of lightness and beauty to the buildings'. The covered balconies, she noted, also had the practical benefit of 'protecting the dwellings from the sun' and rendered them 'agreeable for exercise in the rainy season'.[17]

Upon first impressions, it was tempting to suppose that the British had successfully fashioned a new Rome or Athens in the East. Yet such classical illusions were soon dispelled on closer inspection. The British attempt to construct a formal, anglicised city never quite lived up to the mark. Walter Hamilton was one observer who noted the juxtaposition of European and indigenous dwellings: 'Chowringhee, Park Street, Durrumtollah, the Jaun Bazaar, and Esplanade, now form the European part of the town. On passing along these fine streets, the mixture of native huts with houses of the most noble appearance, like Grecian temples, spoils the effect.'[18] The travel writer Emma Roberts similarly noted the incongruity: 'A mud hut, or row of native hovels, constructed in mats, thatch and bamboos, not superior to the rudest wigwam, often rest against the outer walls of palaces, while there are avenues opening from the principle streets, intersected in all directions by native bazaars, filled with unsightly articles of every description.'[19] The limited extent of Calcutta's 'white town' was also recognised by Bishop Heber. Beyond the Esplanade, Heber noted that the nearby streets of Dhurrumtollah (SN Banerjee Rd.) and Cossitollah (Bentinck St.) were 'pretty equally divided between the different nations', forming what was in effect a cultural transitional zone.[20] As Cossitollah Street followed on to Chitpore Road (Rabindra Sarani), a matter of a few hundred yards, the 'Indianisation' of the European cityscape was almost complete in a scene captured by the artist James Baillie Fraser called *A View in the Bazaar, leading to Chitpore Road*.[21]

For those who dared to explore the city in full, the 'Black town' situated further north formed a stark contrast. William Huggins expressed the dichotomy clearly enough: 'Take it all in all, perhaps no city in the world deserves to be called a mass of misery and magnificence more justly.'[22] Walter Hamilton reckoned that as much as six in eight parts of the city were in a wretched, poverty-stricken state: 'The streets here are narrow, dirty and unpaved; the houses of two stories are of brick, with flat terraced roofs; but the great majority are mud cottages, covered with small tiles, with side walls of mats, bamboos, and other combustible materials, the whole within and without swarming with population.'[23] Yet here too, amidst the squalor, there existed some handsome dwellings. Many Indian merchants and businessmen had become very successful and were keen to flaunt their wealth by acquiring palatial houses and the accoutrements of European culture.[24] Honoria Lawrence noted that 'the richer natives' were keen to imitate 'European manners, equipages, and buildings'.[25] So too did Fanny Parkes who, when invited to a party at the home of the celebrated Bengali, Ram Mohan Roy, observed that 'the house was very handsomely furnished, everything in European style, with the exception of the owner'.[26]

This then was the Calcutta which greeted the Lawrence brothers and Robert Montgomery upon arrival. As civilian officers both John Lawrence and Robert Montgomery would complete their training at Fort William College in an imposing three-storey edifice overlooking Tank Square known as the Writers' Building, the headquarters of the East India Company.[27] The curriculum consisted of Hindustani, Persian, Bengali and Sanskrit as well as European and Classical languages and provided more practical knowledge of the vernacular than Haileybury. Lectures were supplemented by further study with a *munshi* or native teacher. Although the college made provision for the latter, a good *munshi* was much in demand and a competitive market for their services was established.[28] Course duration was usually no more than one year, at the end of which students were required to take an examination. Those who passed could then take up their first posting.

With educational commitments light, much was made of the opportunities for young officers to experience the delights of the city. The archetypal *griffin* of the period was depicted as showing a penchant for 'high-mettled' horses, dressing in the current fashions, going to balls, drinking claret and champagne, and renting expensive houses. In the absence of parental control and with little experience of money matters, sizeable debts could easily pile up within a short space of time. Although Robert Montgomery was no spendthrift, he nevertheless quickly fell into arrears after his arrival in November 1828; a debt that was apparently not fully repaid until he became Lieutenant-Governor of the Punjab many years later.[29]

Robert was greatly impressed by the Bengal metropolis, recounting to his spinster aunts who lived in London Street, Derry, that it boasted 'much grandeur and magnificence' and offered everything that could be desired.[30] He settled in well into his new surroundings and his spirits were lifted by 'a great number of Derry people' whom he met there.[31] Although he missed 'the presence of kind friends at London Street', it seems he had little time to ponder. He threw himself into the quintessential colonial past time of hog hunting, and managed, along with some other officers, to keep a bobbery pack (a mixed pack of dogs) for hunting jackals. One attempt, however, to fit into Calcutta's social scene ended in some embarrassment. At a fancy-dress ball given at Government House, Robert had misconstrued the dress policy by arriving as a chimney sweep and was refused entrance.[32]

Like Robert, John Lawrence was to spend nearly a year at Fort William College continuing to study oriental languages, before taking up his first civil appointment. For much of the time, though, he remained in poor health.[33] When he arrived in February 1830, the cool season had just ended. The rise in temperature, particularly during the rainy season, aggravated his constitution. In such a state, the charms of the city with its balls and dinner parties held little appeal. Homesickness was a natural symptom, and he entertained on several occasions that if a reasonable offer from back home came he would grab it. John nevertheless persevered. Having passed the necessary examinations in Hindustani and Persian, he sought a post in Delhi. According to Charles Aitchison, one reason why John chose the Delhi posting was because of the 'enervating and sickly climate of Calcutta, of which he entertained a hearty dislike to the end of his days'.[34] There were, however, two further reasons. John would be relatively close to both George and Henry who were then stationed at the military cantonment of Karnal, plus there were greater opportunities for career advancement in Delhi rather than in lower Bengal.[35] Far from the immediate orbit of central government, Delhi at that time remained a frontier city. Communication with the rest of India was poor. The Grand Trunk Road did not reach the city until after 1850; the railway by the mid-1860s. Consequently, for John, in early 1831, the 900-mile journey from Calcutta to Delhi was made by palanquin, taking eighteen days to complete.

Elder brother George had similarly little to say of his time in Calcutta where he spent only six weeks in the cadet barracks following his arrival in September 1821. He recorded just two personal events. One was suffering a severe fall when he attempted the first time to mount a horse dressed in full cavalry uniform on the Maidan. George was 'picked up senseless and taken into a good Samaritan's house in Chowringhee' to recover.[36] The other was at a dinner given by the then Governor-General, Lord Hastings, who gave the young officer a friendly piece of advice at the beginning of his career: 'Mind you study the native languages, sir!'[37] In November 1822 George left Calcutta to join the 2nd regiment of Light Cavalry stationed at Keitah, (Bundelkhand) in central India. His journey 'up country' began by boat in a barge-like vessel called a *budgerow* (from the Hindi bajrā). In contrast to John's mode of travel, progress was painfully slow, taking George over two months to complete the journey.

Thankfully more information is available for Henry's time in Calcutta. Having arrived as a second Lieutenant in the Bengal Artillery in February 1823, he was stationed at the regimental headquarters at Dum-Dum, then on the northern outskirts of the city. There he took up residence in a *chummery* along with a fellow artillery cadet called John Edwards who had been on the same voyage. Henry continued to adopt an earnest, upright and introspective way of life as he had done so at Addiscombe. Unlike Robert Montgomery, he did not join in wild game hunting, nor did he gravitate towards the billiard room or the theatre. Apart from his regimental duties, he seems to have spent his time improving his chess as well as delving into the weighty tomes of the day such as Gibbon's *Decline and Fall of the Roman Empire* or the twenty-one volumes of the *Universal History*. He was also cautious over money and scrupulously avoided extravagance. Such parsimony was governed by a heartfelt concern for the financial welfare of his parents who were living in straightened circumstances. Writing to his sister Letitia, he was relieved to learn that his elder brother Alexander was 'now behaving nobly' by sending the surplus of his pay back home. There appears to be the same intention on Henry's part to contribute to the 'Lawrence fund' as soon as possible: 'The proximity of Calcutta is a great incentive to spending money. I know one or two lads who have not been above two years in the country that owe 8,000 or 9,000 rupees. I owe 250, but I hope to be clear of the world in three or four months.'[38]

Reflecting the sentiments of John, Henry's letters also reflect an understandable homesickness. In unfamiliar surroundings, an oppressive climate, and a vast distance away from family and friends, the plea of many *griffins* was to be sent as many letters as possible. Given the length of time it took ships to make the voyage and the fact that only at certain times of the year were voyages undertaken, the delay in hearing from loved ones was undeniably a wrench. Of all the Lawrence brothers, Henry was perhaps the closest to his sister, Letitia, whom he addressed as 'my darling Lettice'. Clearly yearning emotional comfort and advice, he sorely missed the times he would often confide in her: 'I am in a very friendly neighbourhood (that is, I believe I am welcome at all hours at the houses of my married neighbours), but there is still something wanting—a mamma or a sister—in fact, a kind friend to whom I could open the recesses of my heart, and whose hopes and wishes would be entirely in unison with my own.'[39]

After some months Lawrence was forced to find new accommodation due to the illness of Edwards, and later his replacement, a young man named Ackers. Both were forced to return home on sick leave. Henry now joined his old friend Lewin from his Addiscombe days, whom he noted with some admiration had undergone a moral rejuvenation since they had last met: 'It is really wonderful to me the conversion of Lewin, having known him as a worldly-minded lad. His whole thoughts seem now to be of what good he can do. I only wish I was like him.'[40] Lewin was part of a circle of young men at 'Fairy Hall', a large house at Dum-Dum cantonment, under the influence of the Revd George Craufurd, Chaplain to the Artillery station. The atmosphere of Fairy Hall was strongly evangelical. As one not noted for overt displays of piety, it was somewhat surprising that Henry ventured into this intense religious environment. There was of course the obvious advantage of sharing accommodation with his old friend Lewin. But there may also have been a conscious desire to associate himself with such morally upright company. Years later a fellow member of this group suggested that Henry motives were less spiritual and more contemplative: 'It might have been that our quiet habits were in unison with his retiring disposition, and love of reading…I doubt whether religion had reached his heart at the time.'[41]

Whatever the reason for joining Fairy Hall, Henry continued to meet old associates who were not so religiously inclined, while his new housemates endeavoured to pray for the spiritual conversion of 'poor dear Lawrence'.[42] Feeling rather self-conscious, Henry proved unwilling to express his religious feelings openly and certainly not to make an outright declaration of faith. Although he was content to take part in bible readings, he avoided the practice of praying aloud. With a loathing of hypocrisy that would become a lifelong trait, Henry adopted a questioning attitude in his search for religious truth, telling Chaplain Craufurd one day, 'what I want to be assured of is that this Book is God's. Because when I know that, I have nothing left but to obey it'.[43]

This period of soul searching in Henry's life was soon interrupted by the call to active service in Burma. In June 1824 Henry left Calcutta and sailed to Chittagong to take part in the Arakan campaign of what became known as the First Anglo-Burmese War. Lasting two years, the conflict would be financially one of the costliest in British Indian history. A high price was also paid in purely human terms: an estimated one-third of the army (both European and Indian) perished mostly from tropical diseases. The province of Arakan on the west coast of the Burmese empire became synonymous with the war's heavy sacrifice and earned the gruesome sobriquet of 'Death's Bazaar'.[44]

Active combat duty for second lieutenant Henry Lawrence, who was given command of four six-pounders and two five-and-a-half-inch Howitzer guns, was slow in commencing, however. His contingent was forced at first to endure a lengthy wait at Chittagong for the remainder of the army to assemble: 'we were six months preparing to move a force of 10,000 men,' he later wrote frustratingly, 'most of our cattle having been procured from the banks of the Nerbudda in Central India, at least 1,000 miles from Chittagong!'[45] Once on the move, though, Henry faced the arduous task of transporting his guns southwards over rivers, creeks and ravines. It was slow, exhausting work made worse by the hot climate. On one march in January 1825 lasting seven hour, little more than nine miles had been accomplished.[46]

Despite the strenuous effort, the Burmese scenery inspired the poet in Henry. He encountered 'some beautiful streams and glens' as the countryside changed from highly cultivated fields of sugar cane and mustard to 'wild and romantic' hills and jungle. Their route also took them along the coast and seashore, passing by 'bold cliffs with beautiful romantic ravines'.[47] From here they were periodically resupplied by store-sloops anchored offshore. On one occasion, though, the supply ships missed their rendezvous, and the soldiers were temporarily put on half rations. Their march continued until they reached the Razee River. Intelligence had suggested it was easily fordable. But in the event, the horses had to swim for it while Henry and his men's efforts to traverse it proved a notable achievement:

We found only two small, matted rafts to take over the sepoys, troopers, guns, baggage, &c. I was obliged to dismount my guns, take the wheels off the carriages and tumbrils, unstow all my ammunition, and then carry them by pieces through the water to the rafts, to be transported over. My men worked like horses, and I showed them the example…We managed to get everything over by half-past two o'clock, without having wet any of the ammunition, and, to our no small satisfaction, found our tents pitched a short way on the other side. My men had been up to their middles in water

> during the hottest part of the day, and not a man was ill after it, nor did I
> hear a grumble, though they are terrible growlers in cantonments, when
> they have nothing to do...[48]

Henry's 'zeal and readiness' in overcoming these natural obstacles soon won the approval of his superiors.[49] On one occasion, at the end of January, he volunteered to reconnoitre a difficult ravine at the suggestion of his brigadier. The descend to it, he discovered, was 'almost impassable' but after 'a little work' he managed to clear a passage, with his brigadier looking on appreciatively.[50]

By the time British troops had reached the River Naaf at the start of February, Henry had become 'very warlike' in expectation of engaging the enemy. But as they marched further southwards, the Burmese army continued to retreat and for the next couple of months a phoney war was played out where the real challenges remained largely topographical. Another crossing by gun-boats, this time of the four-mile wide Mayu River, in early March, led to the Arakan River via a series of creeks. It continued to be a wearisome undertaking conducted under trying conditions but then on 27th March Henry's guns were at last put into action. Attacking a stockade in the Padue range of hills, they forced the enemy to retreat once more, leaving the final struggle to take place at Mrauk-U, the capital of Arakan. Situated fifty miles from the sea in a valley, Mrauk-U was surrounded by hills which were crowned with temples and pagodas. In the hours before the battle on 30th March, Henry encountered a certain uneasy stillness, 'a momentary expectation of something unpleasant' but this was soon replaced at daybreak by heavy fire from his guns and mortars. 'It was amusing to see,' he later wrote, 'our fellows jumping with delight when a good shot was made. I heard one man tell another that one of my shots knocked one of the enemy's guns six feet into the air.'[51]

In the end sustained firepower throughout the night enabled British troops to drive the Burmese from their positions in the surrounding hills. By 8 a.m. on 1st April they were in full possession. The following day Henry took a tour of the battlefield. 'I...never saw such a picture of desolation, every house completely ransacked, here and there a dead man, goat, dog.'[52] With the fall of the capital, the rest of the Arakan province swiftly came under British occupation. General Morrison, who commanded British forces in Arakan, now looked to join Sir Archibald Campbell's troops at Irrawaddy. Further progress, though, was soon stymied. For in the following month the rains came and in the swampy, humid conditions prevalent to the region, malaria quickly spread. In the short period from June 1825 to January 1826, seventy European officers out of a total of two hundred had died and more were to follow.[53] In these circumstances, Henry could hardly remain immune for long. He was struck down in November 1825 and again in April 1826 with a virulent form of malaria that became known colloquially as 'Arakan fever'. The second bout proved the severest, forcing him to take extended sick leave. In August 1826 he sailed back to England via China in the hope of gaining the health benefits from a long sea voyage.

Becoming a shadow of his former self, the disease would dog Henry for the rest of his life. When he arrived back home in May 1827, his mother in her diary expressed shock at his emaciated figure: 'Returned from Arracan, after the Burmese war, my dearest beloved Henry Montgomery, not twenty-one years old, but reduced by sickness and suffering to more than double that age.'[54] John was equally shaken by the disease's lasting impact on his brother, recalling years later: 'Henry was naturally a bony, muscular fellow, very powerful; but that fever in Burmah seemed to scorch him up, and he remained for the rest of his life very thin and attenuated.'[55] Henry would stay home for nearly two and a half years in an attempt to get over his illness. Throughout this period the fever would return intermittently and suddenly, forcing him back to bed. Only gradually did it dissipate in the temperate climate of home, allowing the young officer to think once more of a return to India.

Part I

Life in the Mofussil:
The Origins of Paternal Governance

The 'confounded zeal' of Henry Lawrence, Revenue Surveyor 1833–38

When Henry returned to India in February 1830, after nearly two and a half years of furlough, he was conscious of the need to improve his career prospects. There were two main impulses at play. Firstly, there was a yearning to find a role that would truly satisfy his energies and temperament. And secondly, such a role should be one of sufficient standing and remuneration for him to make a liberal contribution to the 'Lawrence fund' in support of his mother's future welfare as well as giving him the financial security to marry.[1] The next few years would be frustrating for Henry as he struggled to attain a position which he felt was commensurate with his talents. It was, nevertheless, a formative period during which he made his first move beyond a military career towards more lucrative civil appointments. This change of direction undoubtedly reflected ambition and a strong work ethic, but also the growing influence of romantic paternalism: 'I'll take anything,' he told his sister Letitia in the autumn of 1833, 'political, magisterial, or judicial, and will willingly give up my claim of firing large guns at the black people, or blowing off people's heads… No! I would now much prefer preventing them breaking each other's heads, and be instrumental in leading them into paths of civilization.'[2]

Thoughts of an appealing civil posting, however, were not Henry's immediate concern when he first arrived back in India. Circumstance, at least in the short term, dictated a return to military duties. His first placement was to a company of foot artillery stationed at Karnal, a large cantonment north of Delhi. The location was deliberate; for here his brother George was adjutant of the Second Cavalry Regiment. Fraternal support eased Henry's re-acclimatisation, and for the next eighteen months he stayed with George and his newly married wife Charlotte enjoying the benefits of a home from home. There were other advantages too. Henry availed of the Cavalry regiment's own *munshi* for language tuition – a prerequisite for advancement to staff appointments. The posting also allowed enough leave time for him to explore the possibilities of life beyond regimented routine. In October 1830 he travelled along the Himalayan foothills near Simla, and there is evidence of an emerging literary talent in his journal – *Travels of a Topechee (Artilleryman)* – a travelogue of his experiences penned for the benefit of his sister Letitia. In early 1831 he was again on the move. This time he spent a month with a fellow officer, Capt. P.T. Cautley, who was superintendent of the Doab Canal.[3] Originally built by the Mughals, but undergoing renovation, the canal covered some 130 miles and helped irrigate an otherwise arid region. Cautley's responsibilities of inspecting the canal works and collection of the irrigation revenue gave Lawrence a taste for practical involvement in rural affairs:

> I like the business very much. There is a mingled occupation of in and out-of-door, theoretical and practical, and altogether very much in the way of my pursuits…all this I should consider a pleasing variety, for, though the temper is tried, much is learnt, and, with but little trouble to oneself, much kindness can be done.[4]

So enamoured was Henry by Cautley's work that he made some effort to obtain a canal appointment for himself. Although the attempt came to nothing, it did not discourage him from exploring other avenues for progression. Having improved his equestrian skills thanks to the Cavalry's riding school at Karnal, he was allowed, through George's influence, to transfer to the more coveted Horse Artillery in September 1831.[5] At both these latter stations Henry seems to have eschewed the more social aspects of cantonment life. Although he was obliged to belong to the mess, it was a situation he did not relish. Instead, after completing his regular duties, he spent his time working on his surveying skills, taking strenuous cross-country rides and, above all, improving his language proficiency. 'I certainly have no natural turn for languages,' he told his sister Letitia in March 1832, 'but I have more application than I thought. And whether I pass or not this time I still persist that I am no mean Oriental Scholar.'[7] Despite his linguistic modesty, his dogged determination was rewarded. On 17th July he passed the all-important language examination which involved reading and translating passages of Urdu, Hindi and Persian texts as well as displaying the requisite understanding of more colloquial forms. The examination committee commended Henry's efforts, noting that he had 'most evidently bestowed much labour on his studies' and that he was now 'fully competent to discharge the duties of an interpreter', worthy of the 'notice of his excellency the Commander in Chief'.[8]

Soon afterwards Henry was ordered to take up a position at Dum Dum, near Calcutta. On the way down the Ganges, however, a violent storm capsized the boats in which he and his troops were travelling. There was loss of life, but Henry was praised for helping to save others. In December 1832 he received final ratification of his language qualifications from the College of Fort William, Calcutta, and in the following month he was appointed as an interpreter to an artillery battery based at Cawnpore. The posting proved short-lived, however. For in the meantime, Henry had set his mind on joining the Revenue Survey department whose purpose was to create surveys of agricultural land on which the revenue demand would be based. Although he had received some basic training in surveying at Addiscombe, it was his experience as a volunteer on the *Ordinance Survey of Ireland (OSI)* during his two years of furlough that now proved valuable. As a means of achieving accurate topography measurements, the OSI had employed the scientific technique of triangulation using modern surveying instruments; a system that was also being used by the Great Trigonometrical Survey of India.[9] Strictly speaking, the Revenue Survey in the North-Western Provinces did not use triangulation, but it nevertheless followed similar geometric principles and measuring methods. Armed with the necessary expertise, this was an opportune moment for Henry to change career path. Once more George assisted in promoting his brother's interests by canvassing a fellow artillery officer, George Brooke[10], who in turn provided a glowing tribute to Henry and his fitness for surveying work based on his 'mathematical acquirements' and his experience in 'the Trigo [Trigonometrical] Survey in Ireland'.[11]

Whether it was Brooke who helped George secure a meeting with the Governor-General Bentinck remains unclear. But in any case the elder Lawrence, then on sick leave, was able to advance his brother's claims when he met the Governor-General at the Himalayan hill station of Simla in the summer of 1832.[12] Another officer, Captain J.H. Simmonds, then involved in the Delhi Revenue Survey, also appears to have been instrumental.[13] According to Simmonds, Henry had been lined up become his assistant at Delhi, following his recommendation to the Governor-General.[14] But, for whatever reason, the appointment failed to materialise. Instead, in March 1833, Henry was appointed an assistant revenue surveyor at Moradabad, a district to the east of Delhi.[15] The position offered considerable scope for an industrious, self-reliant young officer, providing Henry with a level of responsibility that simply did not exist in the Artillery. Crucially, the nature of the work necessitated living amongst the rural classes of India during the relatively cooler months of the year (the surveying season was generally between October to May). This afforded him a worm's eye view of village life that was far removed from the segregated environment of the military cantonment. His colleague and biographer, Herbert Edwardes, saw the experience as pivotal in shaping Henry's future career:

> Here he first really learnt to know the natives of India, and the best class of natives, the agricultural population. It was their villages, their fields, their crops, their interest of every kind with which his eyes, hands, thoughts, and heart, were now occupied for five years. Instead of living in a European

station, he pitched his tents among the people, under their trees, and by their streams, for eight months out of twelve. He saw them as military men seldom can see them, as all civilians ought to see them, and as the best do see them, in their homes and daily life, and thus learnt to sympathize with them as a race, and to understand their wants.[16]

Henry's appointment as a revenue surveyor was the direct result of recent land revenue reforms spearheaded by Governor-General Bentinck and Robert Merttins Bird, a former judge, who had been appointed in 1831 to the new Sudder Board of Revenue based at Allahabad. Their aim was to streamline the entire revenue process. At a three-day conference of revenue officials held at Allahabad in January 1833 significant changes were not only made in the way Collectors and Settlement Officers were to calculate their revenue assessments, but also in how the revenue surveys were to be conducted. The changes were enacted as Regulation IX of 1833.[17] Since 1822 the traditional *khusrah* or field survey conducted by Indian assistants had been augmented by professional boundary maps produced by trained British surveyors using scientific equipment. Though acting as an important check or control on the former, the professional survey had come to be seen by Bentinck and Bird as too precise and detailed for what revenue officials required. Moreover, progress was slow and costly (By 1830 only 3,020 square miles had been surveyed).[18] Surveyors spent much of their time settling and recording village boundary disputes, while the professional and field surveys, not to mention the work of collectors and settlement officers, were all too often out-of-sync with one another. Under the Allahabad reforms, both the professional and field surveys now came under the direct supervision of British surveyors. In the production of village, *pargana* and district maps, topographical detail was reduced, while to avoid unnecessary delays, village boundaries were to be settled by the revenue staff before surveying began.

Mapmaking also became standardised. Village maps were to be plotted on a scale of 4 inches to 1 mile, while *pargana* maps [subdivision of a district] were reduced to 1 or 2 inches to 1 mile and district maps reduced to ¼ of an inch to 1 mile. A heavy emphasis was also placed on the proper arrangement of the survey documentation particularly in the production of the village map and associated statistical register 'with a view to the means of securing despatch, economy and uniformity of proceeding among the officers attached to the revenue survey'.[19] A new target for each surveyor of 1,000 square miles per season was now set (the previous average outturn had averaged less than 300 square miles). As a result, the revised system saw an expansion in the number of surveying parties.[20] Indian staff levels substantially increased, some of whom would be trained in professional surveying techniques, while the number of British surveyors was boosted by the secondment of additional military officers. It was this move which now allowed Henry Lawrence a crucial career change.

Henry's role involved supervising the creation of maps and associated statistical information at a district, *pargana* and village level which would in turn facilitate the collector's or settlement officer's assessment of the land revenue. The survey consisted of two main branches – one spearheaded by the revenue surveyor himself called the professional survey; the other being the *khusrah* survey, conducted by Indian surveying assistants known as *amins*. Of all the maps created by the professional survey, the most important was the one based at individual village level as this would be used to check the correctness of the *khusrah* work. With the aid of surveying equipment (theodolite, flagpoles and measuring chains), the village map, statistical details, and surveying calculations were produced using two techniques – the traverse circuit system and Gale's Universal Theorem.[21] The process involved the establishment of a series of observation stations as close to the village boundary as possible. 'Line-cutters' were employed to remove jungle or any other obstacle that impeded the pathway between one station point and the next. 'Chainmen' were then used to measure the distance between each station point using a 'Gunter's chain' (a 20 metres long measuring chain made of iron and consisting of 100 links). At each station a flagman would hold a 20ft long bamboo pole topped with a triangular flag which the surveyor (using the previously surveyed point as a base) fixed within the crosswires of his theodolite to obtain his angular measurements. The process would continue until the circuit had been 'closed' (i.e. by returning to the original station point). To ensure the whole village area was included, 'off-set' men would measure the offsets from the chain line to the actual village boundary. Based on all these measurements, a map would be plotted featuring a meridian line and interior topographical details with Gale's Universal Theorem used to calculate the total internal area of the village.

The *khusrah* Survey was a detailed field-to-field survey of each village. *Amins* recorded in the form of a register [i.e. *khusrah*] the number and name of the proprietor of each field, its size, soil quality, crop type or other mode of occupation, together with the rent of the field if under cultivation. They were also responsible for creating a rough map [*shajra*] on no fixed scale showing the position and boundaries of each field with a corresponding number linked to the proprietor's details in the *khusrah*. In contrast to the professional survey, the *shajra* was completed using more rudimentary measuring equipment such as a rope, rod, or chain. The total area of the village thus measured had to agree with the area defined by the professional survey allowing for only a small degree of error. As well as this check, *'purtal'* *amins* were used to remeasure random fields to correct any errors and to dissuade regular *amins* from committing fraud.

Upon completion of the checks and any corrections, the professional and *khusrah* maps and registers would be handed over to the settlement officer/collector with duplicates sent to the Surveyor-General's office.

An interesting glimpse of Henry's surveying work at Moradabad can be found in the fourth volume of R.H. Phillimore's *Historical Records of the Survey of India* where he and his team surveyed the *mouzah* [village] of Jullalabad (Nujeebabad *pargana*) in March 1834. The subsequent village plan and register confirms that Henry was following the standard practices of professional revenue surveying as laid down at the Allahabad conference of January 1833. On a scale of four inches to a mile, the map clearly shows the traverse lines closely following the village boundary with the meridian line being drawn from one of the station points. The interior village detail has been limited to showing main features only. Above the map is a short statistical table displaying the amount of land under cultivation, land fit for cultivation and barren waste land. Also included are the number of houses and wells, the main crop grown (sugar cane), number of ploughs, and caste affiliation of the village inhabitants. On another page is logged in tabular form the traverse angles, bearings and distances taken at each station, together with the calculation of the total village area in accordance with Gale's system. What is perhaps most noteworthy about this survey is Henry's delegation of responsibility to his Indian subordinates. Although his signature features on the village plan and register for sign-off purposes, both the village boundary and village interior surveys are recorded as having been performed by two Indian assistants – Shaikh Golam Ally and Shaikh Jonub Ally.[22]

This emphasis on the delegation of responsibility was also apparent when, in 1835, Henry went on to survey the Gorakhpur district close to the Nepalese border. By this stage he had been promoted to full surveyor rank, having completed a season of surveying (1834–35) in the Farrukhabad district, southwest of Delhi.[23] One of his assistant surveyors at Gorakhpur was Saunders Alexius Abbott, younger brother of James Abbott, who arrived in the district in 1836 armed with only a rudimentary knowledge of surveying picked up from his time at Addiscombe.[24] Henry was keen to share his knowledge and to instruct, but he was also careful not to cosset his new deputy: 'In teaching me he never spared himself,' remarked Saunders years later, 'but having taught me, he never did anything that I could do for him.' According to Saunders, there were two reasons for Henry's division of labour: firstly, it allowed him to concentrate on the overall supervision of the survey, and secondly, it enabled him to indulge his love of literature 'to which he devoted every moment he could spare from his professional duties'.[25] Given the amount of active work required of him, those instances may well have been all too brief. But according to the Collector of Gorakhpur, Edward Anderton Reade, with whom he formed a life-long friendship, there were nonetheless 'little snatches' during 'less absorbing work' when one could find Henry gathering 'knowledge from a single travel-stained volume under a tree or on the banks of a *nullah*'.[26]

Although Henry regularly took to horseback both to survey and to inspect certain points which required his 'on the spot' attention, much of his time was spent in camp reviewing the work of his subordinates usually in a tent pitched under the shady canopy of a sprawling mango *tope* (grove). Saunders, in one of his first encounters with Henry, gave a revealing sketch of his supervisor's working environment and idiosyncratic habits:

> The tent was of the ordinary size prescribed for a subaltern with a marching regiment, about twelve feet square; but it is not so easy to describe the interior. A charpoy in one corner, an iron stove in another, a couple of tables and three or four chairs, but every superficial inch of each was taken up with papers, plans, or maps; even the floor was covered with papers, carefully placed on certain patterns of the carpet, to aid his memory in certain corrections which each required, but which frequently accumulated to such extent that the object of placing them there was sometimes forgotten. It was undoubtedly unsystematic, or was rather a system peculiarly his own, which, with his wonderful memory, he worked to surprising effect, but it created a great litter, and to the eyes of his new Assistant looked very like chaos.[27]

Under Henry's tutelage, Saunders became 'an exceedingly capable surveyor' to the extent that he was left in charge of the Gorakhpur survey when his superior was forced to take sick leave in March 1837.[28] Henry spent several months convalescing in the Simla hills and only returned to the plains in July in expectation of the impending arrival of his fiancée, Honoria Marshall, then aged twenty-eight. Previously, they had met on a few occasions during Henry's furlough in 1827–28. Each had been attracted to the other. Both shared a romantic temperament, a love of nature and held strong Christian principles. Later, in July 1833 Henry, still smitten, had confided in his sister Letitia: 'I really think I shall be mad enough to tell her [Honoria] my story, and try to make her believe that I have loved for five years, and said nothing of my love. The thing seems incredible, but it is true.'[29] A further four years, however, would pass before Letitia was finally able to reveal her brother's true feelings to Honoria. Why such a painfully long delay? In large part this was due to Henry's natural reticence, but he was also preoccupied over the future financial welfare of his mother as well as his efforts to improve his career prospects. Thankfully, the couple were at last reacquainted in Calcutta and married in the city's Mission

Church on 21st August 1837. After a two-week stay in the capital, they made their way up the Ganges by *pinnace* (an Indian two-mast, shallow-bottomed boat) to Revelganj, and then overland to Gorakhpur by *palkee* and buggy in a journey which took six weeks to complete.

In both her journals and letters, Honoria proved to be an informative and frank observer of her new environment. Of particular interest to her was Henry and his work as a surveyor. Like Saunders Abbott, she was quick to discern her husband's unstructured ways as well as his appearance. 'You bid me describe him, I will try,' she wrote to a friend shortly after her arrival:

> He is thirty-one, but looks older, is rather tall, very thin and sallow, and has altogether an appearance of worse health than he really has. Dark hair, waxing scanty now, high forehead, very projecting eyebrows, small sunken eyes, long nose, thin cheeks, no whiskers, and a very pretty mouth. Very active and alert in his habits, but very unmethodical. As to dress and externals, perfectly careless, and would walk out with a piece of carpet about his shoulders as readily as with a coat, and would invite people to dinner on a cold shoulder of mutton as readily as to a feast. There now, I do think you have an impartial description of my lord and master.[30]

Honoria was equally forthright in her views of Gorakhpur. From an Anglo-Indian perspective, the town was said to have 'a good deal of society', courtesy of a large military cantonment and a well-established civilian presence. But this held little appeal for Honoria who found its social life both tedious and enervating. There were 'few topics of public interest' while the climate, she felt, produced a languor amongst her occidental companions. Perhaps the most discouraging element of Gorakhpur's social scene was the dearth of single women; there were only two living in the station. Dubbed "the big spin" and "the little spin" (short for spinster), their merits or otherwise were the subject of much gossip, leaving Honoria distinctly relieved that she was now happily married. In truth, cantonment life for most European women was a rather stultifying experience. With little variation from day to day, their lives chiefly revolved around an endless cycle of tiffins, dinner parties and the inevitable evening drives 'on the same dirty road where they have driven a thousand times before, meeting the same faces they have met a hundred times'.[31]

Fortunately for both Honoria and Henry, their stay at Gorakhpur was a brief two-week stint. On 1st November, with great relief, they left the civil station to begin the work of surveying the eastern part of the district. 'Every mile we advanced in the jungle,' Honoria recorded, 'I felt my spirits rise. All our annoyances seemed left behind and my mind regained that tranquil elasticity "which in the crowd and bustle of resort" [was] much impaired.'[32] For the next two months, the couple would spend their time journeying from camp to camp, over rivers, through jungles and across plains, swapping their one-horse buggy for a dug-out canoe, a *tat* (an Indian breed of pony) or an elephant as the situation demanded. Earlier the thought of Honoria accompanying her husband on his surveying duties had drawn censure from younger brother John: 'You must try and get some other appointment than in the Survey, which will never do for a married man, as you can't drag your wife about in the jungles in the hot winds,' he firmly told Henry.[33] But he was quickly proved wrong. Honoria turned out to be an all-too-willing travelling companion and was more than happy to exchange the dullness of cantonment life for the adventures of the jungle:

> A lady who shrinks from driving over rough or smooth, riding through a jungle, or crossing a piece of water on the back of an elephant has no business in camp. One who cares much about visiting and parties is out of her place in the *mofussil*, and one who minds living on mutton and fowl for six months in the year had better not marry a surveyor. Our life in camp teaches us how many "indispensables" we can do without…There is perfect freedom, those about you do not understand what you say, so there is no fear of distorted repetitions. We escape all scandal, all censure, all the deteriorating gossip, which one despises, yet is led to join in. There is the fullest enjoyment of nature, perpetual change of air and scene, opportunity for self-improvement, and a general freedom from care. More like the birds of the air than human beings. If we have a chance guest, it is without form or trouble. "Pitch a small tent and grill another fowl," are the only directions needed.[34]

Honoria quickly became a devoted helpmeet who took great interest in her husband's work, accurately recording the survey's *modus operandi*, arranging and copying papers and even helping to plot a number of villages.[35] With their tent becoming the survey's nerve centre and a hive of daily activity, Honoria, sitting quietly in her chair, had the perfect vantage point from which to observe the distinctive characters of a surveying establishment, consisting of 'two or three assistants, about a dozen *crannies* or clerks, and hundreds of natives'.[36] Those catching her eye were the line-cutters and *amins*, the latter returning from the villages with their field-books for Henry to scrutinise. There was also the distinguishing figure of the *mootsuddy*, with his reed pen tucked behind his ear and a small inkstand attached to his waist, 'ready to read and write Persian notes'. And then there was the 'never to be forgotten' wizened appearance of a 'little old baboo'. According to Honoria, he was 'a complete copying machine and a tolerable mathematician' albeit one easily offended if his calculations were called into question: 'Sir, you are my father and my mother. One, two thing I do, no mistake can make, multiple, sine, co-sine. Sir, you are my sucking father. Sir I make no mistake.'[37]

The surveying establishment was augmented by a host of ancillary staff that including a carpenter, a blacksmith, a bookbinder, grain merchants, elephant *mahouts* and bullock drivers as well as servants, their families and camp followers – the latter groups often seizing the opportunity to extort money or goods from the local villagers.[38] Completing this tableau of Henry's 'patriarchal establishment' were the "potent grave and reverend seignors" aka the village elders who would come to make their acquaintance, displaying 'all due etiquette, turbaned and belted, leaving their shoes outside', offering salaams, and either standing or sitting according to their rank. Henry's interaction with these headmen was unusually informal. 'I have smiled at the contrast,' Honoria noted, 'when one of these precise and solemn gentlemen was conversing with Henry in measured tone, and with the proper number of "Sahibs" and bows, while Henry sat without coat, waistcoat or jacket, his legs over the arm of the chair or his feet on the table.'[39]

Henry's daily routine, recorded by Honoria, reflected his vigorous nature. Little time, it seems, was wasted, rising as early as four o'clock in the morning to begin writing, fuelled by the consumption of coffee. When it became light both he and Honoria would go out for their morning ride and then bathe. Breakfast was between nine and ten and then 'shop work' (i.e. surveying work) until about four p.m. Thereafter the couple would go for a drive or a horse ride to a nearby station or village where Henry would talk to the people, picking up 'various kinds of information' in the process. After returning to camp, dinner would be at six and 'then business again, scarcely interrupted by tea till 9 or 10 o'clock, and then to bed'.[40]

Much of the Goruckhpur district, the couple discovered, had a pleasing aspect. The moist climate had produced a fertile environment for vegetation to thrive, helped by numerous rivers, streams and *jheels*. Alongside the cultivation of barley, flax, mustard, hemp and dhal, this lowland region was noted for its large belts of *sal* forests, sprawling mango topes, and tar trees: 'The face of the country has a park-like appearance,' Honoria noted approvingly, 'the boundaries of fields being low, do not break the uniform aspect, and there are moreover large detached bania [banyan] and mango trees, here and there a single tar, and clumps of bamboos.'[41] Their enjoyment of camp life was further enhanced by the accommodating winter season: 'The cold weather is now set in,' she wrote in her diary entry for November, 'nor can there be a climate more delightful than that we are now enjoying, there is seldom any wind, and for months no rain. The sun is too hot to be exposed to during the day, but we can sit out of doors in the tope, and mornings and evenings are delightfully fresh and cool.'[42]

My mid-December they had reached the most isolated part of the district, at a place called Porainya in the *pargana* of Haweli. 'Here we are, in the very midst of the much-dreaded Terai, in the abode of tigers, elephants, bears, hogs and snakes,' Honoria sounded ominously.[43] The Terai was a region of dense jungle composed of tall reedy grasses and interspersed with belts of forest bordering the foothills of the Nepalese Himalayas. Perhaps it was its alluring remoteness which prompted Henry to leave his tent and take up his theodolite. For on this occasion surveying duties were divided between himself and his assistant, Saunders Abbott. As they journeyed further into the Terai, the jungle became thicker and line cutters were deployed to clear long, straight swathes of vegetation along the *pargana* boundary. With the snowy Himalayan peaks in the distance, the clearing formed an impressive vista along which the surveying party, many of whom were wearing scarlet-coloured sepoy jackets, passed in single file. It was a scene which Honoria found particularly picturesque. So too was the profile of Henry who was dressed in a shooting coat, shorts, and a white, wide-brimmed hat. An assistant held a 'huge' umbrella over him as he took his theodolite readings in the midst of what the couple believed to be *terra incognita*: 'No foot of man had ever traversed this ground till our line cutters made the way, and one saw no trace of any human being except ourselves.'[44]

Not far away was Saunders Abbott who had to contend with heavy dews and thick morning fog which had delayed the use of his theodolite. Evenings proved equally challenging. The presence of tigers and wild elephants in the locality led to fires being kept constantly lit throughout the night to deter them.[45] Honoria, though, remained unperturbed at the thought of roaming wild animals, despite having earlier spotted the imprint of a tiger's paw by the side of a stream: 'It is very strange how little formidable danger is, when you are close to it,' she casually remarked.[46] Even so, Henry ensured that she was guarded by 'an old Mussalman chuprassee [chaprassi] with a fine grey beard and a sword by his side'.[47] After three or four days, both surveying parties met up, with Saunders somewhat surprised to see Honoria in tranquil pose: 'She was seated on the bank of a nullah, her feet overhanging the den of some wild animal. While she, with a portfolio in her lap, was writing overland letters, her husband, at no great distance, was laying his theodolite.'[48]

Henry's surveying career reached new heights at Gorakhpur where he had earned a reputation for hard work and impressive results. This was revealed at the end of the 1836–37 survey season when he and his two assistants (Saunders Abbott and John Fitzpatrick) together with seven professional and forty *khusrah* teams had managed to survey a staggering 1,416 square miles, 400 miles more than the target set at the Allahabad conference of January 1833. Of the nine surveying establishments then operating in the N.W.P., only veteran Captain William Brown's was able to surpass Henry's figure at 1698 square miles set during the same season. These results were exceptional, however. Most teams since 1833 had not been able to reach the ambitious 1,000 square miles per season target.[49] Even Henry, despite achieving 1007 square miles in the 1834/35 season, could only manage a modest 839 sq. miles during the following year (1835/36).

The overall pace of surveying was, of course, a matter of grave concern for Robert Merttins Bird who realised that it would have to increase if he was to achieve completion of the N.W.P. settlement within the ten-year period he had promised. The difficulty was that the high technical standards put in place made most revenue surveyors, Henry excepted, hesitant to delegate to junior officers and Indian assistants. A more cost effective and faster way of surveying was thus required which laid less stress on the exacting technical standards and concern over topographical detail, but which was nonetheless sufficient for making revenue assessments. With this objective in mind, Bird now sought out the practical expertise of the survey dept. with the aim of making further improvements to the system.[50] His choice of Henry was no accident. According to John Thornton, Bird's desire, as the driving force within the Sudder Board of Revenue, was to form a group of like-minded subordinates, of whom Henry was undoubtedly one:

> He usually chose young men, as being less encumbered and more manageable than their seniors, and less likely to be imbued with prejudices derived from the dark ages of our earlier administration. With these young officers he kept up constant private intercourse, and thus instilled into them his own views, and animated them by his own hearty temperament.[51]

Henry began discussions with the Board in March 1837 when he passed through Allahabad on sick leave, handing over 'such memoranda and stats, particularly regarding the details of the [surveying] establishment'.[52] Later he met both Bird and James Thomason, then secretary to the Lieutenant-Governor of the North-Western Provinces, at Simla where he discussed a proposed solution. Henry's plan was ambitious and involved a substantial increase in outturn with an equally significant reduction in costs. The target for land surveyed in a season would increase from 1000 to 3,000 square miles per establishment. This would be achieved by having an experienced surveyor supervising a larger establishment of subordinates. Efficiencies would be realised by limiting the professional survey to the traverse of boundary circuits only, while the time-consuming interior professional survey which mapped the cultivated area would be abandoned. Instead, the whole of the area, both cultivated and uncultivated, would now be surveyed and mapped by the less costly Indian surveyors/*amins* whose numbers would be further expanded.[53]

As we have seen from his survey of the Moradabad district, Henry was already relying on his Indian support staff to perform the bulk of surveying work. Under Bird's direction, this was given further official encouragement. By the end of the summer Henry's proposals, known as the Extended Survey Scheme, had won the approbation of the Sudder Board of Revenue at Allahabad:

> Captain Lawrence is one of the most experienced and zealous of the officers employed on the survey and has conducted the complicated process of double survey more successfully perhaps than any other, and has certainly entered more entirely into the Board's views. Captain Lawrence is prepared to guarantee with the establishment stated…a complete survey of 3,000 square miles per annum, where the *mouzas* [villages] average one square mile each.[54]

Sir Charles Metcalfe, then Lieutenant Governor of the N.W.P., also expressed 'a very high opinion of Capt. Lawrence's character as a revenue surveyor'. On 18th September 1837 the scheme was duly sanctioned.[55]

Not everyone, though, was as fulsome in their praise of Henry's abilities and his survey reforms. One unnamed fellow surveyor was heard to express exasperation at his 'confounded zeal'.[56] In 'loud vituperation' he complained that he now had twice as much work to do as previous and had been 'hauled over the coals' by R.M. Bird for not doing more. More sustained and pointed criticism came from Captain James Bedford, Deputy Surveyor-General who had spent the previous sixteen years in the Revenue Survey Department, the last five as its head. Instrumental in implementing the 1833 reforms, Bedford was also candid over its shortcomings. The quality of the surveying, he argued, had diminished with the hurried expansion of the number of surveying parties. Young, inexperienced assistants had attained command of their own survey much earlier than had previously been the case:

> Constant augmentations…have greatly tended to impede progress by withdrawing efficient assistants from the old surveys to aid the new ones. The places of old uncovenanted assistants thus removed have been supplied by young men of various grades more or less educated but all requiring a certain time to qualify them for the various duties of the field and office which they are required to perform.[57]

The use of Indian surveyors, he also viewed, as being 'no light clog on the survey proceedings' whereby a new survey establishment could 'never be fairly considered as properly formed or in full working order before the 3rd season'. Despite these 'impeding causes', Bedford remained sanguine about the prospect of eventually achieving the estimated annual target of 1000 sq. miles. What was needed, he believed, was a couple more surveying seasons and 'the persevering zeal and ability of the surveyors' to bring 'all the establishments into a perfectly efficient state'. Henry's new scheme, however, was not what Bedford had in mind. The prospect of further change aimed, once more, at increasing the speed of surveying dismayed him: 'It is a matter of sincere regret,' he told William Hay Macnaghten, secretary to the Governor-General of India,

> that the Sudder Board in communication with one of the young surveyors [Captain Lawrence] and without reference to myself should have recommended a change which by encouraging undue speed strikes at the root of professional accuracy.[58]

Bedford was both annoyed and personally hurt at the Revenue Board's failure to consult with him over these major operational changes. As Deputy Surveyor-General, the matter was evidently within his professional remit. Indeed, he questioned the Board's right to be involved in what he felt should have been a purely departmental undertaking. Yet not only was he not consulted, news of the scheme only reached him after it had been approved by government despite being in frequent communication with Henry Lawrence during his brief stay in Allahabad and thereafter by letter.[59] This undermining of his authority explains why Bedford took the unusual step of voicing his disapproval to the Governor-General, believing himself to be the victim of a conspiracy: 'The recent interference of the Board in the professional branch of the survey and their secret representations…should be brought to his Lordship's knowledge.'[60]

Bedford did not spare his words with James Thomason either. The Board's high-handedness, he told him, contrasted sharply with the Allahabad survey meeting of January 1833 when 'the whole of the officers consulted together and came to one opinion as to the extent of work which could be annually done and properly superintended with a given establishment'.[61] The Deputy Surveyor-General's anger over the snub was further compounded by the decision to employ the services of Henry Lawrence whose fitness for making survey reforms he now called into question, describing him as 'a young and comparatively speaking inexperienced officer who whatever his zeal [had] exhibited evident marks of over haste' in his work.[62] By contrast, 'some of the ablest and best officers of the Dept.' had been passed over. As to the actual changes themselves, Bedford's main objection centred on the abolition of the interior professional survey, which he argued, removed the only real check on the *khusrah* survey. If 'accelerated general progress' was required, then it should be by the adoption of 'new independent surveys with a responsible officer at their head' rather than by 'imposing on surveyors who have already quite enough to do, a mere nominal responsibility for operations which they cannot effectually check'.[63]

Thomason countered Bedford's main contention concerning the abolition of the interior professional survey. Although admitting that it did remove 'a check upon the extent of cultivated land shown by the Khusreh', the measurements taken by the *amins* of the whole area, he believed, still maintained 'a professional check…over the Khusreh work'. In any case the interior professional survey, it was argued, was by no means a perfect test, and an example was given of a highly regarded surveyor who was forced to reject the professional returns in favour of the *khusrah* measurements. Thomason also tried to allay fears that the topographical character of the survey had been altered: 'In all geodesical purposes its value is as great as ever,' he maintained. Satisfied that quality standards would not be compromised, the new scheme's other advantage (apart from greater outturn) was one of cost with the rate of charge being substantially reduced.[64]

In the end the dispute boiled down to a simple question: What degree of importance should be attached to the surveys as a means of making fair revenue settlements? To Bedford, a stickler for high technical standards, the integrity of the revenue survey was everything. But to Bird and Thomason, a less rigid approach was espoused; one which laid less stress, as Sir Charles Metcalfe once pithily remarked, on the need for 'looking at everything through a theodolite'.[65] Of course accurate surveys were valuable to collectors and settlement officers, but other, more general considerations (e.g. existing village accounts, previous collections, caste differences etc.) needed to be given their due weight. Realising that the Deputy Surveyor-General would not be moved on the matter, Bird chose simply to by-pass him with the aid of Thomason and Lawrence. By the end of 1837, and no doubt to the relief of both sides, Bedford was deputed to advise on the revenue surveys of lower Bengal, based at Calcutta, a move made permanent the following year. He had quickly become yesterday's man and his removal now left all surveys of the North-Western Provinces under the effective control of R.M. Bird as the civilian secretary of the Sudder Board of Revenue.

By December 1837 Henry's surveying duties at Gorakhpur had been completed. His next area of operations centred on the district of Allahabad where the new Extended Survey Scheme would be trialled. On 10th January 1838 after 'a good deal of bustle', Henry and Honoria and their establishment began their 200-mile journey southwards via Azamgarh and Jaunpur.[66] After crossing the Rapti and Gogra (Ghaghara) rivers, the moist, verdant countryside of Gorakhpur gave way to drier conditions.[67] The soil became sandy, and grasses took on a light brown tincture. The great mango topes of further north had disappeared and the only fine tree of any sort, according to Honoria, was the odd large tamarind. Camels now replaced elephants as the common means of conveyance, while Gorakhpur's low thatched-roofed huts draped in attractive creepers were swapped for enclosed, flat-roofed houses often in the shadow of an old mud fort.

On 18th January, after a nine-day march, they arrived at Allahabad where they first viewed the sacred confluence of the great Ganges and Jumna (Yamuna) rivers. A variety of boats were plying the two main channels, while along the beach were vast numbers of pilgrims whose encampments were made 'conspicuous by little scarlet flags'. Afterwards, they made their way into the city where Honoria was struck by the 'many European-like buildings' and 'the beautiful roads all round the station'.[68] Near to the cantonment, and for some distance, there were bungalows, consisting of thatched, sloping roofs, as well as *puckah* houses, built of brick with flat, lime roofs. It was in one of these *puckah* houses where Henry and Honoria first stayed – being the residence of their good friend Robert Montgomery, now Collector and Magistrate of Allahabad, and his wife Fanny (see chapter below). For Honoria, their friendship came as a welcome relief: 'Their society is really a pleasure, and Mrs. M. is my oracle in all domestic matters.'[69]

As at Gorakhpur, the couple's time in Allahabad's civil station was brief. On 22nd January they set off once more for camp and the business of surveying. A direct result of the Extended Survey Scheme was an expansion in the numbers employed in Henry's establishment. Alongside his trusted assistant, Saunders Abbott, he was now joined by another former military officer, Lieut. Henry Stephen, to oversee an increase in the number of surveying parties under his overall supervision.[70] Undoubtedly the challenge of achieving the 3,000 square miles target came with added pressure as noted in both Henry's and Honoria's writings. As he explained to one of Honoria's friends:

> I have now tents in three different places, eight or ten miles apart, and have two other encampments (making five in all) to look after; with such endless vexations and contretemps to encounter as he only can conceive who has engaged to furnish a geographical and revenue map of one-sixth of Scotland in one year, showing not only the features of the country, but furnishing all the statistical details requisite for a land assessment. All this to be done, too, by men who, high and low, take bribes; so much so, that it is perfectly useless discharging a man for it, as his successor will only perhaps be worse.[71]

The enlarged surveying establishment inevitably increased the risk of fraud occurring as the ability to check and control the work of subordinates over a greater area subsequently diminished. On one occasion Henry found an Indian surveyor using his theodolite to extort money from village *zamindars* by pretending that the instrument would not function until some rupees were placed on it.[72] On another occasion it was discovered that an official had taken bribes from a farmer to record his land as poor quality and thereby lower the tax burden. In response Henry's 'object and delight', according to Saunders Abbott, was to come down hard on those found guilty of such transgressions 'however distant, at unexpected times'.[73] One of his punishments involved having the guilty man sit in a tree over his tent for several hours so that he could face the weight of public ridicule and to serve as an example to others. Fraud, however, was only one of the challenges facing Henry. The extra surveying equipment required for the enhanced scheme proved to be in short supply, while famine conditions in western regions, exacerbated by the uncertainties of climate, had the effect of raising local food prices making it difficult to recruit survey workers from cheaper districts.[74]

Despite its hardships, Honoria continued to extol the virtues of their peripatetic lifestyle. 'It is a busy and a wandering life; but we both like it,' she told her friend, Margaret Irwin, in March 1838, '…we live wholly in tents, a week in one place, a month in another, a day in another. We rarely see a European face, or hear a word of English, and are, in fact, almost as much alone together as if we were in a desert island. We have, therefore, especial reason to be thankful that we can be thoroughly companions.'[75] But changes were stirring. By early April they had reached the locality of Kuraon, some forty miles south of Allahabad. The hot winds were now on the rise, and to keep the thermometer below 80°, they swapped their regular tent for a makeshift *taikhana* – a temporary subterranean chamber covered in thatch and wetted *tatties* dug within the thickest shade of a mango tope. By now Honoria was over three months pregnant with their first child. It would be a difficult pregnancy with the expectant mother often sick and listless. Understandably, she soon left the rigours of camp life for the more comfortable surroundings of a furnished house in Allahabad while Henry continued surveying. Although Honoria could now count on the heartfelt support of her good friends, the Montgomerys, illness and her husband's absence inevitably played heavily on her emotions. Nevertheless, when Henry did periodically return from his fieldwork, her spirits quickly lifted, and she found pleasure once more in candidly sketching the interior scenes of her surveyor husband's life:

He is come back! and I am now as happy as I was lonely without him. Here we sit; I am in the drawing-room, and he is in the next room; but there are three large doors open between us, so that I hear and see him. He is seated at one side of a long table, and the skylight overhead shows that he is looking very well. At the same table sits Nawazish Ali, the Deputy-Collector, a bandit-looking Mussulman, with a long nose, great grey beard, gold tissue turban, and white apparel. Behind Henry stands Sookhum Lai, his head Persian writer, a very tall, intelligent, saucy-looking man, with a pen behind his ear and an inkstand stuck in his girdle. The table is surrounded by Ameens, men who measure fields, and bring us reports as to soil, cultivation, &c. A new batch of them have come for service, and Harry [Henry] is examining them. They all look much alike, forming a band of white turbans, black faces, and muslin dresses round the table. In a room beyond are a set of native and half-caste writers.[76]

Henry's time in the revenue survey would eventually come to an end in the autumn of 1838 when news came of the impending military campaign in Afghanistan. On 12th September James Thomason, now secretary to the Governor-General, wrote to the Sudder Board of Revenue informing them that Henry, as one of several officers attached to the Revenue Service, could now 'proceed on military service into Afghanistan'.[77] Henry jumped at the chance of a return to military duties with the prospect of career enhancing opportunities. For, in truth, he had regarded the revenue survey as merely a stepping-stone to greater things, and throughout his time in the service he had remained open to exploring other possibilities. In September 1836, for example, he had made an unsuccessful appeal to F.J. Shore, a district officer, to become one of his assistants.[78] Such efforts, though, should not detract from Henry's well-earned reputation as a hardworking, committed, and resourceful revenue surveyor. Indeed, such was his work ethic that some colleagues felt he was putting his health in danger. His friend and Addiscombe contemporary, Robert Guthrie MacGregor, had already cautioned him in January 1835: 'You must not measure too many villages, nor too long remain abroad in the day; or else anything more you get [i.e. promotion] will not assist you long.'[79] It was a valid concern. For, as we have noted, he was forced to find respite in the Simla Hills during the hot season of 1837. Shortly after leaving the survey, Henry looked back at the work's physical costs: '…this sweet work of ours has reduced me to a perfect anatomy of a man,' he told his fellow surveyor, J.H. Simmonds, 'God be praised it is over; such another [surveying season] would settle [i.e. destroy] me.'[80]

Henry's high standing within the revenue service was confirmed with the presentation of the survey returns for the 1837/38 season. During his final season he and his enhanced establishment managed to survey 2271 square miles of the Allahabad district. This figure, combined with the final 831 square miles surveyed of the Gorakhpur district (under the old system), confirmed that he had surpassed the 3,000 square mile target he had earlier promised.[81] Reaching this important milestone left the Sudder Board of Revenue suitably gratified: 'An examination of the statements now submitted will shew that the favourable anticipations of the Board respecting the surveys on the extended scale have been fully realized and that there can no longer be any doubt that a survey of 3000 square miles can be accomplished with ease within the year.'[82] Further approbation was bestowed when it was revealed that the survey's average cost per square mile had also been reduced from 20 rupees 13 annas and 5 pice to 12 rupees 7 annas 8 pice without, the Board believed, quality being compromised.[83]

By the end of 1842 work on the revenue surveys of the North-Western Provinces would come to an end. Aided by the streamlining changes introduced in 1833 and 1837, the best part of seventy odd thousand square miles were surveyed. It was a considerable achievement that owed much to the energies of R.M. Bird and his small band of revenue surveyors, not least Henry Lawrence. Questions, however, remained over the accuracy of these surveys and their true worth. Seasoned observers from a surveying or scientific background gave scathing assessments. The Victorian geographer, Clements R. Markham, found the Allahabad reforms of 1833 to be 'most disastrous' when 'it was resolved to sacrifice everything to cheapness and rapidity of execution'.[84] Markham lamented the quality of the maps produced which were 'only required to delineate village boundaries and sites, with rough outlines of roads and the courses of rivers and were mere skeleton sketches'. Furthermore, no 'proper connexion' was established between the revenue surveys and the Great Trigonometrical Survey even though it was from the former that 'the sheets of the Indian Atlas' were subsequently produced.[85] A similar view was held by the historian of the Survey of India, R.H. Phillimore:

> The speed-up of work by the methods introduced in 1833, and even more by the relaxation of close professional control from 1837, was no doubt expedient at the time, but resulted in little of long-term value, either for the provision of trustworthy settlement records, or for the effective mapping of the country, for which they long remained the only available material.[86]

Echoing the concerns of Deputy Surveyor-General Bedford, Phillimore agreed that young military officers had been given charge of large establishments without having served adequate apprenticeships. Their assistants and sub-assistants had also been 'recruited hastily and sent on field work with little training'. This had allowed little time for the 'building up a trustworthy staff of Indian surveyors trained on European methods and subject to strict control'.[87]

The ambitious surveying targets certainly allowed less time for detailed topographical mapmaking and quality control. But did this make for poor revenue settlements? From the perspective of the revenue officer, it was argued, that there was no real need for the larger scale, geographical maps. What was crucial, Thomason maintained, was a correct village map showing the landholding on a per field basis together with its taxable value: 'The khusreh map is the important revenue document; the professional map is only the check upon its accuracy.'[88] Correctness of the former, Thomason believed, could be maintained by the checks performed by the Indian *partal* staff under the supervision of the professional surveyors. In practice, however, maintaining quality standards remained a challenge. In the Moradabad district, for example, false *khusrah* figures supplied by 'notoriously corrupt' *amins* had forced the settlement officer to rely on rough and ready reckoning to calculate his assessment.[89] Similar examples could no doubt be found. But so too could cases of well-run establishments. Collector E.A. Reade readily praised Henry's efforts in overcoming 'the contumacious resistance of some zamindars, and the impertinence of some native officers' in the Sulempoor Mujholee *pargana* (Gorakhpur district). 'It is a matter if not of surprise, at least of encomium,' Reade continued, 'that so great a work should have been accomplished with so little trouble to the Collector, and so much real advantage to the settlement officer.'[90] Revenue surveys, of course, were only as good as the quality of British surveyors and their Indian subordinates allowed. Much, too, depended on the accurate workings of individual collectors and settlement officers. Ultimately, though, the making of revenue settlements relied on a host of variable factors. And as we shall see in the following chapters, even with the best of intentions, the outcome could still lead to distress for some agrarian communities.

'Cutcherry on Horseback': John Lawrence and the Making of a Sahib-Zillah 1831–46

In January 1831, aged just twenty years old, John Lawrence took up his appointment as one of five assistants to the British representative at Delhi. It marked the beginning of a long association with the city and its surroundings. His career in the region can be viewed as consisting of two main phases interrupted by a period of furlough. The first phase began with his apprenticeship to the Resident/Agent for a period of almost three years. In December 1833 he then was promoted to Officiating Magistrate and Collector of Delhi.[1] This was followed, in November 1834, by his appointment as Officiating Magistrate and Collector of the Panipat district, a post he held until July 1836 when he moved to the Gurgaon district as Joint-Magistrate and Collector. The following November he was promoted to Officiating Magistrate and Collector of Gurgaon. Two years later, he moved to the Etawah district (east of the Delhi Territory) as Settlement Officer until December 1839 when ill-health forced him to take sick leave. Three months later he left India on furlough. The second phase of his Delhi career began shortly after his return to India in December 1842. A string of temporary positions began with a brief spell as Civil and Sessions Judge at Delhi and ended in his permanent appointment as Magistrate and Collector of the Delhi and Panipat districts; a post he held until the end of the 1st Anglo-Sikh War in March 1846.

Following Lord Lake's defeat of the Marathas and the subsequent Treaty of Surji Arjangaon (1803), the imperial city of Delhi and its environs was formed into an administrative unit known as the Delhi Territory, quite separate from the Bengal Presidency and its Regulation Code – an area of some twenty thousand square miles with, at the time of John's arrival, a population of approximately three million people. Its creation was a direct consequence of Delhi's strategic position, its turbulent history, and unique local conditions. Distinct political responsibilities were established. Foremost was the management of the East India Company's delicate relationship with the Mughal Emperor. Now under British protection, he and his family were to be maintained by the revenues from lands assigned within the Territory. Next was the handling of relations with the numerous *jagirdars* and petty chiefs whose autonomous estates lay within Delhi's borders. And finally, beyond Delhi's immediate orbit, there were diplomatic ties to be established and maintained with the Rajputana principalities, the chieftains in the protected Sikh and hill states as well as the independent kingdoms of Lahore and Kabul. Overseeing these substantial political commitments was the British Resident. Directly responsible to the Governor-General, he ruled on behalf of the emperor who was now styled the King of Delhi and whose authority was confined to the precincts of his palace overlooking the Jumna (Yamuna) River. Although coins in the name of the emperor continued to be cast and official homage paid to the imperial court, Mughal sovereignty had all but disappeared.[2] Real power resided in the Residency with Delhi becoming the crucial frontier base of the Company's growing influence in north-west India.

Alongside these political and diplomatic undertakings, Delhi's long history of civil mismanagement also merited its special, non-regulation status. The territory's best chance of rehabilitation, it was argued, lay under the close supervision of the Resident who, in the early days of British rule, was free to mould the administration according to his own preferences. Under Archibald Seton (Delhi Resident 1806–11) but more prominently under Charles Metcalfe (Delhi Resident 1811–19, 1825–27), the emphasis was on preserving indigenous institutions and customs and only modifying where necessary.[3] Unhampered by the Bengal Regulations, Metcalfe's 'Delhi System' promoted the age-old use of *panchayats* (meeting of elders) to resolve village disputes, continued the practice of collective responsibility for crimes committed within community boundaries, and maintained the existing revenue system by making village settlements with *muqaddams* (village headmen). Metcalfe also upheld the custom whereby land could not be sold or alienated except by the consent of all proprietors. Influenced in part by Romanticism but also by practical considerations, his administrative philosophy was based on his now celebrated description of Delhi's village communities as self-sufficient 'little republics' which had endured political turmoil down through the ages. 'This union of the village communities, each one forming a separate little state in itself, has,' he wrote in 1830, 'contributed more than any other cause to the preservation of the people of India through all the revolutions and changes which they have suffered, and is in a high degree conducive to their happiness, and to the enjoyment of a great portion of freedom and independence.'[4]

It was this rather idealised vision of the Indian village, formed of communal brotherhoods, which underpinned Metcalfe's support for peasant proprietorship and the preservation of village institutions. He saw the sturdy yeoman farmer, the one who tiled the soil, as the natural proprietor of the land rather than large-scale intermediaries as in Bengal: 'The real Proprietors of the Land,' he told Governor-General Lord Bentinck, in March 1831, 'are generally Individuals of the Village Communities who are also, for the most part, the natural occupiers and cultivators of the Land. The great Zamindars, Talookdars &c., whom our Regulation Men recognize as Proprietors, are not so, but Representatives of the Government.'[5] Another notable feature of his land revenue policy was the espousal of moderate assessments. While 'taking the established share of government as a foundation', he hoped that a 'light and easy' settlement would encourage the expansion of cultivation, increase the prosperity of village landholders, and legitimise British rule.[6]

John Lawrence's arrival in the Delhi Territory coincided with several significant administrative changes. The time had come, it was now felt, to remove the distinctive character of its government and bring it more into line with the older provinces of Bengal. In 1832, under Governor-General Bentinck, the Delhi Residency was abolished, and the post of Resident replaced by the less grandiose one of 'Commissioner and Agent to the Governor-General'. Furthermore, responsibility for relations with the Rajputana states was removed, while ultimate control over judicial and revenue affairs within the Delhi Territory was handed over to the Supreme Courts of Justice and the Board of Revenue based at Allahabad. The Agent and his subordinate officers were now required to 'ordinarily conform to the principles and spirit of the Regulations,' and to act according to justice, equity, and good conscience in cases for which no specific rules existed.[7] Although the Bengal Regulations were not formally introduced, the Delhi Territory was now exposed to more legal and civil procedures than hitherto. In 1834 the region became integrated into the Province of Agra which was renamed the North-Western Provinces two years later.

Reforming measures such as the establishment of district courts and the increasing use of police at local level inevitably impinged on village autonomy and threatened Metcalfe's bucolic vision. Yet much of the old ways endured.[8] The system of *panchayats* continued while *muqaddams* still remained the important managers of village affairs.[9] Moreover, an important hallmark of Metcalfe's 'Delhi System' was the role played by the British official who continued to exercise wide discretionary powers through the union of executive (collector) and magisterial (magistrate) functions, a feature that was adopted across the North-Western Provinces and later in Punjab. Drawing inspiration from the Indian tradition of strong, personal government, the district officer's rule was the epitome of paternal governance. 'This officer,' writes Professor Eric Stokes, 'was not to be a distant figure, presiding in his *cutcherry* like a deity in his temple, but a familiar lord, visiting and speaking with them of their quarrels and their crops, and looked up to as *ma-bap*, father and mother.'[10] It was this appeal, according to Charles Aitchison, later Punjab colleague and biographer, which made Delhi such an attractive proposition for John Lawrence:

No finer field than the Delhi Territory could at that time have been chosen for the development of the special characteristics by which John Lawrence was distinguished. There was scope for independent action and opportunity for the display of individuality of character and temperament which the administration of an ordinary British District did not present.[11]

The Delhi that greeted John's arrival in early 1831 was the walled city of Shahjahanabad, now known as 'old Delhi'. Built during the first half of the seventeenth century in honour of the Mughal emperor who had shifted his capital allegedly to avoid the excessive heat of Agra, it was in fact the seventh city of Delhi to have been founded since the eleventh century, each one leaving behind its own set of slowly decaying monuments and ruins. By the fourth decade of the nineteenth century, the latest incarnation was a dense, compact city, dominated by the great walls of the imperial palace, the domes and minarets of the Jama Masjid and the main thoroughfare of Chandhi Chowk. An 1833 census revealed the population of the city, excluding the Palace, to be 119,860.[12] In a census fourteen years later, the city's population had risen to 137,997. Religious affiliation within the city was finely balanced. 71,530 were Hindu while 66,447 were Muslim/non-Hindu. By contrast, in the Delhi district (including the city) at large, an area of 450 square miles, Hindus outnumbered non-Hindus by a ratio of more than two to one. The total population was 306,550, of whom 214,514 were Hindu and 92,036 were Muslim/non-Hindu.[13]

The British had initially established their residences within the old walled city close to Kashmiri Gate to the north and in the Daryaganj neighbourhood near Delhi Gate to the south. Since the days of David Ochterlony, Delhi's first Resident (1803–06), the centre of political and administrative life was the British Residency on Lothian Road. Ochterlony had it constructed around the pavilion of the former palace of Dara Shukoh in classical fashion, complete with a colonnade of Ionic pillars. By 1832, however, due to the Residency needing extensive repairs, the British administration shifted to a gothic, crenelated edifice known as Ludlow Castle, once the home of Samuel Ludlow, a long-serving Residency surgeon.[14] The move marked the growing confidence of the British to go beyond the confines of the old city walls and to set down roots in what would emerge as the city's Civil Lines in the space between Kashmiri Gate and the 'Ridge', a rocky spur running north-east towards the Jumna River, beyond which a military cantonment was established. Near to Ludlow Castle, according to Professor Percival Spear, was John Lawrence's own residence which he shared with the district chaplain, the Revd Robert Everest.[15] Writing in the late 1940s, Spear believed the residence was situated at No. 1 Ludlow Castle Road (now

Raj Niwas Marg), a building which he described as 'a good specimen of an early nineteenth century official's house'.[16] Today a modern school occupies the site.

A notable characteristic of the Delhi Residents in the first few decades of the nineteenth century was their fascination with Indian culture and their fondness for maintaining semi-Indian lifestyles. Delhi's rich cultural milieu and the enduring mystique surrounding the 'fallen greatness' of the Mughals and past dynasties had piqued the newcomers' curiosity. This was further encouraged by its remoteness from the seat of central government, Calcutta. In Delhi, a frontier city where the British presence was much smaller, there was less pressure to maintain a strict adherence to European conventions which characterised the former. Moreover, as they lived cheek-by-jowl with the Indian populace, there was also greater social interaction. Thus, for Ochterlony, Metcalfe and William Fraser (Resident/Agent between 1832–1835), cultural immersion ran deep. Each one lived the life of an oriental nobleman, wearing Indian dress, residing in oriental-styled mansions, while maintaining several *begums* or *bibis* and their offspring. Sanskrit texts and Persian poetry were often the topics of conversation or study while patronage of local artists was *de rigueur*.

There were, of course, character differences. While Ochterlony was the convivial *bon viveur* who regularly enjoyed the delights of the *nautch* and the *hookah*, Metcalfe was the shy, bookish sort who rode poorly and had little appetite for *shikar* (Indian hunting sports). Scottish-born Fraser, on the other hand, was regarded as 'probably the most famous sportsman of Upper India', and was noted for his repeated encounters with lion and tiger on horseback using only spear and sword.[17] Described by William Dalrymple as 'part severe Highland warrior, part Brahminized philosopher, part Conradian madman', Fraser's brusque, obstinate demeanour often put him at odds with those in authority.[18] Nonetheless, in a career spanning thirty-odd years, he was noted for his unrivalled knowledge of Delhi's land tenures and for his deep bonds with its hinterland and people. Lawrence's own judgement of Fraser appears apposite: 'he was a man deservedly popular with the natives of all ranks, and was beloved by them, more particularly by the lower classes, with whom, on many occasions, he showed strong sympathy; but being a man of considerable force of character and decision of purpose, he sometimes made enemies.'[19] These last two traits, as we shall see, would prove to be his downfall.

John's first field of operations, as an assistant to the Resident/Agent, was the central Delhi district; an apprenticeship which would last almost three years until December 1833 when he was promoted to Officiating Magistrate and Collector of Delhi. His responsibilities were wide-ranging and varied. As a magistrate, he was charged with resolving legal disputes, bringing criminals to justice, and regulating the police, while his role as a collector gave him responsibility over the assessment and receipt of revenue. The maintenance and building of roads, drains and schools were also part of his brief. Although John remained at Delhi for almost four years 'working regularly and steadily without any change or intermission', little detail is known about his time in the city. Bosworth Smith attributed this dearth of information to the loss of contemporary official documents during the 1857 Rebellion and the deliberate destruction (for privacy's sake) of John's private letters.[20]

Outside his official duties, there is also little to report beyond some hog-hunting expeditions in the tamarisk jungles along the River Jumna or in the occasional visit to his brothers – George and Henry – then stationed at the military cantonment of Karnal. Personal reminiscences are scarce too. One of the few passing comments comes from his colleague, Charles Trevelyan, who had arrived three years earlier. Macaulay, the Whig historian, discerned the influence of Utilitarianism on the young Trevelyan: 'He is quite at the head of that active party among the younger servants of the Company who take the side of improvement…He has no small talk. His mind is full of schemes of moral and political improvement.'[21] As a strong opponent of the corruption which had permeated the Residency after the departure of Metcalfe, one suspects Trevelyan found a kindred spirit in John whose ethical standards matched his own.[22] Reminiscing years later, he recalled that John 'was in appearance, singularly like what he was in advanced life; nay, he looked, in a manner, older than in after life: the lines in his face were even deeper'. He projected a 'hungry, anxious look' and seemed to have 'a mercurial disposition'. This trait, however, Trevelyan put down to his 'earnest and restless' nature which was reflected in John's habit for riding his horse at a gallop. 'Here,' he noted, 'was the foundation for a man of action.'[23]

John, Bosworth Smith tells us, also became acquainted with the great regional chiefs who had residences in the city and who were accustomed to paying their respects to the representatives of British rule.[24] The perspicacious and colourful character of Begum Samru (Sombre) was certainly one member of the landed elite who would have been well known to John. Beginning her career as a nautch girl, she married a European mercenary, converted to Catholicism, and became immensely wealthy, holding lands in Sardhana near Meerut and Jharsa in Gurgaon. Her imposing, classical inspired haveli on Chandhi Chowk can still be seen today (now the State Bank of India). After her death in 1835, her *jagirs* were resumed by the government – the Jharsa *pargana* being assessed by John in the years 1837/8 (see below). Although Begum Samru became a trusted supporter of the British, John appears to have already taken a dim view of her privileged class: 'In Delhi,' Charles Raikes, his assistant at Panipat, later wrote, 'he perhaps had seen the worst specimens of the idle, debauched Mahomedan quasi-princes and native aristocracy, and I am not sure but that he contracted there a sort of distaste of this class, which he never quite shook off.'[25]

Panipat

A greater understanding of John's work and administrative style can be found when he became Officiating Magistrate and Collector of the Panipat district in the northern division of the Delhi Territory in November 1834. After managing a large city and its hinterland, John was now exposed to what was then an overwhelmingly agricultural district, allowing him to gain broad experience of dealing with all classes and castes. Consequently, he viewed Panipat as the place where he came of age as a civil officer. 'It was a hard one, it is true,' he later recalled, 'but one which I had no cause ever to regret, it facilitated all my subsequent labours, no matter how varied, how onerous.'[26] Still only in his mid-twenties, the posting also allowed John to become the *sahib-zillah* in full charge of his dominion. Little wonder he looked back fondly on his time here: 'These were very happy days. Our time was fully occupied, and our work was of a nature to call forth all our energies, all our sympathies, and all our abilities.'[27]

Spread over an area of almost a thousand square miles, the Panipat district had a population of approximately 280,000 inhabitants of whom two-thirds were Hindu; the remainder mostly Muslim.[28] As a whole, they were drawn primarily from the industrious farming community known as Jats but also included those from the Gujar and Rangur castes who, by contrast, had earned a reputation for cattle stealing and banditry. A tradition of independence and recourse to violence to settle disputes predominated amongst the populace. 'In those days,' remarked Charles Raikes in his reminiscences of Panipat, 'they never went out to plough or herd their buffaloes without sword, shield, and often a long matchlock over their shoulders.'[29] With only himself and Raikes as the sole British representatives, John summarised the challenge they faced:

> To bring people who were impoverished and discontented into order and contentment; to make them pay their land-tax punctually; to deter, if not to wean, them from their habits of life, which were those of their ancestors for centuries; to revise the assessment of the land-tax which had broken down, and at the same time to carry on and improve the general administration, was no light task.[30]

Much of John's time was spent in the saddle and under canvas. For at least half the year, he would tour the district visiting its numerous villages, meeting the elders, resolving boundary disputes between villages, hearing individual grievances, punishing dacoits and petty thieves as well as assessing the land revenue. This mobile system of administration was commonly referred to by contemporaries as 'cutcherry on horseback' – *cutcherry* being the Hindi word for a courthouse or administrative office. Often the impromptu *cutcherry* was under a mango tree or beside a well and made a refreshing change from the often-stifling environment of the central administrative station. Despite the absence of 'English society', John happily flung himself into his work: 'I had in truth so much to occupied me, or, what is pretty much the same thing, made so much occupation for myself, that, though often the sole European in the district, and literally without anyone with whom I could exchange a word in my native tongue, I do not think I ever felt listless for a day.' As he went on to explain, 'there was always some end in view – a village to visit, a new road to be made, or an old one to be repaired, the spot where a murder had been perpetrated to be examined.'[31] John's immersion into the local environment also seemed to produce subtle changes in his habits. He adopted a combination of native and European clothing geared to the prevailing climate, while fellow officers, when they came to visit, noticed that his conversation had become 'so interspersed with Persian words and expressions' that they found difficulty in understanding him.[32]

A central pillar of John Lawrence's administrative style, as noted by Raikes, was his accessibility. For he understood the importance of establishing a direct, personal relationship between ruler and ruled. It also afforded him the opportunity to gather useful information through non-official channels outside regular office hours. When out with his dogs and gun he would frequently talk to locals he met along the way and often, after an evening ride, would hold an impromptu gathering of the village community outside his tent. Clothed in a *chupkun* (an Indian undershirt) and resting on a *charpoy*, these occasions gave him added insight into the habits and concerns of villagers 'from the headman to the barber'. Such was his sponge-like thirst for local knowledge that locals could apparently be heard saying: '*Jan Larens sub janta*' – 'John Lawrence knows everything.'[33] This was the spirit of Metcalfe.

Raikes, clearly in awe of his superior, went on to list several professional attributes that set John apart as the *sahib-zillah par excellence*. When he received intelligence about a murder or a serious robbery, he would be 'at once in the saddle' and off to the scene of the crime no matter what time of the day or night. Similarly, where land boundary disputes or water privileges were concerned, he preferred to go directly to the location to satisfy his understanding of the situation. In such cases he was often heard reciting one of his favourite Persian proverbs: '*Kuzea zumeen buh dir zumeen*' – 'Disputes about land must be settled on the land.'[34] Moreover, John's desire to see things for himself and gain as full a picture as possible on a particular issue, meant that, according to Raikes, he was able to shake off the biased opinions of 'flatterers, sycophants, and informers'. Such behaviour earned him a name for impartiality and a determination to get to the root of the problem.

Lawrence's and his assistant Raikes' ability to hold sway over a wide area, we are told, amazed some locals. 'You Feringhis are wonderful fellows,' expressed an old chief at one of Lawrence's village 'durbars', 'here are two of you managing the whole country for miles around. When I was a young man we should have been going out four or five hundred horsemen strong to plunder it.'[35] Lawrence's apparent success, though, was down to several factors. To begin with, there was no doubt that his sheer force of character and ability to rule with authority played a part in gaining acquiesce. Raikes noted that he exuded 'a quality of hardness, not amounting to harshness, but not short of severity, which made the malefaction tremble at his name. He might or might not be loved – this seemed to be in his mind – but respected he would be at all events.'[36] Similarly, Robert Montgomery recorded the testimony of an Indian assistant in John's *cutcherry*: 'when he is in anger his voice is like a tiger's roar, and the pens tremble in the hands of the writers all round the room.'[37]

Yet John's authoritarian style was not simply based on firm words; it was also backed up by actions. Under his regime, the people took note that 'rules were enforced, rogues punished, and revenue arrears collected'.[38] In one instance when a village had refused to pay its share of the land revenue, Lawrence commanded the local police to surround the village during the night. The following morning when the cowherds attempted to go out to pasture, they were prevented from doing so and a standoff of a few hours ensued. As the cattle became increasingly obstreperous, the village elders, seeing no alternative, finally relented and paid the sum. Hence forth, we are told, the revenue collection in this area passed without incident. Lawrence was also willing to apply pressure by exploiting local tensions. In one instance a recalcitrant chief who refused to pay the land revenue was finally induced to do so by Lawrence requesting a show of force from a rival chief.[39]

Although Lawrence saw himself very much as the 'pivot around which the whole of administration of the district revolved', he also understood the importance of delegation, and much depended on choosing the right assistants.[40] Richard Temple regarded John's ability to accurately assess a man's moral and intellectual qualities as unsurpassable: 'Almost any plan, he [Lawrence] would say, will answer with good men to execute it, with such men even an inferior system will succeed; but with bad or indifferent men to work it, the best system will fail.'[41] Charles Raikes, too, noted that Lawrence was keen to encourage 'a spirit of action and energy in his subordinates'.[42] When Raikes was handed three of the nine *thanahs* or police circuits within the Paniput district to manage, his superior was clear in his expectations: 'if you can keep crime down and collect your revenue in your share of the district, I will not interfere with you,' he told his assistant.

The recruitment of British officials such as Raikes was only a small part of the picture, however. No less important was the contribution made by Indian assistants themselves. Like Henry's revenue survey, John's civil establishment employed a host of local subordinates. In revenue matters, he relied heavily on his Indian assistant collectors at the *pargana* level.[43] In the sphere of law enforcement, according to Raikes, Lawrence had at his disposal armed *sowars* (mounted police), stationed at police headquarters, together with the ordinary constabulary force located at various *thanahs* (police stations) throughout the district. Each *thanah* had a *thanadar* (chief of police), a *Jamadar* (sergeant), a *mohurrir* (clerk) and about a dozen rank and file policemen known as *burkundazes*. This police hierarchy was augmented by the old village watch and ward system which consisted of a *chowkidar* (watchman) and a clerk whose duty was to record and report all crimes and noteworthy events within his village. Raikes believed the system was 'sufficiently efficacious to protect the public' provided it was under an energetic magistrate such as Lawrence. Yet he was also candid enough to admit that it could become 'an apt engine of oppression…under a careless and slothful official'.[44]

In the mid-1840s, with the help of his wife Harriette, John recorded some of his experiences from his Panipat days and his two subsequent postings. Ostensibly penned for the future amusement of their children, they provide a valuable insight into the type of work undertaken by John during this early stage of his career and particularly how he saw himself as an active participant. These carefully crafted accounts, which set forth John's key attributes as a colonial administrator, undoubtedly portray 'brand Lawrence' in the most favourable light possible and suggest that the writer may well have had a wider readership in mind. Tending to avoid humour and self-deprecation, they adopt instead a quite serious, didactic tone, and project an image of a man who, despite adversity, invariably succeeds in what he sets out to do. A murderer is brought to justice, a boundary dispute is ultimately resolved to the relative satisfaction of all parties, and a strike by Hindu traders protesting over cow slaughter is eventually broken thanks to John's problem-solving capabilities. Even in those cases that do not reach a successful conclusion such as a robber evading arrest, it is still an opportunity for John to demonstrate his formidable physical and moral strength. These personal reminiscences, enhanced by Bosworth Smith's gloss upon them, reinforce Lawrence's towering reputation as a heroic 'man of action'.

John's indefatigable zeal in the dispensing of his duties form a common thread throughout these accounts. Yet equally noteworthy is the cool, methodical way he reacts to an emergency and his apparent disregard for his own personal safety. This is exemplified in one such tale entitled 'The Brothers' which concerns the brutal murder of a man close to the magistrate's residence at Panipat in June 1835. Despite the late hour of the incident, John applies a clear structure to his investigations. He begins with the establishment of the initial facts through the firm questioning of an eyewitness, his *khansama*, Ali Khan, who had observed the event from a hidden vantage point. Next is John's speedy arrival at the crime scene, still dressed in his bed clothes and carrying a lighted taper. He finds the bloodied body covered in wounds with its head almost severed. 'As I stooped down to examine the corpse, which was still warm,' he calmly recounts, 'a sudden gust of wind blew out my candle. Seeing therefore that nothing could be done till assistance arrived, I sat down, and after a few minutes which, in my impatience, seemed an hour, I discovered the bearer running along with my pistols.'[45] A hastily assembled group of half-clothed guardsmen follow behind.

As the moon begins to rise, and with the aid of flambeaux and torches, the next phase involves a careful examination of the surrounding area. At first no obvious clues are found; the dead man's identity remains a mystery. Wearing only a simple *dhoti* around the waist, his face has been so badly bludgeoned that it is indistinguishable. Perplexed, John nonetheless orders it to be cleaned as best as possible. Eventually one of the guardsmen recognises the facial features of the dead man. It is Ram Sing, one of their comrades. There soon follows, under John's direction, a group discussion on possible motives for the murder. The discovery of a shoe consisting of an iron heel favoured by *dawk wallahs* (postmen) proves to be a key piece of evidence. 'The dawk wallahs are great runners,' John muses, 'had he (Ram Sing) a feud with any of them?'[46] It quickly transpires that the deceased had a brother called Bulram with whose wife, local gossip it was said, he had been 'rather too intimate'. While some of the guardsmen dismiss the news as idle talk, John is convinced that they have found a plausible motive and suspect.

By this stage, it is already past midnight, but there is no let-up in the investigation. Accompanied by some of his guardsmen, John briskly makes his way first to Bulram's home and then to the post-house where they eventually find the suspect sitting quietly smoking his hookah. His calmness and self-possession under close examination makes John initially doubt himself. But when one of the guardsmen prompts Bulram to show respect to the *sahib* and stand up, he does so reluctantly. His reticence re-ignites John's suspicions, and the interrogation continues. He puts his hand on the suspect's heart and asks, 'what is the matter that your heart beats so violently?'[47] Bulram's explanation that he had been running to arrive on time for work does not fool the inquisitive magistrate who now carefully looks the suspect up and down. Almost immediately his eyes fall on the bloody folds of the suspect's *dhoti*. 'Ah Bulram, what means this?' he enquires. 'Don't trouble yourself, *maino usko mara* [I killed him],' comes the terse reply. The game is up and Bulram, who had been wounded in the frenzied attack, proceeds to confirm why he had murdered his brother: 'He was intimate with my wife, therefore I killed him.'[48] His accomplices are soon after apprehended, and with the help of *khojis* (specialist trackers) the murdered man's turban, necklace, sword, as well as the murder weapons are retrieved. Bulram is eventually hanged while two of his conspirators are imprisoned for life. The case caused a great sensation at the time. But while Ram Sing's death was universally regretted, John found it curious that there was little sympathy for Bulram as the victim of his brother's adultery. 'The general feeling appeared to be,' he observed, 'was not Ram Sing his brother? – how could he murder him?'[49]

The portrayal of Lawrence as an 'intrepid and daredevil ruler' is revealed in another story concerning the nocturnal pursuit of a notorious *dacoit*.[50] In contrast to his Indian assistants, John shows little hesitation when confronted with formidable physical obstacles such as crossing a rapidly flowing river on horseback. Indeed, when it is reported that his *risaldar* has got into difficulties trying to traverse the same river and is feared drowned, it is John, not his Indian subordinates, who readily plunges back into the water to rescue him. Similarly, when his search party closes in on the *dacoit's* lair, it is the future viceroy of India who is seen leading the charge across the rooftops of adjacent houses as the robber tries to make good his escape. Only a misjudged leap and the subsequent dislocation of his ankle forces John to abandon his spirited pursuit. In terms of the moral of the story, though, this matters little. Of more importance is the identification of John with the heroic character traits of courage, compassion, and leadership. Moreover, courtesy of Bosworth Smith, the story is interpreted through the lens of racial stereotyping. John, the high-minded 'Anglo-Saxon' hero, prepared to risk his own life for a subordinate, forms a stark contrast to the 'placid indifference' of his Indian comrades.[51]

John's account of the criminal investigation into the murder of William Fraser, Commissioner and Agent to the Governor-General at Delhi, also reaffirms the former's reputation as a resolute, duty-bound 'man of action'. In contrast to the other stories of the period, this one was published in *Blackwood's Magazine* in 1878, a year before Lawrence's death. The story begins on the evening of 22nd March 1835 when Fraser is returning on horseback to his mansion on the outskirts of the city accompanied only by an unarmed servant.[52] Upon reaching the Fraser domain, an unidentifiable trooper suddenly appears. As he rides past the Commissioner, he shoots him at point blank range in the back.

The balls from the carbine pass through his body, jolting him upwards from his saddle before he falls lifeless to the ground. The trooper quickly gallops off in the direction of the city leaving the 'terror-stricken servant' to raise the alarm. Fraser's household hasten to the spot only to find 'their master dead, but his body still warm'.[53]

The following morning John, then based at Panipat, receives a Persian note from his local police informing him of the tragic news. It comes as a great shock to his close friend and colleague. But, like previous stories, there is little time for mourning. With his extensive knowledge of Delhi, John believes that he can be of assistance in the hunt for the murderer. Without delay, he leaves his Panipat residence to make the forty-mile ride to the house of Thomas Metcalfe, now the senior civil officer at Delhi. Upon arrival, Metcalfe informs him that little progress has so far been made. Professional trackers have been unable to follow the trail of the assassin's horse beyond a certain junction outside the city. A possible line of enquiry, however, is soon revealed when an old chief called Fateh Khan suggests to Metcalfe that his nephew, Shams-ud-din, the Nawab of Ferozepur Jhirka, a district some ninety miles south of Delhi, might be implicated in the murder. While Metcalfe discounts the notion, believing there might be some personal enmity between uncle and nephew, John firmly believes that any lead, no matter how tenuous, requires investigation: 'As in hunting, when the scent is lost,' he remarks, 'one casts about at a venture to recover it, so in this case they must take up any chance clue which might present itself, in the hope of its leading to the object sought for.'[54]

John's open-minded approach soon reaps rewards. A meeting with Simon Fraser, the Magistrate of Delhi and cousin of the deceased, reveals that Shams-ud-din Khan had quarrelled with the late Commissioner who had supported his younger brother's claim to a share of the Ferozepur state's territory. With a possible motive thus established, Fraser and Lawrence's attention swiftly move to the Nawab's Delhi residence where they conduct a search for further clues. With the assistance of a bystander from the Gujar caste (possibly one of the trackers mentioned earlier), Lawrence's inspection of a fine horse in the courtyard raises his suspicions. Its hoofs match the tracks of the murderer's steed, while a comment by one of the Nawab's retainers stating that the horse in question is sick and unable to eat is disproved by Lawrence when he picks up a nose bag of feed and the horse greedily munches from it. John, hiding his true intentions, manages to induce the retainer (whom he mistakenly names as Wassil Khan – his correct name is Kurreem Khan) to accompany him to the magistrate's *cutcherry* where he advises Fraser to arrest him.[55] 'This is an awkward business, this murder of the Commissioner,' John tells Khan, '…it strikes me you must know something of the matter, you shall remain here under restraint until our doubts regarding you are cleared up.'[56]

Other incriminating evidence at the Nawab's residence comes to light. Fraser finds fragments of a note which has been discarded in a bucket of water.[57] Although the ink has become faint through water damage, it is later revived with chemicals supplied by the Ulster-born civil surgeon of Delhi, Dr. Graham. The now reattached Persian note reads: 'You know the object for which I sent you into Delhi; and I have repeatedly told you since, how important it is for me that you should buy 'the dogs'. If you have not yet done so, you must do it without delay; it is most urgent and necessary.'[58] Fraser seeks the opinion of John who is left in little doubt that this is a coded message from the Nawab to Kurreem Khan ordering the murder of the Commissioner. Despite the reluctance of Metcalfe to summon the Nawab to Delhi (on account of his position and influence) to explain himself, Lawrence strongly advocates the measure. Metcalfe eventually complies while further investigations are undertaken by Charles Gubbins, magistrate of the adjoining district of Gurgaon. They result in an accomplice of the murderer, Unyah (Unnia) Meo, eventually giving himself up to the authorities and turning King's evidence. His testimony, revealing the full extent of the plot, proves decisive. Afterwards the supposed murder weapon, a carbine, is discovered by chance in a well near Kabul Gate, while other circumstantial evidence is revealed to further implicate the Nawab and Kurreem Khan. Still maintaining their innocence, both men are tried by a special commissioner, A.J. Colvin, and are hanged in front of large crowds outside Kashmiri Gate. Kurreem Khan is executed on 26th August, while the Nawab is executed on 8th October – the latter, John notes, becomes something of a Muslim martyr and his tomb a shrine for devotees.[59]

In John's foregoing account of the murder investigation, the reader is left in no doubt of the pivotable role he plays in bringing the perpetrators to justice. His sleuthing skills are seen as invaluable. While the new acting Commissioner, Thomas Metcalfe, dithers over possible lines of inquiry, John, by contrast, is resolute in calling for immediate action. Furthermore, the Magistrate of Delhi, Simon Fraser, deliberately seeks out John's opinion at crucial points in the investigation. Yet such an admiring portrayal is rather puzzling since John barely features in the official records of the case and is completely absent from W.H. Sleeman's near contemporary account.[60] In all of the correspondences – including the report conducted by special commissioner A.J. Colvin – John's name appears only once and then only in passing.[61] By contrast, Simon Fraser is referenced numerous times and his contribution spoken of in glowing terms: 'It is impossible for me,' records Colvin on one of several occasions, 'to speak in too flattering terms of the zeal and ability displayed by Mr. Fraser in the investigation of this most important and at first apparently, hopeless case, or of the energy and perseverance he has evinced in following up his enquiries and bringing to light the authors of this most inhuman act.'[62] As Magistrate in charge of law and order within the city, commendation of Fraser's actions is understandable. Yet other, less central figures, such as the Anglo-Indian Colonel James Skinner, or Brigadier Fast, C.O. of the Delhi troops, are praised too. Why not Lawrence? Given the passage of time, it is perhaps understandable that John's account should suffer from some inaccuracies. Yet the dearth of official recognition regarding his contribution must surely cast some doubt on the veracity of his narrative.

Gurgaon

In November 1836 John became Officiating Magistrate and Collector of the Gurgaon district, south of Delhi.[63] Here he continued to practice his robust administrative style in a post which brought its own fresh set of challenges. Covering an area of 1,467 square miles, the Gurgaon district was considerably larger than Panipat (997 sq. m.). It also contained a population of almost twice the size (approximately 460,000 inhabitants). Similarly, the number of villages/ towns within the district was more than double of his former charge (1,274 compared 540). In terms of Gurgaon's religious affiliation, the percentage split between Hindus and Muslims/non-Hindus was 60/40 – a slightly greater representation of the latter than at Panipat.[64] Both here and throughout much of north India, this inter-communal mix could, and did, lead to episodes of inflamed religious tension, particularly in larger urban centres where competition for public space was greater. Often, they were triggered by contentious events – religious festivals and processions, the siting of new temples and mosques or the thorny issue of cattle slaughter. For Hindus, the cow was a sacred animal, a symbol of life and purity, and its slaughter was regarded as a sin. For Muslims, though, the eating of beef held no such taboo, and from a practical standpoint it was cheaper than either mutton or goat. Exercising the right to slaughter cattle therefore elicited strong emotions on both sides which, if left unchecked, could easily erupt into violent protest. In their attempt to maintain civic peace, district magistrates often found themselves placed in the unenviable role of arbiter.[65] John's own experience is recorded in a story entitled 'Passive Resistance', an account which captures, according to Bosworth Smith, his 'courage, his vigour, and his readiness of resource'.[66]

In the spring of 1838, while John is assessing the land revenue in the Rewari *pargana,* the Muslim elders of its principal town (Rewari) petition him in open court to overturn the ban on the slaughter of cattle in their locality – a campaign they had championed over many years but to no avail. John's own feelings on the matter are decidedly pro-Muslim, believing that the origins of the dispute are based on 'a well-known prejudice of the Hindus against the ox'.[67] Nevertheless, he is conscious that whatever decision is taken, it will be unpopular to one side or the other. Better then to deflect personal criticism, he feels, by letting the divisional commissioner, as superintendent of police, make the ruling in favour of cattle slaughter.[68]

Attempting to forge something of a compromise, John fixes the location for the slaughterhouse some three-quarters of a mile outside the town, hoping 'to soften the blow to the Hindus'. But this proves wishful thinking. Instead, the Hindu townsfolk use the Islamic festival of Muharram to attack their Muslim neighbours 'with all manner of weapons, bricks, stones, and even dead pigs and dogs'.[69] The local *tahsildar*, a Brahmin 'of much force of character and self-won influence' eventually restores order but remains convinced that only 'the presence of the magistrate alone can arrest further mischief'.[70] Word is hastily sent to Lawrence who is then currently in camp some forty miles off. 'Here was a pleasant communication for me;' he recounts, 'the hot winds were blowing a perfect simoon, and it required no small spirit of adventure at such a season to face the heat and sand over that wild country.'[71] There is of course no question of him reneging. After an arduous journey over precipitous hills and sandy trackless plains, the unexpected arrival in Rewari of 'Larens Sahib', he tells us, has the effect of cowering the townsfolk who reluctantly return to their homes.[72] On receiving the latest intelligence from his *tahsildar*, he then orders police reinforcements to be placed at key locations throughout the town to deter further unrest.

Although the Hindu protestors have been temporarily subdued, they are far from reconciled. But instead of continuing with acts of civil disorder, they soon adopt a different tactic – an economic embargo. As the Banias (Hindu trading caste) control both the wholesale and retail market within the town, shops are forthwith closed and will only reopen if the cow slaughter order is rescinded. This ploy of 'passive resistance', John admits, 'was by far the most effectual they could have adopted'.[73] The commercial life of the town quickly grinds to a halt and its population, particularly the lower classes, are soon clamoring for relief. John now faces the prospect of widespread rioting and looting. Yet he too soon demonstrates the ability to adapt to changing circumstances. To circumvent the strike, he begins to organise the collection of grain from outlying areas. He also provides letters of credit to retail dealers appointed by himself and who are encouraged to sell their produce in the street. Thus, in the short term at least, his initiative provides for the rudimentary needs of the community. Furthermore, believing that the Hindu community are being manipulated by their priests, he also publishes proclamations warning them of their 'blind allegiance', stating that any violence will be met with 'prompt retribution'. For three weeks the Hindu traders hold out leaving John 'much worn and harassed with the constant work of inspection, repression and writing answers to complaints'. Eventually, though, support for the strike begins to waver as all creeds are made to suffer its ill effects. With no small sense of vindication, John records the moment when the embargo is lifted:

> A crowd of Hindus came to me in a humble frame of mind, owing that they had been led away by their priests, begging for pardon, and solemnly promising never to repeat the offence, and offering to open their shops at once. I agreed to this, and thus a combination which had threatened to produce a general uproar was quietly and peaceably put down. I was able to satisfy the inquiries of Government as to my somewhat independent action in the matter.[74]

Revenue Assessment in the Gurgaon District

While little evidence appears to remain of John Lawrence's revision of the land revenue assessment in Panipat, his time in Gurgaon was dominated by the the completion of no less than six *pargana* revenue settlements – Jharsa, Taoru (Taroo), Rewari, Borah, Shahjahanpur, and Palwal (Pulwul).[75] His well-documented settlement reports shed valuable light on the assessment methodology which had undergone significant modifications in recent years. Back in the early 1820s, the leading proponent on the subject, Holt Mackenzie, had sought to provide a scientific methodology for calculating the government's share of agricultural output. Influenced by Ricardian rent theory, it was based on the concept of 'net produce' or rent which was calculated from the produce of all varieties and classes of land minus the expenses of cultivation, wages of labour, and profits of capital. Although Mackenzie's *Mahalwari* Settlement (Regulation VII of 1822) was laudable in theory, its sheer complexity was to prove unworkable. There was simply insufficient manpower to obtain the in-depth statistical information required, while it was almost impossible to obtain reliable rental figures using the net produce methodology.[76]

In response, Governor-General Bentinck and R.M. Bird's 1833 reforms (Regulation IX of 1833) assumed a less doctrinaire approach – one which aimed at providing a more practical system so that equitable revenue assessments could be completed more rapidly. Gone was the 'interminable investigation into produce, price and minute classification of soil' at an individual field level. Instead, the assessment would be based on the aggregate cultivated area of an entire *mahal* (an estate, usually a village) aided by 'a general acquaintance' with those factors 'taken into consideration when regulating the Government demand' – for example, past revenue demands, receipts and balances, cash rents paid from 'under-cultivators' to proprietors, the state of irrigation, simple soil classification, and caste affiliation.[77] The government's new guidelines were enshrined in R.M. Bird's 1839 *Circular Order by the Sudder Board of Revenue, North-Western Provinces,* an updated version of which was later compiled by James Thomason in his celebrated handbook, *Directions for Settlement Officers (1844).*[78]

Perhaps the most emblematic example of this new approach can be seen in John Lawrence's settlement of the Rewari *pargana* conducted during the cold season of 1837/38. In this *pargana* J.M. Douie, a noted land revenue expert, regarded John's 'aggregate-to-detail' procedure to be 'exactly the method recommended by [R.M.] Bird in his Settlement Circular of 1839'.[79] This was a combination of 'general considerations' and statistical calculation which the Board of Revenue believed followed a robust, systematic methodology subject to local variations.[80] Thus, having found 'the rent and revenue...so mixed up', John Lawrence based his revenue calculations on a variety of sources. 'The rent rates which I have adopted,' he wrote in his settlement report, 'were assumed from the records of the pergunnah; from the accounts of the canoongoes [*pargana* accountants] and zamindars [landholders]: and, lastly, from the opinion of the istumrardars [revenue farmers]; who holding a large number of villages might be considered competent to give an opinion on the subject.'[81]

John also relied on his own empirical findings and those of his *tahsildar.* A heavy onus was placed on the classification of soil type. Having spent a good deal of time on horseback 'traversing and carefully examining the various parts of the pergunnah for two different seasons', he found the usual division into four different kinds – clay (*Chicknout*), good loam (*Nurmout*), sandy loam (*Mugda*), and sand (*Bhoor*) – to be only partially relevant. As the soil was of an inferior kind, and viewing the *amins* as untrustworthy, he directed his *tahsildar* to classify the lands according to the last two categories.[82] Similar exertions were made to gain an accurate picture of the state of irrigation. He found Rewari's wells to be particularly noteworthy: 'In no pergunnah, that I have seen, are wells so frequently sunk, so diligently worked, and the land so well manured as in Rewarree. The soil being barren and un-productive, the attention of the people has been directed to well-irrigation; which, in pergunnahs of more fertile soils, is comparatively neglected.'[83] Further investigations discovered that the water found in Rewari wells could be classified into four types, each varying in the degree of salinity – *Shereen* (sweet water), *Mutwalla* (hard water), *Mulmulla* (brackish water), and *Khari* (very brackish water).

Soil type and the availability of irrigation were two important factors in determining the type and quality of the crops produced and hence their value. Such categorisation enabled John to refine his rent and revenue rates (revenue rates were calculated as a percentage of the rent rates). Set on per acre basis, these rates were then used in conjunction with the amount of cultivated acreage per category to calculate the corresponding rental and revenue values for the *pargana* as a whole. Once these initial rates had been set and the maps and statistical information of the revenue survey had been reviewed, John was able to begin his calculations in what was an iterative, trial and error process. 'After examining all the villages,' John continued in his report,

> I classed them into such as were considered highly, moderately, and lowly, assessed; and by a rough calculation of the probable increase and decrease, in the first and last, was enabled to determine the proper jumma [total government revenue demand] for the whole pergunnah. Having fixed rates for each class of soil and irrigation, into which the land has been divided and ascertained, that the value of the whole did not exceed the proposed jumma, I applied the rates [to the various villages]. The result enabled me to correct my rates, until I obtained such as applied fairly to villages moderately assessed; and by them the assessment of all the mouzahs [villages] was finally calculated.[84]

Historically, many of Rewari's villages were in the possession of 'persons of wealth and influence' [i.e. revenue farmers] whose feuding tendencies had resulted in 'raising, prodigiously, the revenue of all their villages'. When reviewing the fiscal records, John expressed amazement at how these 'excessive assessments' had been realised. But it had come at a cost. The *pargana* was 'generally impoverished' as 'the funds of the capitalist' had been 'too often swallowed up by the demands of the Collector'.[85] Consequently, John's revised assessment (Rs.191,597) gave a reduction of Rs.756 on the previous demand (Rs.192,353). He also oversaw a large reduction in the number of villages under the control of revenue farmers (from 73 to 36 villages). Improvident revenue farmers were removed while the remainder were largely those who had managed their villages responsibly. Of the latter group, John took a practical approach: 'To have at once rejected such men would have been impolitic and unjust. It could only have been effected at an unnecessary sacrifice of much revenue.'[86] Overall, the result left him confident for the future prosperity of the *pargana* which he favourably compared to those adjacent independent states beyond British control:

It is not only more lightly taxed in proportion to its means, but the people having a full confidence that the demand on their labour and prosperity is limited and determined for a long period, (which the people beyond the border can never feel) it may fairly be anticipated that this pergunnah will more rapidly improve, from the exertions of its own population and from emigration from that of the independent states.[87]

Was John's Rewari assessment moderate? A review of the previous revenue demands since 1810 reveals that there were undoubtedly some years when it had advanced beyond a *jama* of Rs. 250,000 and where balances were correspondingly large. Yet from 1821, it is also evident that it had steadily declined to a low of Rs.165,850 in 1830 before rising above Rs.190,000 in the four years prior to John's arrival.[88] From this perspective, his assessment can only be seen as a modest improvement. On the other hand, when calculating his revenue demand as a percentage of the gross rental/net produce (based on John's revenue rate value as a percentage of his rent rate value), the result was undoubtedly high.[89] At 82%, it was substantially more than the two-thirds rule decreed by Governor-General Bentinck in his 26th September 1832 Minute or in what was later prescribed in James Thomason's 1844 *Directions for Settlement Officers*.[90] The figure does, however, accord with the five-sixths rule under Holt Mackenzie's Regulation VII of 1822, which, according to J.M. Douie, was still in operation in the late 1830s.[91] Indeed, the Sudder Board of Revenue's 1839 Settlement Circular, paragraph 116, notes that 'that no increase [in the assessment] shall be demanded, where the estimated net profit to the proprietors shall fall short of 20 per cent.'[92] Nevertheless, this apparent discrepancy is perhaps best explained by Alexander Fraser, a settlement officer writing in the late 1840s, who noted that Rewari had not benefited from 'so large a relief as other pergunnahs of this district'. This he partly ascribed to its early date of settlement when 'officers were not quite so certain of the disposition of the Government to light assessment' and partly 'from the condition of the people in this pergunnah requiring relief less imperatively than they did in others'.[93]

In contrast to Rewari, the small, adjacent *pargana* of Shahjahanpur had not been a victim of over-assessment. Here the revenue had been regularly collected with little balances occurring over the previous fourteen years. Even when faced with the excessive drought of 1837, the revenue had been collected without injury. Lightly assessed, the inhabitants were moderately well off. Keen to maintain the *status quo*, John limited his efforts to ensuring an equalization of the demand which he only slightly increased by 4%.[94]

A similar, relatively positive picture of farming conditions was revealed in the Borah *pargana*. Although the soil was naturally sandy and sterile, it benefited from numerous rivulets flowing down from the nearby hills. Its deposits on *dehur* or flooded land had made the soil more fertile and easier to work compared to other *parganas*. 'In Borah,' John remarked, a 'mere scratch of the plough suffices in the khureef [autumn]; while in the spring, it is only necessary to turn up and sow a light dehur, when the cultivator may rest till the harvest.'[95] Having enjoyed for many years a light assessment, the inhabitants, he believed, were 'now perhaps more affluent than those of any other part of the district'. Although increasing the assessment by 10%, he considered the new settlement to be modest:

> With the experience of thirty years' assessment for my guidance, and the condition of so many pergunnahs injured by over zeal, as a warning, I was careful to avoid the error of over assessment. The pergunnah may therefore be said to be lowly assessed; but taking the character of its people, the local situation, and its past history into consideration, I am inclined to think, it would not have prospered on a much higher revenue.[96]

The ease of cultivation in Borah relative to other *parganas* also led John to slightly alter his perception of caste characteristics as a determining factor in shaping farming practices and general behaviour. The Ahirs and the Jats were almost universally known for their industry and sturdy endurance but in Borah they had become 'inferior to their brethren of other pergunnahs'. Conversely, the Rajput's normally less glowing reputation had become inverted. Influenced by more favourable local conditions, John suspected that the former two castes had become less attentive in their husbandry habits, while the latter's exertions had 'concealed his natural indolence'.[97] Similarly, in the Jharsa *pargana*, he was struck by how Jats and Ahirs had succumbed to following the stereotypical proclivities of Gujars and Rangurs:

> The Goojurs inhabit all the hill villages, and, like all their brethren, are great thieves, and bad cultivators. The Aheers and Jats are frugal and tolerably industrious. The Rangurs are indolent and turbulent as any I have ever seen. All the people however are much given to stealing. In the Goojurs, and even Rangurs, one could expect no less; but it is not a characteristic of the Aheers and Jats. It has however risen from the peculiar situation and circumstances of the pergunnah. Jharsah, surrounded by our districts, and possessing a hilly and almost inaccessible tract of country, was an asylum to all the thieves and plundered property of the surrounding pergunnahs.[98]

Jharsa, which had lapsed to the British in 1836 on the death of the redoubtable Begum Sombre, provided a sorry tale of fiscal mismanagement. The main culprit had been the Begum's *amil* who had taken full advantage of his patron's absence and mental debility in her declining years to impoverish the *pargana*: 'His demand was seldom restricted to that which he might previously have fixed,' John noted, 'the rule being to collect as much as he could: the consequence of which was that the people, losing all trust in his good faith, had no incentive to cultivate their lands regularly.'[99] The absence of local scrutiny had also encouraged village headmen to collect large sums on their own account under the ruse of village expenses. But with the advent of British rule, such fraud had become more difficult to perpetrate: 'The consequence is,' noted John approvingly, 'that, in lapsed jagheers, the headmen regret, but the community rejoice at the change of administration.'[100]

Following the resumption of the *pargana* in 1836, a summary settlement had been made by fellow officer, Charles Gubbins. Based on little more than a review of previous demands and collections, it was superseded two years later by John's regular settlement under the provisions of Regulation IX of 1833. His assessment of Rs.77,873 allowed for only a small reduction of Rs.217 on the previous demand (Rs.78,090).[101] Yet John still considered it to be a light assessment and declared that it was 'collected with great attention to the existing condition of the crops,' ensuring that the people did not desert their lands.[102] Nevertheless, its correctness was soon called into question. Gubbins, after submitting the settlement papers to the Delhi Commissioner, began to suspect the accuracy of the village statements[103], the preparation of which John had entrusted to 'an active and intelligent' *tahsildar* named Rung Rao. Although Rung Rao had unfortunately died soon after completing his work, it did not prevent an investigation from being launched. A new *tahsildar* was appointed to re-examine the statements and amend those found to be erroneous. After much delay, the whole *pargana* was re-traversed and the statements of 18 villages were corrected.[104]

Other settlements conducted by John required revision too. In the Palwal (Pulwul) *pargana*, during the cold season of 1841–2, the then settlement officer, Mr. G.C. Barnes, was shocked to find many *zamindars* reduced to 'extreme destitution' and pointedly blamed his predecessor for his overly optimistic estimation of its agricultural capabilities:

Mr. J. Lawrence, who made the first settlement of the pergunnah under Regulation XI of 1833, undoubtedly rated the resources of the district too highly, and misled, (if I may so presume to speak of an Officer of his known capacity) by the abundance of available waste [land] which each village possessed, assessed each estate at a much higher value than its cultivated area could be brought to pay.[105]

In Barnes opinion, the poor quality of the soil, the poverty of the people, the difficulty of clearing wasteland, and its vulnerability to the seasons were the main impediments to bringing such land into cultivation. Only gradually could wasteland be reclaimed. In the meantime, it made more sense, Barnes argued, to 'allow some villages to escape with a portion of profitable waste land unassessed than to cripple the energies of the people by taxing their cultivation at an exorbitant rate'.[106] Consequently, his revised assessment of Lawrence's 1838 *jama* involved a considerable reduction of 29% from Rs.231,526 to Rs.165,255.

Conditions in the Taoru *pargana* fared little better. The soil was inferior (light and sandy), the means of irrigation limited, and the area of unculturable waste more extensive than in other *parganas*. Most of its fifty-five villages spread over fifty square miles were inhabited by the thriftless caste of Mewatis:

> The villages are small, and the people, being idle and improvident, are poor. They are great thieves and often employed as chowkeedars and burkundazes. Indeed they seem to like any employment better than cultivating….from the wild and isolated situation of the pergunnah, its poor soil, and the daring character of its inhabitants, strangers are unwilling to settle there.[107]

In his 1837 settlement of this *pargana*, John considered the former revenue rates to be 'rather high, and also varying with the supposed distinctions of soil'. He therefore simplified the rates on unirrigated land based on three types of soil and encouraged the construction of more wells by lowering the rates for irrigated lands.[108] In determining the revenue demand of Taoru's different estates, the following criteria was used – the locality, the present condition of the village, the ease or difficulty of collecting previous revenue demands, the extent of cultivation and quantity of culturable land still to be cultivated. Making the necessary allowances, he reduced the assessment overall by 15% from the previous demand and concluded by expressing his 'entire conviction of the probability of the secure and certain realization of the present assessment'.[109]

Unfortunately, John's optimism proved ill-founded and once more a revision of the assessment was required. Taoru, with its deficiency in irrigation and soil quality, had been adversely affected by the severe drought of 1837–8 and by a series of bad harvests. Revenue balances had accrued leading to the forfeiture of some estates to the government as proprietors deserted their lands. Once more G.C. Barnes, the succeeding settlement officer, was forced to make a further substantial reduction of 25% (from Rs. 21,975 to Rs. 16,458) on John's assessment of four year earlier.[110]

Both R.M. Bird's 1839 *Settlement Circular* and Thomason's *Directions for Settlement Officers* warned of the dangers of over-assessment and felt that it was better to under-assess even if it meant monetary loss to the Government. 'Over-assessment,' warned Thomason, 'discourages the people, and demoralizes them by driving them to unworthy shifts and expedients, and it also prevents the accumulation of capital, and dries up the resources of the country.'[111] The challenge for settlement officers like John Lawrence, however, was striking a balance between the financial demands of the government and the resources of the people. In practice, his Gurgaon revenue assessments were far from being considered light or moderate. In Rewari, for example, where the assessment had been calculated at 82% of the net produce (gross rental), F.C. Channing, a settlement officer writing in the 1880s, concluded that it was 'uniformly heavy'.[112] High percentages were also recorded in two other *parganas*. In Shahjahanpur, the assessment was calculated at 75.5% of the net produce, while in Borah it reached 79%.[113] In three *parganas* – Jharsa, Palwal and Taoru, the assessment had to be substantially revised by subsequent settlement officers. Although John's net produce percentages appeared to be in line with the guidelines of Bird's 1839 *Settlement Circular*, the two-thirds rule advocated in Thomason's *Directions* a few years later was a recognition that they had been originally set too high. In any case, the revisions of Palwal and Taoru *parganas* were a clear indication of over-assessment.

The Sudder Board of Revenue was keen to stress the new assessment's scientific credentials and extol the benefits of a professional survey with its host of statistics. But what if some of the figures were inaccurate due either to human error or to corruption? John, as we have noted, ignored the *amins'* soil classification in the Rewari *pargana* presumably because he found it untrustworthy. Instead, the onus was placed on the local *tahsildar* whose returns John 'carefully revised, and was so well satisfied with the work, as to find few alterations necessary'.[114] Not so satisfactory was the work of the *tahsildar* in the Jharsah *pargana* whose village statements subsequently required correction. And what of rent and revenue rates? In the absence of actual cash rents (i.e. the gross rental paid from tenant cultivators to proprietors), the formulation and application of these figures was very much a process of trial and error. However much its scientific credentials were touted, the system remained inescapably one of general estimates of productivity for a village or *pargana*, relying largely on the personal discretion of the settlement officer. No wonder that some settlements were found to have been over-assessed. Well might John stress to his assistants the importance of moderate assessments with a well-used maxim: 'The calf gets the milk which is left in the cow.'[115] Yet the results, as his Gurgaon settlements demonstrate, were often quite different.

Etawah

In November 1838 John Lawrence was appointed settlement officer of Etawah near Agra, a district which had suffered greatly during the famine of that year. Its population had been reduced by a combination of starvation and emigration. With houses deserted and lands abandoned, the revenue settlement had completely broken down. Large *talukdars*, unable to pay, had their estates put up for auction. But with no purchasers, the government bought them at knock-down prices and then settled them with resident cultivators on condition of paying the balances.[116] Although John had the kudos of being specially selected by R.M. Bird for the Etawah role, this was hardly an uplifting situation in which to be placed. Moreover, according to Bosworth Smith, the work was of 'a much less absorbing kind' compared to his Panipat and Gurgaon responsibilities, and before he could begin his principal duties, he was forced to wait for the revenue survey to complete its work.

Despite the lack of active engagement, John's spell at Etawah was nevertheless made more tolerable by his friendship with the local Magistrate and Collector, James Cumine, a fellow Haileybury alumnus. Sharing a house where their 'charpoys at night were under the same punkah', Cumine found John 'as pleasant a companion and friend as I ever met with'. Outside work commitments, both men 'most heartily and happily' took part in the few recreations available in such a 'dull place'. In the mornings there was pigeon shooting 'on the shady side of the house', while in the afternoon there were games of quoits and swimming 'accompanied by some rough horse-play'.[117]

To relieve the boredom, John also sought out employment superintending the survey's field measurements as well as adjudicating on village boundary disputes. The source of such disputes usually centred on common land used for pasture around the edge of ill-defined village boundaries and were often complicated by factors such as caste and religion. With the rollout of R.M. Bird's revised revenue survey, these boundaries now came under the scrutiny of surveyors and settlement officers like John Lawrence. One intractable dispute, which had lasted some twenty years, involved two villages on either side of the Etawah district boundary: one under British jurisdiction, the other under the rule of an independent chieftain. It forms another of John's stories entitled *The Disputed Boundary* which, in the hands of Bosworth Smith, aims to reveal 'the patience, the sagacity, and the resolution of the chief actor'.[118]

In resolving this age-old dispute, John Lawrence's *modus operandi* in this story is characteristically simple and relies on a combination of both moral and physical persuasion. After initial discussions between the two villages prove fruitless, John realises that a different tack is required. His proposal involves the election of a single adjudicator whereby one village chooses a person from the opponent's village to decide the matter. It is a clever ploy as it places the onus on the appointed person who has to swear an oath on his son's life that he will 'faithfully and truly decide the boundary'.[119] When the elders from the chieftain's village eventually choose Sahib Sing as arbiter from the opposing village, it is understandable that his wife attempts to hide their only son fearing that such an oath and her husband's boundary decision will bring calamity upon the family.

At this point John's physical presence and resolution come to the fore. Despite the attempts of a large group of women to stop the procession to the boundary, John is not deflected from the task: 'It was with great difficulty and much delay we finally got free of these ladies,' he rather politely states.[120] Further difficulties arise when they arrive at the boundary in question. With his child in his arms, Sahib Sing's nerve brakes down, pronouncing that he cannot make the decision. But John will have none of it: 'Come, come Sahib Sing! This trick won't do; you shall decide the boundary or face the consequences,' he tells him. In response Sahib Sing throws himself before the district officer and repeats his determination not to cast his verdict. Exasperated, John turns to the headman whom he suspects of 'subterfuge and pretence' and gives him an ultimatum. The headman is given one *ghurree* (24 minutes) to induce Sahib Sing to do his duty or else the verdict will be delivered by John himself.

The position of Sahib Sing is clearly unenviable. Under pressure to support the claims of his fellow villagers, he is also morally bound to the pledge he has taken from the opposing village. Exhausted by the whole ordeal, he eventually lashes out at his own villagers: 'you are a set of double-faced rascals: you want me to kill my child to secure your boundary; you tell the Sahib one thing and me another, you have forced me to it – I will settle the boundary, but in a way you won't like.'[121] As Sing begins to mark the boundary in a way contrary to the views of his villagers, Lawrence is on hand to provide the necessary moral and physical support: 'Well done, Sahib Sing! Don't you be afraid of these fellows, I will protect you: only let us have the true boundary.' The unruly crowd begin throwing stones, leaving the police straining to hold them back. But again, it is John who acts at the crucial moment. Fearing that Sahib Sing will be pulled from his horse, he confronts one of the leading rioters, striking him on the head with the butt of his riding crop. The man drops instantly to the ground, forcing the other rioters to pull back. With this one decisive act, the riot has been quelled. Thereafter the rest of the disputed boundary is marked out without incident. For John, the episode was a notable feather in his cap: 'The decision and the way in which it was brought about was highly lauded far and near, and, what was still better, it facilitated the settlement of many similar disputes. I had not another contested boundary that season.'[122]

John's time in Etawah would culminate in both him and Cumine contracting a severe bout of malaria. While the latter recovered enough to make his way to Allahabad, the former was less fortunate. For nearly a month John's debilitating condition stubbornly refused to improve, and at one point his doctor expressed the fear that he might even succumb to the illness. This news, which Bosworth Smith relates in typical fashion, had a powerful effect on John who 'roused himself to the emergency' and was henceforth 'determined not to die'. Commanding his bearer to bring him a bottle of burgundy he had stored under his bed, he consumed its full contents in the hope of stimulating a recovery. This, we are told, had a miraculous effect. The next day he was back at his desk examining his revenue accounts. Such relief was short-lived, however. Forced to leave Etawah on account of his health, he suffered a relapse at Spence's Hotel, Calcutta in December and was finally ordered by a doctor to go on furlough for three years. After a three months' stay in Calcutta to aid his recuperation, he left India in March and eventually arrived in England in June 1840. Not without good reason, he would later tell his former colleague and fellow malaria victim, Cumine, that he 'took particular care to avoid that hole Etawah' where both men 'were so nearly buried'.[123]

Furlough and Return to India

John's long period of leave was spent visiting family and friends in Britain and Ireland and included two extended trips abroad. In true John style, however, details of this period are scarce. Few personal memories were committed to paper or have survived, leaving a frustrated Bosworth Smith searching, often in vain, to fill the information gaps. Nevertheless, a rough sketch of his itinerary can be compiled. John's first destination was naturally to see his mother at Clifton, Bristol. Now a widow, her situation had been made comfortable by the support of the so-call 'Lawrence Fund' managed prudently by John himself. In August, inspired by the novels of Walter Scott, he took a tour of the western highlands with his Etawah colleague and friend, James Cumine, also on furlough. The following month saw him back in Ireland visiting his relatives and friends at Foyle College – a trip made all the more significant by a visit to the Youngs of Culdaff in nearby Inishowen where he met for the first time the daughter of the local rector, Revd Richard Hamilton, Harriette Catherine Hamilton – the future Mrs Lawrence.

Later in the autumn, John travelled to the continent and stayed for several months in Bonn in the company of his sister-in-law, Charlotte, known affectionately as Charlie (elder brother George was then serving in Afghanistan). There he appeared to enjoy an active social life amongst the city's cosmopolitan student elite. By spring of the following year, however, his funds had dried up, and he was forced to return to England. His next known destination was Bath where he stayed for a couple of weeks in April 1841 with his sister Letitia who was now married to the Reverend Hayes. A Mrs Kensington, then a young girl staying with the Hayes, vividly remembered John's visit. Despite still looking 'rather gaunt and ill', she noted John's 'wonderful energy and his straightforward going at whatever was to be done'. His conversation was 'lively and interesting' filled with curious anecdotes on Indian related topics. The two 'great objects in life' he told them were a return to full health and to find a wife; both of which, it was noted with some mirth, he pursued in a very 'business-like way'.[124] At first John's 'roughness and absence of conventionality' shocked the young Mrs Kensington, but she soon found 'so much force and originality in his whole character' to dispel her misgivings. Given his temperament and ten years fully immersed in Indian life, her first impressions were hardly surprising. For here was a man whom she rightfully observed was 'very indifferent to the luxuries of life or refinements of society' and who was quick to express disdain for those who placed too high a value on them. Despite attending local parties during his stay, John's decided views on future wife material did not, it is fair to say, accord with what the 'ball-going beauties of Bath' had to offer.[125]

Fortunately, John's prospects in Ireland improved in June 1841 when he returned to Donegal to meet once more Harriette Hamilton. Attracted by her solid qualities of simplicity, spirit, and consideration for others, John knew he had at last found his life partner.[126] The engagement lasted a mere two months, and on 26th August 1841 the couple were married. Looking back as Viceroy of India many years later, he recorded, 'In August 1841 I took perhaps the most important, and certainly the happiest, step in my life – in getting married. My wife has been to me everything that a man could wish or hope for.'[127] Their honeymoon was spent aboard where they visited Belgium, France, Switzerland, and Italy. By the time they had reached Rome, though, 'vigorous sightseeing' and the hot climate resulted in a relapse of John's condition. Forced to rest, he expressed his frustrations in a letter to his friend Cumine that he was unable 'to enjoy life in a place where there was so much to see and do as in Rome'.[128] At Naples, in March 1842, they received the shocking news concerning the decimation of the British army in the retreat from Kabul and George's uncertain fate. John wrote to Honoria Lawrence to express his concerns for George's wife, Charlie, and their children. He also revealed his desire to return to active service: 'I wish I was back in India, all my thoughts and feelings are there. I am heartily tired of Italy.'[129] The honeymoon thus ended rather abruptly, and they hurried back to London where John suffered another bout of illness. Against medical advice, and seeing no obvious alternative career at home, he remained determined to return to India: 'If I can't live in India, I must go and die there,' was his characteristically stubborn response.[130]

Their return voyage was now by steamship, traversing the Mediterranean via Gibraltar and Malta to Alexandria. From there, it was an overland route to Port Suez via Cairo before finally taking another steamship to Bombay via Aden. As well as being safer and more reliable, the new service was also much faster than the former means of sailing ship. Leaving Southampton on 1st October 1842, the couple arrived at Bombay on 14th November, a mere six weeks later, cutting the travel time by over two-thirds. Thereafter their journey to the North-Western Provinces, where John hoped to restart his career, was made more arduous due to unrest in the Bundelkhand region. Forced to take a circuitous route via Nagpore, their situation was further hindered by ill health. Soon after their arrival, Harriette contracted cholera, while John's malaria returned. 'We were thus,' wrote Harriette, 'about as helpless a pair of travellers in a strange land as could well be found; but we were young and not so easily frightened, and, as my husband knew what to do on the first appearance of an illness, the alarming symptoms did not increase, and soon he was quite well again.'[131] The challenges of travelling through wild, sparsely populated country also meant that they were unable to rely on regular *dak* transport. As their mode of travel was by palanquin, John was left with the tricky task of procuring and managing some forty bearers who carried them in relays during the relatively cooler hours of the day and at night. Travellers' bungalows were largely non-existent and amenities basic. They usually slept in their palanquins near a village where John did his best to purchase, prepare and cook rough and ready meals of goat and fowl.

Eventually more comfortable accommodation was found at Nagpore and later at Allahabad. At Cawnpore the couple stayed for a month with John's younger brother, Richard, who was then involved in raising troops. All the while the elder Lawrence was seeking out employment opportunities but with little success. In the meantime, he purchased the usual necessities of a sahib-zillah – horses, a buggy, several tents, various stores, as well as hiring domestic servants. Afterwards they moved on to Agra where their tent was pitched just outside the gardens of the Taj Mahal. For Harriette, her new way of life had left her spellbound: 'Great as was then, my joy and thankful pride in my husband, it could not be greater than the delight of those early days, when the world seemed all before us, and the reality of life had yet hardly touched me, and I lived only in the present happiness.'[132]

It was in a large encampment in the Agra district that the couple met, quite by chance, George Lawrence. Still in Afghan dress, he was travelling *en route* to re-join his old cavalry regiment at Cawnpore. The meeting is not recorded in George's *Reminiscences*, but no doubt the rendezvous was the cause of much celebration. On departing, John mentioned his plan of going to Meerut to seek employment; a plan George quickly dismissed: 'Why on earth are you going to a place where you are not known? Go to Delhi, where you are known; you are sure to find work there,' his brother recommended.[133] It was sound advice, for John would soon hold a series of appointments, albeit temporary, in his former patch. He was first appointed, on the Commissioner of Agra's recommendation, Civil and Sessions Judge at Delhi for a one-month period. Next, he took up a post at Karnal, near Panipat, where, on 10th June 1843, the couple's first child, Kate, was born (a second daughter, Emily, was born in November 1844). November of the same year saw him return to Delhi to take up another temporary assignment. Finally, at the end of 1844, he was appointed to the permanent position of Collector and Magistrate of the Delhi and Panipat districts. For the previous two years his salary had been less than half of that he had received before furlough. Now, with some relief, he had finally reclaimed the position and salary he had held before his departure home.

John's work remained, by and large, much the same as it had been during the first phase of his career. His core responsibilities were in the field of criminal and civil justice, supervision of the police, and the management of the land revenue and other taxes. But there were differences. His long period of leave, his marriage and children, had led to a more mature, reflective civilian officer. The spring months of 1845 saw him record, for example, his experiences from his Panipat, Gurgaon and Etawah days. He also engaged in policy debates by contributing to the *Delhi Gazette* on issues such as jail reform and organisation of the police. One article he wrote was against the government's plan to appoint a roving superintendent of jails on 2,500 rupees a month for the North-Western Provinces, believing it would be both expensive and ineffectual.[134] As well as critically assessing the government's proposals, John also suggested his own reforms to the prison system. These included the establishment of central as well as district jails, the classification of criminals, appointment of quality jail doctors, and particularly an increase in pay for those officials doing most of the work. Proper remuneration was essential, John argued, if the standard of Indian officials was to rise.[135]

John's knowledge and understanding of Delhi and its hinterland also continued to impress. His 1844 Delhi Settlement Report provides an important record on mid-century agrarian conditions he found in both the northern and southern *parganas* of the district. The territory consisted of 346 villages scattered across 604 square miles with a further sixty-six villages held in *jagir* – twenty-four belonging to the King of Delhi; five belonging to the King of Oude.[136] A large proportion of the land, about one third, was deemed uncultivated or unculturable. In the southern *pargana* this was due to adverse terrain – a combination rocky hills, wide ravines 'and the debris of ancient habitations,' while in the north high sodium levels were largely to blame. Although the soil quality was generally poor, John considered other factors to be significant: 'The facilities for irrigation, with the character of the cultivators, are the real points, which determine the wealth and prosperity of the community, and their ability to pay their revenue with ease to themselves and punctuality to the state.' On both points, he concluded, the southern *pargana* faired much worse than its northern counterpart. Not only was well irrigation limited and of an inferior quality (less than one-fourth the cultivated area), but the agricultural community also consisted of a large proportion of 'Goojurs and Moosulmans', many of whom John considered to be 'great thieves'. In the northern *pargana*, by contrast, more than two-thirds of the land was under irrigation and cultivated by predominantly hardworking Jat farmers.[137]

Another noteworthy finding concerned land tenures. Although 222 *bhaiachara/ pattidari* (communal brotherhood) tenures were recorded within the two *parganas*, 124 (more than a third) were classified as *zamindari*. John put this down to several factors. Due to the closeness of the imperial court, some influential individuals had been able to oust the ancient village inhabitants and appropriate their lands, while others had simply taken over abandoned villages. Moreover, these *zamindari* tenures were invariably held by revenue farmers – a practice which had become particularly well-established in the district. Of the 346 Government villages, 214 revenue engagements were with proprietors, while 132 were with revenue farmers. Of the latter, John took a dim view and wanted to curb the practice where possible. In his experience, the farmers were not 'men of capital and enterprise' who would take the necessary steps to invest in irrigation to improve the lands. Instead, they depended on 'turning out a profitable speculation, without any exertion on their part'.[138]

By contrast, John held in high esteem those villages under *bhaiachara* tenure. Although admitting that the rambunctious clans of Jats, Rangurs, Gujars, and Mewatis could make life difficult for district officers, he admired their ability to survive poor seasons, epidemics, wars, and other calamities. Moreover, their farming habits were inextricably linked to the welfare of their village in a way that those of *zamindars* or *talukdars* were not. John's poetic description of these coparcener farming communities was worthy of Charles Metcalfe himself:

Bound together by the ties of blood, connection, and, above all, common interest, like the bundle of sticks, they are difficult to break. Droughts may wither their crops, famine and disease may depopulate their houses, their fields may be deserted for a time, but when the storm blows over, if any survive, they are certain to return. If an accident happens to any individual, he is assisted and befriended by his bhy-bunds [brotherhood], but above all the grand advantage, in my mind, of this tenure over the zamindari is that the entire profits are their own, and not that of a stranger. In the hands of the biswadar [coparcener] the rent becomes capital, which directly or indirectly goes to improve his property, or is available on future occasions; while that of the zamindari is too often a mere revenue serving to support a position in the adjoining town to keep up idle servants, horses, elephants and suwary.[139]

In his *Twilight of the Mughals*, Professor Percival Spear considered John Lawrence to be 'the ablest exponent' of Metcalfe's 'Delhi System' – a system whose main purpose was to uphold the ancient village institutions and customs.[140] Certainly, the key elements of Metcalfe's administrative philosophy – the rights of self-cultivators and moderate assessment – appeared to have been safeguarded in John's 1844 Delhi Settlement Report. He asserted that the assessment was 'decidedly moderate' (a 10% reduction from the previous settlement) and had 'little doubt' that the revenue would be collected 'without injury to the people'. He further believed that 'great and marked improvement' had been achieved 'in the measurements, field maps, and the record of rights and interests of the village communities'.[141] Spear also detected 'an echo of John Lawrence's Delhi experience in his Punjab preference for villagers rather than chiefs'.[142] This anti-aristocratic sentiment was yet another tenet he shared with the great Metcalfe who regarded the privileged elite as 'mostly indolent, extravagant and devoid of intelligence'.[143] Well might Charles Aitchison, Punjab colleague and biographer, claim that it was John's training as a revenue officer in Delhi and his 'intimate knowledge of tenures and the economic condition of the peasantry which underlaid all his future land policy'.[44]

Spear, nonetheless, went on to expose certain flaws in the 'Delhi System'. One was over-assessment. Despite Metcalfe's theory of a moderate revenue demand, practice often told a different story. Instances of over-assessment occurred both during Metcalfe's time and, as we have seen in John's Gurgaon settlements, long afterwards. Severe cases ended in whole villages becoming deserted – the very opposite of the system's intended aim.[145] Spear also believed that age-old village institutions were being undermined by the increasing influence of the courts and the police in the pursuit of utilitarian 'improvement'. Corruption could easily find a way into the system and make justice a lottery. For those whose fortunes were overturned, 'the manifold blessings of British rule' appeared to ring hollow. Yet such unforeseen results were by no means universal. Although the authors of the *Final Report on the Settlement of the Land Revenue in the Delhi District (1882)* accepted that village communities had not been unaffected by 'the inevitable tendency to individualism and separation which accompanies the march of progress in India', they still maintained that John's description of these communities held 'for most purposes and intents as true now as it was in 1844'.[146] In that year John proclaimed as pure an arcadian idyll as Metcalfe would have wished:

In a flourishing pergunnah on this side [of] the river we have no large zamindar with his one or two lacs of annual income, but on the other hand, we have thousands of small proprietors, each with his brood mare, his buffaloes, his oxen, in short, with everything that marks a comfortable position in life. In no part of the Western Provinces are the tenures so complete and so well recognized as here, no districts where the ancient village communities are in such excellent preservation, or where the practice of our Civil Courts has hitherto done so little harm.[147]

'The active and judicious measures' of Robert Montgomery, Collector and Magistrate 1829–49

Robert Montgomery's career in the North-Western Provinces during the 1830s and 1840s can be divided into three main parts covering his time as Magistrate and District Collector at Azamgarh, Allahabad and Cawnpore. Each district would bring its own set of challenges whether it was the implementation of the new land revenue settlement, the campaign against female infanticide or crime reduction along the Grand Trunk Road. Like his fellow administrator, John Lawrence, an examination of Robert's early career in the North-Western Provinces allows us to understand more fully the role he would later play in the Punjab after its annexation. Influenced by the reforming impulses of Evangelicalism and Utilitarianism, the period coincided with an expansion in the role of the state with government officials of all grades being held to greater account. Much of this was driven by the practical need to make detailed revenue surveys in preparation for a new agrarian contract. But there was also the desire to reduce crime and improve security in urban areas and along the highways of north India. The provision of vernacular education also came under consideration. During the 1830s the North-Western Provinces was still undergoing a process of integration under Company rule and officials were all too aware of their still fragmentary understanding of indigenous communities. Bridging some of these 'knowledge gaps' were civil officers like Robert Montgomery who provided a valuable array of socio-economic information at the district level and below.[1] Of particular significance were his revenue settlement reports, his published *Statistical Report of the District of Cawnpoor* (Calcutta, 1849) and his memoranda to government on law-and-order matters.

Azamgarh 1829–37

In December 1829 Robert Montgomery swapped the cosmopolitan life of Calcutta for the remote district of Azamgarh in the North-Western Provinces. Situated five hundred miles from the capital, it was bounded on the west by the Kingdom of Oude, to the north by the River Gogra and the district of

Gorakhpur, and to the south and east by the Benares Division. Covering an area of 2,121 square miles, it contained a population of nearly 800,000 people spread amongst five and a half thousand villages.[2] Thanks to easy access to water sources, the district was generally very fertile. The main crops were sugar cane, indigo and opium. Unlike large *mofussil* stations such as Cawnpore and Meerut which enjoyed an active social scene of dinner parties, amateur dramatics, book societies and gymkhana clubs, Azamgarh could boast no such amenities. When Robert arrived as Assistant to the Joint-Magistrate and Deputy Collector there were just three other Europeans residing in the station – a deputy magistrate, a deputy collector, and an assistant surgeon. Only three public buildings existed, two of which were courthouses while the sessions judge, when on circuit, used the third to hold trials. With no private dwelling houses, the civil officers simply lived in the corner rooms of the courthouses while the surgeon occupied the circuit house. Years later Robert recalled in stark terms the sense of remoteness:

> These buildings had the appearance of having been dropped in the middle of a jungle. There were no roads. The station was isolated – separated from all civilization. The nearest place where there were civil residents was Jaunpore, a distant forty miles. The whole [place] presented a most desolate appearance.[3]

In September 1832, however, the station underwent something of a transformation with the appointment of James Thomason as Magistrate, Collector and Deputy Opium Agent of Azamgarh. 'His arrival with his family,' Montgomery was to write, was like 'a gleam of sunshine over the whole place'. The tall, slender features and refined manners of Thomason may well have cut a rather incongruous figure in this remote, provincial station, but, according to Montgomery, he was 'a civilian of eminence' who had 'the power of winning the hearts of all who worked under him'.[4] Born into a strongly evangelical family, Thomason had excelled in his studies both at Haileybury and Fort William College. Over the following decade, he had made a name for himself in several judicial postings in Calcutta where he could easily have stayed for the remainder of his career. But he was not a man to rest on his laurels. Instead, he yearned for practical administrative experience in the *mofussil*. The Azamgarh posting, he later wrote, would prove to be pivotal: 'It was to me a field of victory, where such repute and status as I had in the service was founded.'[5]

Thomason's appointment coincided with the elevation of the district to full collectorship status and its territory was augmented by two additional *parganas* from contiguous districts.[6] At the same time Montgomery was promoted to Officiating Head Assistant to the Magistrate and Collector, while in May of the following year Henry Carre Tucker, a fellow Addiscombe cadet, was appointed as a second assistant. The impetus behind these moves, instigated by the Sudder Board of Revenue, was the need to implement the new land revenue Regulation IX of 1833. Thomason would spearhead its rollout in a series of new land settlements throughout the Azamgarh district over a four-year period (1833–37). This was a considerable undertaking, but expectations were set high that it would usher in an era of improved revenue management and growing agrarian prosperity. The heavy workload necessarily entailed the delegation of authority, and for Montgomery, it led to a pronounced feeling of empowerment: 'His [Thomason's] plan was to give his assistants great power and to hold them responsible. This interested them much in their work,' he later recalled.[7] The extent of Montgomery's involvement can be gauged from the number of revenue settlements he personally undertook. Of the fourteen *parganas* that collectively formed the district, Robert was responsible for the settlement of seven of them, while a further two were settled jointly with Thomason.[8]

For both men, reviewing the fiscal history of the district was an important first step in formulating a new land settlement. The advent of British rule at the beginning of the century had unfortunately ushered in a period of considerable upheaval. The new arrivals had little knowledge of the tenurial makeup of its villages nor had they an accurate understanding of its productive capabilities. With few searching enquiries made and too great a reliance on local officials, it was hardly surprising that instances of fraud had occurred. In the Suggree [Sagri] *pargana*, for example, Montgomery noted 'the great influence obtained by the canoongoes at the cession, and the confusion attendant thereon [had] enabled them to get their names registered in the government records and by degrees to oust the old proprietors'.[9] Earlier revenue settlements had also been set too high which in turn had led to debt defaults. In the Atrowleeah Tilhenee *pargana* no less than 184 out of the 361 villages were sold at auction to realise the government revenue during the first ten years of British rule.[10] It was a similar picture in the Mahol *pargana* where many of the most valuable estates had passed into the hands of 'strangers' who were now recognised as the lawful engagers of the revenue. Despite these unfortunate developments, Montgomery found many of the old village communities still intact with their internal management conducted under the *pattidari* principle.[11] The relationship between the auction purchaser (i.e. the new *zamindar*) and the now subordinate non-proprietary *pattidars* was often a fraught one, however. In Mahol, Montgomery observed, the amount of rent to be paid from the latter to the former had been 'the constant source of quarrels…frequently accompanied with bloodshed and tending to excite in the breast of all parties the deepest animosity'.[12] Confusion also reigned in the *parganas* of Atrowleeah Tilhenee, Kowreeah [Kauria], and Gopalpore where a profusion of small holdings into which the estates were divided had led to great difficulty in collecting the revenue.[13] It was a similar picture in the Nizamabad *pargana*, the largest in the district, where Thomason found a plethora of 'unadjusted rights and disputed claims' which had resulted in large balances accruing over the previous ten years. 'It became an object of great importance,' he later wrote, 'to terminate this state of things as soon as possible.'[14]

To overcome these tenurial tensions, a key requirement of the new settlements was to create a proper record of an estate's proprietary rights. Montgomery fully recognised its importance by his firm insistence on the presentation of a clear, well-maintained rent-roll known in Hindustani as the *jamabandi*. This was a definitive record showing the land held by each *zamindar* as well as the quantity worked by each non-proprietary cultivator together with the rent and revenue rates applied to each field. To ensure that both landholders and their tenants were fully aware of their rights and obligations and that any errors could be corrected at the time of settlement, Montgomery was insistent that the rent-roll be publicly displayed for fifteen days prior to confirmation. This was largely to protect the tenants from the arbitrary designs of an unscrupulous zamindar 'to fix any rate he pleases'.[15] In a similar vein, Robert also requested that the *zamindars* furnish him with a clearly defined *Durkhast* detailing 'the mode in which they might agree to pay the government revenue amongst themselves'. According to Montgomery, this was apparently the first time the document had been demanded, 'altho' the future prosperity of the Muhal [mahal] in a great measure depended upon it'. Like the *jamabandi*, its aim was to remove 'all grounds for future dispute among the shareholders'.[16]

Montgomery's urge to resolve contentious issues and gain common agreement led him not only to define the amount of cultivated land held by each *zamindar* and their tenants, but also to divide up disputed waste land within respective estates, each portion being recorded in the village statement. This was the case in the Atrowleeah Tilhenee, Kowreeah and Gopalpore *parganas* where Robert made use of local *panchayats* to reach agreement.[17] Similarly, much of Thomason and Montgomery's efforts were directed towards resolving village boundary disputes. Formerly the custom had been to measure a village before demarcation of its boundary. But this approach, Thomason noted, had 'given rise to endless intrigues and chicanery on the part of the native ameens'.[18] Henceforth, under the new Regulation IX of 1833, village boundaries would be confirmed before measuring the village, and greater efforts were made to closely superintend the activities of *talsildars*, *amins* and other local officials. Where doubts remained, a personal examination of the boundary was conducted. In the cases of contentious boundary disputes, voluntary arbitration between the parties was the means generally adopted. But, as Thomason discovered, it was a custom which required careful management: 'The venality of the arbitrators became at length notorious, and there were some, who were known to have amassed large sums in this method.' In such circumstances, Thomason argued, it was important 'to tie down the arbitrators within the narrowest limits, and to insist upon a prompt decision in the immediate presence of the superintending officer'.[19] Their combined efforts, Robert concluded, did much 'to allay the animosity long existing between the zamindars in respect to disputed boundaries' which had now been 'accurately defined and marked off, the maps being corrected accordingly'.[20]

When it came to the assessment methodology adopted in the Azamgarh district, Thomason championed the government's new broad-based approach. Instead of 'a minute scrutiny into the assets of each estate' which Holt Mackenzie had earlier espoused, the government's revised assessment was calculated 'from general considerations of former fiscal history, and comparison with neighbouring and similar villages'.[21] This was the method adopted by Montgomery and can be seen in his first revenue settlement report for the Suggree *pargana* – a copy of which exists amongst his private papers.[22] A small number of settlements had been made by Robert's predecessors, Messrs Barlow and Bayley, under the previous Regulation VII of 1822, but the vast bulk was undertaken by himself. During the 1832/33 season, when Montgomery settled 184 villages, his method was to rely on the *jamabandis* compiled by the *patwaris* [village accountants]. These were then checked by reviewing 'the former canoongoes papers, and corrected so as to obviate irregularities of rent occasioned by partiality or favour towards to cultivators'. Montgomery also used as a guide the average rent rates paid by cultivating tenants to their *zamindars*. This *modus operandi*, he favourably contrasted 'to an assessment founded by an arbitrary valuation of the villages according to their quality or capability' which he believed would not have been 'satisfactory to the people or indeed which would in any way obtain their acquiescence'.[23] Even so, his chosen method was far from fool-proof. The following year, when assessing the remaining villages, Robert discovered that many of the *patwari* records were 'notoriously false', forcing him to calculate the new assessment based on his experience of 'the rates paid by other villages in the pergunnah as well as from enquiries on the spot as to the capabilities of the soil etc.'[24]

Despite Montgomery's efforts, the Sudder Board of Revenue, after advice from the Divisional Revenue Commissioner, Frederick Currie, decided to postpone submitting the Sugree settlement for government approval and instead requested that it be revised. The main reason was to bring the settlements fully into line with the new Regulation IX of 1833. The professional survey, absent from the original settlement, was now rolled out while special focus was given to revising Barlow and Bayley's earlier settlements which Montgomery found to be in 'a most imperfect state'. His own rulings on resumed *maafee* tenures (land free from the payment of revenue) also required some redress. Thomason viewed these *maafee* lands as consisting 'mostly of unauthorized grants by amils, or tahsildars, or zamindars, in which the original grantee...had generally demised, and the property had devolved upon the heir, contrary even to the terms of the grants'.[25] Where possible, the resumption of these lands was now the determined object of the Sudder Board of Revenue. In the Suggree *pargana* Montgomery seems to have initially settled with the *maafeedars* (holders of *maafee* land) on rather lenient terms, giving those found in possession life-time engagements on a light assessment. When he returned to the same villages a couple of years later, however, the approach had dramatically changed. Now the emphasis was on making engagements with the village zamindars rather than solely with the *maafeedars*. In Suggree, some sixty-seven *maafee* villages were resumed and accounted for an annual revenue of Rs.8625 or 6.5% of the overall revenue demand for the *pargana* (Rs.127,493).[26] In Mahol the amount of resumed *maafee* land was greater, accounting for an annual revenue of Rs.19,714 or 9% of the overall revenue demand for the *pargana* (Rs.223,485).[27]

Pargana	No. of Villages	Former Jumma (Rupees)	Proposed Jumma (Rupees)	Amount of increase in Jumma (Rupees)	% Increase in Jumma
Nizamabad	1,150	202,727	303,022	100,295	49.5%
Cheriakote*	290	30,110	43,604	13,494	44.8%
Kurriat Mittoo*	66	10,347	14,288	3,941	38.1%
Belhabans	163	33,274	39,937	6,663	20.0%
Deogaon	472	112,271	121,085	8,814	7.9%
Mhownat Bhunjun	64	9,686	11,727	2,041	21.1%
Mahol*	652	171,627	223,485	51,858	30.2%
Mahomedabad	763	133,524	172,535	39,011	29.2%
Atrowleeah Tilhenee*	361	76,511	81,471	4,960	6.5%
Kowreeah*	145	33,326	37,917	4,591	13.8%
Gopalpore *	175	20,583	27,550	6,967	33.8%
Suggree*	672	98,345	127,493	29,148	29.6%
Ghosee*	376	63,987	94,651	30,664	47.9%
Nuthoopoor *	326	42,640	58,650	16,010	37.5%
Total	5,675	1,038,958	1,357,415	318,457	30.7%

* *Pargana* settlements made by R. Montgomery. Source: H.M. Elliot, secretary to Sudder Board of Revenue, to James Thomason, secretary to the Lieutt. Govr., N.W.P., 20 October 1837, N.W.P. Proceedings (Revenue) IOR/P/217/63, No. 249.

Overall, the new Azamgarh settlement saw a substantial increase of Rs. 318,457 in the government demand or *Jama /Jumma* compared to the previous assessment (see table), amounting to an average increase of 31%. In individual *parganas* such as Nizamabad the increase was as much as 49.5% while the smallest rise occurred in Atrowleeah Tilhenee at a mere 6.5%. In no *pargana* was there a reduction from the previous demand. Despite the sizable increase, Thomason maintained that the assessment was 'light' and predicted that it would be 'easily paid'.[28] In one recorded instance, though, the *zamindars* of the Mahol *pargana* had clamoured for a reduction in their assessment which had seen a 30% increase. 'So many applications were made to me for reduction of jumma,' Frederick Currie told the Sudder Board of Revenue, 'that I was induced to examine very strictly into Mr Montgomery's work'. His investigations, however, exonerated Montgomery whose assessment was found to be 'very carefully and judiciously made'. No subsequent reductions were made.[29]

In general, the British authorities justified the new revenue demand based on soil fertility and the high prevalence of water in the district which in turn produced abundant yields of high value crops. Thomason, for example, was effusive over the quality of Mahol's sugar cane: 'The settlement, though showing a high average is very light for the land is exceedingly valuable. The finest sugar land, perhaps, in all India, is to be found here.'[30] He had little doubt that under ordinary seasons, with good management and a healthy demand for the main cash crops, the settlement would hold good. The new assessment (excepting some villages in the Nizamabad *pargana*), it was felt, would encourage more land to be brought into cultivation while ensuring ease of collection by the *talsildars*. Nevertheless, much still depended on the 'firmness of the civil administration' in a district where most of the proprietors were, as Thomason termed them, 'pugnacious Rajpoots':

> If the arrangements made at the settlement are disregarded, the boundaries violated, the rights of proprietors and cultivators neglected, and misrule allowed to prevail, great confusion will ensue, industry will be checked, and improvement stopped. The effect also will immediately be felt in the collections of the Government revenue.[31]

Some concerns were raised by a subsequent collector of Azamgarh, George Campbell, who noticed the high rate of proprietary transfers within the district. He concluded, however, that the cause was not one of over-assessment but rather the excessive subdivision of the land which had created 'a very large class of zemindars, too proud to work, and too poor to live on their profits…

the zemindaree rights become every day more and more sub-divided; a man cannot live on an infinitesimal share, and transfer results'.[32]

Montgomery's land settlements in the Azamgarh district had established his reputation for hard work and high standards. His attention to detail was particularly lauded by his superiors. This was most evident in his work on the creation and maintenance of accurate *Jamabandis* which Thomason regarded as 'the point of greatest importance'.[33] Frederick Currie, Divisional Revenue Commissioner, also commended his work in engaging 'the landowners to apportion the assessment among themselves' and in resolution of 'other questions of internal management'. For these efforts, his monthly salary was raised to Rs. 1000.[34]

Key to the success of the settlement was undoubtedly the close working relationship of Thomason and Montgomery – an association that was intensified by the sheer remoteness of the Azamgarh station. So too was the latter's friendship with the endearing if rather fervent Henry Carre Tucker, with whom he forged a genuine 'bond of union'.[35] Tucker, who often addressed him as 'my dear Monty' (for Thomason it was 'my dear Montgomery'), was a passionate evangelical and, in the absence of a place of worship or resident clergyman, unfailingly assisted Thomason in organising Sunday services. His correspondences were often peppered with Christian thoughts and of the need to give practical expression to his faith. One letter to Montgomery was emblematic: 'I do earnestly wish to work with a single eye to His glory, and the good of mankind, more particularly the inhabitants of this country, and my own district.'[36] Although not as expressive in matters of faith, Montgomery undoubtedly shared the same guiding principles, recognising Tucker as a 'valuable public servant – a bright example – a Christian man and a true Missionary'.[37]

In 1834 the Azamgarh station expanded a little further with the establishment of a small British garrison and the arrival of Frances Mary, the seventeen-year-old sister of James Thomason. Frances, or rather Fanny, was a shy, deeply religious young woman who had hitherto lived a very sheltered life. Beginning a new life in the Indian *mofussil* involved considerable adjustment. There was, however, the expectation that in time she would marry a Company officer of sufficient means and standing. Marital options in Azamgarh were of course extremely limited. Apart from a then young ensign named Arthur Phayre who later became Chief Commissioner of Burma, Robert Montgomery was the only eligible bachelor for miles around (a fact perhaps not lost on James Thomason and his wife). Fortunately, both individuals found each other's company agreeable, and their friendship developed into something of a secret jungle romance albeit firmly within the confines of contemporary social mores. By early December Robert had plucked up enough courage to propose to Fanny who readily accepted. The news came as a complete surprise to Robert's close colleague, Henry Tucker: "You are indeed a close fellow. What a shame not to tell me of your felicity. I shall never forgive you – truth to tell, I congratulate you most warmly and sincerely."[38] Writing to her half-sister, Eliza Hutchinson, Fanny tried to put into words her elated feelings: 'All I know, dear, is, that I am very, very happy!! Who would have thought a few months ago that such a change would have taken place. Love is a mystery indeed, how insensible it works.'[39] Robert, who was soon afterwards working in another part of the district, expressed similar emotions to his intended: 'The whole thing now that we are separated seems to me like a dream and the happiness of being forever united to you seems to me almost impossible.'[40] On 17th December 1834, after a brief engagement of two weeks, they were married in a simple tent. The ceremony was conducted by the Revd Pratt and attended only by Thomason, Tucker and both their wives.

Unlike Honoria Lawrence, however, Fanny took little interest in Robert's official work, and confined herself mostly to household matters. Children soon followed – Frances Mary (born on 10th October 1835), Robert [Robby] Thomason (born on 17th December 1836) and Mary Susan (born 8th November 1838). In her spare time, she kept a 'voluminous diary' recording the small details of family life. Frequent fevers caught by the children and the medicines used to treat them featured prominently. So too was the time when Robert contracted erysipelas in the leg. The doctor's remedy involved the application of leeches to the affected area – a procedure which resulted in Robert fainting at least twice.[41] As well as her diary, Fanny also had a habit of copying long extracts from biblical commentaries, sermons, hymns, and devotional poems. Motherhood, of course, happily consumed much of her energies, and for practical reasons it was necessary to remain at home during her husband's frequent tours of the district. Yet Azamgarh's dismal social life, her inability to speak the local language and Robert's frequent absences inevitably left her feeling very isolated. A palpable sense of this loneliness was revealed in one of her few preserved letters to Robert, dated 21st March 1836:

> My beloved Robert, to think that I am not to see you for a whole week seems dreadful to me, and when I awoke this morning and found you gone, the fact of you having been with me, even for a day, appeared a dream. I could scarcely believe I had been with you at all…I long to hear from you dearest Robert, but will not expect to do so till the day after tomorrow…[42]

Robert, who became Magistrate and Collector of Azamgarh following Thomason's appointment as secretary to the Lieutenant-Governor, North-Western Provinces in March 1837, was not blind to his wife's plight. No matter how long his working day had been or where he was within his district, he insured that he wrote regularly to Fanny. His letters contain the not uncommon day-to-day preoccupations of a district officer. The onset of the hot season, for example, prompted Robert to comment more than once on the means employed to lessen its effect. One method was the fixing of 'tatties' (wetted mats of cuscus grass) on the windows of his *dak* bungalow or across the openings of his tent; the other method was a simple hand *punkah* (hand-held fan) operated by a *punkah wallah*. 'My dearest Fanny,' he wrote in early April,

> I arrived here about 8 o'clock [in the morning] when it was beginning to get very hot but I have tatties up today and with the help of a hand punkah I am very comfortable – I hope you have had up tatties as you will find them very pleasant. If you have not had them today tell Thugeer [one of the servants] to get them as I at least shall be glad of them when I go into the station.[43]

Paternal regard for the welfare of the district's inhabitants was another subject touched upon. Like John Lawrence who, in the absence of dispensaries, carried a medical chest with him to treat the ailments of villagers, Robert was equally disposed to help those in need: 'Pray dear,' he asked Fanny in relation to helping one man suffering from cholera, 'drop 40 drops of Laudanum into a small wine glass full of brandy, put it in a bottle and send it to me – don't be afraid if there are half a dozen drops too much.'[44] Touring the district was not without its own perils either. During one early morning canter when it was still dark, Robert's horse, Sultan, suddenly stumbled on 'a ridge of kunkur [loose gravel] that had been carelessly left incomplete on the road'. Robert was flung out of his saddle and over the horse's head, landing on his back on the loose gravel. 'Most providentially,' he gratefully told Fanny,

> I was not the least hurt nor do I in all my life recollect to have suffered as little from a fall, not even the least bit stunned. Not so alas! poor Sultan, he is marked for life as the kunkur has taken two pieces of flesh out of his knees so large that you might put your fist into the places. I am very vexed about it but it can't be helped.[45]

The conduct of servants was one of Robert's main bugbears while on tour. His spousal correspondences provided a useful release valve for his frustrations over their deficiencies and corrupt practices. At the end of one long day, he peevishly catalogued a list of duties that his bearer had failed to perform:

I told him to awake me an hour before daybreak – He did not – I told him to have hot water ready for my tea before I started, he had none – these were trifles – He had sent ahead my solar topee and map that I had drawn by hand in my packet although I told him particularly not to do so as I intended to take a ride of some 15 miles and was of course entirely dependent on my topee! This I could not stand and I pitched into him properly.[46]

Showing a keen eye for detail and frugality, Robert also carefully scrutinised camp finances, bringing to account those found guilty of wrongdoing such as discovering that the cow-keeper and farmer had siphoned off a large proportion of the milk for personal gain. On other occasion when he felt that an excessive amount of money was being charged for feeding turkeys, his abrupt solution was to tell the cook to 'wring off all their heads'.[47] It was not unusual for Robert to issue small penalties to correct a transgressor's behaviour. Thus, the tent-pitcher was fined for not pitching his tent before he came into camp, while his bearer was fined two annas for forgetting to pack his soap.[48] By contrast, he commended Fanny for her prudent ways of living and had a habit of sending her money back from various parts of the district: 'You are the best wife who ever lived. It is since I married you that my expenses have been so small. I send you one hundred and eighty rupees.'[49]

Despite the long hours, rudimentary accommodation, and the pains of servant ineptitude or even deceit, camp life and the touring of his district provided much satisfaction for Robert. During the working week, he had the opportunity to interact with numerous villagers, to understand their character and their needs and to take note of the varied agrarian conditions. He was also able to find moments of comparative solitude, particularly on Sundays when he gave strict orders not to be disturbed. With his tent pitched on the periphery of a village, an air of stillness descended upon the camp. At such times, he told his wife, he would quietly contemplate his situation and his good fortune:

My own Fanny, I have been thinking very much of you and are dear little ones today whilst sitting alone in my tent, without a sound to be heard but the cawing of a crow, winging its way across the tope. It was a day for meditation, and in looking back on my past life, and on all the blessings and mercies bestowed upon me. I could not but bless God for all the gifts he has given me so abundantly.[50]

Allahabad 1837–43

After seven years at Azamgarh, and having sufficiently demonstrated his capabilities to his superiors, the time had come for Robert to move on. In December 1837 he was appointed Magistrate and Collector of the city and district of Allahabad. Originally known as Prayag or "place of offerings" due to its location at the confluence of the Ganges and the Jumna (Yamuna) rivers, the city was renamed in the sixteenth century to Allahabad meaning abode of God by the Mughal Emperor Akbar.[51] By Anglo-Indian standards, it was regarded as a middle ranking station. Clearly superior to the 'slenderly garrisoned cantonments of the jungles' like Azamgarh but not on a par with the large military depots of Cawnpore and Meerut.[52] Social life, though, remained fairly modest. 'The station has never been remarkable for its festivities,' wrote the travel writer Emma Roberts in 1835. Although its balls and parties were enough to 'attract visitors from smaller and duller military posts,' there was no theatre and 'the chief resource for the gentlemen' appeared to be the billiard table. A 'tolerably well-supported book-club' furnished 'the more studious with the floating literature of the day'.[53] To the Montgomerys, however, Allahabad was a world away from remote Azamgarh and provided a much-needed opportunity to meet a wider circle of colleagues and friends, most notably the Lawrences.

Robert's move to Allahabad also brought with it the accoutrements of promotion, and firmly established him as the *burra sahib*. His residence was now a substantial *pukka* house located a good distance away from the local bazaars in the emerging Civil Lines district to the north of the city. This presumably was the same District Magistrate's residence painted by Sita Ram in 1815 but which was most likely destroyed during the 1857 Rebellion.[54] Reflecting the Anglo-Indian attempt to lessen the harsh effects of climate and disease, the emphasis was on space and the free movement of clean air. Although the *pukka* house's flat stone roof was considered less effective than the pitched, thatched version normally associated with bungalow construction, its high ceilings, interconnecting rooms, and substantial verandas were proven features designed to mitigate the high temperature during the hot season. Little if any vegetation was allowed in the immediate vicinity of the house. This, together with its elevated position, aimed to lessen the effects of low-lying miasma (bad air emanating from organic matter) which contemporary medical opinion considered to be the cause of fevers such as malaria.[55]

Among the main responsibilities as Magistrate and Collector of Allahabad, Robert Montgomery continued the rollout of the land revenue settlement under Regulation IX of 1833. This time, though, his new appointment brought him into close cooperation with Henry Lawrence who, as we have seen, was given responsibility the revenue survey of the Allahabad district at the beginning of 1838. For both men, their new roles provided fresh challenges. For Henry, it was a test of his new Extended Survey Scheme, while for Robert, it was the first opportunity to be in sole charge of a district's settlement. Furthermore, geographically, it was substantially larger than Azamgarh, covering an area of 2808 sq. miles and containing fifteen *parganas* grouped under three divisions. In the Trans Ganges division (those *parganas* to the north of the Ganges), home to the most valuable lands in the district, sugar cane and rice predominated, while in the Jumna-Ganges doab (those *parganas* located between the two rivers), it was opium and tobacco. Both these divisions were in general superior in terms of fertility, soil, and irrigation to the Trans Jumna division (those *parganas* to the south of the Jumna) where the main crop was cotton grown on largely stony ground.

In his *Report on the Settlement of the district of Allahabad*, Robert went to some lengths to explain his settlement methodology. His involvement began in June 1838 when he started receiving the field measurements of the first few *parganas* from Henry and his revenue survey teams.[56] This was the cue for the *peshkars* [superintendents of revenue] to prepare statements or abstracts detailing the capabilities of every village in terms of soil type, crops grown, prevalence of irrigation, and the former revenue assessment. Its purpose was to enable Robert as settlement officer 'at a glance to see the actual condition of each estate'.[57] Like Henry's Extended Survey Scheme, Robert's settlement work was now performed on an extensive scale. Where formerly only one establishment had been in operation, now there were ten working simultaneously in various parts of the district. The extra responsibility of handling multiple establishments, however, did not faze Robert. For, as he was keen to point out, 'they all worked upon one system, which the superintendents were acquainted with before they were entrusted with the duties'.[58] By October, the *peshkars'* settlement abstracts for the first few *parganas* were ready for use, prompting Robert to begin a rapid tour of the region. Little time, it seems, was wasted:

> I moved my camp twice every day, which enabled me to see a great deal of the country in a short time, and this plan I invariably pursued throughout the season. During my progress I gave my attention entirely to one object, that of finding out the capabilities of the different estates.[59]

From the abstracts, Robert asserted that he could quickly tell which estates were either over or under assessed. He paid particular attention to the quality and variety of soil, the state of the crops grown and whether the amount of irrigated land matched the information supplied by the *amins*. 'In fact,' he continued, 'I made notes of everything that struck me as worthy of notice, and that would afterwards be useful to me in fixing my assessment, and before I left an estate I was generally well acquainted with its capabilities.'[60] With a *pargana* containing between 30 to 60 estates, Robert believed that about ten days for each one was sufficient 'to come to a correct conclusion as to the amount of juma' he should apply.

During this whistlestop tour further assistance, we are told, came from the local landholders with whom Robert was 'in constant communication' and who were allowed to visit his tent 'at all hours'. From 'private interviews with the zamindars' he managed to obtain 'the correct information…relative to the capabilities of the numerous estates'.[61] Initially he was rather startled with how 'they confirmed each other's testimony'. But from the information he had gathered through his own observations, he soon found that their statements invariably matched his own. For those that did not, he bluntly declared his objections. 'Had I not visited the several estates, I could not of course have urged my reasons with such force, and they knowing that I had visited them (even had they before been inclined to mislead me) would not have ventured to do it.' Thus, by following this plan, Robert believed he was able to form a reasonable idea of what the *jama* should be. But, like John Lawrence, he proceeded to apply his rent and revenue rates as a check on his initial findings. These were based on three different soil classifications, sub-divided into irrigated and un-irrigated groupings which, prior to his perambulations, Robert had calculated from the prevailing money rates paid by cultivators to their proprietors. 'On applying this second test,' he tells us, 'it was generally found that my previous impression was correct, but when otherwise, a reason could generally be assigned, and hence nothing further was requisite.'[62]

Once the *jama* was fixed, Robert left its distribution on the different villages of the *pargana* to the proprietors to manage – a process which was generally completed in one day. In only a few cases where this was not possible, he either decided it himself or referred it to the local *panchayat*. Thereafter, Montgomery handed over responsibility to one of his two deputy collectors to finalise the settlement arrangements while he went on to assess another pargana. In the meantime, the *peshkar* and his establishment remained to complete the *jamabandis* [rent-rolls]. 'This business', remarked Robert, 'was a work of time and could not be hastily done.' For, as in Azamgarh, ensuring that the *jamabandis* were correct and well-publicised was paramount – a procedure which encountered heavy resistance from *zamindars* who now found their ability to manipulate the records drastically curbed:

I have paid particular attention and endeavoured as far as I was able to make the village rent-rolls, perhaps the most important part of the whole settlement arrangements, as perfect as possible. I have experienced great opposition on the part of the landholders in effecting this, I can now however say that there is not a single estate in the district, the rent-roll of which has not been received.[63]

In line with the anti-aristocratic thrust of Regulation IX (1833), the settlement of the Allahabad district also favoured village *muqaddams* (headmen) or cultivating communities at the expense of *talukdars* (large landholders). In his settlement report, Robert paid special notice to the Kheyragurh *pargana* where the inhabitants had suffered years of oppression at the hands of the local Raja. Now the impetus was on making settlements with the old village communities and only where they did not exist was direct engagement with the Raja allowed (a *malikana* allowance of 18% was given to the former *talukdar* as compensation). This *pargana*, however, defied simple categorisation. Robert found it impossible to fix any standard rates for different kinds of soil located here and instead took the average of ten years' collections and the previous rent-roll as the basis of his assessment.

Overall, the revised *jama* for the Allahabad district amounted to Rs.2,189,957; an increase of Rs.264,799 or 12% based on the previous settlement (Rs.1,925,158). Taking into account the *malikana* allowance for *parganas* Kheyragurh and Bara of Rs.80,780, the *jama* was reduced to a final total of Rs.2,109,176 – making an increase of Rs.184,018 or 8.7%.[64] This was a modest increase compared to the settlement of Azamgarh and was presented as such by Robert:

The settlement that has now been made is, I think, equal and fair, and I believe the people are contented with it. It certainly is by no means a heavy assessment, nor am I aware of a single objection having been preferred against the juma of any estate, notwithstanding the peculiar facility for appealing they possess at this station. Under ordinary seasons and good management, I doubt not but that the revenue will always be punctually realized.[65]

The official judgement on Montgomery's work was once again highly commendatory. The settlement, Robert Lowther, Revenue Commissioner of the Allahabad Division remarked, had been carried out 'with great care and judgement' and was 'by no means heavy'. Indeed, he believed that the assessment could have been set 'somewhat higher' but for a conscious desire not 'to sacrifice the interests of those whose welfare the resettlement' was intended to promote.[66]

This favourable view, however, would prove to be at odds with later findings. F.W. Porter, who conducted the succeeding settlement of the district in the

1870s, took issue with several aspects of the 1839 settlement. On methodology, he questioned the accuracy of Montgomery's rent and revenue rates which appeared to have been fixed prior to visiting the locality. 'Rates thus framed,' Porter contended, 'must of necessity have been of the roughest descriptions.'[67] He also believed that the classification of soil type was insufficient to accurately represent 'so large and varied a tract as the Allahabad district'. More general criticisms were voiced too. The limited time set for the inspection of each *pargana* prevented 'the attainment of such a thorough knowledge of each estate as an assessing officer should possess,' while allowing the *zamindars* to organise the 'hurried distribution' of the *jama* amongst themselves could 'only result in the inequality of assessment'.[68]

Porter's underlying contention was not that the overall *jama* had been set too high but that it had been distributed unfairly across the district. Some *parganas* were more adversely affected than others. Uthurbun (Atharban), for example, was one of the poorest but its rates were fixed at the highest level, while in Kuralee (Karári), a more prosperous *pargana*, the rates had been set much lower. A similar picture emerged in Kheyragurh where the Raja was said to have caused the highest revenue to be put on the poorest estates which had remained under his control. These were then mortgaged to one of his dependents, 'a man of straw' who quickly fell into arrears. The estates were subsequently put up to auction but realized nothing. 'Against a plot of this kind,' Porter argued, 'nothing but a thorough inspection of each individual village would have been of any avail, and this Mr Montgomery could not possibly have undertaken in the limited time he was employed.'[69]

Kheyragurh and another *pargana* called Bara, both located in the Trans Jumna division of the district, had witnessed significant increases in their revenue demand. Compared to the previous assessment, the former had increased by Rs.44,992 (11.7%); the latter by Rs.83,215 (42.9%). In 1860 substantial reductions were belatedly made to both leading Porter to conclude 'that the assessment in portions at least of these two *parganas* was perfectly unbearable in its severity'.[70] Remissions, of course, were the most obvious admission of overassessment. But there was also a possible correlation between an excessive *jama* and the extent of forced transfers of landed property and the coercive processes employed to retrieve the government's revenue demand. What portion of these actions was due to over-assessment, and what was due to 'the extravagance and thriftlessness of proprietors' was for Porter a moot point. Nevertheless, an indication of heavy assessment was detected in the earlier years of Robert's settlement for two *parganas*, Mah and Kiwai which had exhibited higher than expected sales for arrears. By the 1850s, however, these pressures had eased, and the revenue demand was collected thereafter without difficulty.

Aside for these individual cases, the assessment for the remaining *parganas* appears to have been moderate in its incidence. Its punctual payment reflected the rise in the price of grain in recent years and the corresponding high demand for land in these portions of the district.

Robert's Allahabad settlement report can be seen as a well-crafted piece of self-advertisement. It presented an image of a highly efficient operation, achieving accurate results in record time. Here multiple establishments worked seamlessly and simultaneously together under the watchful eye of the settlement officer and his deputies who were 'most unwearied in their exertions'.[71] The report, of course, performed a singular purpose, aimed at justifying the new assessment to the Sudder Board of Revenue and the Lieutenant-Governor of the North-Western Provinces. It stuck rigidly to the narrow limits of settlement requirements. History and geography attracted only the briefest of mentions while sociological detail, such as caste affiliation, was avoided entirely. Speed was of the essence both in the narrative and in the field. As for the assessment methodology itself, there was an undeniable Thomasonian thread running through it. Hence only a cursory discussion of rent and revenue rates and a greater emphasis on touring the district and understanding the agricultural capabilities of a village at first hand. In fixing the district's *jama*, art and not science was transcendent.

Porter's criticisms, however, remained pertinent. The most obvious flaw concerned the time allotted for *pargana* inspections. The example of the Kheyragurh *pargana* was illustrative. This tract contained 693 villages spread over 675 sq. miles. Allowing only ten days to cover such a widespread area was clearly inadequate. Heavy reliance must therefore have been placed on the work of the Revenue Survey and Robert's hard-pressed subordinates. As for the results across the district, Robert admitted that the rent-roll had provoked 'thousands of petitions against the rates'; a fact confirmed by Porter:

> These rent-rolls showed the rents in future proposed to be collected from the zamindars, and were based on the rent-rates fixed by the settlement officer. Their receipt occasioned a general outcry. More than 8,000 petitions of objection were lodged and the papers were delayed for two years.[72]

Female Infanticide

Another notable feature of Robert's time at Allahabad was his involvement in the campaign against female infanticide. Deeply rooted within certain sections of north Indian society, the killing of female infants was based on marriage custom, family honour and caste rather than religion.[73] The practice was largely confined to certain high caste families whose primary aim was to forge hypergamous unions for their children. A daughter could only marry someone of equal or superior status, but never an inferior sub-caste as this would entail a loss of status. Bitter rivalries developed over the years, particularly amongst the Rajputs, as different sub castes claimed superiority over others thus making intermarriage a very troublesome affair. Alongside this matter of pride, was one of purse. Wedding expenses, particularly dowries, could be exorbitant. High caste families marrying their sons, and wishing to ensure their status was maintained, demanded extravagant weddings and large dowries. The higher the boy's social standing, the greater the expectation to spend lavishly. Equally for the bride's family, extravagance became synonymous with honour, and often had profound consequences. It was not unknown for large portions of hereditary land to be transferred to the bridegroom's family leading to financial ruin for the bride's family. For such families a daughter was seen as a heavy burden, both financially and socially. Consequently, female infanticide was seen as a ruthless way of avoiding both the potential disgrace of marrying girls to inferior rank boys and excessive wedding expenses.

Although the British had first discovered the practice of killing female infants towards the end of the eighteenth century, little had hitherto been done to combat it.[74] Aside from the difficulty in detecting the crime in the first place, the British had neither the appetite nor the resources to implement a crusade against it. By the 1830s, however, the mood had changed. Proponents of the twin strands of reform – Utilitarianism and particularly Evangelicalism – were to pursue an active agenda against what was perceived as perverse indigenous customs. Female infanticide, sati, and the burying alive of lepers were deemed inimical to the Christian values of the Empire and there was therefore a moral duty to eradicate them. No doubt for some fervent evangelicals, there was the hope that Christianity would spread in the wake of these endeavours.[75] But government officials were obliged to tread a more delicate path. In the interests of 'strict neutrality', they could not use their professional position to promote the faith however much ardent evangelicals would have wished. Instead, the official line against sati, female infanticide and the killing of lepers was 'guided purely by philanthropic and humanitarian aims'. This stressed the need to focus on them as social ills to deflect any suggestion that such efforts were driven by purely religious motives.[76]

Despite their abhorrence of female infanticide, however, the Indian Government was disinclined to sanction official measures against it, fearful perhaps that a social policy involving active interference within the homes of powerful Rajput families might be counterproductive. They hoped instead that the spread of education and knowledge would eventually lead to its eradication.

In the meantime, efforts against female infanticide in the North-Western Provinces were left to the inclinations of individual district officers, such as James Thomason and Robert Montgomery. In 1835, while implementing the revised land revenue settlement in the Azamgarh district, Thomason had discovered the custom being practiced by the *Bais Rajputs* in the Deogaon *pargana*. Although appalled by what he saw as 'so inhuman a practice', its entrenched hold amongst certain clans led Thomason to believe that purely coercive measures would be futile: 'As it arises out of their social state, a police [force] is powerless for its correction. So long as the society in which the perpetrators of the crime move can tolerate and palliate such enormities, the civil power must fail to prevent or correct them.'[77] Consequently, Thomason adopted a persuasive approach by having conciliatory meetings with the local *zamindars* to encourage them to put an end to the practice. Key to his success was the support given by the local *tahsildar*, Meer Muksood Ali, who was able to use his influence amongst his kinsmen to check the prevalence of the custom. In return Thomason deputised Montgomery to reward Muksood Ali by presenting him with a *Khillat* [dress of honour] for his efforts. Those *Bais Rajputs* who spared their daughters were also given rewards of shawls and *parwanas*. Aside from the registration of female births, no coercive action was undertaken. Results, in these early years, were encouraging. In 1845 it was recorded that there were 284 girls existing amongst the *Bais Rajputs* of Azamgarh. Yet by 1855, the figure had slipped to 89.[78] It seemed that without the continued exertions of an active magistrate those communities with a history of infanticide tended to fall back on old habits.

It was reasonable to expect that Robert Montgomery, when he became Collector and Magistrate of Allahabad, would continue to adopt the crusade against female infanticide with the same indefatigable zeal as his former superior if instances of the custom became apparent. In this regard he did not disappoint. In 1840 Robert discovered the custom being widely practised amongst three clans of Rajputs (the *Purhars, Kuchwars* and *Bedourias*) within the *Bara pargana*. At first, he followed the Thomasonian conciliatory method by calling an assembly of clan chiefs where he urged them through moral pressure to end the practice. Yet their stubborn adherence swiftly convinced him to shelve the idea: 'I soon saw that exhortations would be of little avail, and I determined to adopt prompt measures.'[79]

Robert believed that a more coercive approach was necessary, albeit one that relied on the prospect of rewards as well as the threat of penalties. The key was to harness the services of local officials who would form a network of surveillance at village level.[80] A *chaprassi* was to be appointed to each village whose sole responsibility was to report the birth of a female child within the clans following the custom. This was reinforced by the further appointments of a *gorait, chowkidar* and midwife who would report independently of each other the birth of a girl to the local *thana*. Each official would act as a check upon the other and were under pain of penalty if they failed to comply. Furthermore, Robert charged the *thanadar* to hold an inquest into the death of any baby girl within his jurisdiction. This would then be referred to the civil surgeon for further investigation. As a means of giving greater superintendence to the campaign, he charged the *tahsildar* to work closely with the *thanadar* and offered them both rewards if it could be proved that their efforts had led to eradication of the practice. Robert was also not averse to using paid informants in the detection of cases. One man called Taboo Singh, a *Chandel Rajput*, proved to be an invaluable source of intelligence. Indeed, this was the man who had first alerted Robert to the existence of the custom in the Bara *pargana*. At Robert's instigation, he received the substantial amount of 500 rupees for his services: 'Taboo Singh is a poor man,' he recorded, 'and has followed out his plans with a degree of perseverance and energy quite uncommon to a native, and apparently without looking for any return.'[81]

After just two months in operation, Robert confidently asserted to the Divisional Commissioner of Allahabad, Robert Lowther, that his measures were already bearing fruit. Of the four baby girls registered during this period, only one had subsequently died. In this instance suspicions were soon raised after the midwife had initially declared the child 'strong and well'. Upon further investigation by the civil surgeon, however, it was discovered that the baby girl had in fact been poisoned after the midwife's visit. The confession of a household maid revealed that, despite initial opposition from the baby's mother, it was the grandmother of the child, at the instigation of the father, who had administered the poisonous juice of the madar plant; a fact subsequently confirmed by the surgeon's post-mortem results. The accused were now awaiting trial and Robert hoped that this would send out a clear message to the rest of the district that the custom would no longer be tolerated. His strict measures, though, had one unintended consequence: It forced some pregnant women across the border into the nearby independent state of Rewa, out of reach of the authorities. In response Robert enlisted the support of the Raja of Rewa to stop his territory being used as a sanctuary: 'I addressed a communication to the Raja on the subject, and he has readily promised to do all in his power to put down the practice.'[82] For his part, the Raja issued a 'strict prohibition to its continuance' and believing that the high costs of marriage were the cause of the custom, 'he would afford the necessary aid' to those parents could not afford 'to defray the marriage expenses of their daughters'.[83]

A little over a year later, in February 1842, the facts appeared to vindicate Robert's strategy. Fourteen baby girls were now alive within the Bara *pargana* and only one had died from natural causes according to the civil surgeon. Robert, while optimistic, remained cautious and stressed the need to maintain a close watch: 'The greatest vigilance is still requisite; and, on my twice visiting the *pargana* this year, I was most particular in looking into and inquiring after the arrangements I had made for putting it down. I receive weekly reports from the *pargana* head officers, both revenue and judicial,' he informed the Divisional Commissioner.[84] By November 1842 further progress was recorded. The number of girls had risen to the more substantial figure of twenty-eight, and for Robert a tipping point appeared to have been reached: 'Now that so many girls are alive, the minds of the people are beginning to get reconciled to the custom of sparing them.'[85] Indeed, such were his efforts that they came to the pleasing attention of the Court of Directors: 'Mr Montgomery, the Magistrate of Allahabad, deserves great credit for the active and judicious measures taken by him for the detection and prevention of infanticide; and we trust they have proved entirely successful.'[86] A subsequent magistrate of Allahabad, M.H. Court, also confirmed Montgomery's legacy in the mid-1850s: 'When Mr Montgomery undertook the measures, female children were unknown; and there are now close upon a hundred, from fourteen years downwards.'[87]

Death, Furlough and Remarriage

Robert's time in Allahabad was sadly touched by personal tragedy. It was unfortunately a grim reality for many Company officers and their families as they battled in vain against the rigours of Indian life and the limitations of contemporary medical provision. Childbearing women were particularly vulnerable. Robert's elder sister Annie, who had married Alexander Heyland, a judge stationed at Ghazipore, died during childbirth in 1839. James Thomason's wife, Elizabeth, had also passed away following a prolonged illness in the same year. Most heartrending of all was the fate of Fanny herself who had been dogged with 'enteric fever' or recurrent typhoid. In a poignant diary entry for 1st February 1842, she had expressed hope for a change of fortunes: 'May this year now entered upon be better than those that have gone.'[88] But it was not to be. In the following month, on 23rd March 1842 and having just miscarried for the second time in two years, Fanny died of smallpox aged only twenty-six years. The marriage had lasted a little over seven years and her sudden death left Robert bereft. Finding solace in his faith and the support of his brother-in-law, James Thomason, Robert wrote of their 'uninterrupted happiness together' the day after her death:

She was not formed to shine in the assemblies of the gay in which her soul did not delight, but she had what was far more estimable "the ornament of a meek and quiet spirit" and for these qualities she was beloved by all who knew her.[89]

Robert, however, had little time to grieve before his mind was forced to turn to the welfare of his motherless children. What was to become of them? It was seen then as impractical for a widower to bring up his offspring single-handedly. Fortunately, for Robert, the matter was settled with Fanny's eldest sister, Mrs Hutchinson, offering to take charge of them. 'I feel,' he told Mrs Hutchison, then staying at Boulogne, northern France during her husband's furlough, 'that my prayers and those of my beloved Fanny have been fulfilled, and that in committing my precious children to your care, her oft expressed wishes will be accomplished, and I have the fullest confidence, that they will be brought up as she would have desired.'[90] Robert admitted that his six year-old son Robby posed the 'greatest difficulty' for the new surrogate mother who had a family of only older girls: 'Poor Robby is the idle boy, so full of spirits, and in appearance is the only one like his dear mother.' His two daughters, nevertheless, offered a more manageable prospect. Fanny, aged seven, was described as 'a sweet, tractable child, most anxious to please', while Mary, aged four, was deemed 'more lively than Fanny' but still 'most tractable'.[91]

Robert planned to go home on an extended period of furlough (of 3 years duration), to rest and to rebuild his life in the company of family and friends. His departure, though, was not immediate, and it took him a further six to eight months to settle his affairs at Allahabad. Finally on 12th November 1842 he left the city with his children, travelling by river steamer to Calcutta. Thereafter they boarded the *Southampton* for the voyage home, accompanied by a Miss Sparrow who was employed to look after the children. He endeavoured to fill his time by reading a lot, including Fanny's journal, and by trying to learn French. 'A certain amount of excitement is necessary to keep me in health,' he recorded in his diary.[92] But there was little to pique his interest in what he found to be a monotonous few months of sailing via the Cape and St Helena. They eventually landed at Southampton on 4th May 1843. The next two and three-quarter years were spent in peripatetic fashion in Britain and Ireland as well as on Continental Europe. In Boulogne he handed over the care of his children to the Hutchisons but continued to visit them periodically. His interests on all these journeys were wide-ranging and purposeful. He visited Worcester to learn about its bone china, Derby for its spinning mills and Sheffield for its cutlery. He kept a keen, observing eye on the countryside he passed through noting the types of crops grown in each locality. In Shropshire he fell in with the great and the good of the county, where he went shooting, visited the races, and attended a ball, finding 'a polite ease and elegance' that he had 'never before witnessed'.[93] By contrast, back in Ireland, festivities at Kilfane House, Kilkenny, the country seat of Sir John and Lady Power, were of a more relaxed, socially inclusive nature. 'I danced one set with cowherd's wife and the other with the dairymaid. Susan Staples [a friend] danced with the butcher and the cowherd.'[94]

The most momentous event of his leave occurred on Saturday 5th October 1844 when Robert was invited to the home of Mr Lambert of Woodmansterne, Surrey, a former Calcutta merchant, and his family. There he met the twenty-year-old Ellen Jane Lambert for the first time – the future Mrs Montgomery. On the 29th of the same month, he wrote succinctly in his diary: 'An eventful day. Dearest Ellen engaged to be mine.'[95] They were married on 2nd May 1845 and, after a honeymoon spent in northern England, they sailed for India, arriving on 4th October.[96] On the 18th of the same month, Robert was appointed Officiating Collector and Magistrate of Cawnpore through the patronage of James Thomason, now Lieutenant-Governor of the North-Western Provinces. The position was made permanent the following March.[97]

Cawnpore 1845–49

As befitting the Collector and District Magistrate of Cawnpore (Kanpur), Robert Montgomery's official residence was a spacious bungalow erected on a tall stone platform along the banks of the Ganges River. The travel writer Fanny Parkes, who resided in the house in the early 1830s when her husband was acting collector of customs, noted its generous proportions: 'The rooms of our house are lofty and good; the dining-room forty feet by twenty-eight, the swimming-bath thirty feet by twenty-one, and all the other rooms on a suitable scale. There is a fine garden belonging to and surrounding the house, having two good wells, coach-house, stables, cow-house, &c.'[98] From its elevated position, the bungalow looked out over the Ganges. In the cool season, when the water was low, islands would form at various points in the river and where the locals would cultivate melons, cucumbers and wheat. When the rains came and the river was in full flood, 'white-crested waves' lapped beneath the veranda. During the hot season, temperatures reached almost unbearable levels. 'In the open air,' Fanny recorded in the month of June, 'the thermometer stands at 130 [degrees Fahrenheit]; in the drawing-room, with three tatties up, at 88. The heat is too oppressive to admit of an evening drive.'[99]

The house is still in existence today and continues to be inhabited by the current Collector and District Magistrate of Kanpur.[100] Inevitably the building has undergone alterations over time. The roof that Fanny described in her journal as 'tiled over a thatch' was most likely destroyed during the 1857 Revolt.[101] It has been replaced by one made of flat stone, giving the appearance of a *pukka* house instead of a pitched-roof bungalow. The surrounding verandas have also been enclosed, while the residence has been given a grander facade with the addition of a pillared portico and ornamental roof balustrades. Much, however, remains to evoke a tangible sense of the past. Numerous subordinates continue to support the present *burra sahib* both in his house and nearby *cutcherry*. Peacocks grace the foreground of the spacious, enclosed domain, which stills boasts a fine garden and extensive vegetable patch. The view across the Ganges also remains largely as it was during Robert's time. Like their forebears, locals continue to wash their clothes at the nearby ghats while farmers work the fertile islands that temporary form during the cool season.

A major focus for Robert Montgomery during his time at Cawnpore was the creation of a detailed anatomy of the district's administration. Published in 1849 under the title *Statistical Report of the District of Cawnpoor*, the inspiration for the work can be directly attributed to his influential friend and mentor, James Thomason, who, on becoming Lieutenant Governor of the North-Western Provinces, urged his district officers to collate and publish pertinent information on the various branches of local civil government under their jurisdiction. 'An official history of each district,' Thomason believed, 'would enable the public officers of Government to understand the peculiarities of the district and conduct of the administration.'[102] To such men, it was axiomatic that increased knowledge led to better governance as the presentation and analysis of data brought greater accountability and the thirst for improvement. Thus 'minute directions' were given on how to arrange the subject matter that would include details on 'current [land] tenures, the rise and fall of [notable] families, the operation of special measures or laws, and the effect of the revenue and judicial systems'.[103]

Thomason's vision was undoubtedly laudable, but his call to action fell largely on deaf ears. In practice, Robert was one of only a handful of civil officers who had 'the energy and skill to work out the plan'.[104] Indeed, it would take until the last quarter of the century for district gazetteers to become the *vade mecum* that Thomason envisaged. Nevertheless, Robert's *Statistical Report* can be seen as one of the earliest attempts by government officials to disseminate an ever-increasing body of official knowledge to a wider audience. In doing so, it established a pattern for other publications to follow – most notably another Thomasonian inspired work – the multivolume *Selections from the Records of Government*. Although partly a response, as Professor C.A. Bayly has noted, to public and parliamentary criticism, the propagation of such material also acted as a 'permanent and public' testimony to 'a vast variety of most useful and suggestive papers on all official subjects – revenue, police, judicial, engineering, statistical' which, for the most part, presented a picture of an India progressing benignly under Company rule.[105]

The impetus behind this information expansion largely arose from the land revenue reforms of the 1830s. This had required a vast body of socio-economic data to be compiled from an individual village level upwards. Robert's *Statistical Report* was no exception, and throughout its five hundred-odd, generously tabulated pages, it drew heavily on revenue related material to present both a high-level district summary as well as a detailed *pargana*/village view.[106] Almost half the book (250 pages) was assigned solely to the 'Register of Mouzas' within each *pargana*. This showed the current *jama* for each village, the assessed area, both cultivated and culturable, as well as the population spilt between Hindus and Muslims and between cultivator and non-cultivator.

For contextual purposes, the report began with a general account of Cawnpore's fiscal history since the inception of British rule at the beginning of the century. Formed from a former portion of the Oude territory which was bounded on the north by the Ganges and on the south by the Jumna, the district covered some 2337 sq. miles and contained a population 993,031 spread over 2258 villages. Drawing on the records of Mr A. Welland, Cawnpore's first district officer, the territory had suffered greatly from the predatory habits of the *amils* [the revenue officers in the pre-British period] who were 'said to have always taken the utmost which the stock and produce would afford'.[107] The beginning of British rule, however, did not mark an immediate transformation in its fortunes. Quite the opposite. As in other districts within the North-Western Provinces, like Azamgarh or Allahabad, Montgomery revealed a familiar tale of socio-economic upheaval caused by 'the ignorance of Government European Functionaries' and the fraudulent activities of unscrupulous local officials who had deprived the old co-sharing tenurial communities of their estates.[108] One of Montgomery statistics – the *Statement Shewing the Mutations of Property since the Cession [1802] up to 1846–47* – highlighted the scale of the problem. Of the 2258 villages comprising the district, 405 or 18% had been sold for arrears of revenue, most of which had been disposed of in the first few years of British rule.[109] Holt Mackenzie's reforms of the early 1820s had aimed to solve the haphazard approach to land revenue settlements but the amount of detail required meant that none of the *parganas* in the Cawnpore district had been completed under his scheme. Despite the gallant efforts of a few former Collectors, it was only by 1842, when a new settlement was made under the provisions of Regulation IX of 1833, that Robert could feel justified in lauding Cawnpore's revenue arrangements:

When we look back to our ignorance at the commencement of our legislation, and then contemplate the present period, now that we have a record of every boundary, and every proprietary right, that each cultivator knows his fields, and that he cannot be ejected without good cause, that the Government demand has been fixed for 30 years, and that at a glance the whole history of any village may be known, it appears that past errors have been atoned for.[110]

Robert took note of the efforts to clamp down on revenue fraud and general mismanagement. There was now greater supervision of *tahsildars* and their work. Corrupt local officials were removed and the office of *lambardar* was made elective with shareholders having the power to remove those unfit. Following the Circular Orders of the Revenue Board, the onus was on a tightly run Collector's Office where 'the papers of any particular case, or the entire papers relating to any village from the period of the Cession to the present time' could be 'taken out in a few seconds'.[111] Of course, as in other parts of the North-Western Provinces, Bird's revenue reforms did not herald the complete end of over-assessment. In a district which had been adversely affected by recent famine, two years' experience of Cawnpore's new assessment had convinced the revenue authorities that it was still too high. Not only had it been 'paid with great difficulty', the very low prices paid for land sold on account of revenue arrears also suggested that the estates had been over-assessed.[112] Consequently, a remission of Rs.32,326 was made to 307 estates by the mid-1840s.[113]

Besides revenue matters, Robert went on to highlight improvements in the provision of law and order and credited one of his predecessors, the 'energetic and vigilant' Mr Caldecott, for effecting reform during the 1830s.[114] Under his direction, the workings of the central and local police now came under greater scrutiny, a more rapid and frequent communication with the *thanahs* was instituted (improving the *dak*), and a code of conduct for officials was enforced. Caldecott also encouraged greater cooperation with the other departments of the district, both civil and military, and took great care in his appointment and dismissal of subordinates. Of some significance was his successful campaign against *dacoity* (gang robbery) within the district. The capture of their leaders and the breakup of the gangs led Robert to boast that no other district was 'more free from the open and daring crimes of dacoity and highway robberies'.[115] Later reforms in the 1840s saw the Revenue and Police jurisdictions assimilated and reorganised in line with changing population density.

Although the *Juma Wasil Baqee* or the *Account of Demands, Collections and Balances of Land Revenue* (Appendix No. I) could present an unbroken record of returns for the years between 1802 and 1846, most of Robert's data collection was of a more recent period. In terms of crime statistics, for example, reliable records on the type and number of offences committed such as homicides, highway robberies, burglaries, affrays, etc., only stretched back to 1830. Similarly, his efforts to understand the prevalence of crimes committed against either persons or property covered just a three-year period (1844–46). Despite its paucity, Robert clearly saw the potential for much greater use of official data in future. 'There are many statistical facts regarding crime,' he noted sagely, 'which hereafter it will be possible to obtain from the accuracy with which our records are now kept and preserved.'[116]

One of the greatest potential improvements lay in the field of penal reform. 'Nothing could exceed,' Robert lamented, 'the utter want of discipline, order, and classification that existed generally within our jails, till a few years ago.' Until as late as 1835, all types of prisoners, whether murderers, thieves, vagabonds, men, women etc, were invariably crammed into just a single ward within Cawnpore central jail. Regular uniforms were unavailable, while the ventilation and sanitation provisions were 'very imperfect'. However, since the appointment of a Superintendent of Jails in 1844 substantial improvements had been made. Prisoners were now categorised by gender and type of crime while efforts were made to improve environmental conditions by adding new windows, raising the height of cell walls, and removing toilets and drains to more suitable locations. In charting these improvements, the collection of relevant data was crucial. The dietary requirements for the prisoners were now recorded and presented in tables as was the itemisation of jail expenditure – the latter a vital tool in promoting economy.[117]

Other weighty topics in Robert's compendium included an 'Abstract Statement of Annual Imports and Exports of the District of Cawnpoor', the Abkaree or excise showing the demands, collections and balances on 'spiritous liquors and intoxicating drugs', and reports on the state of education and 'the rise and progress of the poppy cultivation in the zillah of Cawnpore'. There were also statistics on crop type, its acreage and value, population breakdown by caste and religion and, of course, the all-important government treasury statement showing receipts and disbursements. The range of subjects reflected the expanding scope of colonial rule in India. To govern effectively, the regular compilation and presentation of official information was now seen as critical. Through data analysis, trends could be discerned, comparisons made, shortcomings highlighted, and improvements made. At a higher level, policy decisions could be taken on how best to manage resources. This growing reliance on the power of data marked another important chapter in the birth of the modern state.

On a personal level, Robert's *Statistical Report* also amply demonstrated those skills by which he would become synonymous – namely attention to detail, a head for figures and a strong work ethic that focused on results – qualities that were increasingly prized by those in the upper echelon of the Indian administration. When James Thomason reviewed a draft version in November 1847, he acknowledged 'a vast deal of very valuable information contained in the report,' and its 'importance to make public'. This was indeed a project very dear to Thomason who annotated the draft report 'very fully and freely', suggesting greater brevity of some sections and the inclusion of important cases such as 'the rise, progress and termination of the Special Commission in Cawnpore'.[118] His constructive criticism was, as always, tempered with an appreciation. 'I hope what I say will not discourage you,' he told Robert,

> I desire and intend to assist you. I wonder at your diligence and perseverance in accomplishing what you have done. If I would lead you to aim still higher, it is not in forgetfulness of what you have done, but in acknowledgement of the importance of your object and your own high qualifications for its accomplishment.[119]

That Robert's work at Cawnpore should also feature in *Selections from the Records of Government* was no surprise. A key aim for magistrates during this period was to reduce criminal activity along the main roads of their district, and in particular the Grand Trunk Road (GTR) which ran from Calcutta to Peshawar and cut through two-thirds of the North-Western Provinces. One of Asia's oldest thoroughfares, it was regarded by the British, particularly before the advent of the railway, as a crucial channel of communication for both military and commercial reasons. During his time as Lieutenant Governor of the N.W.P., and amongst his wide array of development projects he spearheaded, James Thomason demanded improvements in the security for travellers along its route.[120]

Much of the practical detail and implementation of Thomason's directives fell to the likes of Robert Montgomery who as Magistrate of Cawnpore was responsible for a sixty-mile stretch of the GTR running through his district. In seeking to improve safety along its route, Robert focused on the nature of criminal activity being committed. Most crime, he discovered, involved the theft of traveller's belongings at night. Further inquiries revealed that only a small number of travellers stayed in caravanserais – lodgings which could offer a secure overnight stay. In practice the majority, after a long day's journey, would simply set up camp by the side of the road, leaving their goods and belongings largely unprotected. Robert's investigations next turned to the system of policing then currently deployed. Although there were police stations situated every few miles along its course, Robert found that there was no regular system of night-time patrols by *burkundazes* or *chowkidars*. It was little wonder then that crime levels spiked during nocturnal hours. Robert had no illusions as to the extent of the problem as he surmised that such crime went largely unreported. Most travellers would grudgingly accept their losses rather than endure the prospect of being detained by the police from their onward journey. As most stolen property was quickly spirited away to 'receiving houses' in Cawnpore or Futtehgurh, there was little hope of ever retrieving it.[121]

From February 1846 onwards, and only a few months since taking up his Cawnpore appointment, Robert began to tackle the problem in several ways. He now established a series of *puraos* or halting places at regular intervals along the GTR. The aim was to provide travellers and merchants with a 'safe asylum' at night when the risk of robbery was at its greatest. The *puraos*, situated at every three miles or so, were unenclosed places which afforded good tree cover, a plentiful supply of water and, where possible, a bazaar offering food and goods. Most important was the provision of an effective night watch, composed of *burkundazes* and *chowkidars*, who would patrol around the encampment and be subject to regular inspections from the *thanadar*. The overall management of the *puraos* would be under the strict supervision of the local *tahsildar* and both he and the *thanadar* were to report directly to Robert. For added security, he hoped to institute a system of patrols between the puraos by *sowars* subject to government approval. In the meantime, these simple measures appeared to have their intended result: 'I soon found that the halting places were thronged of an evening, and that robberies were rare,' Robert reported in April 1847.[122] In 1845, prior to the changes, the amount of property officially reported stolen on the Grand Trunk Road at night was valued at 2,350 rupees. By the following year, however, the figure had dropped to 346 rupees.[123] Much of the improvement undoubtedly rested on the careful management of the district's law enforcers by the incumbent magistrate – a point implicitly acknowledged by Lieutenant-Colonel J. Steel, Superintendent of Police and Supplies on the Grand Trunk Road, who found that 'Mr Montgomery's police behaved better than those of any other zillah'.[124]

The Tashma-baz Thugs

'Thuggee and Meypunnaism [kidnapping children for sale] are no sooner suppressed than a new system of secret assassination and robbery is discovered, proving the truth of Colonel Sleeman's remark, that "India is a strange land; and live in it as long as we may, and mix with its people as much as we please, we shall to the last be constantly liable to stumble upon new moral phenomena to excite our special wonder." As anticipated, at least one set of new actors have to be introduced to the public, and these are the *Tashma-baz* thugs.' *The Agra Messenger, 2nd December 1848*.[125]

The most high-profile example of Montgomery's crime reduction work occurred in early February 1848 when, acting on intelligence from the Bulandshahr district close to Delhi, he gave orders for the arrest of nineteen members of a criminal gang based in his own district of Cawnpore. The gang had been operating a gambling racket using a game called *Tashma-bazee*. A form of thimblerigging, also known as 'pricking the garter', it involved a long strap being first doubled and then folded around many times to form a coil.[126] The aim of the game was to insert a stick into one of two central loops within the coil so that, when the ends of the strap were pulled, it was still held in its doubled state. Unsuspecting bystanders were encouraged to try their luck at this seemingly simple game. But, as with all confidence tricks, the odds were stacked against them. In practice, it proved almost impossible to win without the consent of the trickster (based on how he unwound the coil). Victims were usually lured by early wins before being ultimately fleeced of their valuables.

What was noteworthy about these practitioners of *Tashma-bazee* was that they had not merely been arrested as petty swindlers, but that they had been indicted on the more serious charge of *thuggee*. Derived from the Hindi word *thugna*, meaning to deceive, *thugs* were characterised in traditional colonial representations as a close knit, secret cult of professional murderers. Sanctifying their grisly work by worshipping the Hindu goddess Kali, they plied their trade along major highways and at fairs and religious festivals, tricking unsuspecting travellers and pilgrims. It was through the deposition of one gang member, a man called Sheikh Ghazee, that Robert Montgomery revealed the intriguing world of the *Tashma-baz thugs* and their place in the criminal underworld of north Indian society.

One of the revelations uncovered by Montgomery was that the roots of the scam were not Indian at all, but rather of British or Irish origin. A soldier by the name of Creagh, stationed at Cawnpore cantonment, was believed to have passed on 'the art of *Tusman-bazee*' to three Indian acquaintances at the beginning of the century. Over subsequent years the game, it seems, became a well-established fixture amongst the petty criminal fraternity, and by the late 1840s those involved in the scam had grown to around fifty active participants. Account books of the gang examined by Montgomery showed that it was a lucrative venture. Gang members had pawned 'ornaments to a considerable value' in return for money advances, while *hoondees* (bills of exchange) amounting to 750 rupees had accrued over the previous year.[127]

Although based in Cawnpore, their operations extended over a wide area which included the territories of Delhi, Gwalior and Etawah. In terms of organisation, Robert discovered that the *Tashma-bazees* were divided into two main gangs, although membership was fluid enough for individuals to form smaller groups depending on personal circumstances. Each operation followed a set procedure. After setting up a temporary base at a local caravanserai, the gang would choose a suitable location to entice their prey. To play out the charade more effectively, they adopted the disguise of different characters acting as complete strangers to one another. Their cover was further aided using slang language, a notable feature of the thug fraternity, which allowed gang members to surreptitiously alert one another of potential dangers or swindling opportunities.

Although well known to the authorities and punished numerous times for their gambling activities, the *Tashma-baz* gangs had not been previously labelled as dangerous criminals. Indeed, for much of their existence the local police had tolerated their gaming habits in return for a percentage of the profits. What changed this *modus vivendi* were the measures taken by the local magistrate, Mr Plowden, in the Bulandshahr district near Delhi in December 1847. Acting on rumours circulating of 'budmashes and suspected thugs' operating in his district, Plowden had deputed the local *tahsildar* and *cotwal* (police chief) to investigate. Before long fourteen members of the *Tashma-baz* gang, including its two leaders, were arrested.[128] Through the disposition of one of those seized, a man named Gungadeen, Plowden concluded that the gang were not merely petty criminals but 'belonged to the thug fraternity' who were using the 'pretence of Tusma-bazee....for the purpose of committing other crimes, and administering poison to travellers'.[129] With the recent discovery of a headless corpse in the locality and Gungadeen's admission that other *Tashma-baz* gangs were operating throughout the Ganga-Jumna Doab, Plowden decided to widen the investigation by calling on the assistance of Major J. Graham, Assistant General Superintendent of the Thuggee Department who instructed his assistants to gather further intelligence from other districts; a decision which had led to Montgomery's involvement two months later. Graham, like Plowden, was convinced that these gangs were not simply involved in swindling activities but 'used the denomination merely as a cloak for darker deeds'.[130] As he explained to his superior, the celebrated anti-thuggee crusader, Colonel W.H. Sleeman:

> Their art and their vagrant habits gave them peculiar facilities for selecting their victims; they appear to have well chosen their positions on the Grand Trunk Road, and must have seen all travellers passing along; their game attracted attention and proved an excellent snare to catch the unwary; the impunity given by the police, made them less suspected; from those seduced to play they were able to ascertain who had any thing to lose, and what they failed to obtain by their art, they appear to have got by the administering dhutorah [poison], and by more violent means when necessary.[131]

With the active support of Plowden and Montgomery and a network of informers, Graham built a damning case against the *Tashma-bazees* in which almost all were implicated either directly or indirectly in cases of *thuggee*. The identification of the *Tashma-baz* gangs with serial homicide was a key component of the charge against them. Montgomery maintained that it was 'easy to conceive that gangs of this kind would not, when the opportunity offered, resist the temptation to rob, or even murder'.[132] Graham went further, intimating that many of the unexplained corpses found along the Grand Trunk Road were most likely their victims:

> It is a remarkable fact, that up to the time of the apprehension of these people, cases of dhuttoreeah [poisoning] and reports of bodies found in the vicinity of the Trunk Road, were numerous and defying all proof. It is not long since the Commissioner of Agra reported, that they were greatly on the increase, but since their apprehension not more than two cases have been heard of.[133]

Did the *Tashma-bazees* constitute another strand of the *thuggee* cult? Based on the literal interpretation of *thuggee* – that of deception and confidence trickery – they might be said to qualify. Like other forms of *thuggee*, they were also part of a wandering community, which operated with a clear sense of identity and camaraderie. This could be clearly seen in the adoption of "honour amongst thieves" rules and in their use of slang language. Nevertheless, it is doubtful whether any of those arrested would have seen themselves as *thugs*. More importantly, on the evidence supplied by Plowden, Montgomery and Graham, there is little to suggest that they followed anything close to the religiously inspired murdering ideology of *thuggee*. James Hutton, writing in the late 1850s, clearly disputed the classification: 'To call them *thugs* was evidently a misnomer, for they had none of the observances of that ancient fraternity, nor did they lay any claim to religious motives. They were simply organized bands of vagrants of the most worthless characters, who preferred fraud to labour and murder to industry.'[134]

As for the murders allegedly committed by *Tashma-baz* gang members, their confessions should be treated with caution. Some gang members had quarrelled over their share of loot, threatening to betray one another, while others had turned Queen's evidence to avoid the full force of the law. The real impetus behind the campaign against them is perhaps less sensational. More plausible was the British desire to clamp down on itinerant communities in general, particularly those deemed to be actively engaged in petty crime along the Grand Trunk Road.[135] There was also the determination to stamp out endemic police corruption. As

Graham noted, 'had the police not winked at their proceedings, it would have been impossible for these people to have carried on their depredations for so long a time'.[136] With the Company's reach extending ever deeper into north Indian society, such flagrant abuse by government officials together with the crime itself were an affront to the concept of *Pax Britannica*. By labelling the *Tashma-baz* gangs as *thugs*, British officials took advantage of recent Thuggee Suppression Acts to eradicate this itinerant group and their activities. Due to the efforts of Montgomery and his colleagues, and after a long period of connivance, the occidental import known as *Tashma-bazee* swiftly came to an end in the North-Western Provinces.

Part II

Conquest and Loss – George and Henry Lawrence's Afghan War

1. Statue of John Lawrence, Waterloo Place, London.

. Statue of John Lawrence, Foyle College, Londonderry.

3. Robert Montgomery by William Carpenter, Lahore (1854).

4. Lieutenant Henry Lawrence, oil on canvas, attributed to James Heath Millington (1828).

5. George St. Patrick Lawrence, Cavalry Officer and Military Secretary to Sir William Hay Macnaghten.

6. John Lawrence by T.W. Knight.

. Foyle College, Londonderry, early 19th Century.

. The East India College at Haileybury by Thomas Medland (1810).

9. The East India Company Military Seminary at Addiscombe (c.1859).

10. The gothic, crenelated edifice known as Ludlow Castle, once the home of the long-serving Residenc
surgeon Samuel Ludlow, became the British Residency from 1832 and the centre of the Britis
administration during John Lawrence's time in the Delhi Territory.

11. James Thomason, Lieutenant-Governor
of the North-Western Provinces.

12. Honoria Marshall (Lawrence), aged 21, from a
portrait miniature.

13. Henry Lawrence painted by Delhi artist
Ghulam Husain Khan (c. 1847).

14. The District Magistrate's residence at Allahabad by Sita Ram (1814–15).

15. The Collector and District Magistrate's residence at Kanpur (Cawnpore).

16. Dost Mohammed, the Amir of Kabul by an
East India Company artist (c. 1835).

17. Akbar Khan, son of Dost Mohammed, by an
East India Company artist (c.1840).

18. Shah Shuja ul-Mulk, head of the Sadozai
clan, by Louis and Charles Haghe after Jas
Atkinson (1842).

19. Prison sketch of Captain George Lawrence
in Afghan dress by Lieutenant Vincent Eyre
(1842).

20. The Fort of Shewaki, near Kabul, where George Lawrence and his fellow British hostages were held by Akbar Khan.

21. The British Residency in Kathmandu, Nepal. According to Sir John Lawrence's 'Lawrence of Lucknow: A Biography (1990)', the scene depicts Henry Lawrence's family in the foreground with an ayah holding the infant Henry (Harry) Waldemar Lawrence while Honoria appears to be on the roof surveying her surroundings using a telescope.

The Great Game

Once the East India Company had extended its rule to the Delhi Territory at the beginning of the nineteenth century, there was a corresponding need, given the proximity of Ranjit Singh's growing Sikh empire, to make its north-west frontier stable and secure. Ranjit's desire to expand southwards to take control over the Cis-Sutlej states was one potential source of conflict. Another was the perceived threat of a French invasion of India. The first issue was largely resolved by the signing of the Treaty of Amritsar (1809) – an agreement based on 'perpetual friendship' between 'the British government and the Raja of Lahore'. The latter was now recognised by the former as the sole sovereign ruler of Punjab. Moreover, he was free to expand his empire northwards of the river Sutlej without the risk of British interference. For his part, the Sikh ruler renounced his claim to sovereignty over the Cis-Sutlej territories. His southwards expansion was thus halted, and the River Sutlej now became the frontier between the two empires. Although there were no specific articles defining the nature of this Anglo-Sikh alliance beyond 'being anxious to maintain relations of perfect amity and accord', the treaty nonetheless effectively established the Sikh kingdom as a buffer state in defence of India's north-west frontier.[1] As for a French invasion of India; it never materialised and interest in frontier affairs subsequently waned.

It would take another twenty years before the security of India's north-west frontier was placed firmly back on the agenda. British ministers, Company officials and military officers' concerns over French designs were eventually replaced by Russia's imperialist ambitions. Following victories in wars with the Persians (1826–28) and the Ottomans (1828–29), the Tsarist empire had quickly expanded south and eastwards along the Black Sea Coast and into the Caucasus.[2] Would it extend further into Central Asia, to Afghanistan, and thereby threaten the very border of India itself? Although there was little evidence of any Russian plans to do so, a wave of Russophobia soon enveloped British foreign policy circles. It marked the beginning of a long period of Anglo-Russian rivalry and diplomatic intrigue rather loosely referred to by later commentators as 'the Great Game'. One contemporary observer, Colonel George de Lacy Evans, concluded in his influential book *On the Practicability of an Invasion of British*

India (1829) that Russia was most likely contemplating 'advancing a force towards the most vulnerable frontier of our Indian possessions' and that there existed 'no insurmountable obstacle to the execution of such a project'.[3] Lord Ellenborough, then President of the Board of Control (for Indian affairs) and later Governor-General of India, took Evans' book to heart, noting hawkishly in his diary entry of 3rd September 1829: 'I feel confident we shall have to fight the Russians on the Indus, and I have long had a presentiment that I should meet them there and gain a great battle.'[4]

Despite the hyperbolic language, Ellenborough's initial efforts to combat the perceived Russian threat took the form of a non-belligerent strategy; one of security through commerce with the aim of exploiting the River Indus as an important trading route.[5] By supplying British goods to the likes of Kabul and Bukhara, and supplanting, where possible, those of Russian merchants, Ellenborough hoped that British commercial influence would negate tsarist attempts to gain dominance.[6] Supporting this strategy was the despatch of diplomatic missions to the region's indigenous rulers. Little was then known of the Central Asian Khanates, so an increased understanding of the region's geography and power dynamics was seen as essential. One such mission, in 1831, involved the young, gifted linguist, Alexander Burnes, travelling to Lahore by boat ostensibly to present a collection of dray horses and a bespoke carriage to Maharaja Ranjit Singh. Its prime intention, however, was to ascertain the navigability of the Indus. Burnes' mission was extended to include a journey through Afghanistan and into Central Asia and became the source material for his celebrated *Travels into Bokhara*. The charismatic Scotsman formed an easy rapport with both Maharaja Ranjit Singh and the Amir of Kabul, Dost Mohammed Khan of the Barakzai clan of Pashtuns. Of the latter, he was impressed by the Amir's ability, regarding him as 'doubtless the most powerful chief in Afghanistan'.[7] Moreover, his amenability to British overtures made Burnes believe that an Anglo-Afghan alliance was both eminently possible and the answer to India's north-west frontier policy. Another visit to Kabul in autumn 1837 re-affirmed this view. But by spring of the following year hopes of an accommodation foundered over an Afghan-Sikh dispute involving possession of the city of Peshawar in which British policy favoured Lahore.

Burnes' diplomatic efforts were ultimately undermined by the influence of other Company officials. Both Major Claude Wade, the long-standing British agent at Ludhiana, and William Hay Macnaghten, political secretary to the Governor-General, Lord Auckland, had little time for Dost Mohammed whom they thought lacked popular support and who was predisposed to Persian and Russian intrigue. Undoubtedly there was an element of jealousy over Burnes' meteoric rise to fame and favour, but there was also the strong urge to maintain the Sikh alliance at the expense of the Barakzai dynasty. This was clearly in Wade's interest. For to remain relevant, the Ludhiana agent needed to maintain cordial relations with Lahore.[8]

After Burnes' empty-handed departure from Kabul in April 1838, the government's Afghan policy looked set to be one of continuing non-interference, limited to cultivating commerce. Auckland's recent arrival in the alpine summer retreat of Simla suggested so. For here, it seemed, the cool, fresh climate would encourage a spirit of serene contemplation. But there was little time for relaxation. By early May, two issues came to the fore. One was the threat posed by a Russian agent named Ivan Vitkevitch, then currying favour with Dost Mohammed in Kabul; the other, was the perilous state of the western Afghan city of Herat, besieged by the Persians since November 1837 with Russian backing. Sir John MacNeill, the British Ambassador to Persia, then with the Persian camp outside the city, called for resolute action by the Governor-General.[9]

Auckland's response to these challenges was the abandonment of 'commercial diplomacy' in favour of the much more radical policy of regime change. In helping him reach this decision, Wade and Macnaghten, neither of whom incidentally had ever set foot in Afghanistan, undoubtedly played a crucial part.[10] Both men had for some time been keen to promote the claims of Shah Shuja ul-Mulk of the rival Sadozai clan, despite having lost the Afghan throne some thirty years earlier and having already failed in an attempt to regain it as recently as 1834. These uncomfortable truths were conveniently ignored, however. Only by installing a compliant ruler in Afghanistan, the Governor-General now believed, would India's defences be secure. In July 1838 a tripartite agreement between the British, Maharaja Ranjit Singh and Shah Shuja was signed, setting in motion the invasion of Afghanistan. Using a largely Anglo-Sikh force, the aim was to oust Dost Mohammed and restore the former king from his exile in Ludhiana to his old throne in Kabul.

The reasons for prosecuting the war were enshrined in the Simla Manifesto of 1st October 1838. The document was an unashamed piece of propaganda designed to justify an unprovoked war. It began by emphasising that benign, altruistic interests ('to facilitate the extension of commerce') lay at the core of Britain's Central Asian policy, but swiftly moved on to denigrate Dost Mohammed's character and actions.[11] The 'chief of Cabul' had demonstrated 'the most unreasonable pretensions' and 'avowed schemes of aggrandizement and ambition, injurious to the security and peace of the frontiers of India and that he openly threatened, in furtherance of those schemes, to call in every foreign aid which he could command.'[12] In order to arrest the 'rapid progress of foreign intrigue and aggression towards our own territories', the manifesto concluded that the moment had now come to champion the claims of Shah

Shuja 'whose popularity throughout Afghanistan had been proved….by the strong and unanimous testimony of the best authorities.'[13] He would return to Afghanistan 'surrounded by his own troops' and 'supported against foreign interference and factious opposition by a British army'. The Governor-General confidently looked forward to his speedy re-enthronement by his own subjects, and once secured in power and 'the independence and integrity of Afghanistan established', British troops could then withdraw. So, at least, ran the theory; the reality would prove otherwise.

For George St. Patrick Lawrence, the 1st Anglo-Afghan War would mark a turning point in his largely hitherto humdrum career.[14] Since first joining his cavalry regiment at Keitah, Bundelkhand in January 1822, his life, by his own admission, had been 'one of common routine in an Indian cantonment, merely diversified by a change of quarters'.[15] Indeed, it was a period that remained wholly unaccounted for in his autobiography, *Reminiscences of Forty-three Years in India*. By contrast, George's part in the 1st Anglo-Afghan War, which covered only a four-year period (1838–42), would fill over two-thirds of his memoirs.[16]

There were three main reasons for the Afghan war's literary predominance. Firstly, aside from George's first opportunity of active service, the war enabled him to move beyond a strictly military career and into a diplomatic role where the responsibilities were more interesting and varied. From the modest position of a cavalry captain, he became military assistant to the British Envoy in Kabul, William Hay Macnaghten, who was himself of Ulster extraction. Secondly, and more importantly, after the successful uprising by insurgents in Kabul in November 1841, George would occupy a central role in the unfolding crisis. Taken hostage by Dost Mohammed's son Akbar, he became a leading light in the small group of British officers and their wives who managed to survive the dreaded retreat from Kabul in January 1842. Lasting over eight months, George's captivity, alongside his fellow hostages, was a remarkable tale of endurance and courage. It was no surprise that a growing readership back home was eager to read of the heroic exploits of embattled Company servants on the frontiers of its empire.[17]

Thirdly, the legacy of the 1st Anglo-Afghan War had a profound effect on contemporary British public opinion. The war ended in military catastrophe and marked the first major occasion of the British suffering an ignominious defeat on the Indian sub-continent. 'No failure so total and overwhelming as this is recorded in the pages of history…It was, in principle and in act, an unrighteous usurpation, and the curse of God was on it from the first,' was the bitter conclusion of the Victorian historian, J.W. Kaye.[18] Of the 5,000 troops and 10,000 camp followers who retreated from Kabul in the bitterly freezing conditions of January 1842 only a tiny fraction survived. The war continued to cast a long shadow into the 1870s. In the preface to George's *Reminiscences*, published in 1874, the editor, W. Edwards, saw the 1st Anglo-Afghan War as providing a salutary lesson for those statesmen who advocated 'a return to that policy which bore so bitter fruit in 1839–40'.[19] Four years later, though, the 2nd Anglo-Afghan War began.

The First Anglo-Afghan War would also be an opportunity for Henry Lawrence's career to progress, albeit in a less dramatic fashion. Like his brother George, he too would move beyond a military career by gaining the first rung on the political department ladder as an assistant to a frontier agent. The responsibilities of the frontier or political agency in North-West India were wide-ranging and included conducting diplomatic relations with sovereign powers beyond India's frontier, gathering intelligence on their affairs and, where necessary, organising the civil administration in newly acquired territories. As the eyes and ears of the Indian government, frontier agents and their assistants occupied an important role not only in implementing Company policy, but also influencing it. Such roles were therefore highly coveted, attracting young, ambitious Company army officers who could demonstrate a high degree of resourcefulness and self-belief.

Among those officers who could demonstrate those attributes, at least in embryonic form, was Henry Lawrence. When the order was given in August 1838 for his company of Horse Artillery to prepare for active service in the forthcoming Afghan campaign, he immediately made efforts to secure a rapid release from the Revenue Survey and a return to military duties.[20] Even then he was already looking beyond a regular artillery posting. Within the same month of the call-up, he submitted a proposal for the formation of a 'Corps of Guides', a specialist intelligence-gathering unit, designed to help the war effort. Henry believed his years of surveying experience had amply equipped him with the necessary skills of 'ascertaining the position of the enemy, the resources of the country, the state of the roads, passes, and fords, and the numerous etcetera necessary to the success of an army'.[21] Unfortunately, the military's top brass did not share his vision, nor did they take kindly to his brazen recommendation of himself as commander along with a list of officers who should be appointed.[22] Although his efforts on his occasion came to nothing, his proposal was eventually brought to life eight years later when a 'Guide Corps' was raised in the Punjab under his direction.

Another incident during this time served not only to underline Henry's breadth of interests and sense of conviction but also an impulsiveness and a careless disregard for loved ones. It concerned his critical review of a biography of an Indian army veteran, General Sir John Adams, and led to a long running war of words with the book's author who accused him of peddling lies.[23] With passions running high, Henry's acute sensitivity and quick temper got the better of him and he responded with the challenge of a duel. Fortunately, the good sense of Henry's fellow officers prevented it from taking place. But the episode nevertheless caused much anguish to Honoria.[24] She had just given birth to their first child, Alexander (Alick) Hutchinson on 6th September 1838 after what had been a difficult pregnancy.[25]

With one trial over, Honoria still had to contend with Henry's impending departure to join his regiment. His hastiness, together with a lack of empathy for his wife's condition, was again reflected in his insistence that he would no longer wait for the military order to come through but would leave for the large military station of Karnal on 1st October. Honoria accompanied Henry as far as Meerut on a journey in which her health and that of her new-born baby suffered considerably. They remained at Meerut with George's wife Charlotte, regaining their strength, while Henry, accompanied by his elder brother, continued the journey to Karnal and eventually to Ferozepur.

Much to his disappointment, though not Honoria's, Henry and his troop of artillery were ordered to remain at Ferozepur when news came of the lifting of the Persian siege of Herat in western Afghanistan. The siege had been one of the main reasons for prosecuting the war due to Russia's support of Persia. But with its ending came the decision to scale back the number of troops involved in the invasion force. There was now little hope of active service for Henry. Desperate to remain on the frontier and be at least within earshot of the action, he fortuitously heard of an opening – as an assistant to George Clerk, formerly the Frontier Agent at Ambala but now the Officiating Political Agent at Ludhiana in the absence of Claude Wade. Through the influence of his former colleague, Frederick Currie, the former Revenue Commissioner of Gorakhpur, then a secretary to Lord Auckland, Henry was appointed in January 1839 to the frontier agency with responsibility for the civil administration of the Ferozepur district. 'Now I have helped to put your foot into the stirrup,' Currie told him, 'It rests with you to put yourself into the saddle.'[26] His brother John was one of the first to congratulate him: 'I am delighted to hear of your success. You are well out of the Survey. Besides, the Political is the best line. One can get on in it if he has mettle.'[27]

Although the career change offered greater opportunities to advance, professionally, it made Henry worse off financially. After sixteen years in the army Henry was still only receiving 700 rupees a month, 200 rupees per month less than as a surveyor. By contrast, John with nine years' experience as a civilian officer was drawing 2000 rupees. Despite the appointment being the breakthrough that Henry desperately needed, the modest salary was clearly a sticking point, and one which led him to sound out Frederick Currie on the possibility of an increase from the Governor-General. But the latter was not receptive. His view of political officers was hardly complimentary, believing that there was 'a great deal of difference between knocking about with a theodolite in all the hot weather, living in tents nine months out of the twelve,' compared to 'sitting with one's heels on the table, playing civilian'.[28] Faced with the alternative of a return to the more limited prospects of the revenue service, Henry would have to be patient and look to the prospect of future promotion within the political line for more acceptable remuneration. The next three years, however, would show that Henry would be the very antithesis of Auckland's fanciful description of a civilian officer 'sitting with one's heels on the table'.

The Army of the Indus

George and his regiment, the 2nd Bengal Light Cavalry, were part of the Bengal contingent of the grandly termed 'Army of the Indus'. Its purpose was to oust the existing Amir of Kabul, Dost Mohammed and restore the pliant former Afghan King Shah Shuja.[1] As the army departed from the frontier base of Ferozepur on 10th December 1838, morale and expectations were set high. Active service offered career-defining opportunities – of promotion and prize money – as well as the chance to enhance British prestige at large. 'We have gained a golden opportunity for confirming ourselves in a position across the Indus and establishing a just impression of our power throughout Central Asia,' wrote Lord Auckland's private secretary, John Colvin.[2] The campaign was talked of as a 'grand military promenade'; the prospect of hard fighting was barely considered.[3] As if to underline this hubristic approach, British officers spared themselves little in bringing with them the comforts of cantonment life. Despite orders to the contrary, the amount of personal baggage and paraphernalia reached epic proportions. Even low-ranking officers did not stint on clean linen, personal dressing cases, cigars, and wines. Transporting this bloated excess fell to camp followers and their animals. The number of camp followers for the Bengal division alone was estimated to be a staggering 38,000 while the number of camels approached 30,000.

For the first couple of months there was little to dent the army's optimism. George reported that their march to the island fortress of Bukkur on the Indus passed 'without any incidents of importance'.[4] Even the next stage of the expedition, which began on 23rd February 1839, proved easier than expected. Fellow officers like Henry Havelock might have felt justifiably despondent as they 'traced upon the map the vast tracts of impoverished plain, and absolute desert' of the one hundred and forty mile stretch which lay before them from Shikarpur to Dadur, the entrance to the Bolan Pass.[5] Yet George made light of the challenges, noting that the desert of Rajgan 'presented little difficulty to troops marching across it'.[6] In large measure this was due to travelling in February rather than high summer when the worst extremes of climate were unleashed. Even so George did acknowledge the 'scarcity of water and grain' on the march. Where water was available, much of it was brackish and unfit for consumption, while his task of organising the collection of forage was undoubtedly made difficult in a region comprising little more than course grass and tamarisk bushes.[7]

Only when the army reached the entrance to the Bolan Pass, did their confidence begin to wane. The pass was a sixty-mile series of narrow, winding defiles that ascended to over 5,000 feet above sea level.[8] George's regiment, which formed part of the advance guard, had to contend with harsh topographical conditions. Sharp flint stones and boulders were strewn across the route, while the rapidly flowing Bolan River had to be traversed numerous times. Large numbers of camels died due to the 'severity of the marching and the difficulty of the road'.[9] The army was also forced to endure violent wind and rainstorms as well as searing heat. Furthermore, Baluchi tribesmen were intent on plundering their possessions. Straggling camp followers faired the worst with many being wounded or killed, while considerable numbers of *syces* and *dooley* bearers simply deserted.

Once through the Pass and nearing Quetta, the situation improved little. The inadequate preparations of the commissariat were now fully exposed. The decision for the army to live off the land had taken little account of local conditions. With farming at near subsistence levels, it proved difficult, as George discovered, to procure enough supplies of grain to support such a large force. When they arrived at Quetta at the beginning of April, then a 'village of some 500 houses, with a miserable mud fort', the troops were put on half rations. Fatigue and starvation blighted the army's progress towards the southern provincial capital of Kandahar. Many of the horses from the artillery and George's own cavalry regiment had become 'completely worn out' leaving no option but for them to be destroyed. As they passed through the even narrower defile known as the Khojak Pass, further baggage, including tents and stores were abandoned, while many of the camp followers suffered terribly due to the intense heat and lack of water. 'I saw a trooper of the 16th Lancers,' recorded George, 'who had a soda-water bottle half full of water, pour the whole contents down the throat of a poor native woman's child, who was just dying of thirst. I could have hugged the fellow for his noble and disinterested act.'[10]

Eventually on reaching the Dori River, a tributary of the Helmand, the terrain became more forgiving and allowed for much needed replenishment of supplies. There was no denying that the march had taken a heavy toll on troops and camp followers alike, yet George remained surprising stoical in the face of such adversity. Despite witnessing the misery and hardships of others, he appeared to take it all in his stride and expressed little in the way of personal sufferings. Fortunately, when the struggling army approached Kandahar, the lure of *firangi* gold proved sufficiently enticing for the city's chiefs to abandon the Barakzai cause. The defection of one chief, Haji Khan Kakar, acted as the tipping point for others to desert, leaving the way clear for the Sadozai monarch to enter the city unopposed.

The Envoy, William Hay Macnaghten, maintained that Shah Shuja would be 'cordially welcomed by all classes of the people' once in Afghanistan and events at first appeared to vindicate him.[11] On 25th April Kandahar's inhabitants turned out to greet the returning king enthusiastically. As the royal cavalcade made its way through the city's busy streets, flowers were strewn before the horses' feet. The air was filled with music accompanied by the celebratory crack of gunfire, while onlookers shouted out 'welcome to the son of Timur Shah'.[12] Two weeks later, though, at a grand durbar to formally mark Shuja's installation as King of Afghanistan, the mood appeared to change. Relief that the Kandaharis had now been spared the oppressive rule of the Barakzais soon gave way to either sullen indifference or active opposition against their Sadozai successor.

At least that was the interpretation of the historian, J.W. Kaye, who regarded the ceremony as a painful failure: 'the miserable paucity of Afghans who appeared to do homage to the King, must have warned Shah Soojah, with ominous significance, of the feebleness of his tenure upon the affections of the people.'[13] George, likewise, noted that 'none of his [Shah Shuja's] own subjects came in to pledge their allegiance,' and swiftly concluded that 'the country was clearly against us'.[14] Both remarks, however, should be treated with caution as they appear to have been made with the benefit of hindsight rather than contemporaneous with events. Other eyewitnesses recollected Shah Shuja's entrance as far from being an abject failure. Although admitting there was nowhere near the immense crowd expected, Major William Hough observed, that there were still 'about 3,000 or 4,000 Afghans assembled to view the scene'.[15] In retrospect, it was tempting to portray, as Kaye did, the policy of regime change as an unmitigated disaster from the very beginning.[16] Yet, at this early stage, many Durrani chieftains in Kandahar and its environs, who had no cause to love the Barakzai chiefs, were at least willing to adopt a 'wait and see' approach in the hope of reclaiming their former wealth and status. Indeed, Shah Shuja made encouraging signs to this effect, as Kaye acknowledged, by promising to reinstate them to the offices they had previously held at court, giving them back their sequestrated lands, and granting them allowances and remission of taxes.[17]

George's doubts over the level of support for Shah Shuja were perhaps more plausible when the Army of the Indus approached the formidable fortress of Ghazni, situated some ninety miles southwest of Kabul. In contrast to the more accommodating and relatively sophisticated Durrani tribes to the south, this region was home to the Ghilzais, who were a more rustic, warlike sub-tribe of

Pashtuns. Here, George met a 'well-dressed Afghan horseman' who castigated their foolish attempts to replace the Afghan monarchy:

> You are an army of tents and camels: our army is one of men and horses. What could induce you to squander crores of rupees in coming to a poor rocky country like ours, without wood or water, and all in order to force upon us a *kumbukht* [unlucky person], as a king, who, the moment you turn your backs, will be upset by Dost Mahomed, our own king?[18]

Unlike their good fortune at Kandahar, the fortress at Ghazni would be their first military test. Occupying a commanding position on the western end of a range of hills, it was defended by a deep ditch and appeared impregnable. British efforts were put at a distinct disadvantage by the decision to leave the battering train back in Kandahar as Commander-in-Chief, Lieut. Gen. Sir John Keane had been led to believe, quite mistakenly, that the fort would offer little opposition. Fortuitously, however, intelligence from a deserter, a relative of Dost Mohammed himself, revealed a weakness: the fortress's Kabul gate was the only entrance which had not been reinforced. In the early hours of 23rd July, and with the help of some diversionary tactics, a small contingent of engineers placed twelve large bags of gunpowder at the foot of the gate. Just before daybreak, the charge exploded, and the assault began. By five a.m. British regimental colours could be seen fluttering from the top of the ramparts.

The fortress had been taken with the loss of only 17 men and 165 wounded on the British side. But casualties on the Afghan side were extremely heavy in what appeared to be a bloodbath. George estimated that a total number of 600 Afghans had been killed and 1,600 taken prisoner. He paid tribute to their fighting spirit: 'The Afghans, when driven to bay, had fought gallantly with their swords, and succeeded in wounding several of our men, even when themselves transfixed with the bayonet.'[19] Although not included in the storming party, George coolly related how his regiment had 'succeeded in killing and capturing many of the Afghans' as they tried to escape the fortress. As he led his troops through the town afterwards, he found the sight of hundreds of dead bodies of men and horses strewn along the streets 'most sad and deplorable'. Even so, it seemed that there was little time for clemency or remorse. To the victors the spoils; George was appointed a prize agent, responsible for distributing the plunder.

The fall of Ghazni was closely followed by the capture of the strategic fort of Ali Masjid in the Khyber Pass by a Sikh force led by Lieutenant Colonel Claude Wade whose sights were now set on taking Jalalabad. Both events served to encourage a rising of Kohistani tribesmen against Barakzai rule. Faced with a string of setbacks, Dost Mohammed offered a settlement whereby Shah Shuja would be installed as King if he could hold the position of *wazir* (prime minister). But the British dismissed the proposal out of hand and by early August the army had left Ghazni and were heading for Kabul. As they were approached the capital, news came that Dost Mohammed and his family had fled north in the direction of Bamian. 'His escape,' George remarked, 'was regarded with dismay by the Shah and the Envoy, and it was determined to make every effort to follow, and if possible, to capture him.' George was part of a small contingent of British troops invited to make the attempt.

The mission proved to be a frustrating game of cat and mouse as they gave Dost Mohammed chase through the precipitous, mountain terrain of the Hindu Kush. Progress was continually hampered by the unwillingness of a contingent of Afghan horsemen under the command of Haji Khan Kakar to keep sufficient pace and provide the necessary guidance. George regarded the chief as 'a notorious scoundrel' and had 'no confidence or faith' in him or his guides.[20] At various times when intelligence told them they were within striking distance, he recorded with exasperation that his 'Afghan friends could not be prevailed upon to budge further than they liked'.[21] The Haji, of course, had no desire to see the Amir captured, declaring at one point to the mission leader, Captain James Outram, 'if you do encounter Dost Mohammed Khan, not one of the Afghans will draw a sword against him, nor will I be responsible that they do not turn against you in the melee.'[22] Although he wished to be seen as cooperating with the British as the best way to survive the current political upheaval, he was also conscious that circumstances could change. If the Dost was ever to regain power, the chieftain could still hope to salvage his fortunes having allowed the former ruler to escape. In the event, his delaying tactics proved sufficient. Outram's search party was forced to give up the chase at Bamian when they heard their prey had gone beyond the limits of the Shah's territory to seek refuge with the Amir of Bokhara. Despite the frustration of not capturing the Kabul chieftain, the 'hunting trip' had provided a good dose of excitement and camaraderie for George and his companions:

> You would have laughed as much as we did could you have seen us [thirteen officers] seated in a small tent, round a blanket, with a huge *dekchee* [degchi – cooking pot] in the centre, filled with four or five *moorghies* [chickens], half a sheep, peas, beans culled from the fields, all stewed together, with mountains of chupatties for our dinner. I declare I have not enjoyed myself more for many a day.[23]

Meanwhile, Shah Shuja and his entourage had made their triumphal entry into Kabul on 7th August, taking up residence in the dilapidated citadel and palace of Bala Hissar after a thirty-year absence. For the Bengal army, Kabul marked the campaign's final destination, after a march of 1,500-odd miles from Karnal cantonment (their first assembly point).[24] Although the primary objective had been achieved, Shah Shuja's arrival in the capital, as in Kandahar, was depicted by George Lawrence as an embarrassing failure. The inhabitants showed 'the most complete indifference to their new sovereign…expressing no sign of welcome or satisfaction at his accession to the throne. Evidently their hearts and affections were with their previous sovereign, now a wanderer beyond the Hindu Koosh.'[25] Once again, however, we must question George's account. For crucially he was not an eyewitness. After his unsuccessful attempt to capture Dost Mohammed, George's own arrival in Kabul was in fact on 17th August, some ten days after Shah Shuja had made his return. By contrast, Capt. Henry Havelock gauged a more positive mood at first hand. Although acknowledging that there was probably less personal affection for Shah Shuja than Dost Mohammed, he detected clear 'public satisfaction at having got rid of the exactions and oppressions of the Barukzye dominion, and of delight at receiving any king at the hands and under the auspices of the Ungreeze [Angrezi] Feringees.'[26] Similarly, in Major William Hough's account, the reception was considered respectful: 'The people were very orderly; there were immense crowds, every place in the town was filled with them. As the king advanced, they stood up, and when he passed on, they reseated themselves.'[27]

The Simla Manifesto had explicitly mentioned the withdrawal of the army once 'the independence and integrity of Afghanistan' had been established, but it was soon evident that Shah Shuja could not be left without some degree of British protection. Even Macnaghten admitted that there was insufficient support to guarantee his security. The new king, it was argued, needed time to win the affections of the Afghan people, and as Dost Mohammed still lurked beyond the Hindu Kush, there remained the possibility of his return to raise the flag of rebellion. It was decided therefore that most of the Bengal division would remain in Afghanistan for the winter, while the Bombay column would make its return to India by mid-September. The following month Sir John Keane, who, like Macnaghten, received a baronetcy for his efforts, handed over military command to Sir Willoughby Cotton and returned via the Khyber Pass accompanied by the remaining Bengal contingent.

The prolonged stay in Kabul also meant promotion for George. He now became the Envoy's military secretary thereby occupying a central role in the British administration. Although nominally military in character, George's responsibilities were to all intents and purposes political. Tasked with mastering the art of diplomacy, Afghan style, he was called up to act as coadjutor between the Envoy and the restored king:

> The transition from purely regimental to civil duty was sudden and complete and at first not a little embarrassing. My position was by no means the sinecure the secretary of an embassy is represented generally to be, who has only to look solemn and mysterious; on the contrary, my employment was incessant, and any leisure I could snatch had to be devoted to the study of Persian, as without an intimate knowledge of that language it would have been impossible for me to carry on the multifarious duties devolving on me.[28]

From November 1839 to May 1840 George and the Envoy attended Shah Shuja and his entourage at Jalalabad to escape the worst of the winter. It was a period of relative tranquillity as the threat of Dost Mohammed had temporarily receded. When they made their way back to Kabul, George noted that the king's return was greeted 'amidst the acclamations of crowds of his subjects, whose demonstrations of welcome, although tardy, might still lead to the conviction that he was the most popular of sovereigns.'[29] Even a brief show of resistance by Ghilzai tribesmen at Tazi, near Qalat-i-Ghilzai on the road between Kandahar and Ghazni, was swiftly dealt with by a combination of General Nott's forces based at Kandahar, and the offer of an annual subvention from the British in return for the promise of good conduct.[30]

But then came the news in August that Dost Mohammed had escaped the confines of Bukhara and was intent on raising the standard of holy war or *jihad* amongst the various tribes along the Bamian frontier, northwest of Kabul. The scale of the rebellion took the British off-guard and served to encourage some Afghan levies to abandon their colours and join the Barakzai cause. Reinforcements were requested and on 18th September a force led by Colonel William Dennie engaged Dost Mohammed and his Uzbek allies near Bamian. Despite their superior numbers and control of several forts dominating the valley, Dennie's troops managed to disperse the enemy by sustained artillery fire followed by a cavalry charge. The British viewed it as a watershed moment, with George expressing a palpable sense of relief: 'This success was very opportune, for the disaffected among the townspeople at Cabul had spread many evil reports of serious disasters having happened to our force at Bameean.'[31] On 20th September George was given charge of offering congratulations to Shah Shuja on the 'defeat of Dost Mahomed and the dispersion of his allies'.[32]

Although Dost Mohammed's forces had been scattered, the disposed Amir continued to provide encouragement for others to rebel. The chiefs of Kohistan, a region to the north of Kabul, had become increasing disillusioned with the new regime and its failure to reward them for their part in fermenting opposition to Barakzai rule.[33] Tapping into this discontent, Dost Mohammed now provided the focal point in a guerrilla war aimed at attacking government outposts. In response, a brigade under General Sale spent much of October employing slash-and-burn tactics against rebel held villages. In one assault on a stronghold George's good friend, Edward Conolly, was killed. In the absence of a chaplain, George did his best to conduct the funeral service: 'it was all I could do to read the service over the remains of my valued friend without breaking down.'[34]

Despite the high number of casualties and wanton destruction, the campaign appeared to be heading towards a long, drawn-out stalemate. Until, that is, the morning of 2nd November when Sale's force arrived in the small valley of Parwan Darra where they came suddenly face to face with Dost Mohammed and a few hundred of his horsemen. Realising that this was their best chance to capture the Amir, a few of the officers quickly led the charge only to find that their cavalry squadrons had not followed them – partly the result, according to George, of countermanding orders given by Perceval Lord, the local political agent. Now exposed amidst the enemy and without support, those officers at the forefront were soon either killed or severely wounded. Despite this initial fiasco, the British managed to recover their composure, and through the actions of the 37th Native Infantry they were able to drive off Dost Mohammed's forces. But once more the Amir had evaded capture.

In the end the surrender of Dost Mohammed was all rather civilised and happened when the British Envoy had least expected it. On 4th November Macnaghten and Lawrence were returning from their usual evening ride and had been mulling over the depressing news from Parwan Darra when a horseman in the courtyard of the Envoy's residence surprised them. Riding up to Lawrence, he asked if his companion was 'the Lord Sahib'. Upon confirmation, the stranger reached for the Envoy's bridle and exclaimed: "the Ameer, the Ameer!" A startled Macnaghten and Lawrence instinctively turned around. 'Looking behind me on the instant,' recorded the latter,

I saw another horseman close to us, who, riding up, threw himself off his horse, and seized hold of the Envoy's stirrup leather and then his hand, which he put to his forehead and his lips as a sign of submission. Sir William instantly dismounted, and said to the Ameer, "You are welcome, you are welcome;" and then led him through the Residency garden to his own room. Dost Mahomed, on entering, prostrated himself in Oriental fashion, and taking off his turban, touched the floor with his forehead. On rising, he delivered up his sword in token of surrender, saying "he had now no more use for it." The Envoy, immediately returning him his sword, assured the Ameer of every consideration being shown to him, notwithstanding he had so long opposed the views of the British Government. To which the Ameer replied that "it was his destiny, and he could not oppose it."[35]

The Dost told Macnaghten that he had already made up his mind to surrender prior to the engagement at Parwan Darra, notwithstanding 'his temporary success in that affair'. For the moment the Amir calculated that the time had come to submit to the British presumably in the hope that at some future date he would be able to revitalise his fortunes. After some further discussions, he was then put under the temporary care of an anxious George Lawrence:

I scarcely closed my eyes during the two nights he remained under my charge, every now and then getting up and looking into the tent to see that he was still there; it seemed all so much like a dream that at last we should have the Dost safe in our hands, that I could hardly credit it except by frequent visits to the tent.[36]

The British could feel justifiably gratified by this unexpected turn of events. The main source of opposition in Afghanistan had been taken into their custody without the need for further military exertions. As 1840 drew to a close, Macnaghten and his colleagues could now look forward with some confidence to the new year and the hope of a stable Afghanistan under Shah Shuja. Dost Mohammed and his large family were packed off to India and thus removed from making further mischief in the country. Indeed, as Sir Willoughby Cotton handed over the chief command to his successor, General Elphinstone, in December 1840, his farewell remark reflected a not uncommonly held view at the time: 'You will have nothing to do here. All is peace'.[37] It was a similar response from George: 'The wild tribes seemed suddenly to forget their old feuds and lawless habits, and to subside into peaceful subjects, while our European soldiers were able, for the first time since our arrival, to walk out in all directions for miles, unarmed, with the most perfect safety.'[38]

Political Agent at Ferozepur

Meanwhile, Henry had been performing his duties as the Political Agent at Ferozepur since January 1839. The British had taken over the small Cis-Sutlej state in 1835, through the doctrine of lapse, when Rani Lachmi Kaur had died without heir.[1] Occupying an area of about one hundred square miles on the southern bank of the River Sutlej and to the west of Ludhiana, the state had gained a deserved reputation for crime and poverty. Cattle-stealing was widespread and boundary disputes between villages were numerous. Watchtowers, wrote Henry, 'were the most striking points in the landscape, and gave fearful proof of the insecurity of all around'.[2] Set within what was then a barren region with precious little land under cultivation, the town itself was noted for its squalidness, consisting of 'little more than an assemblage of zamindars' huts, mixed up with a few banyas' shops, and overhung by a crumbling fortress'.[3] Within the fort where Henry and Honoria's *state apartments* – the latter's mocking description of their accommodation which was little more than a couple of rooms that had neither window or fireplace and where the doors could not be shut properly. 'We suffered much from cold for three months, and then the heat was excessive,' recounted Honoria.[4]

This unedifying backwater, however, was in the process of transformation. With the advent of the Anglo-Afghan War, Ferozepur quickly became an important frontier post for the Army of the Indus. Troops, military supplies and food provisions were assembled at the sprawling military station, before making their way through the Punjab and onto Afghanistan. Much of Henry's duties during the first half of 1839 were focused on procuring enough boats and camels needed to transport supplies. On 22nd March, for example, he informed Capt. Woodward, the station's commissariat officer, that '60 or 80 Sutlej boats' were to be 'expected at the [Ferozepur] ghat tomorrow or the next day'.[5] A few days later he confirmed that twelve boats had been repaired, with four or five now available for daily use. By early April a further twenty-five boats were ready. Supply, however, did not keep pace with demand, and by June Henry was seeking assistance from other stations: 'May I request,' he told one officer, 'that you will do me the favour to send me as many boats as you can command, and further that you will inform me what assistance I may expect from you…as boats are just now urgently required and government is desirous of securing a bi-monthly dispatch from the Ferozepur ghat.'[6] The unrelenting nature of the work led to strained relations with some colleagues. On the delivery of one consignment of boats, Henry struggled to keep his temper in check as he tried to allay the safety concerns of one officer: 'I am just now on my way to the ghat and hope to set matters right, but as I do not wish to have yet more responsibility than is my due, I hope General Duncan will send the [military supplies] by land or overwise if Major Jones continues to think the boats unsafe.'[7]

Securing the services of boatmen and camel drivers proved equally challenging, and was largely the result, Henry believed, of insufficient remuneration: 'The boatmen are very badly off and are daily deserting,' he told Woodward in early April, 'unless an advance is made to them I see little chance of any remaining, when we shall have great difficulty in procuring others.'[8] It was a similar picture for camel drivers. When Henry offered favourable terms to one group, it drew him 'into a long and vexatious correspondence' with the commissariat officer.[9] In a dispute that became increasingly acrimonious and conflated with other petty matters, Henry argued that it was pointless to penny-pinch if the government wanted to attract or retain these vital support services.

The management of the local treasury was also included in Henry's remit. This became a particular bugbear as financial bookkeeping, by his own admission, was never his *forte*. Furthermore, he had inherited an under-staffed office, with no writers except a treasurer who was as inexperienced as himself. The 'heavy duty and great responsibility' of this position, he told Col. C.M. Wade in January 1840, involved him 'making advances and paying up arrears … to all comers and goers; whether officers or private soldiers'. Although he had little issue undertaking the regular monthly payment to the troops at the station, it was the 'constant adjustment of small sums' performed on an ad hoc basis that irked him the most. The time-consuming burden of reconciling these accounts with different paymasters based elsewhere forced him to seek Wade's permission 'to have a responsible writer on a fair salary' to cope with the extra work. Failing that, he wished 'to be relieved of the duty of paying up arrears or making advances in the military department'.[10] By this stage, Henry had already incurred the censure of the Accountant General over the wrong numbering of bills in his weekly statements, a charge he did his best to refute: 'In your remarks on my conduct,' he told the Accountant General, 'you seem to have overlooked the fact when I took charge of this office an erroneous system was in play and that with a majority of the questionable bills I had nothing whatever to say, having acted to the best of my understanding.'[11]

Unsurprisingly, a tone of exasperation can easily be detected in much of Henry's correspondences during this period. With limited resources, he battled hard to provide the necessary logistical support and banking facilities, not to mention organising postal services for soldiers in Afghanistan – an onerous task, he estimated, that could take up to ten hours a day and was only manageable with the help of his devoted Honoria.[12] For all this, he felt he had received precious little gratitude, plenty of criticism and inadequate financial reward. He vented his frustrations to his friend and mentor, James Thomason, then Secretary to the Government of the North-Western Provinces, who was at first sympathetic: 'I am sorry to hear you have been so badly treated in the matter of allowances. What can be done? Don't injure yourself by over-work and let us hope for better days.'[13] Henry placed his faith in Thomason's ability to alleviate his circumstances but in his then current role there was no patronage to offer.[14] After several letters had passed between them on the subject, it was evident that Henry's peevishness and strong sense of injustice had begun to grate on his counsellor who, in a letter dated 20th June 1840, cautioned his friend's use of language and told him to count his blessings: 'You might have told me your mind a little less tartly, [for] you risked by your bark the loss of a very dear friend…I cannot help directing your attention in one alleviation of your lot, for which I would gladly exchange all I have. Your wife and child are with you and well. Is that nothing?'[15]

As a measure of his frustrations, Henry began to explore other possible career openings. His focus turned to opportunities in Afghanistan and once more his brother George provided a useful link. The latter's appointment as Military Secretary to the Envoy had left his former role as Auditor vacant, and at Rs 1000 per month, it was Rs 300 more than the Ferozepur salary. Henry was keen to be considered for the role, although it placed George in an awkward position. While wishing to help his younger brother, he fully sympathised with Honoria's objections to Henry's potential transfer to Afghanistan. For it was assumed that the move would entail bringing Honoria. George, though, was adamant that the country was no place for European females while he also feared for Henry's safety. Much better, he felt, was for his brother to place his faith in George Clerk to aid his promotion prospects.[16] In December 1839 Henry appeared to discount the role when writing to his sister Letitia.[17] But by July 1840 he was still lobbying for the position to John Colvin, Private Secretary to the Governor-General.[18] Colvin's reply, however, soon quashed the idea on the basis that there were already enough claimants for the role currently employed in Afghanistan.[19]

Whatever his career frustrations, Henry still flung himself into his work. In an 1841 report to Thomas Metcalfe, Agent to the Governor-General in the North-West Provinces, he proudly listed the improvements he had spearheaded at Ferozepur. The town's population had 'nearly doubled within the last two years' while commercial activity had correspondingly increased with the creation of a 'sudder bazaar of 500 shops'. The old fort had been repaired, and a new wall built around the town. A hospital and courthouse had also been constructed, while streets were widened, new roads laid out, and drainage improved. To reduce crime, *chowkidars* were appointed, regular police patrols instituted and *lumberdars* [village headmen] were held responsible for the conduct of their tenants. 'It has been my object,' he told Metcalfe, 'to reclaim the *Dogurs* and other pastoral classes from their lawless habits, by making the jail a real punishment to those convicted and by offering the well-disposed every inducement to cultivate their lands; the great increase of cultivation within the territory and the removal of some of the worst characters from my jurisdiction show that something has been done.' During the period cultivators were removed from Ferozepur town to populate nineteen new hamlets in the neighbourhood, while 'a very light [revenue] settlement for 5 years' was introduced.[20]

Equally significant was Henry's boundary settlement of the neighbouring state of Faridkot, another Cis-Sutlej principality under British protection though still ostensibly independent. Disputes over the boundary had led to long-running blood feuds with no less than nine other contiguous states including Ferozepur. Many outrages took place during the planting season while, throughout the year, border raids and cattles thefts were common; all of which, it was estimated, claimed some five hundred lives annually.[21] The prospects for an amicable solution must have seemed slight when agents of the Faridkot chief first requested Henry's services. For Henry, however, the assignment provided a welcome challenge and release from less savoury aspects of his Ferozepur duties. Covering the period September to December 1839, his *modus operandi* was instructive. This was no desk-bound sinecure but required him to spend long hours in the saddle armed with all his experience as a revenue surveyor. Having found that the boundary depositions sent to him at Ferozepur varied 'egregiously', he was anxious to ascertain the situation at first hand: 'I confess I learned more in the field by looking at the ground and talking to the people than I did in *cutcherry*,' he informed his superior, George Clerk, in his boundary settlement report.[22] Earlier adjudications passed in favour of one or other of the contending parties often left him 'at a loss to reconcile them to the present status'. At one location, the previous officer, Capt. Murray, it seems, had merely inspected a portion of the boundary through a telescope positioned on a distant tower. Henry, by contrast, 'rode in all directions, and got a good acquaintance with the localities'.[23]

In defining the boundary, the preferred outcome was for arbitrators to be appointed from each side to reach agreement on where the line should lie. Often, though, Henry had to intervene and firmly steer the parties towards a resolution. On one occasion when both parties procrastinated, he reached for his theodolite and began to fix the boundary himself. This prompted them into action, and they carried on the boundary demarcation in the direction originally set until other diversionary tactics were deployed: 'each side making the most absurd claims, showing imaginary sites of old towns, and fictitious towers and tanks, making me constantly ride two or three miles right or left to see what they knew perfectly well never existed.' In the end, Henry took matters into his own hands and proceeded to complete marking the boundary himself 'giving as equal a division as possible, regarding as hitherto, natural marks and actual possession, however brief, of lands that had not before been cultivated.'[24]

Some portions of the boundary which had suffered only minor infringements from one side's cultivators or the other were easily resolved by simply ordering that a ditch be cut between boundary pillars. Other proposed demarcations, however, were initially greeted with howls of injustice by one or other of the aggrieved parties. Henry invariable dismissed these outcries, convinced that there were mere ploys designed to dupe him into making favourable alterations. Only on one instance when 'considerable opposition was made' did he feel it necessary to slightly alter the boundary pillars to the advantage of one party.[25] Despite the challenges of reaching a settlement, Henry found that once due enquiry was made and the boundary marks established, his decisions were invariably respected: 'At least among the many outrages committed within the last 18 months,' he would later write, 'I know of none occasioned by disputes on those borders, where formerly so many lives were yearly sacrificed, but on the contrary I have since been warmly greeted by many who at the time were most violent.'[26]

A key factor in the success of the Faridkot boundary settlement was the perception of Henry as an impartial moderator. Before carrying out the demarcation based on the principle of equitable division, he tells us, he would listen patiently to all parties concerned and then measure the disputed land in their presence. Another crucial element was his resolute action: 'I have not gone the common and usual way [of] issuing decrees never to be executed,' he explained to his sister Letitia, 'but almost at the bayonet point, certainly at the spear and sword edge. I have enforced my own orders and while on the spot put up [boundary] pillars all around the territory.'[27] Part of Henry's success must also be attributed to his Indian assistants which he gratefully acknowledged in his settlement report. *Munshi* Golab Singh proved to be 'a valuable public servant', while *Ameen* Ally Baccus 'who, though much fatigued, very patiently performed good service without imputation'. The *Amin* [Indian surveyor], he pointedly told Clerk, 'gave me much assistance, without which I should have found difficulty in getting through my work.'[28] Henry's Faridkot settlement bears an uncanny resemblance to John's boundary work at Etawah. Both men deployed similar techniques and encountered the same initial hostility. Yet their steadfastness and apparent impartiality paved the way for settlements that were almost universally accepted. Similarly, both men gained notable kudos for their efforts, and in Henry's case led to a demand for his services elsewhere: 'I have been several times entreated by the Mundote [Mamdot] and Khye Agents, as well as cultivators, to settle their boundaries with one another, the Lahore Vukeel has in like manner urged on me to do so, and also to define the limits of his own jageer.'[29]

During Henry's three-year stint at Ferozepur, domestic arrangements were dictated by the Indian climate. Honoria had suffered greatly during her pregnancy (Jan-Sept 1839) and any thought of her or her young child remaining on the plains during the hot Punjab summer was now firmly discounted. From March to November each year, both she and son, Alick would spend their time in the Simla hills, particularly at Sabathu, close to where a military hill station had been established. For Honoria it was a relief to be placed in such pleasant surroundings: 'Here we are, enjoying together this lovely climate,' she told a friend in May 1841, 'our improved health, our children's well-being, and the very great luxury of perfect quiet, which, after the whirl of Ferozepoor, is unspeakably grateful.'[30] Henry, for the most part, continued his work at Ferozepur, with sporadic visits when he was able to do so. In March 1841, however, he suffered a serious relapse of his recurring malaria and was ordered to spent six months recuperating in the hills with his family.

Time spent at Sabathu, however, was a mixture of both joy and sorrow. On 16th November 1840, Henry and Honoria were blessed with the arrival of a baby girl, who they christened Letitia Catherine. But tragedy was not far off. Their peaceful idyll was shattered when both their children contracted malaria in the summer of 1841. Under a treatment of leaches and warm baths, Alick recovered, but Letitia did not. In the words of Honoria, she 'fell asleep' on 1st August, and was buried in the local garrison cemetery. Heartbroken by the loss, the Lawrences moved later that summer to the nearby but higher elevated hill station of Kasauli (above the 'malaria belt') where they built a small cottage called 'Sunnyside' which is still in existence today. 'From our house,' Henry later wrote, 'we can see the burial-ground at Subathoo, where the mortal remains of our little angel lie. It is on a solitary hill above Subathoo, ten miles from Kussowlee.'[31]

At both Ferozepur and Sabathu, Henry and Honoria still found time to devote themselves to literary pursuits. Their combined efforts produced a work then entitled, *Some Passages in the Life of an Adventurer in the Punjaub*. Serialised anonymously in the *Delhi Gazette*, it would later be fashioned into book form four years later during their stay in Nepal. Another notably effort was *Anticipatory Chapters of Indian History* also published in the *Delhi Gazette*. Based on the reminiscences of a fictitious Irish soldier called Darby Connor, it was a simple, literary device for Henry to express his own criticism of the Afghan War by questioning the quality of the army's manpower and its decision-making abilities. Yet what was remarkable about the piece was the prescient storyline: An Afghan revolt had subjected the British to a crushing defeat and had forced their retreat to India. Darby Connor told his readers that few soldiers 'recrossed the Attock' and those that did brought tales of misery and despair. 'All Hindustan was in a blaze; the cry of "The Feringhee raj is over!" resounded from one coast to another.'[32] Within a matter of months, Henry's *Anticipatory Chapters* would become fact.

The Rising

If the British had expected the new year of 1841 to continue in the same peaceful manner as the previous one had ended, they were to be sorely disappointed. Discontent soon broke out in the Afghan provinces. The restored monarchy of Shah Shuja had raised the expectations of the Durrani chieftains of Kandahar who believed the oppressions of the former Barakzai regime would be overturned. They had now become impatient. Unrest centred on Zamindawar, a district situated to the right of the Helmand River and northwest of Kandahar. Initial attempts to collect the land tax had met with opposition, forcing revenue officers and a contingent of the Shah's horse to beat a hasty retreat. To restore order, a detachment of General Nott's troops was able to disperse a sizeable force of some 1500 Durrani horse in early January. According to the local political officer, Major Henry Rawlinson, the cause of the unrest was not simply the result of the land tax demand but rather more worrying, it was the product of a changing mindset. Rawlinson believed that the agitation had been encouraged by 'his Majesty's clemency' which gave the tribes the impression that the Shah was eager 'to manage the Douranees through the agency of their hopes rather than of their fears'.[1] The insurgency continued throughout the spring and into early summer until a temporary lull in August. Meanwhile, the Ghilzais were rebelling in eastern Afghanistan in and around the town of Qalat-i-Ghilzai. The source of this unrest was linked to the British rebuilding of the town's fortress with the intention of establishing a strong garrison. Located on the main Kandahar-Kabul route and within the heart of Ghilzai country, the work was viewed as an act of provocation. Several bloody encounters throughout spring and summer ensued until early August when British forces forced the Ghilzais to come to terms.

Throughout 1841 it was apparent that Macnaghten had adopted an overly sanguine view of the British position in Afghanistan, and had flatly refused to believe the reports of Rawlinson and other political officers who warned of growing discontent. Indeed, the Envoy blamed Rawlinson for taking 'an unwarrantably gloomy view' of British control over the country.[2] From his distant post in Kabul, without the benefit of first-hand knowledge, it was perhaps easy for the Envoy to be lulled into a false sense of security. Afterall he could plausibly argue that both the Durrani and the Ghilzai revolts had been suppressed by mid-August, while two months later, a military expedition to put down rebellion in the north-western districts of Afghanistan (Tereen and Dehrawat) had successfully led to the capture and execution of the rebel chief. It is equally noteworthy that George Lawrence gave no hint in his *Reminiscences* of the unrest taking place in southern Afghanistan. Instead, as another winter was spent at Jalalabad with Shah Shuja and his entourage, he merely took note of the king's increasing exasperation over his circumscribed role.[3] Apart from some tribal disturbances in the Nuzeran (Nazian) valley in February, this was the only case of unrest reported by George in the year up to October 1841, leaving him to conclude that 'the country was at this time tranquil, and everything seemed so secure'. His thoughts now turned to personal matters as his 'health had begun to fail for incessant labour'.[4] On medical advice, he now looked forward to taking a year's furlough, while Macnaghten also made plans to take up the lucrative Company position of Governor of Bombay. Events, however, would soon dictate otherwise.

For much of 1841 Governor-General Auckland and his Indian administration had become all too aware of the crippling costs of governing Afghanistan. By October the demand to make economies was forcing Macnaghten to make some painful choices. Yet instead of cutting back on obvious areas such as the Shah's household expenses, he chose to halve the annual subsidies of 80,000 rupees to the eastern Ghilzai tribes. It was a critical miscalculation and its repercussions, as George recounted, were quickly felt:

> The chiefs, indignant at what they regarded, and with some justice, as a breach of faith, flew to arms, and commenced operations by plundering a rich kaffila (caravan) at Tezeen (Tezin), and then taking up a strong position in the Khord Cabul defiles, closed the pass, and bade defiance to the Shah and his European allies. Thus commenced a conflagration which soon spread over the length and breadth of Afghanistan, producing most unlooked for and disastrous results.[5]

Despite the unrest, which a force under General Sale unsuccessfully endeavoured to subdue, George still maintained that the atmosphere in Kabul was relaxed; there were no signs of panic. He noted, for example, that the property of General Elphinstone, who was to return to India on account of ill health, fetched high prices at auction. Similarly, when George had breakfast with Sir Alexander Burnes in the heart of the city on 24th October, he found him to be in 'high spirits at the prospect of succeeding Sir W. Macnaghten and exercising *at last* the supreme authority in Affghanistan'.[6] For the remainder of October, the city had the appearance of 'complete tranquillity'.[7] But it would not last for long.

On 2nd November George had just returned home from his regular early morning walk and was about to begin his work for the day when a messenger suddenly arrived in a frenzied state. The news was not good. The city's shops had closed and its streets were filled with groups of armed men who had surrounded the houses of Alexander Burnes and Captain Johnson, paymaster to Shah Shuja's army. George immediately went in search of the Envoy whom he found in deep discussion with General Elphinstone and three other officers. Macnaghten handed George a hastily written note from Burnes who had urgently requested help. When asked his opinion on the course of action, George strongly advised that 'not a moment should be lost' in despatching a regiment to Burnes' house within the city and that the ringleaders of this disturbance, believed to be Aminullah Khan Logari and Abdullah Khan Achakzai (two disgruntled chieftains), be quickly apprehended. It was a seemingly sensible proposal but, according to George, it was dismissed out of hand as being 'one of pure insanity, and under the circumstances utterly unfeasible'.[8] Despite the knockback, George ventured another suggestion: that Brigadier Shelton's forces, then currently positioned on the outlying Siyah Sang hills, be moved immediately to the citadel of Bala Hissar where they could more usefully deployed 'to act as circumstances required'. Yet again, his fellow officers procrastinated. Although the second proposal was agreed in principle, General Elphinstone insisted that the force be merely put on standby, only to act if Shah Shuja required its presence. It appeared that only the George Lawrence appreciated the gravity of the situation – a pattern that would become all too familiar in the days and weeks ahead.

In the meantime, George was tasked with making the two-mile journey to the Bala Hissar to inform Shah Shuja of the plan to utilise Sheldon's brigade subject to the king's request. There was now a palpable sense of danger in the air: 'I started forth-with, mounted on a powerful horse of Sir William's,' George recounted, 'and taking four troopers of the escort with me, directed them to keep close up to me, to use their spurs if necessary, but on no account to pull up or stop.'[9] This was sound advice. For on the way he was suddenly confronted by an Afghan rushing towards him, brandishing a large double-handed sword. The assailant made a 'furious lunge' towards him, but George instinctively threw his stick at him, drew his own sword, and made his horse thrust towards him. The attacker was then shot dead by one of the troopers. Soon afterwards the party came under fire from another group of men concealed in a nearby ditch. But fortunately, thanks to their hard galloping, George and his escort escaped unscathed.

On reaching the royal citadel, George found an agitated king lamenting the outbreak of violence but quickly pointing the finger at Macnaghten for not executing certain refractory chiefs: 'Is it not just what I always told the Envoy would happen if he would not follow my advice?' It was then revealed that a force under Shah Shuja's son, Fatteh Jang and his prime minister, Osman Khan, had already entered the city to confront the rebels. 'I have no doubt they will suppress the tumult,' the King confidently told Lawrence who was encouraged by early reports indicating that the King's forces were gaining the upper hand. This optimism, though, was soon crushed by the sudden, bloody arrival of Lieutenant Sturt, the garrison engineer, who had been given the task of liaising with Brigadier-General Shelton. Sword in hand, he was 'bleeding profusely' after having been stabbed at the citadel's gate. The effect of seeing Sturt's injuries was to play on the King's mind and his concern for his son and prime minister. Although George was insistent that they should remain in the city, Shah Shuja after some hesitation decided to recall them. It was to draw an angry and ominous response from Osman Khan: 'By recalling us just in the moment of victory your troops will be defeated, and evil will fall on all.'[10]

Soon afterwards George went to the Siyah Sang hills near to the cantonments to summon Sheldon's force to the Bala Hissar. He then proceeded to the Residency to update the Envoy on the current situation. The latter was relieved to see his military secretary in the flesh as rumours had circulated of his death. George, however, was very much alive to events now unfolding. For when he returned to the Bala Hissar, he expressed exasperation over Sheldon's inactivity:

> Shelton, on my joining him, seemed almost beside himself, not knowing how to act, and with incapacity stamped on every feature of his face. He immediately asked me what he should do, and on my replying 'Enter the city at once,' he sharply rebuked me, saying, 'My force is inadequate, and you don't appear to know what street firing is.' 'You asked my opinion,' I rejoined, 'and I have given it. It is what I would do myself.'[11]

Realising that further argument on this point to be futile, George requested the repositioning of two artillery guns to a more elevated spot so that they could fire more effectively on the part of the city then currently in revolt. But while Sheldon agreed, his subordinate officer, Captain Nicholls, refused on account of his horses being incapable of dragging the guns up such a steep ascent. At this point, George lost his patience, exclaiming to Shelton: 'Really, sir, if you allow your officers to make objections instead of obeying, nothing can be done.' In the end it was two companies of the Shah's own Native Infantry who repositioned the guns. The Envoy's military secretary then left the Bala Hissar to return to the Residency, irked by both Shelton's and Nicholls' inaction.[12]

That night the news came that Sir Alexander Burnes, his brother, Lieutenant Charles Burnes, and Captain William Broadfoot had been 'cut to pieces' by the angry mob, while Johnson's treasury of £17,000 had been plundered. Two small outposts in the city commanded by Captains Trevor and Mackenzie were, however, still managing to hold out with only a handful of men. Like Burnes before, they too had sent messages asking for aid and once more George called for action. Yet his suggestion to send out two companies led by himself to reinforce Trevor and Mackenzie drew a predicable response: 'My proposal was condemned by the staff as most imprudent, as they feared exposing their men to street firing.'[13] Another opportunity of nipping the rebellion in the bud had been missed:

> Vacillation and incapacity ruled in our military councils, and paralysed the hearts of those who should have acted with energy and decision. By their deplorable pusillanimity an accidental *emeute*, which could have been quelled on the moment by the prompt employment of a small force, became a formidable insurrection.[14]

Did Macnaghten show sufficient understanding of the crisis and was this clearly communicated to the military authorities? In these first few critical moments of the uprising George Lawrence strongly defended the conduct of his superior: 'the Envoy alone comprehended the gravity of the crisis and showed his usual resolution and energy of character.' The underlying problem was the limited scope of the Envoy's powers: 'He could do no more than urge his views, which were for immediate action, on the chief military authorities,' but 'he had no power to enforce their obedience,' it was maintained.[15] This sympathetic view, however, was not shared by Lieutenant Vincent Eyre, Commissary of Ordinance: 'Unhappily, Sir William Macnaghten at first made light of the insurrection, and, by his representations as to the general feeling of the people towards us, not only deluded himself, but misled the General in council.'[16]

Lawrence was also willing to absolve General Elphinstone of ultimate responsibility for the tardy British response. The general, aged fifty-eight, had not seen active service since Waterloo and had no prior Indian experience. Although he believed the General to be 'a skilful soldier, well versed in all branches of his profession, and a naturally brave man,' he was unfortunately dogged by severe rheumatic gout making him 'perfectly incapable of exertion'. Instead, criticism was directed towards those who had pressurised Elphinstone into accepting command of British forces in Afghanistan in the first place. Without naming him, he clearly meant Lord Auckland.[17] Lawrence's greatest censure, however, was reserved for Elphinstone's military staff who were characterised by the 'most deplorable vacillation and absence of energy'. By the end of the insurrection's first day, there little cause for optimism: 'Thus the 2nd of November slowly waned away, and at last closed in apathy and confusion. Sorely cast down in mind and greatly fatigued in body, I went to rest, with many a sad foreboding for the coming day.'[18]

Such foreboding appeared justified when on the following day a vain attempt to establish a line of communication between the cantonments and Bala Hissar once more exposed the ineffectualness of the military authorities. Even the relatively simple task of taking over the nearby gardens, Shah Bagh, and the Mohammed Sharif Fort, which would have made the commissariat stores (bizarrely located in another exposed fort beyond the cantonments) more secure, was ignored. Both locations were soon occupied by the rebels. Meanwhile, Captains Trevor and Mackenzie were eventually forced to evacuate their outposts in the city when their plea for reinforcements went unheeded. Intelligence from Trevor, revealing that certain communities within the city, such as the Qizilbash (Persian descendants of Nadir Shah's troops) who had initially held aloof from the rebels, confirmed Lawrence's conviction 'that had troops been thrown into the town on the 2nd and 3rd November, the insurrection would have been stifled at the commencement'.[19]

As the Envoy's right-hand man, Lawrence would ruefully witness a frustrating pattern of procrastination and inactivity over the coming days and weeks. Elphinstone's indecision over a plan to secure the commissariat fort, for example, quickly led to the inevitable: The fort fell into rebel hands without a struggle on 6th November, and its loss was quickly felt. Half-rations were put in place, while Macnaghten was forced to negotiate supplies of grain from the chief of the village of Bemaroo, situated a short distance to the rear of the cantonments. Recent events had now exposed the vulnerability of the British position. Incredibly, the cantonments had been built on low-lying swampy ground overlooked by a low range of hills and by several small forts and buildings. All within musket range. Yet Macnaghten and Lawrence's 'earnest entreaties' to General Elphinstone for the takeover of the Bemaroo and Rikab Bashi Forts and for demolishing the outlying buildings were met with 'apathy and indifference'.[20] When Macnaghten made a subsequent request for Elphinstone to send troops to secure the Rikab Bashi Fort on the morning of 10th November, it was met with the customary refusal. Only the Envoy's persistence on this point eventually forced the military authorities into action. Later that day British troops under Brigadier Shelton were able to retake the Rikab Bashi Fort while four other forts nearby were destroyed after large quantities of grain were taken back to the cantonments.

The action had the effect of temporarily quelling insurgent activity, and for the following three days Lawrence was able to walk three miles from the cantonments 'without seeing an enemy'. It was a crucial moment for the British to press the advantage. But the recent fighting had come at a price – two hundred soldiers mostly European had been killed – making the military authorities more reluctant than ever to take further military action. Soon the emboldened rebels returned. On 13th November they had positioned two guns on the Bemaroo hills overlooking the cantonments and had commenced firing. Yet again the Envoy's request for urgent military action was meet with 'the usual excuses and objections'. This time, though, Brigadier Shelton's 'stubborn opposition' raised the Envoy's ire to bursting point: 'Brigadier Shelton, if you will allow yourself to be thus bearded by the enemy, and will not advance and take these two guns by this evening, you must be prepared for any disgrace that may befall us.'[21]

When a force was eventually mustered, their engagement with the enemy was portrayed by Lawrence as 'a brilliant success'. Forcing the Afghans to hastily abandon their guns, British troops, he believed, could have 'easily followed them into and taken the city, had not the night come on'.[22] J.W. Kaye, however, depicted a less convincing British performance and argued that it would have been 'a mere shadow of a victory' had the enemy's guns not been taken. For many, on both sides, had fallen during what was at times a frenzied battle. 'It was the last success,' recounted Kaye, 'even of a doubtful and equivocal character, which the unhappy force was destined to achieve.'[23] Even Lawrence was forced to admit that Shelton's 'previous procrastination had rendered it impossible to reap any real advantage from the victory'.[24] Thereafter, there was little news to cheer. Towards the end of October rebellion had erupted in the Kolistan district which ultimately led to the abandonment of the British post at Charikar and the massacre of its Gurkha garrison. An injured Major Eldred Pottinger, the local political agent, and a handful of survivors were the only ones to stumble back to Kabul on 15th November. This tragedy was soon followed by reports of another – the massacre of Captain Woodburn and one hundred and fifty troops at Shekabad near Ghazni. Furthermore, having sent messengers to the other British posts of Ghazni, Qalat-i-Ghilzai, Kandahar and Jalalabad, there was still no word of reinforcements heading to relieve Kabul.

Meanwhile, Henry Lawrence, having returned to Ferozepur after six months sick leave, was one of the first on the frontier to receive news of the Kabul revolt. Both Henry and Honoria had been entertaining guests when they received the despatch announcing the murder of Sir Alexander Burnes and the 'fearful extend of the insurrection'. 'Henry was called out of the room,' recounted Honoria, but returned immediately, and merely gave me a look to go into the next room (Alick's crying soon gave me an excuse), where I found the letters just come, with his directions to copy them. I made the requisite copies, and left all ready, merely requiring his signature. Strange feeling at first it was, to copy out the lists of killed and wounded people we had seen, as if but yesterday and to dwell on the preparations for death and destruction.[25]

In the absence of clear direction from both Governor-General Auckland and Commander-in-Chief Sir Jasper Nicolls, Henry's superior, George Clerk, now Agent to the Governor-General for the affairs of the Punjab, took the initiative to mount a relief operation. Four regiments from Ferozepur and Ludhiana under the command of Brigadier Wild were ordered to march to Peshawar, then a border outpost of the Sikh kingdom. To facilitate their safe passage through the sovereign Sikh state, Clerk selected Henry to accompany the brigade and to liaise with their Sikh counterparts:

I feel much confidence in your knowledge of the Sikh authorities – in their reliance on your fair dealing – in your experience as a district officer and a people's protector, – and in your activity and decision to meet emergencies of every shape, that I have selected you to proceed for the present to Peshawur.[26]

Henry's stint at Ferozepur had been largely office based, where he had been harassed by 'petty but incessant demands on his time'.[27] His new role, by contrast, offered the prospect of exciting challenges in the field. This was the opportunity he had been craving: 'My earnest desire,' he told his superior only a few weeks earlier, 'is to be employed in any capacity in which you may deem my services most useful, in the event of operations being now, or at any other time, undertaken on the frontier.'[28] He had now got his wish. Moreover, in keeping with the political department ethos, Clerk had given him only the briefest of instructions thereby allowing broad scope for personal initiative. True to form, Henry quickly set to work organising logistical support for the brigade with one young officer, J.R. Becher, noting his vigorous contribution: 'All day long Lawrence was busied in measures calculated to hasten our progress – especially in throwing a bridge over the Sutlej – I remember how we were impressed by his energy…We all recognised in him the leading man of the camp. He was always sanguine, and ardent for an advance.'[29]

Back in Kabul, two weeks after the start of the rising, the Envoy in consultation with General Elphinstone considered their weakening position. According to George Lawrence, 'Sir William strongly urged holding out to the last, and vehemently opposed the idea of retreat, already broached, which would not only be disastrous but dishonourable, to be contemplated solely in the very last extremity.'[30] If the British were ultimately to retreat, it would mean sacrificing valuable property and abandoning Shah Shuja, 'the main object of our original entrance into Afghanistan'. Furthermore, retreat would expose the troops and camp followers to the harsh winter weather. Inevitably many would perish. It was therefore agreed that they should maintain their present position for the next ten days or so while Macnaghten tried to split the enemy using bribery. Through Mohan Lal, a government agent based in the heart of the city, money was offered to the Qizilbash and to some Durrani and Ghilzai chiefs.

In the meantime, the insurgents continued to probe the fringes of the cantonments. On 22nd November they took over the nearby village of Bemaroo. This was a direct threat to British security and the ability to procure food from outlining areas. A speedy and firm response was essential. Yet attempts the following day to do so were marred by delays, missed opportunities and poor tactical decisions. Crucially the rebels, following an initial British assault, were given time to regroup. Having taken up an exposed position on the brow of a hill overlooking the village and being in closely formed ranks, the British became easy prey for the long-range Afghan jezail rifles. The situation then went from bad to worse when the insurgents managed to capture the sole British gun. Only after some heroic efforts was it retaken. At this point, according to George, Shelton missed a chance to charge the enemy but for 'some unexplained cause nothing could induce him to stir from the hill'.[31] Instead it was the Afghans who now rushed the British formation, which eventual broke, forcing infantry, cavalry, and artillerymen to flee in confusion back to the cantonments. From the relative safety of its ramparts, George watched in horror as the tragedy unfolded: 'I could see from my post our flying troops hotly pursued and mixed up with the enemy, who were slaughtering them on all sides: the scene was so fearful that I can never forget it.' The British lost three hundred men during this fiasco, and once more the blame was firmly laid on one man's shoulders:

Nothing of course could justify the conduct of our troops; but the total incapacity of Brigadier Shelton, his reckless exposure of his men for hours on the top of a high ridge to a destructive fire, and his stubborn neglect to avail himself of the several opportunities offered to him throughout the day – by the temporary flight of the enemy, to complete their dispersion and prevent their rallying – go far to extenuate the soldiers, who had lost all confidence in a leader who had proved himself so incapable to command.[32]

Insult was added to injury when it was observed that the insurgents were mostly 'tradesmen and artisans of Cabul' and not the 'soldier tribes of the country' which could command at least a modicum of respect. This ragtag group now taunted the besieged by saying that 'the war was now over'. It was not far from the truth. The rout had a demoralising effect on the garrison leaving little appetite for fresh military initiatives. When the insurgents brazenly began destroying the bridge over the Kabul River linking the cantonments to the Bala Hissar, only a stone's throw away from the parapets, no attempt was made by the British to prevent them.

In the wake of this disaster, Macnaghten had invited a rebel delegation to the cantonments on 25th November, hoping to negotiate some sort of honourable outcome. Yet what the insurgents proposed amounted to nothing less than an unconditional surrender and the abandonment of Shah Shuja who had maintained his loyalty to the British cause despite offers to defect. It was too much for Macnaghten who broke up proceedings proclaiming: 'I prefer death to dishonour, and leave the issue to the God of battles.'[33] A two-week hiatus followed during which the Envoy continued to hope that a relieving force would liberate them. But by the end of the first week of December news came that heavy snow had blocked the route from Kandahar and via the Khyber Pass. Moreover, both General Sale's force at Jalalabad and the garrison at Ghazni were in a state of heavy siege and could offer no assistance. Their worst fears were confirmed: Macnaghten and his colleagues were now on their own.

Amongst this increasingly gloomy setting, a frosty meeting was held on 8th December between the Envoy and his military commanders. Elphinstone and his colleagues re-affirmed their opposition to further military operations and their belief that the only option, given the precarious state of the garrison, was a negotiated retreat to India.[34] Despite the General's unbending position, Macnaghten and Lawrence continued to pressurise him into action. An operation to capture the Khwaja Rawash Fort, some four miles from the cantonments, which contained large supplies of grain was eventually agreed only for it to be abandoned at the last minute.[35] The following day, at another conference, a proposal to abandon the cantonments and occupy the more secure Bala Hissar was predictably opposed by Elphinstone and Brigadier Shelton who continued to press for a negotiated retreat. According to Lawrence, Macnaghten 'most strenuously opposed' the idea, arguing that a retreat would bring annihilation for the British due to the freezing conditions as well as the untrustworthiness of the insurgents themselves. Such arguments were in vain, however, and the Envoy was reluctantly forced to abide by the views of the military authorities.

Cognizant of a severe lack of provisions and many wounded and sick, Macnaghten was forced to resume negotiations with the insurgents on 11th

December. Captains Trevor, Mackenzie, and Lawrence accompanied him to a location some 200 yards beyond the cantonment's ramparts overlooking the Kabul River where, for the first time, they met Akbar Khan, Dost Mohammed's favourite son, who had taken over the mantle of chief leader of the revolt. In preparation, the Envoy had produced an eighteen-point draft treaty, which made provision for the safe evacuation of all British troops from Afghanistan. Shah Shuja and his family would be given the option to either remain in Afghanistan or else return to India, while Dost Mohammed would be released from his confinement at Ludhiana and allowed to return home. After meeting for two hours, Akbar Khan and the chiefs ostensibly gave their consent to the articles. It was agreed that food and supplies would be given to the British who would then depart from the cantonments within three days, while hostages would be exchanged to ensure the treaty's compliance. Afterwards Macnaghten expressed what to many seemed like undue optimism:

> The terms I secured were the best obtainable, and the destruction of fifteen thousand human beings would little have benefited our country, whilst our government would have been almost compelled to avenge our fate at whatever cost....We shall part with the Afghans as friends, and I feel satisfied that any government which may be established hereafter will always be disposed to cultivate a good understanding with us.[36]

In preparation for their departure, the order was given for the British troops to evacuate Bala Hissar and return to the cantonments. But there were already worrying signs that parts of the treaty were being undermined. An attempt on 15th December by Akbar Khan to force his own troops into the citadel instead of a contingent under the command of Aminullah Khan Loghari forced Shah Shuja and his personal guard to deny them entrance. The king's efforts won the applause of Lawrence who compared 'the promptitude and courage he had displayed on this very critical occasion' with the paralysis of his own military commanders.[37] Another warning sign occurred the following day when the retiring British force came under fire from insurgents despite promises of safe passage. For Lawrence it reinforced the belief that their assurances counted for little. Furthermore, there was still no evidence of the insurgents supplying the necessary provisions which had by now reached critical levels. When the Envoy raised this issue, the insurgents responded by demanding that the British now give up control of the few remaining forts close to the cantonments held in British hands as a sign of their willingness to leave Afghanistan. Annoyed by this further condition, Macnaghten proposed to Elphinstone that the troops should 'march out in order of battle, and enter Cabul, or fight the enemy beneath its walls'. But the General predicably refused and the forts, witnessed Lawrence, were soon in enemy hands:

> The Envoy and I stood on a mound near the mosque while the forts were being evacuated by our men, and I am not ashamed to say it was with eyes moistened with tears from grief and indignation, we witnessed these strongholds, the last prop of our tottering power in Cabul, which it had cost us so much blood to seize and defend, made over, one after another, to our treacherous and exulting enemies.[38]

The insurgents soon issued another demand during a conference held on 20th December – that the British surrender all of their 9-pound guns. The Envoy rejected the request out of hand and the meeting broke up. In its aftermath, he once more proposed to Elphinstone ending all negotiations and for the troops to attack the insurgents. Yet again the General declined. Another inconclusive conference followed the next day leading Macnaghten to surmise that the insurgent leaders could not be trusted collectively. Meanwhile the Envoy continued to intrigue with those lukewarm supporters of Akbar Khan in the hope of splitting them. Then, unexpectantly, on the evening of 22nd December Macnaghten received new 'secret' proposals from Akbar Khan, sent via Captain James Skinner, an Anglo-Indian officer who had remained in the city since the beginning of the revolt. The new proposals, in place of the recently agreed treaty, stated that Shah Shuja would continue as king, with Akbar Khan acting as his *wazir* or chief minister and that British forces would remain in Afghanistan until the spring when they would evacuate the country. As a reward Akbar would receive 30,000 rupees along with an annual pension of Rs 40,000, while Aminullah Khan Logari, the chief instigator of the rebellion, would be handed over to the British. Given the lack of British bargaining power, it all seemed too good to be true.

Was Macnaghten deluding himself by accepting these new terms at the expense of the original treaty? George Lawrence, in his *Reminiscences*, made a strong defence of the Envoy's actions despite his own reservations. Macnaghten was 'perfectly justified' in breaking with the other chiefs as their conduct had proved 'so faithless'. There were also 'abundant good and sufficient reasons' for accepting Akbar's offer. He was a man of 'great weight and influence' whose self-interest would ensure that he remained faithful to the agreement. His father, Dost Mohammed, was after all under house arrest in British India, and there was the threat of an avenging British army, which would no doubt return to Afghanistan if the terms were not honoured. Furthermore, the treaty would give Akbar great power and wealth through the lucrative position of *wazir* and provide him with the opportunity of getting rid of his rival Aminullah Khan Logari.[39] George's accepting view, however, was not shared by Capt. Colin Mackenzie who was in no doubt that Macnaghten was being duped and that Akbar Khan's 'wild proposal' counted for nothing. To him the Envoy 'was like a drowning man catching at straws' whose 'strong mind had been harassed until it had in some degree lost its equipoise'.[40] Events would shortly prove that Mackenzie's suspicions were fully justified; a trap was about to be sprung.

At noon on 23rd December a conference with Akbar Khan was arranged to conclude the details of the new treaty. Captains Lawrence, Trevor, and Mackenzie accompanied the envoy together with an escort of sixteen troopers who, according to Lawrence, 'appeared unusually flurried and excited in manner'. There was undoubtedly a feeling of foreboding in the air. Mohan Lal had already written to the Envoy the previous evening arguing that Akbar could not be trusted, while just before departing Mackenzie had warned that there was a plot against him.[41] Upon leaving, Elphinstone also expressed 'some fear of treachery'. The Envoy, however, responded by throwing down the gauntlet: 'If you will at once march out the troops and meet the enemy, I will accompany you, and I am sure we shall beat them; as regards these negotiations, I have no faith in them.'[42] The General declined, giving the excuse that the troops could no longer be relied upon. As they continued their way to the rendezvous point some 300 yards from the cantonments, Lawrence too highlighted 'the risk of treachery' at which point the Envoy's reply laid bare their bleak predicament:

> 'Treachery!' he replied, 'of course there is but what can I do? The General has declared his inability to fight, we have no prospect of aid from any quarter, the enemy are only playing with us, not one article of the treaty have they fulfilled, and I have no confidence whatever in them. The life I have led for the last six weeks, you, Lawrence, know well; and rather than be disgraced, and live it over again, I would risk a hundred deaths; success will save our honour, and more than make up for all risks'.[43]

At first Akbar Khan, accompanied by Sultan Jan Barakzai (Akbar's cousin), Mahomed Shah Khan Ghilzai, and other Ghilzai chiefs, greeted the British delegation amicably. Pleasantries were exchanged and the Envoy was thanked for his gift of a fine horse as well as a pair of pistols that had formerly belonged to Lawrence. With their escort a short distance away, the Envoy and his officers were then invited to dismount and sit down on some horse-rugs, which covered a small mound sloping towards the river. Rather worryingly, Lawrence had already noticed the large number of armed Afghans congregating around them. Instead of sitting down at the request of Mohamed Shah Khan, he cautiously knelt on one knee and voiced his concerns that the meeting's confidentiality was in danger of being compromised. Akbar tried to lighten the mood: 'we are all in the same boat, and Lawrence sahib need not be in the least alarmed.' But no sooner had the chief spoken those words than the cry of 'Bigir! Bigir!' (seize! seize!) was heard.[44] Lawrence suddenly found his pistols and sword snatched and his arms grabbed by Mahomed Shah Khan who said, 'if you value your life, come along with me.' Trevor and Mackenzie were similarly pinned down while Lawrence caught a glimpse of the Envoy 'with his head down the declivity, struggling to rise, and his wrists locked in the grasp of Akbar Khan, horror and consternation being apparent on his face'.[45] Apart from one courageous *jamadar*, the whole escort simply fled in panic back to the cantonments.

In the meantime, Lawrence had quickly followed his abductor and had leapt onto his horse to escape the *ghazis* (Muslim holy warriors) who shouted 'Drop the infidel! Why spare the accursed! Let us shed the Kaffir's blood!' Despite blows to his head and body, Lawrence managed to make it safely to Mahomed Sharif's fort on the back of the chieftain's horse. Not so fortunate, it was later revealed, was his friend and colleague Captain Trevor. He too had mounted a chief's horse, but the poor animal had slipped on ice and he had been brutally cut to pieces by the baying mob. Lawrence, who was soon followed by Mackenzie, was placed in a cell with only a small, grated window. Outside a crowd had congregated and began taunting them. At one point they displayed a severed hand, which was clearly that of a European. Later Aminullah Khan Logari, the rebel chief who had been used as bait in Akbar's secret proposals to Macnaghten, bluntly told them that they would be blown away from guns, while Dost Mahomed Khan (Mahomed Shah's brother) relieved them of their silk handkerchiefs, watches, and rings. As the night drew in Lawrence and Mackenzie were given sheepskin coats to keep out the cold while the Ghilzai guards shared their dinner with them. Despite 'the awful events of the day' and their as yet unknown fate, the two men quickly fell asleep 'thoroughly exhausted in body and mind'.[46]

Their repose did not last long, however. For at midnight both were awakened and ordered to proceed to the house of Akbar Khan. Lawrence rode behind Mahomed Shah Khan through the quiet and deserted streets of the city. At one point he briefly thought of throwing himself off the horse and making a dash for the Bala Hissar. But the notion was soon discounted as he feared it would put Mackenzie's life in danger. After arriving at their destination, Akbar Khan arose from his bed and received both men in a gracious manner, 'lamenting the sad occurrence of the day' but giving no hint as to the reason for his mournful tone. Instead, he let it be known that Captain Skinner was staying in a nearby room should they wish to see him. Skinner soon revealed the reason for the sombre mood. 'The Envoy is dead,' he gravely told his fellow officers, 'I saw his head being brought into this very courtyard.' Lawrence was horrified: 'Thus suddenly came upon me the dreadful and astounding intelligence of the murder of the man I loved and revered as a father.'[47] With cruel irony, Lawrence also learned that Akbar Khan had killed the Envoy using one of his old pistols that been presented to the chief as a gift earlier. Like Alexander Burnes before him, no respect was accorded to the deceased Envoy. Without hesitation, the mob had quickly mutilated the corpse before it was dragged through the city streets. Eventually his head was 'stuck up for all to gaze upon in the Char Chowk', the most frequented part of Kabul.

The following day, clothed in Afghan dress on the advice of Akbar Khan, Lawrence and Mackenzie were escorted through the city's streets. Their disguise, however, fooled no one: 'the savage mob,' George noted, 'yelled and screamed on all sides, demanding our blood'.[48] Eventually they arrived at the house of Nawab Zuman Khan where a council of all the chiefs had assembled. A new draft treaty had been compiled in which they were prepared to offer safe passage of the army to Peshawar provided the British surrender their all treasure, ammunition and guns. Lawrence and Mackenzie 'endeavoured to propose some modifications to it, but, as prisoners, [their] remonstrances had no weight whatever'. The treaty was then sealed by all the chiefs and sent to the cantonments for review. In the meantime, both men returned to Akbar Khan's house where they endured a 'very sad Christmas'. At one point the chief insensitively asked George to fix the pistol he had used to kill the Envoy, while Sultan Jan, although personable, 'inveighed most bitterly against our occupation of the country, and the indignities to which his countrymen, and women especially, had been subjected by our troops, and by some of our officers whom he named'.[49]

On 26th December, and with some trepidation, Lawrence found himself being taken into the care of the infamous chief Aminullah Khan Logari. Having labelled him 'a monster of cruelty' for his unbridled use of torture and 'contempt for human life', Lawrence was surprised to find the chief courteous. Other chiefs had congregated at Aminullah's house to discuss the terms of the new treaty and in particular which British officers would be made hostages to this agreement. When the chiefs put forward a mere sergeant called Deane as one of the potential hostages, Lawrence was quick to highlight its inappropriateness. His candid views, it seems, were to win the approbation of the group: 'Lawrence Sahib is truthful and to be depended on,' he overheard them saying, 'he might easily have passed off Deane on us as an officer quite fit for a hostage, but he would not deceive us. We shall trust him; he is a man of truth.'[50]

It was shortly afterwards decided that Lawrence would be allowed to return to the cantonments, though there was some delay as Akbar Khan had opposed the gesture. Nevertheless, Aminullah Khan was adamant that his promise to

Lawrence should hold firm. Before taking his leave, the chief had one piece of advice: the retreating army should avoid the Khord Kabul Pass, a five-mile-deep gorge, which was controlled by Akbar Khan and his Ghilzai tribesmen, and instead proceed via Zurmat which was under Aminullah's control.[51] On 29th December Lawrence, with no small sense of relief, returned to the cantonments where he was greeted with both surprise and delight by his fellow officers, their wives, sepoys and his old Hindu bearer who 'wept with joy'.[52]

Thoughts soon turned on what to do next. Fellow Ulsterman, Major Eldred Pottinger, now the chief political authority, was against any further negotiations, believing that the only two realistic options available was either to evacuate to the Bala Hissar or else march swiftly to Jalalabad without baggage. Both were firmly rejected by the military authorities who instead accepted the treaty proposed by the Afghan chiefs. As the new year opened amidst heavy falls of snow, Lawrence noted that 'the confusion in the cantonments was fearful'.[53] Efforts to purchase provisions and cattle for transport were now being urgently made, as was the bartering of articles and goods to lighten the baggage for the intended retreat. There was also much plundering of Afghan traders beyond the ramparts, though there was no attempt to stop it. Rumours, warnings, and counteroffers were rife. George heard reports from 'several of the native officers of Anderson's horse' who spoke of the treacherous designs of the insurgents and their intention to massacre. An alternative offer from the Kohistanis to escort the army back to Peshawar was made to General Elphinstone but declined. Then there was Shah Shuja's urgent message to Lawrence to advise Elphinstone not to leave the cantonments. If they did, they would be 'dead men'. A similar warning came from a Qizilbash chief. On the 5th January Lady Macnaghten received an offer from Shah Shuja for her, and as many ladies who wished, to seek asylum in the Bala Hissar. The move prompted Pottinger to propose that when the army was to leave the cantonments, they should march straight to the citadel instead of the road to Jalalabad. The plan won the support of George who believed the King would warmly welcome them. When the proposal was presented to General Elphinstone he asked if they could guarantee supplies. 'We cannot guarantee,' replied Pottinger and Lawrence, 'but we are pretty sure of sufficient supplies.' The answer was insufficient for the General's assent. 'No, we retreat!' was his final and fateful decision.

Meanwhile back in India, Henry Lawrence had spent twelve days marching with Wild's brigade from Ferozepur through a then sparsely populated and uncultivated region of northwest Punjab to finally reach Peshawar on 28th December. Despite the critical state of the British position in Afghanistan, it soon became clear that Auckland was loath to bolster rescue efforts with more troops. After the Kabul rising, he had become convinced that his 1838 Afghan strategy was now untenable; the costs had outstripped the benefits.[54] In any case, he was about to leave his post and did not wish to burden his successor with further Afghan commitments.[55] The British response thus remained modest. Only one brigade then mustering at Peshawar with the addition of a contingent of Sikh troops would be allowed to come to the aid of General Sale's garrison at Jalalabad and those survivors from Kabul. There would be no largescale attempt to re-take Afghanistan.

For those officers on the frontier, however, it was obvious that such a meagre force was insufficient for even this modest objective, forcing George Clerk to use all his influence with the Lahore Durbar to gain more resources. Under the command of the Italian General Avitabile and Raja Gulab Singh, they reluctantly agreed to give 5,000 troops and some pieces of artillery. After making the necessary arrangements, the plan was for the relief force to advance via the Khyber Pass. The Sikh soldiers, however, were in no rush to help their tripartite allies and their tardiness soon exasperated Henry: 'There is clearly no help to be had from the Sikhs as long as we want it,' wrote Henry to Honoria on New Year's Day (1842), 'Avitabile himself is our ally, but he is afraid to act; afraid of his men, and afraid of his Government, and of ours too; of support, in short, there is none.'[56] Much of early January was spent coaxing the Sikh gunners to release their guns and make them serviceable. On 5th January Henry had managed to test some of them at a Sikh camp eight miles from Peshawar, though one had been damaged in the process. When inspecting other guns at Jamrud, the gateway to the Khyber Pass, the Sikh troops' mood was one of indifference. He sensed that 'they should not like to give up their guns, or to enter the Pass, being so little cared for by their Government.'[57] Nevertheless, in predictable fashion Henry persevered and by 8th January he was able to report that he had 'got the guns into pretty good order'. While waiting for the go-ahead to advance through the Khyber, he busied himself making further preparations which included organising extra supplies of ammunition, procuring grain and fodder, and finding extra camel drivers to transport materials beyond Peshawar. He even used his persuasive skills to defuse a potential mutiny of the 64th Bengal Native Infantry Regiment over pay and better winter clothing.

Alongside these headaches, morale was further dented by the shocking news of Macnaghten's murder as well as George Lawrence and Colin Mackenzie's captivity. Henry expressed little hope for those who remained at Kabul. 'Their fate, I fear, is sealed,' he told his wife on 5th January, 'and the question now is, how or what to do as regards Jalalabad; for the orders of Government seem to look no further (in the event of losing Cabul) than to insure the retreat of the troops at other points.'[58]

Retreat from Kabul

Around 9 am on 6th January approximately 700 British troops, 3,800 Indian sepoys and some 12,000 camp followers began their doomed retreat from Kabul back to India through heavy snow. Melancholy gripped George Lawrence as he looked at the troops about him: They were not 'the smart, light-hearted body of men they appeared some time ago,' but 'a crouching, drooping, dispirited army'.[1] Even at this late stage he still wistfully hoped that in some manner they would proceed to the Bala Hissar rather than risk 'plunging into the dreadful defiles' which now awaited them. He did his best to banish such thoughts by riding his horse hard and by giving encouragement to the clearly frightened women and children over whom he was given charge for the duration of the march. But the column soon came to a halt at Siyah Sang on the orders of General Elphinstone, after news came that the promised Afghan escort was still not ready. Colin Mackenzie, however, was in no mood to wait and instead galloped to Brigadier Shelton to tell him to resume the march.[2] Even so, a delay of over an hour ensued before they were on the move again. For George, there was no escaping the bleak situation:

It was bitterly cold, freezing hard, and I pitied from my soul the poor native soldiers and camp followers, walking up to their knees in snow and slush. It was no easy task to keep all my charge together, some of the bearers hurrying on, others lagging behind with the palanquins and doolies containing the women and children.[3]

As the night drew in, after marching only four miles with a further eighty miles still to go, they set up camp at Bagramee. Most of the women remained inside their doolies and palanquins due to the freezing conditions. George was fortunate to escape the elements in a tent pitched by his servants which he shared with two other officers; a situation made more comfortable with the supply of some cold meat and sherry courtesy of Mrs Macnaghten.

The rear-guard was not so lucky. Even before they had left the cantonments in the afternoon, they were already suffering many casualties from being fired at by *ghazis* who had gained access to the adjacent Mission Compound. The delay in departing had been largely due to the creation of a makeshift bridge over the Kabul River. As no other fording point was used, it quickly resulted in a traffic bottleneck. The accompanying camp followers and their animals 'became at once mixed together in an unmanageable mass'.[4] Much of the baggage, ammunition and commissariat stores were simply abandoned; a situation made worse by the predatory activities of Afghan marauders and fire from the *ghazis' jezails*. During the remainder of the day, the rear-guard was to fight all the way to the overnight halt at Bagramee while passing 'a continuous lane of poor wretches, men, women and children, dead or dying from the cold and wounds'. Reaching their halt at two in the morning, they found no shelter, food, or fuel. Many quietly succumbed during the freezing night. 'The silence of the men,' George noted, 'betrayed their despair and torpor, not a voice being heard.'[5]

One scene epitomised the hopelessness of their exodus. In the morning, close to his tent, Lawrence came across the stiff corpse of 'an old grey-haired conductor named Macgregor' dressed in full regimentals with his sword still drawn in his hand. Completely exhausted by the previous day's events, the old veteran had simply laid down and had frozen to death. A depressing conclusion was drawn: 'Such was the first march of the retreat, proving but too surely how correct was Sir William Macnaghten's conviction, that the measure which the military authorities regarded as the only one for ensuring the safety of the force, must, if persisted in, end in its annihilation.'[6]

By the second day little semblance of order remained. Soldiers, camp followers and what little remained of the baggage had become a jumbled, disorganised muddle. George reckoned that more than half of the sepoys had thrown away their muskets unable to handle them due to cold and hunger, while the bulk of the Shah's 6th Infantry and sappers had simply deserted, making their way back to Kabul, resigned to become prisoners rather than endure further misery. The rear-guard continued to suffer heavy casualties from groups of Afghan horse and foot who were moving in parallel with the retreating column. Meanwhile, the women and children under George's charge remained unharmed, although it was no easy task to keep the palanquin and doolie bearers in check. Lady Macnaghten's bearers were the first to quit and she was forced to ride with George for part of the way before being transferred to a camel fitted with *kajahwahs*.

On reaching Butkhak at the end of the second day, only a further five miles had been achieved, and with heavy hearts and broken bodies, the British were left wondering what had happened to the promise of safe conduct. In a meeting that evening with Captain Skinner, Akbar Khan explained the British mistake: they had left the cantonments before the escort had joined them. Had they not been so impatient they would have avoided their recent misfortunes. It was hardly a credible explanation since Akbar had earlier been seen with the very same Afghan horsemen who had attacked the column. Nevertheless, the chief now promised that he would personally escort them to Jalalabad on the condition that six hostages would be handed over as guarantee to ensure the force would not march beyond Tezin before General Sale evacuated Jalalabad. At the conclusion of the meeting the firing on the British camp ceased. That night the temperature reached minus ten degrees. Once more George had the benefit of a tent and further provisions from Lady Macnaghten. This was in stark contrast to most of the officers and all the soldiers who were 'forced to lie down upon the snow, without food or fuel'.[7]

By the beginning of the third day's march, on 8th January, the remaining palanquin and doolie bearers could no longer be relied upon and George organised for the rest of the ladies to be transferred to *kajahwahs*. As they began their march towards the infamous Khord Kabul Pass, it wasn't long before the Afghans resumed their firing: 'Suddenly the whole mass of soldiers, camp followers, and cattle appeared convulsed' and began 'to roll towards the rear like an enormous wave.'[8] George ordered his mounted troopers to close further around the women and children for extra protection. Towards the front he could see Jezail riflemen taking long shots at the 44th Regiment. Looking in vain for a senior officer to give orders to advance, he eventually received the go-ahead from Major Thain, the aide-de-camp. The cavalry then charged at a body of Afghan horsemen forcing them to flee until they found cover behind some hillocks which were occupied by their jezail riflemen. 'Even at this, the eleventh hour,' George recorded, 'we might, if properly led, have driven the enemy like sheep into Cabul, and ourselves have occupied the Bala Hissar.'[9]

Abkar Khan now reappeared to demand his hostages as part of the deal to escort the column to safety. Lawrence, Mackenzie and Pottinger were chosen. Having been escorted through crowds of insurgents, they were brought before the chief who had his men relieve them of their firearms, though Lawrence was allowed to retain his sword. Amid the unfolding chaos, the meeting had an unreal air of civility. Situated on the side of a hill, they were invited to have breakfast: 'We then sat down and partook of breakfast, not without a shudder I confess on my part, at eating from the same dish with the man who had been so lately the murderer of the Envoy.'[10] The chief then gave orders for the firing to cease.

Chaperoned by Akbar Khan, Sultan Jan and some Ghilzai chiefs together with their horsemen, Lawrence, Mackenzie and Pottinger now followed the rear of the retreating army. Almost as soon as they recommenced their march, Ghilzai tribesmen renewed their plunder of the baggage at the rear of the column. Akbar directed his horsemen to fire on the plunderers, but this only halted their activities momentarily. According to Eldred Pottinger, Akbar Khan was playing a double game. Pottinger, a noted linguist, had told Mackenzie that while he had heard Akbar call to the Ghilzais to stop firing in Persian, he had also overheard the chief shout 'slay them' in Pashto.[11] Events would appear to confirm Pottinger's suspicions. As they approached the Khord Kabul Pass, they began to confront 'at every yard the mangled corpses' of camp followers. At this stage Lawrence counted only three Europeans amongst the dead, but further along their number increased. Gruesome scenes continued throughout the Pass:

> Sepoys and camp followers were being stripped and plundered on all sides, and such as refused to give up their money and valuables were instantly stabbed or cut down by the ruthless enemy with their long knives. On seeing us the poor creatures cried out for help, many of them recognising me and calling out to me by name. But what could we do? We ourselves were quite helpless.[12]

Lawrence and the other hostages now had to endure the taunts of the Ghilzais brandishing their blood-stained knives and telling them that they would be shortly joining the 'heaps of carcases' around them. 'It was most difficult to restrain oneself,' Lawrence recalled, 'and involuntarily my hand grasped my sword-hilt; but I controlled my anger, knowing that any offensive movement on my part would insure our instant destruction.'[13] In order to avoid unwanted attention, the party departed from the road and sheltered for some time under an overhanging rock where they were joined by the youngest son of Captain Boyd and Mrs Bean, wife of a private, both of whom had become separated from their loved ones. The group continued their journey until they came across an injured sergeant of the 44th who recognised George. 'For God's sake, Captain Lawrence, don't leave me here!' he cried out. At first sight it appeared the soldier had only lost his left hand. But when George tried to lift him, he discovered deep cuts from the nape of his neck and along his backbone. Realising that nothing could be done to save him, the sergeant cried out to be shot; a request George was unable to fulfil, and they were forced to leave him. Eventually the group made it to a small fort for the night where the guards were generous enough to share their 'scanty meal' with them. Thereafter they laid down in a circle with their feet towards the fire and quickly fell asleep.

The next morning, on 9th January, according to George's account, the hostages made their way to the Khord Kabul Fort where they met Akbar Khan. The chief addressed George directly. He now proposed that the ladies and their husbands, their children, and the wounded officers should be handed over to him, and he would provide protection for them, and afterwards forward them under escort to Jalalabad. The offer, of course, only related to British wives and children, and not the wives and children of sepoy and camp followers. Akbar may well have talked to George about 'reasons of humanity', which prompted him to make the offer, but his real interest was to increase his group of valuable hostages whom he could later use as bargaining chips. As the past few days had all too clearly shown, however, he was devoid of any sympathy for the Indian sepoys and camp followers. George undoubtedly recognised Akbar's true motives, but he was also aware of their grim circumstances. Thus, the proposal was 'promptly and cordially approved' by both him, Pottinger and Captain Skinner acting on behalf of Elphinstone. By evening the European women and children had been brought to the fort, and for George, moved by patriarchal concern, it was a moment of grudging acceptance:

> It was distressing beyond expression to see our countrywomen and their helpless children thus placed in the power of these ruffians, but there was no help for it. The extreme suffering of mind and body they had endured since the 5th was apparent in their worn and grief-stricken faces. Many of them during these four wretched days had tasted nothing but some dry biscuits and some sherry or brandy.[14]

Having rested a further day, and relieved that their situation had become more secure, the group set off on the morning of 11th January. But their spirits soon plummeted when they came face to face with the horrific spectacle of death and suffering on the road to Tezin: 'It was strewn in every direction,' George recounted, 'with the stripped and mangled bodies of our late companions, exhibiting every variety of the ghastliness of death.'[15] The scenes of carnage continued as they marched through the Tezin valley where Lawrence had to endure the harrowing experience of recognising some of his fallen comrades. One 'venerable old subahdar' who had 'eaten the Company's salt' for over forty year lay on the road beside his horse; the body of Dr. Cardew, 'a most gallant and fearless officer', who had planned to meet his betrothed in India, lay near an abandoned horse artillery gun.[16] Perhaps the most shocking discovery was that of Captain Skinner who had been shot while delivering a message from General Elphinstone to Akbar Khan. 'A high-minded, manly soldier…loved and respected by all,' Lawrence 'mourned for him with unfeigned sorrow.'[17]

Skinner had died near Jagdalak where the carnage had been particularly brutal. Indeed, Lawrence noted that 'the last two miles into Jagdalak were literally lined with bodies of Europeans and natives, all stripped, and lying just as they fell, side by side.' From amongst the survivors, George managed to save two Indians of rank. One was a subedar from the 37th Native Infantry, the other 'an old Hindu treasurer' from Captain Bygrave's regiment. Yet for the great mass of rank and file, the situation had become truly hopeless. Hundreds of sepoys and camp followers, having been stripped naked by the Afghans, were huddled together beside the road pleading in vain for help. Could something have been done to stop this war crime? George argued that his own position as a hostage precluded intervention: 'I could not even do anything for them by supplicating Mahomed Akbar on their behalf, as otherwise I would have done, for the Sirdar had warned me not to come near him unless he sent for me, and I was surrounded by a guard of his own retainers.'[18] He had also argued that by the time they had arrived on the scene many victims had already reached a state of being 'beyond all human help'. Undoubtedly George and his fellow hostages were in a weak position. But not to raise any objections beyond expressing a sense of horrified pity was surely a damming indictment of the officer class and its inability to look after all those under its command.

At Jagdalak the hostages were reunited with General Elphinstone, Brigadier Shelton and Captain Johnson. From Johnson, George heard the dreadful news of what had happened to the army since the time he had been taken hostage. In their march to Tezin the army once more had come under fire from the Afghans despite promises of protection. Yet bizarrely the military authorities had ordered that on no account should they return fire. A predictable bloodbath ensued. When the depleted force reached Tezin, a deputation was sent by General Elphinstone to make terms. But when Akbar Khan offered them safety and protection, provided the soldiers surrendered and gave up their firearms (the officers would be allowed to retain their swords), it was rejected by Elphinstone on the grounds of dishonour. After Tezin, the army was further decimated by a combination of Akbar Khan's forces and the Ghilzais. By the time they had reached Jagdalak, it had been reduced to less than two hundred men with practically all ammunition expended. There was a last-ditch attempt at negotiation. Akbar Khan proposed that the surviving Europeans should be separated from non-Europeans, and each mounted behind one of his horsemen. Tragically, even in these desperate circumstances, the General and Shelton baulked at the chief's proposal, again on a nonsensical point of honour. George was astounded by their complete disregard for the welfare of their troops and their impending obliteration:

> They had abandoned their post, their stores and treasure, when they had a well-equipped army of 5,000 men to defend them, had allowed some 8,000 camp-followers to be butchered and their fighting men to be reduced to less than 200 – it was surely too late then to talk of honour, when to surrender was the only measure which could avert the annihilation of this remnant.[19]

Despairing of the indecision of Elphinstone and Shelton, the remaining troops continued their march. At the Jagdalak Pass many were to die, leaving a mere twenty officers, fifty men of the 44th, four Horse Artillery and cavalry troopers, and three hundred camp followers to make their last stand at Gandamak. 'Thus perished our Cabul army,' George wrote, 'sacrificed....to the incompetency, feebleness, and want of skill and resolution of their military leaders.'[20]

Captivity and Deliverance

On 14th January Lawrence and the rest of the group, chaperoned by Akbar Khan's escort, recommenced their march north from Jagdalak. The terrain now proved the most challenging so far. Climbing through a very steep, narrow chasm, just wide enough for their camels laden with *kajahwahs* to pass, their ascent continued along the precipitous Budurnuck Pass. As they journeyed through the barren range of mountains, they again encountered groups of frostbitten sepoys and camp followers who had managed to escape the recent massacres, but whose days were numbered. After a twenty-five-mile march they reached the banks of the Panshir River, where they were forced to bivouac in the open. Lawrence used his trunk and that of Mrs Macnaghten's as shelter for the women and children against the cold, biting wind, while during the night they were sustained by a meal of 'boiled mutton and half-baked cakes'. Crossing the Panshir River, they continued north passing forts and high-walled villages whose inhabitants only offered abuse to the passers-by.

Throughout the journey, George was active in ensuring the safety of the convoy by fending off groups of armed Ghilzais who were intent on plunder and murder. He also helped an old servant to cross a river and one of the ladies who had fallen off her pony to remount. As for himself, he seems to have adopted an almost blasé attitude to the prospect of danger. At one point, when he was at the rear of the convoy, a Qizilbash horseman expressed surprise to find him riding alone 'so unconcernedly' and suggested, as they approached a village, the possibility that any one of the inhabitants might choose to shoot him. 'Fortunately no one molested us,' George reported insouciantly, 'and we jogged on together in friendly conversation until we overtook the column.'[1]

Having endured physical hardship and the psychological trauma of experiencing so much death and suffering, it was with great relief that on 17th January their peripatetic way of life came to a temporary halt when they arrived at the newly erected and imposing fort at Badiabad. Akbar Khan, ever the courteous host as far as British officers and their wives were concerned, welcomed his 'honoured guests', proclaiming that 'they should want nothing he could supply them with' and assured them that 'as soon as the roads were safe enough he would escort them to Jalalabad'.[2] In order to encourage their continued wellbeing, George gifted Akbar his fine grey horse (formerly the Envoy's) and a gold repeater watch; to his fellow chief, Sultan Jan, a diamond ring was presented, while the man who was left in charge of guarding them, Musa Khan, received a silver hookah pipe and shawl.

Lawrence's concern for the welfare of his fellow captives during their arduous journey continued as they settled into their new surroundings. Akbar handed him the task of allocating the accommodation amongst the group, which now comprised the precariously ill General Elphinstone, Brigadier Shelton together with seven officers, ten officers' wives and fifteen children as well as several soldiers and servants. The six rooms within the fort were divided amongst the officers, women, and children, while able-bodied soldiers had to make do with the stables. George also took the lead, assisted by his servants, in the ordering and distribution of staple food items such sheep, flour, rice, ghee, and wood. For the most part, he freely accepted such responsibilities, though at times it could be burdensome. When Akbar sent supplies of tea, sugar and chintzes to the fort, George found the task of distributing to be 'very disagreeable and invidious'. As much as he might act 'without favour or partiality,' it proved 'impossible fully to satisfy' the needs of his fellow captives.[3]

Of their nearly three months' stay, there was little worthy to report. Although a powerful earthquake on 19th February did manage to rock their humdrum existence, fortunately there were no injuries. The main challenge facing the captives was to find ways to stem the boredom and to keep their spirits from flagging. Fellow officer Colin Mackenzie found Lawrence to be 'ever cheerful and never despairing'.[4] His positive demeanour was helped in part by the adoption of a daily routine. Alongside his commissariat responsibilities, George engaged in regular exercise, which consisted of racing against his Afghan guards every morning around the courtyard. Boasting that he generally managed to beat his competitors, he felt 'all the better for the excitement as well as the bodily exercise'. George also organised regular drill practices with the children to give them 'exercise and amusement', while on Sunday both he and Mackenzie conducted church services. Several of the inmates, like Lawrence and Mackenzie, also filled their time recording a diary of their ordeal, while the tedium of incarceration was occasionally relieved by the arrival of a small number of other prisoners who had escaped the massacres at Jagdalak and Gandamak.

How much did the experience change George and his fellow captives? There is no doubt that circumstance forced them to adapt their habits and manners. The prison sketches of his fellow officers drawn by Lieutenant Vincent Eyre at Badiabad are perhaps the most obvious indication. In Eyre's portrait of George Lawrence, there is little to suggest that the subject matter is a British army officer. The bearded Ulsterman is depicted wearing a turban on his head and sitting cross-legged. His body is clothed in an Afghan choga with a cummerbund round his waist, while over his shoulders is draped a loose-flowing shawl. In the introduction to Eyre's *Prison Sketches*, the editor gave a clear reason for this transformation: British officers adopted Afghan costume as a precaution, 'to avoid attracting inconvenient observation in their wanderings among hostile people'.[5] Yet this seems hardly plausible. Both Mackenzie and Lawrence had been recognised previously in Kabul despite wearing Afghan attire. Furthermore, the captive ladies of the group mostly continued to wear European dress. No doubt for some officers there was a romantic inclination to adopt oriental garb but there was also a more practical reason. Apart from George and Mrs Macnaghten, almost all had lost their baggage in the retreat from Kabul so they were inevitably forced to wear whatever they could.

The usual table manners and food habits inevitably underwent modification. Vincent Eyre 'soon learned to consider spoons, forks, and other table gear as effeminate luxuries' and instead used his fingers when eating 'a greasy pilao' from a common dish which he shared with several others.[6] Similarly, George noted that there was initially little enthusiasm among the hostages for the Afghan staple of just rice and ghee, yet 'all learnt very speedily to appreciate the full value and sustaining properties of the dish'.[7] Even when Henry Lawrence later sent some bottles of sherry and brandy, the captives 'had been so long without these stimulants' that few of them availed of the kind gesture.[8] Forced to live in cramped, basic conditions with little sanitation, it was inevitably that standards of cleanliness would suffer too. Lieutenant Eyre once more noted the hostages' changing perspectives: 'The first discovery of a real living l-o-u-s-e was a severe shock to our fine sense of delicacy; but custom reconciles folk to anything, and even the ladies eventually mustered up resolution to look one of these intruders in the face without a scream.'[9]

Morale was raised within the fort by the ability to send and receive letters and newspapers via messengers and Afghan acquaintances. Regular communication with the Jalalabad garrison situated only thirty miles away was now possible, and soon letters were received from General Robert Sale and Captain George Macgregor. George was gratified to learn that his brother Henry was at Peshawar assisting in the preparations of General Pollock's relieving force, named menacingly as the Army of Retribution. Meanwhile, they were also kept informed of Akbar Khan's unsuccessful attempts to overcome the besieged garrison of Jalalabad. By mid-March a request by the fort's commander, Mirza Baha-ud-Din, for a certificate to be signed by all the captives testifying that he had treated them well was a timely admission that future political fortunes remained in the balance and that it was prudent to make the necessary arrangements.[10] This became more concrete when news reached the fort that General Sale's garrison at Jalalabad had made a successful sally against Akbar Khan's forces on 7th April, capturing tents and guns, and only narrowly missing the opportunity of taking the chief prisoner. In its aftermath Mohamed Shah Khan told Pottinger and Lawrence that a council of war had been hastily assembled where the chiefs had proposed that all the captives be killed. But Akbar, fully aware that he needed to keep his 'bargaining chips' alive, would not hear of it. Instead, the captives would be moved from Badiabad to a more remote location to avoid the possibility of a rescue attempt from Jalalabad.

Henry, in the meantime, had been supporting the efforts of Wild's Brigade to force its way through the Khyber Pass following Major Frederick Mackeson's (Henry's fellow political officer) failure to reach agreement with the Afridi tribes. One interim objective was to relieve the besieged garrison at Ali Masjid Fort situated some five miles from the Pass's entrance. An attempt on 19th January was scuppered by the mutiny of the Sikh Najeeb (Muslim) regiments the previous evening. Despite their absence, Henry advised Wild to advance in what turned out to be a costly mistake. Over a hundred men were killed and wounded by the turbulent Afridis, while the Ali Masjid Fort remained unrelieved. Henry did his best to stop a couple of the guns falling into enemy hands as well as stemming the retreat of Wild's two regiments but the day's events afforded little consolation: 'I've witnessed a shameful sight today,' he told Honoria on a scrap of paper, 'our troops behaving ill before a handful of savages.'[11] Another abortive attempt on 24th January, in which Henry performed the duties of 'general, artilleryman, pioneer, and cavalry' resulted in some three hundred casualties. On this occasion he castigated the timidity of his fellow officers for not advancing further through the Pass: 'I was quite sickened; for all the morning, and the morning before, I had alone, against every officer's opinion and will, wanted [Colonel] T – to move on; but no, he would not stir beyond what is called the "tungee," or narrow defile…With few exceptions, there is not a man with head and heart in the force; but Pollock will bring some, I trust.'[12]

As a result of these embarrassing failures, it was decided that no further action would be attempted until the arrival of the main relieving force under General George Pollock. The General, who reached Peshawar in early February, was regarded as an unassuming but able man, whom Lawrence held in high esteem. 'General Pollock is about as good a commander as could be sent,' he told Honoria.[13] His appearance on the frontier boosted morale amongst Wild's weary brigade and invigorated Lawrence who was keen to assist him in any capacity 'as a clerk, as an aide-de-camp, artilleryman, quartermaster-general, or pioneer'.[14] Pollock, however, was not a man to be hurried. Indeed, he would spend two full months preparing his relieving force, bringing in extra supplies of clothing and equipment as well as reinforcements of British Dragoons and Horse Artillery from India.

Notwithstanding the impending arrival of Pollock's army, obtaining the Sikh troops' cooperation was pivotal to the success of the Company's relief effort both in terms of manpower and in the context of projecting a united front against its enemies. Under the treaty terms in aid of Shah Shuja, the Sikhs were bound to cooperate with the British and supply 5,000 men. Yet for much of February and March 1842 Henry continued to wonder if the Sikhs would oblige: 'I am so puzzled to know,' he told Honoria, 'if our sepoys will advance, and if the Sikhs will, of the latter I have not a hope that I am quite bothered.'[15] By the end of March conditions in Jalalabad were becoming increasing fraught. Rations for the soldiers were cut to two-thirds of salt meat, while camp followers were reduced to eating salt camels and horses. As preparations for the relieving force were reaching completion, there was still no agreement with the Afridi chiefs for safe passage through the Khyber. The Khyber would have to be taken by force. It was decided that Major Mackeson, as the senior assistant, would go with the relieving force into Afghanistan, despite Henry's earnest desire to do so. A keen rivalry existed between the two political officers and Henry was naturally disappointed not to be at the centre of the action. Nevertheless, he still managed to persuade Pollock to allow him to take a couple of guns for use inside the Khyber Pass.

The prospect of Henry's participation, however, turned out to be precarious. In the early hours of 5th April Pollock went to Henry's tent in preparation for the assault on the Pass later that day only to find him seriously ill from an attack of fever. The General genuinely feared for Henry's life, but thankfully the illness proved fleeting. For a few hours later Henry was seen actively manning the guns at the entrance to the Pass having had, according to Herbert Edwardes, 'all bodily infirmities subdued by force of will and sense of duty'.[16] Reinvigorated by the heat of battle, he later organised the evacuation of wounded men and arranged for the supply of water to the rear-guard. By the end of the first day of action, the British after some hard fighting had overcome the Afridis. Writing to Clerk, Henry reported approvingly that ten Sikh infantry regiments and two Sikh cavalry regiments, amounting to some 15,000 men, had been heavily involved in the assault. The Sikh troops 'appeared to have advanced willingly, and [were] improving in spirits', while some of them even boasted to Henry that they would now 'go all the way to Cabul, sahib!'[17]

Overall credit for the Sikh's eventual cooperation was undoubtedly due to Clerk's diplomacy at the Lahore court.[18] Yet on the ground Lawrence was equally influential in maintaining a Sikh rear-guard that would keep the Khyber open as far as Ali Musjid following General Pollock's advance. Henry's tireless efforts in organising the Sikh troops and ensuring adequate supplies of men, ammunition, water, grain, and fodder were noted by his superiors. General Pollock's despatch of 6th April acknowledged, 'the very great assistance…received from Captains Mackeson and Lawrence'.[19] Clerk, too, praised Henry's efforts: 'All along this frontier praises are loud of your exertions, alacrity, and spirit.'[20]

Pollock's Khyber Pass success was soon followed by the breakout of Sale's garrison at Jalalabad on 7th April and the retreat of Mohammed Akbar's forces. Yet despite the storming of the Khyber Pass and the relief of Jalalabad, there followed a period of procrastination when British fortunes still hung in the balance. The fate of the British prisoners in Kabul remained uncertain and for Henry and Honoria it was an anxious time wondering if they would ever see George again. Throughout April, May and June, there remained the real possibility that the captives would be abandoned to their fate and that, subject to the vagaries of government policy, the army would return to India with only half the mission completed. Auckland's final instructions to Pollock before leaving office were ambiguous. The General was ordered to withdraw the garrison from Jalalabad and to do what was required to 'procure the safe return of our troops and people detained beyond the Khyber Pass'.[21] No specific mention was made of the Kabul captives. Auckland's successor, Lord Ellenborough, appeared equally pusillanimous. After receiving reports in early April that a British force had been repulsed at the Khojak Pass, he sent instructions for General Nott, then based at Kandahar, to withdraw via Quetta and for General Pollock to withdraw from Jalalabad as soon as possible. Thankfully, however, both generals, keen to salvage some degree of honour, opposed any immediate retreat, and gave the excuse of the hot weather and lack of transport for their decision to remain *in situ*.[22]

Meanwhile, after eleven weeks, and with 'much regret' the captives prepared to leave their refuge at Badiabad on 10th April. Mahomed Shah Khan took this as an opportunity to relieve George and Lady Macnaghten of some of their remaining valuables. The former was forced to hand over his 'pouch, belt, epaulettes, and some stars of the Dourannee order' while the latter gave 'some of her best shawls' and, on the advice of George, some of the jewels she had 'secreted about her person'. This time 'the poor private soldiers' would not be allowed to accompany the officers, their wives and children. While George expressed regret, it appears there was little effort to remonstrate. As for the servants, many, including one who had been with Lawrence twenty years, now decided voluntarily not to follow their masters as they viewed their 'position as desperate'.[23]

Unsure of their destination, the captives, once more, had to endure the hardships of life on the road for the following six weeks. They encountered further challenging mountain terrain such as the Badpush Pass where the women were forced to temporarily ditch their *kajahwahs* and instead ride ponies along the precipitous rocky path. At one point they crossed the rapidly flowing Kabul River on rafts inflated with bullock hides, while Lawrence himself undertook the march via the Udruck Pass solely on foot having given his two horses to injured soldiers. For parts of the journey, they retraced some of their former steps of early January. At Tezin, George noted gruesomely that the air was still 'pestilential from the decomposed bodies' of the retreating British troops. In some places the corpses lay in high piles, 'having probably perished by famine and exposure to the cold'.[24] At the ill-fated Khord Kabul Pass, he also observed 'many of the bodies, from being imbedded in the snow, were little altered, but most were reduced to skeletons'.[25]

Where previously the freezing cold had been the cause of acute suffering, they now at times had to endure being drenched with rain. Accommodation was in tents and in local forts, often for no more than a few days at a time. At Mahomed Khan's fort, which had been badly damaged by the recent earthquake, the sleeping arrangements were a cramped, one-room affair. George, without mattress or rug, managed to find a spot by Lady Sale's feet and commiserated with 'the poor ladies [who] had to pass the night in their wet garments'.[26] For General Elphinstone, the recent marches and the painful memory of the army's annihilation were to take their toll. 'Worn out in body and mind,' he told George that 'he repeatedly wished, and even prayed for death, as, he said, sleeping and waking the horrors of that dreadful retreat were before his eyes.'[27] He died at the fort on 23rd April.

What was striking throughout this period was Akbar Khan's concern for the welfare of his captives. At one point of the journey, Akbar gave up his own palanquin to Lady Macnaghten and Lady Sale in the absence of camels with *kajahwahs*, while on another occasion he was seen giving small gifts of bread and sugar to the children. He even gave one thousand rupees for George to distribute amongst the hostages. The chief formed a particularly good relationship with George with their marches often punctuated by friendly chats: 'The Sirdar always took in good part whatever I said to him, and treated me invariably with marked distinction, rising on every occasion of my entering his durbar, and placing me on his right hand, above all his chiefs.'[28] Indeed, following Sale's victory at Jalalabad, Akbar Khan, though looking pale and carrying his hand in a sling (the result of an assassination attempt), greeted Lawrence 'in a free and soldierly manner' praising the 'gallant bearing' of the British troops, while admitting that 'his force was fairly surprised' and that he had been lucky to avoid capture.[29]

To a degree, Akbar was even amenable. A decision on the second day of the march to divide the captives in two – married men and ladies in one group; bachelors in another – provoked a vigorous response from Lawrence. Meeting Akbar face to face, he strongly objected on the grounds that ladies who had no husbands to look after them, such as Lady Macnaghten and Lady Sale, would be helpless. In response Akbar proposed that both he and another officer should then accompany those ladies. Lawrence, however, remained adamant that the captives remained as one group. After a brief pause, the chief relented. No doubt there was some degree of selective compassion directing Akbar's actions, but there was also the realisation that the end game was fast approaching. In the light of Sale's success at Jalalabad and the impending advance of General Pollock's forces, Akbar was eager to project a magnanimous image. At one point he told Lawrence that he deeply regretted the part he had taken in recent events, and that he had 'peremptorily refused to deliver up' any of the hostages to the other chiefs who were intent on killing them.

When the time came for making terms with the British, Captain Colin Mackenzie (and later Captain Colin Troup) was selected to be the intermediary in negotiations between Akbar Khan and General Pollock at Jalalabad. The chief's proposals entailed a prisoner release (including the return of Dost Mohammed and his family from India) in return for the withdrawal of British forces from Afghanistan. By the middle of May, Mackenzie had conducted two missions to Jalalabad returning with money, letters and papers but still no agreement on the hostages' release. Eventually on 24th May the captives were once more to find a sort of semi-permanent residence at the Fort of Shewaki, located on the outskirts of Kabul. At first the group was offered cattle sheds as the only accommodation available. But this proposal, we are told, 'greatly incensed' the indomitable Lady Sale and upon George's protest to Akbar Khan, the owner's family were ordered to give up their apartments for the new arrivals. It was a vast improvement on their previous accommodation to date. Their quarters were found to be 'roomy, clean and comfortable', while attached to the fort was a large, attractive garden including a stream in which to bathe. Here they would wait on developments that would hopefully secure their release, while being periodically updated by Captains Troup and Mackenzie as they shuttled between the Jalalabad garrison and Akbar Khan's camp.

Meanwhile, during the continued vacillations following the Khyber breakthrough of early April, Henry was playing an important, though largely thankless, role in supplying Pollock's army at Jalalabad with food, transport, and money. A lack of clarity concerning roles and responsibilities left the political officer shouldering much of the burden: 'I don't see how the grain collected here [at Ali Masjid Fort] is to be got on,' an exasperated Henry told Clerk on 27th

April, 'for we have but little carriage…the comt [commissariat] officers look on the grain as political [i.e. political officer's responsibility], so I am left to do all.'[30] Forced to organise transportation, he also had to ensure that it had adequate protection, which again he felt was the responsibility of other commanding officers. Moreover, to complicate matters further, the Sikh regiments were again proving unreliable in keeping the Khyber Pass open against the marauding Afridi tribes. By the end of May Henry reported that 'the insolence of the [Sikh] troops was again exceeding all bounds; no British officer could pass them without being insulted.'[31] By early June he complained to Clerk: 'I declared I have ate more dirt at Peshawur than I shall get out of my mouth in the next seven years.'[32] The decision to move the Sikh contingent to Jalalabad, however, improved matters. As they marched out of the Khyber, reaching Jalalabad by 10th June, Lawrence noted thankfully that their previously sullen behaviour had fizzled out. Much of this changed outlook, as Clerk recognised in a special letter of commendation, was down to Henry himself: 'I am very sensible of the persevering exertions, patience, and care that must have been exercised on your part to induce them to move forwards, in the condition of efficiency and proper spirit, in which they appear to have departed.'[33] The situation, though, remained unpredictable, and for this reason Pollock cautiously accepted Henry's continued management of the Sikhs troops, while his rival Mackeson returned to Peshawar.

Back at Shewaki Fort, little had changed during the months of June and July, apart from George Lawrence and some of his fellow captives contracting fever. At the end of July, however, Lawrence received a request from Akbar Khan for him to accompanied Captain Troup, who replaced a sick Mackenzie, on a mission to Jalalabad. Despite being barely recuperated himself, the prospect of seeing his brother Henry, then in charge of Sikh troops at Jalalabad, made the mission too tempting to refuse: 'Although strongly advised by Dr. Campbell, Lady Sale and others, not to make the attempt, as I was in their opinion far too weak to travel, I gladly intimated my willingness to accompany Troup, feeling assured that once on horseback and in the open country, I should speedily recover my strength.'[34]

The aim of the mission was to obtain ratification in writing of an earlier verbal agreement between General Pollock and Akbar Khan, which would allow for an exchange of prisoners and the evacuation of British troops from Afghanistan. After a two-day ride Troup and Lawrence, together with a small escort, reached Jalalabad. Entering General Pollock's camp, George finally met Henry. It had been an interval of nearly three years since they had last done so: 'It is impossible,' George later wrote, 'to describe my feelings of intense thankfulness and delight at meeting my brother, and finding myself once more among British soldiers.'[35] His Afghan escort, Haji Bukhtiar, however, expressed surprised to see that their reunion comprised little more than a shaking of hands. 'We do not feel the less, although we make but little show,' was George's phlegmatic retort.

Both officers then proceeded to General Pollock and passed on Akbar's conditions, requesting that the General fix a date for leaving Afghanistan. By this stage, however, talk of a direct withdrawal from Afghanistan was replaced by a plan of 'retiring via Kabul' following Lord Ellenborough's go-ahead. Consequently, the General's reply to Akbar was deliberately illusive, declaring that he would leave Afghanistan at a time of his own convenience. This response, however, placed George and Troup in an unenviable position, the delivery of which could well amount to a death sentence for both men and the rest of the hostages. Given his recent sickness, Henry offered to take George's place as a hostage 'arguing that if anything fatal happened to him, as he had only one child, it would be of small consequence' compared with George, who was a father of five.[36] Henry's selfless proposal was, needless to say, declined, and on 6th August both George and Troup left Jalalabad with 'a sad foreboding' wondering if they would ever see their colleagues and loved ones again. Predictably, when they arrived back at the Bala Hissar in Kabul on 10th August, Akbar Khan's response was anything but pleasant. The chief angrily waved General Pollock's reply in his hand, and exclaimed:

> Why, what is this you have brought me? It is no reply to my letter! I see the General is playing with me! He in no way confirms the verbal message he sent me by Troup Sahib respecting a mutual exchange of prisoners and evacuation of the country by the British. I had thought you English were men of truth; that your word once given was as good as law. I now see I was in error, and so end all my hopes of an amicable arrangement, and now it must be war.[37]

Even after Akbar Khan had eventually calmed down, it was by no means clear what the future held for the hostages. But, as the meeting neared its end, George told Akbar of Henry's offer to take his place as a hostage. Asked whether he would have accepted Henry instead of George, the chief replied, 'no, no, I prize yourself too much'.

Meanwhile, on 7th August, General Nott's relieving force of 6,000 troops began their march from Kandahar onwards to Kabul. Two weeks later, on 20th August, General Pollock and his 8,000 men from Jalalabad did likewise. In personal command of 200 Sikh horse and 300 infantry, Henry joined the main army at Gandamak. The thought of him now being able to go all the way to Kabul energized him: 'The air is heavenly, and I am all the better for knocking about,' he told Honoria.[38] As for the hostages, the effect of these manoeuvres forced them on the move again. On the evening of 25th August, after another three-month stay, a gloom-laden band of inmates (who had now been joined by the British hostages from Ghazni that included fellow Ulsterman John Nicholson) left Shewaki and began their march, heading westwards. Uncertain as to their fate, George could not escape a crushing sense of despondency while placing his fate in the hands of the Almighty.[39] Their escort was drawn from a regiment of Shah Shuja's infantry under the command of a former subedar called Saleh Mahomed whom George tried in vain to bribe.

On 2nd September, after a very fatiguing week that involved crossing the challenging Hadji Yak Pass at 12,500 feet, they arrived at Bamian, pitching their tents near to the then colossal figures of the Buddhas which, George noted, their guards fired upon 'cursing them as idols'. For the next ten days little of note occurred apart from the circulation of various rumours. But then finally, on 11th September, the breakthrough came when Saleh Mahomed, sensing that the Afghans were about to be defeated by Nott and Pollock's forces, approached Pottinger suggesting that he was now amenable to a settlement that would liberate the hostages. Pottinger, Mackenzie, Lawrence and two other officers wasted no time in holding a conference. After some discussion, the officers agreed under oath to guarantee Saleh Mahomed a pension for life of 1,000 rupees per month, plus a lump sum 20,000 rupees when they returned to Kabul. For his part Saleh Mahomed handed over a written order from Akbar Khan which had directed him to send the hostages to Khulum in the event of Kabul falling to the British. George was under no illusions that, had the order been carried through, the hostages would have been sold into slavery in Turkestan. Saleh Mahomed then 'hoisted the flag of independence' on the fort where they had come to stay. The prisoners were now free.

On 16th September, with their spirits lifted, they left Bamian and began their return to Kabul. On the same day Pollock's forces entered the capital unopposed after defeating Akbar Khan's forces at Tezin where once more Henry's efforts were duly noted by Pollock: 'The Lahore contingent under the able direction of Captain Lawrence, has invariably given the most cheerful assistance, dragging the guns, occupying the heights, and covering the rear-guard.'[40] On 17th September Pollock's military secretary, Sir Richmond Shakespeare, along with a few hundred Qizilbash horsemen, finally reached the hostages. For George, it was an emotional end: 'Oh, what a joyful moment was that when I saw my old friend Shakespeare, and felt that we were really delivered! We made the hills around us ring again with our cheers of delight and thankfulness.'[41] By the 20th he was reunited with his brother Henry and other officers on the approach to Kabul. The following day they entered the city, walking through the Char Chatta, the Great Bazaar of Kabul, until reaching General Pollock's camp. It was finally the end of George's eight and a half months' ordeal and with great relief he expressed his thanks accordingly: 'May the God who so graciously preserved me through so many dangers sanctify His great mercies to me.'[42] By the beginning of November both he and Henry made their way back to India with Pollock's army in circumstances much changed from a few months previous: 'We bowled through the Khyber as if it had been the road between Hammersmith and London,' a jubilant Henry told George Clerk.[43]

Soon after George's liberation, the Army of Retribution had inflicted its vengeance in two acts of wanton destruction – the Great Bazaar of Kabul was razed to the ground while the fortress of Ghazni was blown up. The stain of humiliation, however, remained indelible. Not only had the experiment of regime change been an abject failure, it was also reversed. The loyal Shah Shuja, who had been assassinated in April 1842 by his own godson, Shuja al-Daula, after the British Army had abandoned him in their retreat from Kabul, was replaced by the once demonised figure of Dost Mohammed. The Barakzai clan had triumphed over the Sadozai. After two years of enforced residence in British India, the Dost was restored to the Afghan throne with both the British and the Afghans promising in future not to meddle in each other's affairs.

That George Lawrence had managed to survive his Afghan ordeal tells us much of his personal attributes. He had displayed coolness under pressure and had rapidly reacted to changing circumstances. From the very beginning of the Afghan uprising, and in marked contrast to General Elphinstone and Brigadier Shelton, George was vociferous in campaigning for swift action to defeat the insurgents. Had his views been acted on, the revolt would most likely have been suppressed in its infancy. As the crisis developed, some might have dwelt on the idiocy of inactivity and to have become obstinate. But George wasted little time pondering 'what if?' Instead, he proved himself to be both practical and, given his predicament, unusually sanguine as noted by his brother Henry in an unpublished article entitled *Defence of Sir William Macnaghten*: 'In captivity, as during the siege, his face was ever cheerful. He would give up his horse or his clothes. He would carry a soldier's wife on his pony, or for a whole march a child in his arms. He would serve out the rations, and beard the jailor to his face on behalf of his fellow-captives.'[44] No doubt George's naturally bullish, straightforward temperament helped him to face the various challenges during these critical times, but he also displayed political astuteness, endeavouring to build a rapport with a number of the rebel chiefs – something which Macnaghten had categorically failed to do and had paid the price for it. Yet like so many others, George did not escape unscathed. Eventually, 'the anxieties and exposure of the preceding year' were to take their toll, forcing him to return home on sick leave.[45] He would not return to India until September 1846.

As for Henry, the Anglo-Afghan War had provided an important stepping-stone in his career. He had managed to leave the Revenue Survey and his regiment to join 'the Politicals' – a department which enjoyed greater kudos and career opportunities of which he was most appreciative: 'I do not know how to tell you how much I am obliged for what you have done for me,' he told George Clerk in November 1842, 'to you entirely I owe not being sent back to my regt. or turned into an A.D.C. and I thank you accordingly most heartily and most warmly.'[46] At Ferozepur he had begun to develop his own administrative style, and took the credit for improvements to the town and local economy. He had also enhanced his reputation amongst local Sikh chiefs for his handling of the Faridkot boundary dispute. Such dealings, within the relative proximity of Lahore, enabled him to build up an impressive understanding of Sikh politics and society. As we shall see in the next chapter, he would use this knowledge as research material for published articles and a historical novel. Henry had also worked tirelessly providing logistical support for the Army of the Indus and later in relief measures following the Kabul Revolt. Admittedly, for much of the time the experience was a frustrating one – stymied by a lack of resources, bad military planning and a contingent of Sikh troops who were often obstreperous. Yet Henry had not only managed to overcome these challenges; he had also won the approbation of his superiors and could thus look forward with confidence to further promotion. For both Lawrence brothers, once recuperated, the future looked bright.

Nepalese Sojourn

In the wake of the Afghan campaign, Henry Lawrence had hoped, with good reason, for recognition and promotion. Yet instead of being appointed to a reputable position in which he could make his mark, he was forced to accept a brace of temporarily assignments on low pay. Initially there had been grounds for optimism. In early 1843 he was appointed Superintendent of Dehra Dun, a lucrative post bordering the southern foothills of the Himalayas. But the appointment was soon rescinded when it was discovered that only a covenanted member of the Indian Civil Service was eligible and not a political officer such as Henry. In response, a position based at Ambala was hastily arranged. George Clerk did his best to console Henry by highlighting the post's closeness to the nearest hill station and to the Punjab frontier.[1] But it did little to salve his disappointment: "'My distaste for my present appointment" may appear undue; but it seems to me to be very natural, being by no means a distaste for the work of a civilian…but an unqualified disgust at the manner I have been treated, shoved about … when I had a right to expect consideration and promotion.'[2]

His gloom intensified following the discovery that he had been passed over succeeding Clerk as the Governor-General's agent on the north-west frontier: 'I ought to succeed him here, if knowing anything about the work has aught to do with the matter,' he complained to his sister Letitia.[3] Then, after only two months at Ambala, Henry was forced to shift again when he was sent by Clerk to handle the British takeover of the neighbouring state of Kaithal (Khytul) where the incumbent Sikh Raja (Bhai Ude Singh) had died without heir in March 1843. He did so again in grumbling fashion as it was a modest appointment at no more than 1,000 rupees per month. James Thomason, then foreign secretary to the Indian government, as always tried to temper Henry's career frustrations by urging restraint on his friend's aggrieved passions: 'Any hasty or intemperate action will greatly prejudice your cause, and put it out of the power of your friends to serve you. I entreat you still further – put a bridle on your words as well as your actions,' Thomason advised.[4] With no alternative, it was a case of getting on with the job before a more suitable post came his way.

In the event, the handover of Kaithal to British forces proved to be no formality. In April retainers of the old Raja had at first refused to surrender to a small contingent of British troops sent by Clerk. In response, the latter turned to Henry who, with the help of his brother John, hastily organised reinforcements from the Karnal cantonment, thirty-five miles west. News of their impending arrival was sufficient to convince the Raja's followers that further resistance was futile. The fort and palace of Kaithal were quickly abandoned, leaving the British to enter unopposed. 'It was a strange scene of confusion,' recalled one young officer, Henry Yule, as he set foot within the citadel, 'all the paraphernalia and accumulation of odds and ends of a wealthy family lying about and inviting loot.'[5] The temptation did indeed prove too much for some British officers who began helping themselves to the contents of the palace treasury. But when Henry caught wind of this free-for-all, he swiftly issued a stern rebuke and demanded that they 'give up every article of property that they may have taken possession of since their arrival'.[6] During the commotion, Yule was on hand to capture a revealing vignette of the man who would one day rule the Punjab:

When the news of this affair came to him [H. Lawrence] I was present. It was in a white marble loggia in the palace, where there was a white marble chair or throne on a basement. Lawrence was sitting on this throne in great excitement. He wore an Afghan *choga*, a sort of dressing-gown garment, and this and his thin locks, and thin beard were streaming in the wind. He always dwells in my memory as a sort of pythoness on her tripod under the afflatus.[7]

Henry was to spend a busy six-months as 'Malik of Khytul', Clerk's light-hearted description of his role. Most of the time involved making a summary settlement of the land revenue.[8] It was a task made more difficult by the recent disorder. Henry found that the central revenue records of the state were 'almost entirely either destroyed or abstracted', and even after hiring the help of two *munshis* very few accounts were uncovered or were in a useable state. Consequently, he was forced to look to the various *parganas* of the district to supply village revenue accounts. This proved more fruitful, and he was able to procure 'tolerably correct statements' for the years 1827 to 1837. He also managed to obtain some village accounts in each *pargana* covering the most recent five years even though they served to confirm his worse fears 'that the estates had been year after year deteriorating; and that much of the territory was in a fair way of becoming perfectly desolate'.[9]

While the revenue papers were being collated, Henry embarked on three extensive tours of the district during April, May and July: 'I visited almost every village in the territory, thoroughly inspecting every one of those most decayed, and requiring most attention and making notes on their condition.'[10] His investigations revealed that revenue collection under the previous government had been in the hands of revenue farmers or middlemen who were anxious to continue in the same capacity. By instinct, Henry sought to promote the interests of the owner cultivator or village *zamindari* class at the expense of these middlemen as the best means of increasing the amount of land under cultivation. In practice, however, reaching a settlement with the former required some gentle coaxing: 'I found the zamindars at first to hang off altogether, or to offer in some instances hundreds were they could pay thousands; and almost in every instance at first offering fifty or a hundred percent less than they eventually agreed to, when inundated by the offers of the expectant [revenue] farmers.'[11]

In his summary settlement report, Henry stated that he had taken the average of ten-year's worth of available revenue records as the basis for his three-year assessment. He also removed some onerous charges – capitation tax, levies on buffaloes, use of grass and wood, payments to local government officials – which had previously been collected as part of the government demand. But in some villages the poor state of cultivation forced Henry to offer revenue remissions albeit under certain obligations: 'in all these instances I have bound down the zumindars to dig or prepare new wells, to repair old ones – and to bring in a certain number of ploughs before the expiration of the present lease; indeed what I held out to all was the improvement of the lands, as the price of their present moderate assessment.'[12] By the end of his time at Kaithal, and similar to his efforts at Ferozepur, Henry presented a picture of rapid agrarian improvement under his direction:

> Such indeed was the desolate condition of the district that in April and May last when looking at the country from the tops of towers…I could often see miles and miles of good land, without a single acre of cultivation; the remissions made by government of thirty per cent on the last rubbee [spring] crop in consequence of the report I then made, have been the main cause of the improved cultivation of the district.[13]

Henry estimated during his tenure that the number of ploughs in use had 'increased fifty per cent' while incentives had been given to farmers to grow potatoes, sugar, cotton, and trees for timber. Leading by example, he had ordered the planting of 'some miles of road with trees and given out large quantities of seed for plantation'.[14] He had also advocated the availability of small advances for the purchase of seed and cattle, made suggestions for canal construction to increase irrigation, and 'urged the necessity of opening out good roads' as well as a system of drainage to improve 'the salubrity of the country'.[15]

The reputation of Kaithal 'as lawless a tract of country as any in India' was swiftly overturned too. Many offenders had been placed into confinement or had simply fled the district. Within a week of British rule being introduced, Henry proclaimed that 'two flagrant instances of wholesale cattle driving [stealing], in which more than a hundred men were concerned' had been discovered and most of the culprits apprehended. 'No other instance has since happened, although under the late government, they were of daily occurrence.'[16] Other measures included the taking of security bonds from 'all villages of bad or doubtful character' to pay for stolen property tracked to their lands, with headmen made responsible 'for the acts of all residing within their bounds'.[17] Cases of violent crime were apparently reduced by Henry's order that all firearms be handed into the local police station and that only one sword per ten households could be retained. 'I have now the pleasure of thinking,' he told the Governor-General's Agent, Colonel A.F. Richmond, 'that while almost the whole of the boundaries of the district have been settled, not only has no life been lost, but I am not aware of a single affray having occurred, in a country where it has not been unusual in a single village for ten or twenty men to be killed.'[18]

Henry's self-publicised improvements in the fortunes of the Kaithal district were notable, but not everyone found his record so satisfactory. One later British settlement officer, J.M. Douie, was to cast doubt on Henry's revenue assessment methodology, believing that 'he did not follow his [ten-year *pargana*] figures at all closely, but trusted a good deal apparently to his personal inspection of villages'. More pointedly, Douie regarded his 'moderate' assessment, as being 'too severe' as only a few years later was a subsequent settlement officer obliged to reduce the *jama* [revenue total] by one-fifth. Douie also believed that Lawrence had been unrealistically sanguine in forecasting substantial material improvement over the course of his three-year settlement. In practice, progress was slow: 'the seasons were unfavourable both as regards health and crops; and men's minds were disturbed by the fear that Khytul would be handed back to Bhai Ude Singh's widow, or to his nearest collateral relative, the Bhai of Arnauli.'[19]

Despite the engrossing nature of the work at Kaithal, Henry nevertheless remained frustrated over his career prospects. He had resigned himself, he told General Pollock in late August 1843, to 'fag away…for another year on the same pay', and questioned Governor-General Ellenborough's distribution of honours: 'One man gets praise, another pudding; I have had neither.'[20] To add to his miseries, the Governor-General had shortly afterwards mistakenly addressed a package to Henry as Major Lawrence C.B.[21] Its contents, however, revealed no Order of the Bath, only a modest looking Kabul medal. The typo left him crestfallen, and at one point he even considered returning home.[22] But thankfully his disgruntlement did not last long. Within a matter of days,

Henry received news of his appointment as Resident at the Court of Nepal –
an independent kingdom on India's northern border where a British presence
had been established earlier in the century.[23]

The Nepalese Residency was a prestigious post on a substantial salary of Rs
3,500 per month, and with responsibilities that were far from onerous. Moreover,
Nepal's invigorating climate afforded Henry the chance to restore his health.
'I happen to know,' James Thomason informed him, 'that Lord Ellenborough
selected you for it, in a great measure, because he hoped the climate would agree
with you, and enable you to stay in the country.'[24] There was one drawback,
though. It removed him from his preferred milieu of the northwest frontier
where career-enhancing opportunities for budding soldier-administrators like
himself were more likely. Nepal, by contrast, offered little such hope, and for this
reason Henry could not help feeling a tinge of despondency: 'My appointment
was most unexpected, and not as welcome as it ought to have been,' he would
later record in his Nepalese journal.[25] Indeed, shortly before making the journey
to the kingdom, the ill health of Colonel A.F. Richmond, Clerk's successor on
the northwest frontier, prompted Henry to propose swapping places.[26] Clerk,
who was now briefly Lieutenant-Governor of the North-Western Provinces,
swiftly quashed the idea, believing that Henry's health would not have withstood
another hot summer on the frontier.

Henry arrived in the Nepalese kingdom on 30th November 1843, smoothing
the way for Honoria and their young son Alick to join some six weeks later.
Previously, no Resident had been allowed to bring his wife with him. This time
the kingdom's rules were relaxed giving Honoria the honour of becoming the
first white woman to visit the country. The Lawrences soon came to appreciate
their new surroundings. Henry likened the climate of its capital, Kathmandu, to
Montpellier, 'never hot, never very cold'. This aspect combined with sweeping
views of richly cultivated valleys, winding rivers, Buddhist temples, and snow-
capped mountains greatly raised their spirits: 'a lovelier spot than this the heart of
man could scarce desire,' he told one friend in February 1844, 'in every direction
we choose to ride we have lovely or sublime prospects. Every day and every hour
a new scene opens upon us…the towns, the temples, the people are all fruitful
in interest to us.'[27] Thoughts of labouring as head of the Punjab Agency were
dispelled, albeit temporarily, and there was an acceptance that Clerk's refusal had
undoubtedly been the correct one. Instead, as he explained to another friend,
John Marshman, a sense of relief and gratitude now prevailed:

> Our own lot has fallen in a goodly land, at a time, too, when we most wanted
> and least expected it, my wife delicate, our one surviving child unable to
> live in the plains – myself the wreck of two Arrakan fevers, and almost

yearly fevers ever since. We were preparing for England without the means of paying our passage home, when we were sent here. In our thankfulness for this change of fortune, for quiet, ease, health, and competence, in lieu of toil, discomfort, and sickness and for years having literally no home, no place of retirement – when it was comparative rest and comfort to go out to camp in the hot winds, or to ride off 50 or 60 miles at a stretch, to exchange the daily and nightly toil of cantts [cantonments] for village work – all this we have exchanged for a paradise.[28]

Henry's appointment as Resident was an opportunity, on the part of the Calcutta government, to reset Indo-Nepalese relations. Ellenborough had dismissed his predecessor, Brian Hodgson, after a long stint in Nepal, on account of his undue involvement in the country's internal politics, and the perception that he had become the victim of court manipulation.[29] Calcutta was now insistent that the new man avoid such intervention. James Thomason, recently appointed Lieutenant-Governor of the North-Western Provinces following the ill-health of George Clerk, explained the Nepalese brief to Henry. His duties, he told him, were principally twofold. He was to observe the goings-on at the Nepalese court and to report and remonstrate against anything detrimental to British interests. Secondly, he was also to offer measured advice if sought or if it was 'likely to be acceptable and useful'. It was this 'duty of advice' which Thomason regarded as 'the most important and delicate' task a Resident could perform: 'The main object is to identify oneself with the real and best interests of the State. When they feel that such is really the case, and that the object is worked out in a kind, conciliatory, and single-minded manner, considerable influence will probably be obtained.'[30]

From the beginning, Henry was highly critical of the path trodden by his predecessor. During the handover in early December he had quickly detected, he told Honoria, a subservient relationship between Hodgson and the Nepalese royalty: '...they are canvassing my character & they made such a fool of Mr H. [Hodgson] that they are puzzled about me. Mr H. mixed up in their intrigues, and with outstretched hands in my presence called himself the Raja's servant; so you can fancy the system that has prevailed.'[31] After introducing himself to the Raja and declaring his 'non-interference creed', the new Resident soon revealed that 'as the *Elchee* [ambassador] of a Government' his relationship with the Nepalese authorities would not be an obsequious one.[32] Over the first few months, Henry spent a good deal of his time reading the Residency papers. He was appalled to find that except for the letters of the last two years, they were in 'open bookshelves in the Residency dining room' and surmised that 'copies of all political documents' were now in the hands of the Nepalese Durbar.[33]

In Hodgson's letters to the Maharaja and his ministers, he also found 'plenty of interference and dictation' but in 'a style of humility' that was 'extremely unbecoming'. In sum, he told Frederick Currie in October 1844, 'Mr H. seems to me to have sought dignity, or excitement, or some unknown good, by mixing himself up in Nepal affairs and to have endeavoured to ingratiate himself with the Raja by personal subserviency.'[34]

Although much of Henry's time in Nepal was officially uneventful, the one notable feature of Nepalese politics was a power struggle played out between the Maharaja, the Rani, their son and an ambitious minister called Matabur Singh. The affable Matabur had made repeated efforts over several months to forge an alliance with the new Resident in opposition to the Raja. But Henry flatly refused to be involved in intrigue, anxious to establish his non-partisan credentials in the light of his predecessor's perceived meddling. In November 1844 events took a brutal turn with the execution of nineteen army officers, summarily charged with plotting against Matabur. Although the affair temporarily strengthened the minister's hand, it ultimately sowed the seeds of his undoing. Despite warnings from Henry, Matabur did not 'wear his honours meekly' nor use 'his influence judiciously'.[35] Lulled into a false sense of security, his pursuit of vanity projects such as the building of an ostentatious residence by enlisted soldiers, or lavish spending on clothes merely served to alienate the chiefs and the military.[36] Eventually the Raja took advantage of the growing animosity towards his minister, and late on the evening of 17th May 1845, under the ruse of urgent business, had Matabur assassinated: 'Twelve hours after the murder,' recorded Henry, 'not a word was to be heard in favour of the man who, the day before, had been everything.'[37]

Despite the country's domestic political turmoil, Henry remained confident that Nepal did not pose a serious threat to the security of British India. 'There is not a soldier in Nepal, scarcely a single man that has seen a shot fired and not one that could lead an Army,' he told Lord Auckland on 25th May 1845,

The chiefs are a very poor set, effeminate, debauched creatures wanting in all respectable qualities...The Goorkhas will always intrigue; and will generally be as insolent as they are permitted to be, but they know our power too well to molest us unless in some such catastrophe as would cause a general insurrection in India.[38]

Even so, such a view did not stop Henry considering the possibility of another conflict. At the beginning of 1845, he told Clerk that 'a poke in the ribs of Nepal might do good' and act as a corrective to the ill-judged policy of his predecessor: 'we have allowed ourselves so long to be humbugged that I much fear their doing something some day that we will not stomach. Hodgson always told the Government that we had everything to lose and nothing to gain by quarrelling with Nepal. I differ in opinion on every point.'[39] Henry estimated that Nepal could be taken within three months by an invasion force of some thirty thousand men, and 'that it would be more valuable to us than the Panjab, giving us the snowy range for our eastern boundary, and Sanataria all along the Oudh'. The country could then be held by a combination of troops from the Cawnpore, Dinapore, and Benares divisions and the drafting of Gurkha soldiers into Indian regiments. In these musings, there was a strong element of Henry craving an active foreign policy. But in cooler moments he thought that the British stance should be robust but non-combative: 'I can thus see the advantages of the country to us, but I think the fair and honest way of dealing with the Goorkhas is to let them distinctly know our power, so that they may not commit themselves, for hitherto their vanity has been so flattered that they are up to any absurdity.'[40]

Henry's watching brief on Nepalese political affairs no doubt frustrated his energetic instincts. Yet there were other aspects of his situation which took the sheen off the Lawrences' alpine idyll. One was the Nepalese government's restriction on their movements. They were confined mostly to the capital, save for a small summer cottage at Koulia, located barely fourteen miles away at a height of 1800 feet. More importantly, however, was the 'want of some society'. The British community at Kathmandu, beside themselves, consisted only of the station doctor, Dr Christie, and the commandant of the Resident's small escort of Indian troops, Captain Smith. At first relations with the two men were cordial. 'I like the Dr. and Smith well, both are quiet and well behaved and desirous of being agreeable,' he told Honoria on arrival in December 1843.[41] Four months later, though, interactions had become decidedly strained. According to Honoria, Captain Smith was now seen as 'overbearing and crouching' with 'a zig zag up and down notion of the truth' while Dr. Christie, although 'harmless and inoffensive' was 'ignorant on most general subjects'. Mealtimes with the two men were painful affairs and were kept as brief as possible. 'I see no glimmer of principle in either,' lamented Honoria, 'of any motive higher or broader or deeper than "my own advantage" or "what the world expects."'[42]

Matters, however, were to go beyond irritating character traits. In fact, Captain Smith would cause Henry a good deal of trouble. Not only had he built up considerable financial debts, his failure to disclose their full extent (despite Henry's financial assistance) and his 'total disregard' in fulfilling numerous administrative duties left Henry with no other choice but to seek his removal.[43] He was particularly irked by Smith's 'dictatorial tone' and the 'ceaseless, vehement protestations of his willingness, nay anxiety to help' that gave the impression of him being the injured party.[44] Relations reached breaking point when he purloined Henry's cook but still demanded that his dinner be sent to him: 'You call my Table a public one,' an exasperated Henry told Smith, 'and you have certainly found it so, whether you chose to dine at your own house or at the said table; however as you took away my cook you could hardly expect me to continue to send you dinner.'[45]

Smith was eventually replaced by Captain George Ottley who had decided to take up the post even after Henry had described conditions at Kathmandu in less than favourable terms. Although Nepal's fine climate was a definite advantage compared to other parts of India, he told his prospective assistant, the real drawback was the isolation and the lack of active employment: 'you must however calculate on having a good deal of your own company and if you don't like that you had better not come, as you would soon get dissatisfied.'[46] But Ottley, who was accompanied by his wife, had no intention of staying long in Nepal. When his own leave plans collided with those of Henry's, relations between the two men quickly soured, ending in Ottley's resignation. 'He has behaved very shabbily,' Henry informed Frederick Currie on 28th October 1845, '...I attribute his conduct chiefly to his foolish wife who was left some 30,000 Rs. a few months ago which had turned her weak head.'[47] Henry, alas, was once more forced to find a replacement. The experience led him to stipulate one key requirement: the next candidate should be unmarried: 'I can manage the husbands,' he told Currie, 'but not the ladies.'[48]

During their Nepalese stay, Honoria was forced to endure long bouts of severe illness during her pregnancy and after the delivery of her third child, Henry Waldemar (also known as Harry) who was born on 24th January 1845 (named after Prince Waldemar of Prussia, a noted traveller and explorer who had visited the Nepalese kingdom during their stay). Her illness appears to have been exacerbated by Dr Christie's incompetence and by the end of 1845 it was decided that she should leave Nepal and return to England for the sake of her health taking Alick and Harry with her.[49] In the meantime, despite her afflictions and encouraged by Henry's light official duties and lack of social life, the couple still managed to devote much of their time to their own personal projects. Based on their firm religious beliefs, one important philanthropic venture was their plan to provide schooling for the children of British soldiers in India. There were two main reforming impulses behind the move. One was physical – both Henry and Honoria understood barrack life was particularly challenging for children and their young uneducated mothers who were ill-equipped to cope with the climate and unaware of the importance of hygiene. The other was moral – cramped barrack conditions and the lack of privacy often led to the corruption of girls, many of whom were forced into prostitution or untimely marriages; for the boys there was little prospect beyond an early regimental enlistment. A blind eye was generally turned to their plight, but the Lawrences were intent on offering a practical solution.

The idea of founding an educational establishment had first germinated in late 1842 when Henry had visited a school run by a Mr. Mackinnon at the hill station of Mussoorie where he was 'much struck with the robust, active appearance of the pupils, as well as with that gentleman's management'.[50] Based on this experience, both Henry and Honoria were convinced that a school, or rather an asylum, set in the hills would provide the most appropriate environment in which both boys and girls could thrive. Use of the term asylum was deliberate. For this was a place of retreat – a secure, healthy establishment for children to develop into responsible adults. In its first official history, Henry outlined the asylum's purpose:

> The object of the institution is to provide for the orphan and other children of soldiers serving or having served in India, an asylum from the debilitating effects of a tropical climate, and the demoralizing influences of barrack-life; wherein they may obtain the benefits of a bracing climate, a healthy moral atmosphere, and a plain, useful, and above all religious education, adapted to fit them for employment suited to their position in life, and with divine blessing to make them consistent Christians, and intelligent, and useful members of society.[51]

Key to its success, he believed, was the assistance of regimental commanding officers in its management and supply of teachers. For this reason, the asylum would be situated near an existing military hill station and would also be non-denominational. In July 1845, he wrote to Colonel Stuart, Secretary to the Government Military Department, outlining his proposal, and stressed that it was 'no sudden freak of wild enthusiasm, but the sober result of long acquaintance with the condition of barrack children, and of the especial degradation of girls'.[52] Many, however, remained unconvinced of the venture. Even his good friend and colleague, James Thomason, poured 'cold water on the scheme', arguing that it would be difficult to set up an efficient management committee to run the school.[53] Despite the lukewarm response, Henry and Honoria remained committed to seeing the project through. Having laid the groundwork during their Nepalese stay, the breakthrough eventually came in the immediate aftermath of the 1st Anglo-Sikh War. Armed with the backing of Lord Gough (Commander-in-Chief) and Lord Hardinge (Governor-General), sufficient support was given at an officers' meeting held in Lahore on 10th March 1846. By the following August a site for the new school had been chosen on the hill of Sanawar near to the military hill stations of Sabathu and Kasauli. Funded by subscriptions and donations from not only the Anglo-Indian community but also from several Punjabi chieftains, most notably Maharaja Gulab Singh who gave one lakh rupees, the asylum opened in March 1847.[54]

Another key focus for Henry and Honoria during their Nepalese stay was the pursuit of various literary ventures. Their creative energies were channelled through the timely establishment of *The Calcutta Review*, a periodical on Anglo-Indian related subjects founded by J.W. Kaye in 1844. The *Review* proved to be an ideal platform for the couple to express their views, albeit anonymously, across a wide range of topics. Henry's contributions, according to Kaye, 'were gravid with matter of the best kind – important facts accompanied by weighty opinions and wise suggestions'.[55] They did pose some editorial challenges, however. Despite the assistance of Honoria, his poor handwriting, and a tendency to leave sentences unfinished led at times to what Kaye described as 'ludicrous confusion' when the proofs returned 'from the hands of the native printer'.[56] By today's standards, the articles are convoluted, digressive affairs. But they are, nonetheless, the reflections of a man who had read widely and thought deeply. Henry may well have secluded himself in his Nepalese mountain retreat, yet it is clear from the subject matter of his pen that he was constantly thinking of India and the role Britain was playing in its governance.

That the northwest frontier remained in the forefront of his thinking can be seen in no less than three articles published in 1844: *Recent History of the Punjab*, *The Seikhs and their Country*, and *Kashmir and the Countries around the Indus*. These timely articles, published against the backdrop of growing volatility within the Sikh state, provided a critique of recent historical literature and drew heavily on Henry's experience as a frontier political officer. As he explained to George Clerk, they had been written 'with a view of inculcating right notions' as he feared that 'at home as well as in India' there was 'a strong propensity to crush poor Khalsajee'.[57] Thus in *Recent History of the Punjab*, Henry expressed no desire to see the boundary of British India extended to the Indus, 'much less to see interference forced upon the Punjab'.[58] Although accepting the argument for the existing border to 'be still further strengthened with troops and material' as a means of rendering British India 'safe from insult', he nonetheless believed that an excessive build-up of military forces and belligerent talk gave the Lahore government 'a pretext for war'.[59]

Despite the vehemence expressed by Henry in his *Calcutta Review* articles for maintaining the status quo vis-à-vis the Sikhs, privately at least he was willing to become fully involved in a conflict should it arise. 'Pray tell His Excellency the C-in-C., that, if my services would be thought at all useful, I shall be too happy to join and serve during the campaign, in any capacity, A.D.C., guide, artillery or political,' he told one officer at staff headquarters in March 1844.[60] By the end of October 1845, with rumours of war abounding, Henry also reminded Frederick Currie of his readiness to take part: 'I again ask to get as much warning as possible if I am to be called on – if my services can in any way be useful I am at all times ready should I be called.'[61] Henry's seemingly contradictory stance was perhaps best explained in a letter (29th November 1845) to his friend, John Marshman, in which he questioned whether the Punjab could remain an effective buffer state, fulfilling the security needs of India's north-west frontier. If it was weak, he told Marshman, it provided no barrier, but if it was strong and acted like Afghanistan, it would be a threat: 'No native power that dared,' he argued, 'would hesitate to try for Hindostan.' He reiterated his belief that the Punjab should be 'let alone, as long as possible', but if there was to be a conflict it should be conducted 'effectually'. Comparisons were drawn with how British had 'only clipped' the likes of Burma, Nepal, and Mysore and had 'thought to make them friends by taking half their territory; or at any rate to render them harmless'.[62] But this, Henry argued, was a mistake; there should be no half measures when it came to involvement in the affairs of another contiguous state. It was a point he also made in the final few lines of his *Recent History of the Punjab* article:

> Interference is easy to talk of, but no one knowing the miseries it engenders will advocate its application. The first step taken, and the Rubicon is passed; we cannot halt; we must go on; we must take the country for ourselves; or a far worse measure, we must perpetuate in the Punjab the tales of the Deccan (Hyderabad), of Mysore, Arcot and Oude.[63]

One subject of enduring interest to Henry was the state of the India army and its importance to the continuance of British rule in India. In *Military Defence of our Empire in the East,* he candidly admitted that however light 'the yoke of the stranger' happened to be, the British in India could not maintain their position 'without sword-government': 'we must know that, differing in colour, caste, language, habits – everything; having indeed nothing in common with our subjects, our rule can scarcely be a loved one.'[64] It was therefore imperative that the army, composed of both British and Indian soldiers, was a well-maintained, disciplined and trustworthy force. For Henry, though, there was much scope for reform. He saw the Engineer Corps 'too little engaged during peace in the functions that would best prepare them for war' and advocated more practical training in techniques such as surveying and mapping.[65] As a former artillery officer, he also called for improvements in the organisation of the Foot Artillery and for it to be placed on a par with the more prestigious Horse Artillery 'as to all emoluments, equipment, and officering'.[66] Similarly, his frustrating experience of organising logistics during the 1st Anglo-Afghan War led him to demand an overhaul of the Commissariat dept. For both health and moral reasons, he also strongly recommended that European troops and their families be garrisoned as much as possible at military hill stations linked with good road connections.

A notable bugbear of Henry's was the army's system of promotion and its bias towards length of service. 'We are strongly of opinion,' he declared, 'that old age is but a negative virtue, and should not without positive merit be rewarded in soldiers.'[67] Among the measures demanded were a weeding out of invalids and those found to be incompetent, for a maximum age limit to be set, and greater opportunity for both Indian and British soldiers to rise within the ranks. In the recruitment of sepoys, he advocated that they should be drawn from a wider range of castes and classes as well as from different parts of India in an effort to reduce clannishness and potential disaffection. Indeed, with an uncanny sense of the prescient, Henry was one of the few to fully appreciate the dangers of disregarding the welfare and feelings of Indian soldiers.[68] His generosity of spirit and his willingness of telling hard truths to power were prophetically revealed in the final paragraph of the article:

> We cannot expect to hold India forever. Let us so conduct ourselves in our civil and military relations as when the connexion ceases, it may do so, not with convulsions, but with mutual esteem and affection; and that England may then have in India a noble ally, enlightened, and brought into the scale of nations under her guidance and fostering care.[69]

The strength of his feeling on military matters would be confirmed over a decade later with two further *Calcutta Review* articles entitled *The Indian Army* (1855) and *Army Reform* (1856). In the meantime, his broad interests were demonstrated in other articles of a more personal nature. In *Romance and Reality of Indian life*, a piece he co-wrote with Honoria, the intellectual and emotional impulses of both Henry the writer and the colonial administrator are revealed. The piece amply demonstrates the strong influence of early nineteenth century Romanticism. Described by one historian as 'combining a strong introspective bent, a sensibility for natural beauty and for historical associations, with an imaginative urge for release in action and adventure,' Romanticism in India offered an emotional appeal against the rising influence of stern Utilitarianism.[70] Thus the Lawrences wrote: 'We set little store by the dry Utilitarians who can see only the dark features of the chronicles they unravel, who hearts kindle not at tales of gallantry and devotion, however clouded by errors of faith – who have not a tear of sympathy for the brave man, dying in defence of his hearth, or the maiden, preferring death to dishonour; even though the scene of such heroism be in India, the actors in such tragedies Heathens.'[71]

While Utilitarianism championed uniformity, regulation and an impersonal bureaucracy, Romanticism stressed a belief in upholding indigenous institutions wherever possible, and an espousal of strong, but sympathetic paternal rule. The chief exponents of this Romantic school were an earlier breed of Anglo-Indian administrators. Men such as John Malcolm, Mountstuart Elphinstone, Charles Metcalfe and Thomas Munro sanctified the role of the district officer as the *ma-bap* (compassionate father and mother) of the Indian peasantry.[72] Of the four figures, Malcolm would arguably form the deepest impression on Henry and the development of his administrative ethos. Like his contemporaries, Malcolm thought deeply and sensitively about the nature of British rule in India:

> We must divest our minds of all arrogant pretentions arising from the presumed superiority of our own knowledge, and seek the accomplishment of the great ends we have in view by the means which are best suited to the peculiar nature of the objects…All that the government can do is, by maintaining the internal peace of the country, and by adapting its principles to the various feelings, habits and character of its inhabitants, to give time for the slow and silent operation of the desired improvement, with a constant impression that every attempt to accelerate this end will be attended with the danger of its defeat.[73]

In *Romance and Reality* Henry and Honoria believed that many of the British arrivals to India suffered from excessively romantic expectations. Fed on 'splendid delusions, learned from the Arabian Nights, and the scenic melodramas of the London stage', the 'romance' of India was soon dispelled upon arrival.[74] 'There is glare and dust; and both are to be shut out; and the luxuriant herbage is condemned as jungle, suggesting thoughts of dire disease…'[75] India was not the beguiling place as previously imagined. Disappointment led to a stifling of poetic sensibilities. Offering a different perspective, however, the Lawrences sought to show that there was much in Indian life that was both 'picturesque and attractive'. It all depended on the proper intermixing of romance and reality:

> When the two faculties are duly blended, Reality pursues a straight though rough path to a desirable and practicable result; while Romance beguiles the road by pointing out its beauties, by bestowing a deep and practical conviction that even in this dark and material existence, there may be found a joy with which a stranger intermeddleth not – a light that shineth more and more unto the perfect day.[76]

Of those deemed to be 'excellent examples' of following such a path, John Malcolm was a clear favourite. In Henry's opinion, the Scottish born administrator 'possessed probably larger and more diversified experience than any other British Officer ever attained in the East'.[77] His esteemed career, it was argued, was based fundamentally on the romantic elements of enthusiasm, imagination, feeling and character:

> He [Malcolm] carried with him everywhere the freshness of feeling, the enthusiasm of character, that enabled him to enter heartily into the feelings and peculiarities of the many interesting races with which he was brought into contact. The sympathy that qualified him to enter into conversation as readily with the peasant as with the peer, with the rude Seikh soldier, Pindarie or Mahratta, as with the Nawabs and Rajahs of the land, proved to all, that his was not mere lip-service, but that in his heart he aimed at their welfare.[78]

Likewise, Sir Thomas Munro had the 'romance of feeling and character' which stirred him to overhaul the land revenue system in Madras: 'Miles apart from any European, he laboured with a singleness of heart that impelled him to do good for its own sake, and for the blessings it wrought out for a long-distracted country.'[79] Lieutenant Colonel James Tod was another lauded for his unstinting efforts in canal construction within the Delhi Territory as well as for his monumental *Annals and Antiquities of Rajasthan* – a work much in keeping with Romanticism's fondness for chivalric history. In all these examples it was 'imagination', 'poetry of thought' and 'enthusiasm' which fashioned improvements and renovations, and drew satisfaction in 'substituting peace and plenty, for plunder and poverty' – qualities, the couple argued, that were 'indispensable to the attainment of the highest goodness and greatness of human character'.[80] Here was the inspiration for Henry's paternalism.

If the influence of Romanticism on the couple's writings had found a fertile outlet in *The Calcutta Review*, it was soon given greater vent in a more ambitious literary offering. Around the same time, and again with Honoria's assistance, Henry was preparing for publication a historical novel set towards the end of Ranjit Singh's reign. Entitled *Adventures of an Officer in the Service of Runjeet Singh*, it followed the exploits of a romantic adventurer called Colonel Bellasis. Drawing inspiration from the careers of foreign mercenaries employed in the Maharaja's army and the literary style of Sir Walter Scott, Henry utilised his first-hand frontier knowledge together with contemporary historical works on the subject.[81] Originally serialized anonymously in the *Delhi Gazette* as *Some Passages in the Life of an Adventurer in the Punjaub*, he decided this time to forego anonymity in an effort to establish his reputation as one of the leading British authorities on Punjab affairs. In doing so, he no doubt hoped it would pave the way for his eventual return to the region.

As a historical novel, *Adventures of an Officer in the Service of Runjeet Singh* is, at the very least, as much about fact as it is about fiction. For although the protagonist Bellasis cautions the reader early on not to regard his 'rough notes as materials for history' but rather as 'first impressions and crude gatherings', it soon becomes clear that the work is a serious contribution to Anglo-Indian literature on Punjab history and culture.[82] In the book's preface, it is revealed that the 'slight story' of the fictional Bellasis has been 'adopted merely as a convenient vehicle for conveying to the reader characteristic illustrations of the border country, its people, its manners, its rulers, and their modes of ruling'.[83] To aid the reader, there are numerous explanatory footnotes as well as a significant amount of purely historical information inserted directly into the narrative. Character sketches of the leading political figures of the day are also supplied, together with details on the factional makeup of the kingdom's chieftains. Under the strong appeal of Romanticism, the choice of a straightforward historical monograph is shunned in favour of a more vibrant depiction of the Sikh polity – a decision made implicit in the concluding chapter where a distinction is drawn between 'history' and 'historical romance':

> History gives (or ought to give) a well-proportioned *Map* of events, while historical romance…offers *pictures* of men and manners, and seeks to sketch the interior scenes of life, and details that escape the casual observer, rather than to chronicle occurrences already recorded in official documents.[84]

In *The Calcutta Review*'s appraisal of the book, the reviewer, possibly J.W. Kaye, clearly saw the historical novel genre as leaving a deeper impression on the reader's imagination. Major Lawrence is 'a master of all the intricacies of Sikh affairs' whose narrative is 'so skilfully constructed as to convey…a vast deal of interesting and authentic intelligence, of a varied character – statistical, historical, geographical and political,' the reviewer effused. In addition, there is 'all the vividness of a dramatic representation. Everything is so natural— so true— so painted to the life— that the reader is made as it were an eye-witness of every scene, and a partaker in the evolution of every striking incident and stirring event.'[85]

Much of the book naturally revolves around Bellasis's relationship with Maharaja Ranjit Singh. His characterisation of the great man is one that would have been familiar to most contemporary European observers – namely a figure of apparent contradictions.[86] While Bellasis describes the Maharaja in the twilight of his career as a man of 'mean appearance' whose constitution has been 'much worn out by hard living and debauchery', he clearly finds him worthy of study if not admiration.[87] 'For his age and country,' he remarks, 'he may truly be called great, and, in some respects, even a good king. He is active, enterprising, and, to a certain extent, just. Kind and liberal to those within his sight, he is much beloved by his personal followers.'[88] Bellasis makes allowances for the Maharaja's 'grasping rapacity' based on 'his education and temptations', and believes 'that the worst parts of his rule are those common to oriental despots, while the favourable points arise from his individual character'.[89] Although illiterate, the Maharaja's 'great natural intelligence, and a wonderfully quick apprehension and retentive memory' are duly noted.[90] His success is measured by his ability to not only draw 'all around into his wishes' but also to know 'when to yield and how to contract his measures' in reference to his shrewd dealings with the East India Company.[91] To Bellasis, his overall achievement is one of bringing peace and security to a region where once each petty chief was 'a legalised plunderer and murderer': 'Runjit has made life comparatively secure, and he must have done something for property, or we should not see the existing wealth of Lahore and Amritsar, nor would his subjects shew so little anxiety to locate themselves under the neighbouring British rule.'[92]

Despite his penchant for nocturnal revelries and sporting pastimes, the Maharaja maintains a firm personal grip on his empire. Long hours are spent hearing provincial reports, dictating correspondences to scribes, holding daily durbars, and conducting annual circuits. Revenue accounts, Bellasis notes, are of particular importance and the subject of intense scrutiny: 'A true statement he does not reckon among possibilities; so that when the accounts seem all fair and square, and the revenue rendered even exceeds the stipulated sum, he always disallows a certain percentage, the tenacity of his memory enabling him to follow out the most complicated statements.'[93] He, nonetheless, relies heavily on delegation and in the careful selection of subordinates. Bellasis discovers that his court is composed not only of Sikhs, but Brahmins, Dogra Rajputs and Muslims, and reflects the polymorphous nature of his kingdom. Among the most prominent are Diwan Dina Nath, a Kashmiri Brahmin, who is the kingdom's 'Accountant and Auditor General' and Faqir Aziz-ud-din, a Sufi Muslim, who assumes the role of foreign minister, interpreting 'Runjit's meaning at once into beautiful language, embellishing sound sense with rich and appropriate imagery'.[94]

Bellasis pays particular attention to the meteoric rise of the Hindu Dogra brothers from Jammu – Dhian, Gulab and Suchet Singh – though questions the political expediency of doing so: 'Each in turn, by the basest subserviency to the Maharajah, and being men of business and courage, made their way into his permanent favour. All three became Rajas, acquired jagirs and contracts that have enriched them beyond count, and with their own ability, make them dangerous subjects.' Dhian as 'prime minister, commander of the forces, and chief aide-de-camp' carefully restricts access to the Maharaja at Lahore, while, in the provinces, Gulab's monopoly of the salt contracts 'interferes directly with the bread of every man in the country'.[95] Of the European officers in the service of Ranjit Singh, General M.M. Court is seen by Bellasis as 'a scientific man, modest and honourable' who 'has feathered his nest less than any of his brethren'. On the other hand, General Avitabili's draconian rule in Peshawar leaves him open to the charge of acting 'as a savage among savage men'.[96]

As for the character of Bellasis, it soon becomes evident that this *wilayeti* or foreigner is really an idealised version of Henry himself. Drawing on his experiences at Ferozepur and Kaithal, the novel reveals much of Henry's personal traits as well as his espousal of paternalistic government. In short, the *beau ideal* of a soldier-philosopher. After impressing the Maharaja with his horsemanship, courage and plain-speaking, Bellasis is given the task of administering the Kot Kangra district, a mountainous region in Northern India composed of unruly hill tribes. The district, having fallen into mismanagement, needs to be brought under firm control so that its revenues can be restored. Just as Henry had swapped his military career for a civil one, Bellasis is keen to do likewise:

> Though I was not averse to feats of arms, and in my hotter youth had loved the battle-field, it was now my ambition to build up a city of peace, an exception to the rule of those around me, and commemorate my name rather by preservation than destruction.[97]

He, too, is acutely sensitive to the personal feelings and social position of local chieftains:

> I need hardly note that many Europeans, low-born, low-bred, and low-minded, think fit to Lord it over all Asiatics, and to show their own dignity by refusing the usual civilities to those in every way entitled to them, whose feelings are hurt, and their position among their own countrymen lowered, by such rough contact with overbearing foreigners.[98]

Henry's defining hallmarks of autocratic but kindly rule, cultural openness and a strong work ethic are also mirrored in Bellasis's *modus operandi*. His vigour and 'eccentricity', we are told, baffle the locals who suggest instead that he should 'get married and enjoy life'. But rather than lolling on a *charpai* taking life easy, we see an intensive drive by Bellasis to gain command of his brief. It is the epitome of Henry's way of doing things:

> I now occupied myself day and night in getting acquainted with my people of all degrees; with examining the country, its passes and its fells, its weak and its strong points, and for whole days, leaving my trustiest in charge of the garrison, would I wander over the hills, try every footpath, and investigate the minutest features of my extensive and important charge.[99]

While Henry seeks to contrast Bellasis' indefatigable nature with perceived notions of eastern indolence, our hero's daily habits also reveal an acceptance of conducting business on oriental terms. When not touring his district, Bellasis rises before dawn to 'saunter about the works' [i.e. Kangra Fort]. Afterwards, he holds his *durbar* where his accounts with the *raiyats* [cultivators or farmers] as well as police matters are discussed and settled. A brief respite in the early afternoon, when Bellasis devotes himself to reading European literature and attending to personal correspondences, is followed by the appearance of his 'principal followers and landowners'. Taking up their places on a large outspread carpet, the chiefs seek his assistance on a variety of matters – 'having a plea to offer, an excuse to make, protection, assistance, remission, or other favour to demand, or the track of a tiger or of a robber to point out'. The free expression of opinion by those attending initially takes Bellasis aback, when compared to more formal, occidental modes of government. Yet he soon admits that 'this oriental nonchalance has its conveniences'. It allows for greater understanding of the wants and needs of his district, while ensuring that the chiefs are given ready access to their governor. The day is rounded off by a relaxed perambulation that provides further opportunities for paternalistic endeavour – inspecting his troops and encouraging local farmers in their cultivation.[100]

Clearly reflecting the ethos of a Malcolm or a Munro, Bellasis's approach is one of accessibility and the attainment of local knowledge through direct engagement. Though this, it should be noted, is not simply an exercise of benign rule. On the contrary, Bellasis declares, at one point, that 'despotism is good, if it can be pure and energetic'.[101] On another occasion, he expounds on both the liberal and authoritarian aspects of his paternalistic creed:

> The true philosophy…is to cultivate their better qualities, and make the best of their defects; treating them with what indulgence is possible, respecting their religious prejudices, but, at the same time…keeping them strictly to their duty, even though it be a matter of routine, mindful that…what men

are not taught in ordinary times to do as a matter of course, they may, in time of need, look on as a hardship.[102]

Bellasis's efforts in Kangra soon bring tangible results. By encouraging the development of bazaars and clamping down on crime, the district's economy booms, attracting traders from neighbouring hill states. A moderate land revenue demand of one-third of the produce is introduced, and onerous capitation taxes removed. Complaints on fiscal matters become rare while the amount of land under cultivation doubles. Bellasis's management of Kangra's accounts is also seen as a shining example of financial probity within the Sikh state. 'We know it, Colonel Sahib; the appearance of everything at Kangra bespeaks your activity and your honesty,' the Maharaja concludes.[103] Gratitude within the local community is not lacking either. When the time comes for Bellasis to leave the district, officials, traders and *zamindars*, he tells us, express 'real grief…not perhaps for any personal affection for me, but at losing one who had protected and fostered them, and under whose care their businesses had thriven'.[104]

Yet not everything goes according to plan. At the outset, Bellasis is forced to wrestle control of Kangra Fort from the previous governor. Once installed, he soon must contend with court intrigue as various interests, most notably the Dogra Rajas, seek to undermine his position. His *vakil* at the Lahore Durbar, Chand Khan, is murdered, and at one point he himself falls victim to an assassination attempt and is badly injured. He recovers, but then must defend Kangra from an attack by Raja Suchet Singh's troops. He succeeds but is later forced again to defend it from an assault by a confederacy of hill chiefs. During the unrest his wife-to-be, Mahtab Kowr [Kaur], the local Raja's daughter, goes missing and falls into the hands of Raja Dhian Singh. Unsurprisingly, these episodes leave Bellasis disillusioned: 'I began to see the folly of hoping to effect anything permanent on a shifting sand, such as was the government I served; and my eyes suddenly opened to the impossibility of one man working out the plan that I had desired for my principality.'[105] Even when he does find contentment, by reuniting and marrying Mahtab, it proves short-lived. On a journey to Bahawalpur with her new husband, she is tragically killed by bandits.

Throughout the novel, which comprises two volumes and covers over five hundred pages, Henry is keen to demonstrate his considerable knowledge of Punjab affairs and beyond. A fact-finding mission by Bellasis along the southern flank of the River Sutlej, for example, leads to a full description of Ferozepur and its surroundings based on Henry's time there as a political officer. Pet subjects such as fortress construction are discussed and unflattering character descriptions of East India Company deserters serving in the Punjab are offered. With the benefit of hindsight, Henry also manages to criticise British policy on Afghanistan by stating the case for supporting Dost Mohammed prior to the 1st Anglo-Afghan War. The Afghan chief, Bellasis tells Governor-General Bentinck during an imaginary meeting, is 'as good a man as they [the Afghans] are likely to get' while his intended replacement, Shah Shuja, is dismissed as a mere dotard.[106] Similarly, Henry, having witnessed the end of Ranjit Singh's reign and the subsequent internecine struggles amongst the Sikh aristocracy, has Raja Dhian Singh 'predict' that 'Runjit Singh's death would be the signal, if not for total anarchy, and a rush on the *toshah-khana* [treasury], at least for much bloodshed and many masters.'[107]

The prospect of an Anglo-Sikh war, then very much a topic of discussion, is also addressed. On an official visitation to Kangra, Ranjit Singh asks Bellasis whether his army could successfully confront their East India Company counterparts. In a candid reply, which reflected a commonly held view by contemporary British officers,[108] Bellasis doubts its prospects: 'I may be wrong, but there are many reasons; the Europeans have superior discipline and better leaders, and their gradations of rank are more complete.'[109] Echoing Henry's *Calcutta Review* articles, British territorial expansion is again discouraged: 'I am the well-wisher of the Khalsa, heartily so,' Bellasis tells Ranjit, 'for I am not ungrateful to your Highness's favours; and, as I love the English banner, I would rather, for its own sake, see its lust of conquest restrained, and that the British Government should consolidate their already huge possessions than extend them.'[110]

As the novel draws to a close, Bellasis reflects on his experiences. Although he concludes that the Punjab is 'not the country in which an honest man should choose to serve', he admits that he has found in Ranjit Singh's service 'less of slavery than perhaps in any European army' and that he was less likely to have to act against his conscience 'than if serving with more civilised powers'.[111] Moreover, he has enjoyed excitement, quick promotion (contrast this with Henry's own career frustrations), and 'above all, opportunity of following the bent of one's heart, whether for good or for evil'.[112] At the time of writing, Henry would have had little inkling of how far his own life would emulate his literary creation. But fact, once more, would have a strange way of imitating fiction. Within a matter of months, Henry would be handed the chance of following 'the bent of one's heart' in the former kingdom of Ranjit Singh.

Epilogue

By the early 1840s, the three Lawrence brothers and Robert Montgomery had all firmly established their careers in India. They had become *burra sahibs* with the prospect of greater things to come. It had not been an easy path, however. Fortunate though they were to have received the all-important East India Company nomination, their progress thereafter had entailed a good deal of grit and hard work. In fact, their achievements were all the more remarkable when considering how the odds were often stacked against them. Besides their modest backgrounds and self professed lack of education, many physical demands were placed upon them. There was, to begin with, the arduous voyage of some five months to India during which they had to endure bouts of seasickness, cramped conditions, a lack of fresh food and a monotonous daily routine. Navigating the high seas of the Atlantic and Indian oceans via the infamous Cape of Good Hope was by no means plain sailing. Shipwrecks were not uncommon.[1] For those passengers who had successfully completed their journey, the prospect of tropical diseases and an unforgiving climate awaited. John Lawrence's arrival in Calcutta in 1830 was soon marked by contracting a fever during the rainy season, while Henry's first taste of conflict in the 1st Anglo-Burmese War resulted not in battle scars but in a virulent form of malaria that was to plague him for the rest of his life.

Such were the rigours of the Indian environment that they largely dictated how the Lawrences and Montgomery went about their official business. In summer, travel during the hottest period of the day was to be avoided at all costs, while numerous techniques were deployed to mitigate the worst effects of the heat. Periodic escapes to a hill station gave much needed respite. Revenue surveying and touring the district were confined to the cold season. Long journeys in the *mofussil* were often laborious, uncomfortable affairs. John's 900-mile journey from Calcutta to Delhi in 1831 was undertaken by palanquin. Travelling mostly at night, it took eighteen days to complete, averaging a rather rapid fifty miles a day. By contrast, Henry and Honoria's 1837 trip from Calcutta to Gorakhpur was of six weeks' duration using a combination of boat, *palkee* and buggy. Some journeys proved more treacherous than others. An earlier excursion down the Ganges by Henry ended in tragedy when a violent storm capsized the boats in which he and his troops were travelling. Some did not survive. Travelling on horseback over unfamiliar terrain could be equally hazardous. During one early morning canter, Robert Montgomery was suddenly flung from his saddle when his horse stumbled over loose ground. Although landing on his back uninjured, it could so easily have been otherwise. The same could be said when John's favourite horse, Chanda, saved him one evening from falling into an open water tank some thirty feet deep.[2] The future Viceroy of India, however, was less fortunate during another nocturnal escapade when his pursuit of a notorious robber in the Panipat district ended in the dislocation of his ankle. These events, though, seem almost minor when compared to George's perilous moments during the First Anglo-Afghan War.

As we have observed during the Lawrences and Montgomery's time at the East India Company's training colleges of Addiscombe and Haileybury, there was little attempt to prepare young men for the actual challenges of working life in India. Both institutions largely avoided offering anything in the way of practical training and only the dedicated few retained their rather theoretical knowledge for some later use in India. Consequently, much rested on when these callow youths reached Calcutta – a city of palaces whose architecture briefly inspired newcomers to think they had discovered a new Rome in the east. Such impressions, however, soon wore off once visitors noticed the unattractive hovels leaning against the walls of the stately homes in Chowringhee. Despite the aspirations of the city fathers, the 'Indianisation' of the imperial metropolis was never far from view. The Lawrences held little affection for the city, though Robert Montgomery believed it had 'much grandeur and magnificence' and offered everything that could be desired.[3] Both John and Robert attended Fort William College where, with the aid of a *munshi*, they obtained sufficient proficiency in the local languages. True fluency in colloquial Hindustani, however, could only be attained further up the Gangetic plain where its usage predominated. Indeed, only when they took up their first postings in the *mofussil* under the watchful eye of an experienced officer could it be said that their real training had begun.

By far the most important mentor to the Lawrences and Montgomery in their early careers was James Thomason. With the exception of George Lawrence, Thomason was to exercise a towering influence over Henry, John and Robert. Since sharing a cabin on their outbound voyage to India, Henry had maintained both a personal and professional relationship with Thomason who would often act as a patient sounding board for the former's career anxieties. Both, as we have seen, worked closely on streamlining the Revenue Survey methodology with the involvement of R.M. Bird. Similarly, in John's revenue work at Delhi, the influences of both Bird and Thomason have been noted. Indeed, Richard

Temple saw John as foremost amongst a group of civil officers who had been 'brought up in the great official school of the North-Western Provinces,' and 'who thoroughly agreed with Thomason's principles and ideas'.[4] Next in line to John, Temple believed, was Robert who was to work intimately with Thomason at Azamgarh. Tasked with carrying out the new land revenue settlements, Robert imbibed Thomason's principles in unison with the work of Bird. Other areas of Thomasonian influence included improvements in the organisation of the police, the campaign against female infanticide, and the creation of in-depth administrative reporting. The closeness of their relationship was revealed on a personal level by Robert's first marriage to Thomason's sister Frances whose untimely death exemplified the fragility of life in India.

The Lawrences and Montgomery, nevertheless, remained very much their own men. Henry, while fully in sync on revenue survey methodology, did not share Bird and Thomason's ardent attack on the *talukdars* and the great magnates. Their 'levelling' views, he would argue, needed to be tempered by the sentiments of John Malcolm and his sympathy for the 'fallen greatness' of the aristocracy.[5] It was a point of difference which would become more apparent during the Lawrences' Punjab rule and in post-annexation Oudh. Robert, too, would follow his own path in combating female infanticide. Although fully agreed on the aims of the campaign, he differed with Thomason on the means to tackle it. Such points of difference, however, should not overshadow their common administrative philosophy which stressed the importance of strong paternal governance as a moral, civilising force for good. Based on the Indian tradition of personal rule, direct involvement in the lives of villagers was conducted through the concentrated authority of the district officer. He was, in the traditional sense, the *ma-bap* of the peasantry. Knowledgeable and sympathetic, he acted as a benevolent autocrat, eschewing complex legal forms and procedures in favour of dispensing simple justice under a banyan tree.

Few personified this characterisation of the district officer more so than John Lawrence. As his recorded stories of the period reveal, much of his early days were spent in the saddle and under canvas getting to know his district. In his interactions with villagers, he championed the importance of accessibility. Even when the working day was done, there was still the chance to glean some useful information by holding impromptu gatherings of the village community outside his tent. During his time at Delhi, he adopted the principles espoused by former British Resident, Charles Metcalfe – support for peasant proprietorship, low assessments, and the preservation of village institutions. This was the ideal, yet in practice both Metcalfe and Lawrence fell prey to the iniquities of over-assessment. Assessing large tracts of land within a narrow timeframe using finite resources inevitably led to discrepancies. Moreover, the methodology was by no means infallible. Robert's Allahabad settlement suffered from similar issues. In both the implementation of detailed revenue surveys as well as the revenue assessment and collection, much relied on the delegation of authority and the quality of those employed. Large numbers of Indian support staff were required from the district headquarters to the base level of the village. The same was true of other branches of the administration such as law and order. Civil officers such as John Lawrence may well have been the 'pivot around which the whole of administration of the district revolved', but without the cooperation of a large, indigenous support staff, local government could simply not have functioned.[6]

As revenue surveys churned out ever increasing amounts of data, Robert Montgomery was on hand to collate and analyse. Combined with other areas of administration such as judicial and police reporting, a comprehensive anatomy of a district could be revealed. Robert's *Statistical Report of the District of Cawnpoor* represented the beginning of a modern, professional approach to the business of governing. It was the power of data which could lead to improvements in the efficiency of the state for the benefit of its inhabitants.

Yet beyond the domestic arena, on the broader topics of defence and foreign relations, sagacious decision-making remained woefully sub-standard. Nowhere was this more apparent than in the genesis and conduct of the 1st Anglo-Afghan War. This sorry episode revealed how the sway of individual political agents such as Claude Wade and William Hay Macnaghten could lead to disastrous policy outcomes. When combined with the chronic ineptitude of the military high command and intelligence oversight, the trumped-up merits of regime change were tragically exposed. Following the British invasion, the faithful Shah Shuja was reduced to the position of a quisling king bereft of Afghan support. Had someone of the calibre of George Clerk been Envoy and not Macnaghten, perhaps the outcome would have been different. But in the event the British authorities were to be found wanting when confronted by the surprise outbreak of the Kabul revolt in November 1841. George Lawrence's account of the Afghan debacle reads like a litany of missed opportunities and military blunders. The sheer incompetency and lack of vigour by senior British officers is as breath-taking to the modern reader as it was to George. Had his opinions been acted on, the Kabul revolt may well have been put down at its inception.

In reviewing their careers to date, none of the Lawrences or Montgomery could ever have been accused of lacking vigour. Quite the opposite. All had energetically applied themselves during their apprenticeship years. In numerous instances, they had outperformed their peers, receiving many accolades. Henry's revenue survey reforms had won plaudits from the Sudder Board of Revenue, while his resolution of the Faridkot boundary dispute had led to a demand for his services elsewhere. Moreover, his novel, *Adventures of an Officer in the Service of Runjeet Singh*, and his *Calcutta Review* articles, had made him the pre-eminent authority on Punjab affairs. John, too, was lauded for his settlement of a boundary dispute in Etawah, while his stories of his Panipat and Gurgaon days elevated him to the position of *sahib zillah par excellence.* Robert Montgomery's achievements were hardly less impressive. Frederick Currie, then Divisional Revenue Commissioner, found his Azamgarh settlements to be 'very satisfactory and highly creditable' while the Court of Directors praised his 'active and judicious measures' in the campaign against female infanticide in Allahabad.[7] As for George, he was awarded £600 by the East India Company for his courageous services in Afghanistan.[8]

Despite such fulsome praise, the reader of this book has been offered a critical re-evaluation of these four men's careers. As we have seen, not every personal reminiscence can be taken at face value. The views of other civil and military officers have provided a useful corrective while what has not been said has been equally noteworthy as in the case of John Lawrence's supposed role in the murder investigation of William Fraser. Furthermore, their own official records, such as in the field of revenue assessments, can be used to test the success of their administrative performance. Taking such qualifications into account, a more rounded picture of the Lawrences and Montgomery emerges. A picture that is still highly impressive, but one that also reveals their limitations, their frustrations, and their mistakes. Yet whatever their shortcomings, it was their ability to learn from their experiences which would prove crucial. Rather than being stifled by the oppressive constraints of the cantonment or the central *cutcherry*, most of their profitable time had been spent 'in the field' interacting at first hand with a wide Indian populace. Consequently, the knowledge and skills developed by this quartet of talented Company servants would put them in good stead for their next challenge in the former kingdom of Ranjit Singh. The Punjab – the land of five rivers – would, in time, become the scene of their greatest triumphs.

Notes

Prologue

1. The Builder (1882), 42:632, op. cit. Mark Stocker, *Royalist and Realist, The Life and Work of Sir Joseph Edgar Boehm*, (Garland Publishing, New York & London, 1988) p. 125. One British official, writing in the 1920s, remarked 'The pose has been not infelicitously described as that of a foreman haranguing a gang of coolies,' quoted in D. Gilmartin, *Empire and Islam, Punjab and the Making of Pakistan* (London: I.B. Tauris & Co. Ltd, 1988) p. 11.
2. Athenaeum, 3 June 1882, p. 706, op. cit. Mark Stocker, *Royalist and Realist*, p. 127.
3. Leslie Linder, ed., *The Journal of Beatrix Potter from 1881 to 1897* (London: Frederick Warne, 1966), note 1566.
4. 'Apparently the statue you now possess was originally erected in Waterloo Place in 1882 but was not well received. It was given to the Municipality of Lahore and the artist produced another, in less truculent attitude, to take its place in 1884.' J. Darlington, London County Council Librarian and Archivist to W.S. Ferguson, Foyle College Old Boys Association, 20 February 1963, Foyle College Archives.
5. New York Times, 11th November 1921.
6. 'It is not intended that the very words of my letter were suggested by the Commissioner, for such was not the case, but at that period I was so imbued with the spirit of his example and his teachings, his principle of firmness of purpose, and decision of acting, accompanied by a never-failing love and tenderness to the people, while still in rebellion, that, if it was I who penned the words, the conception and the sentiment were his. My works were his.' R.N. Cust, *Pictures of Indian Life Sketched with the Pen from 1852 to 1881* (London: Trubner & Co., 1881), p. 266.
7. See Milton Israel, *Communications and Power: Propaganda and the Press in the Indian National Struggle, 1920–1947* (Cambridge: Cambridge University Press, 1994), pp. 26–29.
8. 'Four Sikhs are on trial in Lahore Jail for disfiguring the Lawrence Statue', 4 May 1932, *The Indian Recorder* (Calcutta, April-June 1932), p. 15.
9. See Mary Ann Steggles, *Statues of the Raj*, (BACSA, London, 2000).
10. Michael Silvestri, *Ireland and India: Nationalism, Empire and Memory*, (Cambridge Imperial and Post-Colonial Studies Series), (New York: Palgrave Macmillan, 2009), pp. 143-5.
11. John Nicholson's statue was unveiled by Lord Mountbatten, India's last Viceroy, on 13 April 1960.
12. Foyle College Board Governors to Ministry of Education, 6 February 1961, Foyle College Archives.
13. Letter from the Pakistan Minister of the Interior, Lt. Gen K.N. Sheikh to Sir Olaf Caroe, 14 October 1959, Foyle College Archives.
14. The statue was later removed to a new school site at Springtown in 1967 and then to the present site on the Waterside in 2018.
15. Foyle College Times, June 1963, p. 106.

Acknowledgements

1. Amid the ruined remains of the British Residency in Lucknow can be found the modest tomb of Henry Lawrence whose brief epitaph reads: 'Here lies Henry Lawrence who tried to do his duty.' In St. Paul's Cathedral, Kolkata a marble memorial by the sculptor J.H. Foley records Henry as a 'Christian Statesman, Philanthropist and Soldier, who, in the Punjab, Rajpootana and Oudh, taught how kindly subject races should be ruled.' There are Lawrence Roads in Amritsar, Delhi and Lahore, the latter also has a road named after Montgomery. Situated between Lawrence Road and Mall Road, Lahore, in botanical gardens previous called Lawrence Gardens, there are two impressive neo-classical buildings built in the 1860s in honour of Robert Montgomery and John Lawrence (called Montgomery Hall and Lawrence Hall). They now form the Quaid-e-Azam library. Alongside the Lawrence School, Sanawar, three other schools were established: The Lawrence School at Mount Abu, Rajasthan (now the Internal Security Academy) was opened in 1856; The Lawrence School at Lovedale in the Nilgiri hills, Tamil Nadu was established after his death in September 1858; Lawrence College at Ghora Gali, Murree, now in Pakistan, was established in his memory in 1860.

Introduction

1. H. B. Edwardes & H. Merivale, *Life of Sir Henry Lawrence*, (London: Smith, elder & Co., 1872), Vol. 2, p. 185.
2. R. Temple, *Lord Lawrence* (London: Macmillan and Co., 1889), p. 136.
3. R. Bosworth Smith, *Life of Lord Lawrence*, (London: Smith, Elder & Co., 1883), Vol. 1, p. 66.
4. See R.N. Cust, *Pictures of Indian Life*, p. 249; R. Temple, *Lord Lawrence*, p. 44.
5. Bosworth Smith, 1, p. 112.
6. Ibid., p. 198.
7. R.N. Cust, *Pictures of Indian Life*, p. 246.
8. Edwardes & Merivale, 2, p. 154.
9. J.W. Kaye, *Lives of Indian Officers, Illustrative of the History of the Civil and Military Services of India*, (London: A. Strahan & Co., Bell & Daldy, 1867) Vol. 2, p. 348.
10. Ibid., p. 349.
11. J. J. McLeod Innes, *Sir Henry Lawrence: the Pacificator* (Oxford: Clarendon Press, 1898), p. 8.
12. H.B. (Mrs), Edwardes, *Memorials of the Life & Letters of Major-General Sir Herbert B. Edwards*, (London: Kegan Paul, Trench & Co., 1886), Vol. 1, p. 58.
13. R. Temple, *Lord Lawrence*, p. 48.
14. Bosworth Smith, 1, p. 1.
15. L. J. Trotter, *Life of the Marquis of Dalhousie*, (London: W. H. Allen & Co., 1889), p. 62. See also Lewis D. Wurgaft, *The Imperial Imagination, Magic and Myth in Kipling's India* (Middletown, Connecticut: Wesleyan University Press, 1983) chapter 3, British Heroism in India: History as Mythology.
16. Edwardes & Merivale, 1, 117.
17. R, Temple, *Lord Lawrence*, p. 1. Bosworth Smith, 1, p. 148: 'The man who had done more than any other single man to save our Indian Empire.'
18. R. Temple, *Lord Lawrence*, pp. 2-5.
19. 'The Life of Lord Lawrence, tree-calf, two vols., nine rupees, eight annas.' Rudyard Kipling, *Kim* (Penguin, London, 1987) p. 212.
20. J.L. Morison, *Lawrence of Lucknow*, (London: G. Bell and Sons Ltd, 1934), p. 3.

21. P. Woodruff, *The Men who Ruled India*, 2 Vols. (London: Jonathan Cape, 1963), Vol. 1, p. 13.

22. Ibid., p. 325.

23. N.M. Khilnani, *British Power in the Punjab 1839-58*, (Asia Publishing House, Bombay 1972), p. 25.

24. Ibid., pp. 28-29.

25. B.J. Hasrat, *Anglo-Sikh Relations 1799-1849: A Reappraisal of the Rise and Fall of the Sikhs* (Hoshiarpur: V.V. Research Institute Press, 1968), pp. 297-298.

26. John Lawrence, *Lawrence of Lucknow* (London, Hodder and Stoughton, 1990) p. xvii.

27. Ibid., p. xviii.

28. Harold Lee, *Brothers in the Raj, The Lives of Henry and John Lawrence* (Karachi: Oxford University Press, 2002), p. 6.

29. Ibid., p. 420.

30. J.L. Morison, *Lawrence of Lucknow*, p. 199.

31. George Lawrence, *Reminiscences of Forty-Three Years in India* (London, John Murray, 1875, 2nd edition).

32. Ibid., preface, p. vii.

33. B. Montgomery, *Monty's Grandfather, A Life's Service for the Raj* (Poole: Blandford Press, 1984), p. 31; F.W. Sale, *A Journal of the Disasters in Afghanistan, 1841-2*, (New York: Harper & Brothers, 1843), p. 39.

34. G. Campbell, *Memoirs of my Indian Career*, (London, Macmillan & Co., 1893), Vol. 2, p. 8; John Beames, *Memoirs of a Bengal Civilian* (London: Eland, 1984), p. 103.

35. R. Temple, *Men and Events of my time in India* (London: John Murray, 1882), p. 65.

36. H.L. to Colonel Stuart, Secretary to Government Military Dept., 23 July 1845, Mss. Eur. F85/5A, p. 109.

Imperial Connections

1. C.A. Bayly, *Indian Society and the making of the British Empire, The New Cambridge History of India*, II, 1 (Cambridge: The Cambridge University Press, 1988), p. 120.

2. S. Bandyopadhyay, *From Plassey to Partition: A History of Modern India* (Delhi: Orient Longman, 2004), p. 56.

3. Governor-General Wellesley's motivations were strongly influenced by the threat of French intrigue. See J. Holmes, *Administration of the Delhi Territory 1803-1832*, unpublished Ph.D. thesis, pp. 5-9.

4. D.L. Drake-Brockman, Hamirpur District Gazetteer (Allahabad, 1909), p. 152.

5. In 1816 the Himalayan foothill districts of Kumaon and Dehra Dun were surrendered in the aftermath of the Anglo-Nepalese War and became part of the Ceded and Conquered Provinces. In 1836 the districts of the Benares division were transferred to the North-Western Provinces from Lower Bengal. Imperial Gazetteer of India, Vol. XXIV, 1908, p. 158. For the sake of convenience, I have called it the North Western Provinces (N.W.P.) throughout.

6. John Thornton, *Settlement of the Land Revenue in the North-Western Provinces, The Calcutta Review*, July-December 1849, Vol. 12, p. 415.

7. Table No.3, An Account of the Revenues and Charges of the North-Western Provinces, Accounts respecting the Annual Territorial Revenues and Disbursements of the East India Company, for the Years 1838-39, 1839-40 and 1840-41, in *Accounts and papers of the House of Commons*, Volume 35, 2 February – 24 August 1843, p. 55.

8. Table No.10, General Abstract View of the Revenues and Charges of India, ibid., p. 65.

9. J.W. Kaye, *The Administration of the East India Company* (London: Richard Bentley, 1853), p. 155.

10. Minutes of Evidence Taken Before the Select Committee into the affairs of the East India Company, House of Commons (16 August 1832), Vol. 5, Appendix A, p. 195.

11. Bernard S. Cohn, *The Recruitment and Training of British Civil Servants in India* in *An Anthropologist among the Historians and Other Essays*, (Oxford: Oxford University Press, 1990), p. 514.

12. B. Crosbie, *Irish Imperial Networks, Migration, Social Communication and Exchange in Nineteenth Century India* (Cambridge: Cambridge University Press, 2012), pp. 90-92.

13. The Irish military Tradition and the British Empire, in K, Jeffrey, ed., *An Irish Empire? Aspects of Ireland and the British Empire* (Manchester: Manchester University Press, 1996), p. 94.

14. L. Colley, Captives: *Britain, Empire and the World, 1600-1850* (London: Jonathan Cape, 2002),p. 310.

15. H. Morse Stephens, *An Account of the East India College at Haileybury (1806-1857)* in A. Lawrence Lowell (ed.), *Colonial Civil Service* (London: Macmillan & Co., 1900), p. 249.

16. Bernard S. Cohn, *Recruitment and Training of British Civil Servants in India*, p. 516.

17. The period 1802-1833 saw the appointment of 1190 writers in total. Ibid., p. 514.

18. John Michael Bourne, *The Civil and Military Patronage of the East India Company, 1784-1858*, unpublished Ph.D thesis (University of Leicester, 1977) p. 174.

19. B.S. Cohn, *Recruitment and Training of British Civil Servants in India*, p. 518.

20. 'East India postings became the foundation for bringing more political stability to Scotland and forging a stronger union.' T.M. Devine, *Scotland's Empire, The origins of the Global Diaspora* (London: Penguin, 2004), p. 269.

21. John Michael Bourne, *Civil and Military Patronage*, p. 178.

22. S.B. Cook, *The Irish Raj: Social Origins and Careers of Irishmen in the Indian Civil Service 1855-1919* in Journal of Social History, 20 (Spring, 1987). p. 510.

23. Kevin Kenny, *The Irish in the Empire*, in Kenny, Kevin. ed., *Ireland and the British Empire* (The Oxford History of the British Empire, Companion Series; Oxford: Oxford University Press, 2004), p. 106.

24. Introduction Caledon Papers, PRONI, 2007, p. 4 (Northern Ireland P.R.O., D2432/5/4/2).

25. R. Alexander, *Account of the Family History of Rev. Robert Alexander and other Notes of the Families of Alexander and McClintock* (Londonderry, 1946), p. 6.

26. Unfortunately James died in Simla on 18th April 1843 from wounds received at the Tezin Pass during the 1st Anglo-Afghan War. He was aged only twenty-five.

27. L.J. Trotter, *The Life of John Nicholson, Soldier and Administrator*, (London: Thomas Nelson & Sons, 1897), p. 27.

28. George Pottinger, *Sir Henry Pottinger – First Governor of Hong Kong* (Stroud: Sutton Publishing Ltd., 1997), p. 8

29. A.T. Harrison (ed.), *The Graham Indian Mutiny Papers* (Belfast, Public Record: Office of Northern Ireland, 1980), pp. ix-x.

30. Twelve children: George Tomkins (1799-1803), Letitia (1892-65), Alexander (1803-68), George St. Patrick (1805-84), Henry (1806-57), Honoria (1807-89), James (1809-27), John (1811-79), Mary Anne (1812-77), Charlotte (1814-85), Marcia (1815-83), and Richard (1817-96).

31. 'Names of the Gentlemen both Masters and Pupils of the New Free School', Foyle College Archives. After Foyle College, Henry also briefly attended Mr Gough's school, College Green, Bristol (the family was then living in Clifton) between 1819-20.

Education and Training

1. Robert Simpson, *The Annals of Derry*, (Londonderry, 1847), p. 259.
2. W.S. Ferguson, Our School Times (1924?), Mss. Eur. D1019/1, p. 14.
3. Ibid., p. 15. 'The school was no special home of learning', J.L. Morison, *Lawrence of Lucknow*, p. 15; 'It does not seem to have been a very good school', Edwardes & Merivale, 1, p. 14.
4. Sir Richard Temple, *Lord Lawrence*, p. 10.
5. C. Allen, *Soldier Sahibs: The Men who made the North-West Frontier* (London: John Murray, 2000), p. 47.
6. J.L. Morison, *Lawrence of Lucknow*, pp. 14-15.
7. Edwardes & Merivale, 1, p. 14
8. Bosworth Smith, 1, p. 18.
9. Bosworth Smith, 1, pp. 19-20.
10. W.F.B. Laurie, *Sketches of Some Distinguished Anglo-Indians* (London: Wm. H. Allen & Co., 1887), p. 217.
11. Revd James Knox to Colonel Alexander Lawrence (Senior), 31 July 1819, Mss. Eur. F85/21, p. 207.
12. Edwardes & Merivale, 1, p. 19.
13. Bosworth Smith, 1, p. 22.
14. R. Temple, *Lord Lawrence*, p. 10.
15. J.L. Morison, *Lawrence of Lucknow*, p. 15.
16. R. Temple, *Lord Lawrence*, p. 10.
17. B. Montgomery, *Monty's Grandfather*, p. 1.
18. R. Temple, *Lord Lawrence*, p. 36.
19. J.W. Kaye, *Lives of Indian Officers*, Vol. 2, p. 277.
20. *The Lahore Chronicle*, 19 October 1864, copy in the Montgomery Papers, Mss. Eur. D1019/5, p. 378.
21. F.P. Gibbon, *The Lawrences of the Punjab* (London: J.M. Dent & Co., 1908), p. 295.
22. On the exterior east front of the classically styled building was carved the Latin inscription, *Non faciam vitio culpave minorem* ("I will not lower myself by vice or fault"), H.M. Vibart, *Addiscombe its heroes and men of note* (London: Archibald Constable & Co., 1894), p. 12.
23. Ibid., p. 56.
24. *The Calcutta Review*, Oct-Dec 1844, Vol. 2, p. 128.
25. H.M. Vibart, *Addiscombe its heroes and men of note*, p. 126.
26. *The Calcutta Review*, Oct-Dec 1844, Vol. 2, p. 129.
27. George Lawrence to Mrs L. Lawrence Senior, 26 August 1820, Mss. Eur F85/21, pp. 209-210.
28. The Lawrence family moved to Clifton in 1819, then on the outskirts of Bristol.
29. Edwardes & Merivale, 1, pp. 22-23.
30. J.L. Morison, *Lawrence of Lucknow*, p. 19.
31. One exception to this was when he nearly drowned while swimming in the Croydon Canal with his fellow cadets. He was saved thanks to the efforts of fellow cadet, R.G. Macgregor.

32. Edwardes & Merivale, 1, p. 28.

33. Ibid., p. 27.

34. H.M. Vibart, *Addiscombe its heroes and men of note*, p. 41.

35. Ibid., pp. 71-72.

36. Ibid., p. 150.

37. *The Calcutta Review*, Oct-Dec 1844, Vol. 2, p. 139.

38. "Army Reform" in H.M. Lawrence, *Essays, Military and Political, written in India* (London: Wm. H. Allen & Co., 1859), p. 481.

39. Edwardes & Merivale, 1, p. 30.

40. Bosworth Smith, 1, p. 19.

41. H. Morse Stephens, *An Account of the East India College at Haileybury (1806-1857)*, p. 259.

42. Bosworth Smith, 1, p. 28.

43. Sir George Campbell, *Memoirs of my Indian Career*, Vol. 1, p. 10.

44. Danvers, F.C. et al, *Memorials of old Haileybury College*, (London, Archibald Constable & Co., 1894), p. 47.

45. G.R. Elsmie, *Thirty-five years in the Punjab*, (Edinburgh: David Douglas, 1908), p. 9.

46. John Beames, *Memoirs of a Bengal Civilian*, pp. 64-67.

47. Danvers, F.C. et al, *Memorials of old Haileybury College*, p. 61.

48. G.R. Elsmie, *Thirty-five years in the Punjab*, p. 9; *John Beames, Memoirs of a Bengal Civilian*, p. 66.

49. H. Morse Stephens, *An Account of the East India College at Haileybury (1806-1857)*, p. 313.

50. Bosworth Smith, 1, p. 28.

51. Danvers, F.C. et al, *Memorials of old Haileybury College*, p. 391.

52. Batten only achieved one prize during his time at Haileybury. It was an essay prize, 'The Power of the Romans in the West compared to the British in the East', in his 3rd term. He passed out sixth place in his last term. His Indian career spanned thirty-seven years reaching the position of Commissioner of Agra. Ibid., p. 391; Bosworth Smith, 1, p. 30.

53. Bosworth Smith, 1, p. 30.

54. Ibid., p. 31.

55. George Campbell, *Modern India: A Sketch of The System of Civil Government. To which is prefixed, some account of the natives and native institutions* (London: John Murray, 1852), p. 265.

56. L.Pelly, ed., *The Views and Opinions of Brigadier-General John Jacob, C.B.*, (London: Smith, Elder & Co., 1858), p. 13.

57. John Beames, *Memoirs of a Bengal Civilian*, p. 64.

58. R. Temple, *Men and events of my time in India*, p. 19; G. Trevelyan, The Competition Wallah, (London: Macmillan & Co., 1895), pp. 7-8.

First Impressions: Calcutta in Regency Times

1. John Lawrence's seasickness lasted several weeks, leading Richard Temple to conclude that it 'must have aggravated any constitutional tendency to nervous irritability in his head.' Richard Temple, *Lord Lawrence*, p. 15.

2. F. Parkes, *Wanderings of a Pilgrim in search of the Picturesque*, (London: Pelham Richardson, 1850), Vol. 1, p. 3.

3. Edwardes & Merivale, 1, p. 43.

4. Montgomery Papers, Mss. Eur. D1019/1, p. 187.

5. B. Montgomery, *Monty's Grandfather*, p. 9.

6. William Huggins, *Sketches in India* (London: John Letts, 1824), p. 4.

7. 'Calcutta has been styled the City of Palaces, and it well deserves the name.' F. Parkes, *Wanderings of a Pilgrim*, Vol. 1, p. 20.

8. Robert Montgomery Martin, *Statistics of the Colonies of the British Empire* (London: Wm. H. Allen & Co., 1839), p. 289.

9. Reginald Heber, *Narrative of a Journey through the Upper Provinces of India*, (London: John Murray, 1846), Vol. 1, p. 56.

10. Esplanade Row (East) was renamed Sidhu Kanu Dahar. Esplanade Row (West) has not been renamed.

11. William Huggins, *Sketches in India*, p. 6.

12. Walter Hamilton, "*Calcutta in 1820*" in Calcutta in the 19th Century (*Company's Days*), ed. P. Thankappan Nair, (Calcutta: Firma KLM Private Limited, 1989), p. 223.

13. Reginald Heber, *Narrative of a Journey*, Vol. 1, p. 56.

14. Chowringhee Road is now named Jawalharlal Nehru Road.

15. Geoffrey Moorhouse, *Calcutta* (London: Weidenfeld and Nicolson, 1971), p. 59.

16. Honoria Lawrence's Journal, Mss. Eur F85/78, p. 21.

17. Fanny Parkes, *Wanderings of a Pilgrim*, Vol. 1, p. 20.

18. Walter Hamilton, *Calcutta in 1820*, p. 307.

19. Emma Roberts, *Scenes and Characteristics of Hindoostan*, (London: Wm. H. Allen & Co., 1835), Vol. 1, p. 2.

20. Reginald Heber, *Narrative of a Journey*, Vol. 1, p. 56.

21. James Baillie Fraser's aquatints were part of a collection called '*Views of Calcutta and its Environs*'.

22. William Huggins, *Sketches in India*, p. 8.

23. Walter Hamilton, *Calcutta in 1820*, p. 224.

24. Ibid., p. 234.

25. Honoria Lawrence's Journal, Mss. Eur F85/78, p. 21.

26. Fanny Parkes, *Wanderings of a Pilgrim*, Vol. 1, p. 30.

27. Tank Square was later called Dalhousie Square and is now called B.B.D. Bagh.

28. John Beames, *Memoirs of a Bengal Civilian*, pp. 80-81.

29. Montgomery Papers, Mss. Eur. D1019/1, p. 46.

30. Ibid., p. 36.

31. One was Ross McClintock who was an Assistant Surgeon on board the *Princess Charlotte*, another was the nephew of a Helen Harvey, while a third was the son of a Mr Grant. Ibid., p. 35.

32. Ibid., p. 39.

33. Bosworth Smith, 1, p. 36.

34. C. Aitchison, *Lord Lawrence*, (Oxford, Clarendon Press, 1892), p. 22.

35. R. Temple, *Lord Lawrence*, p. 16.

36. George Lawrence, *Reminiscences*, p. 1.

37. Ibid., p. 2.

38. H.L. to Letitia Lawrence, 2 August 1823, Edwardes & Merivale, 1, p. 39.

39. H.L. to Letitia Lawrence, 8 October 1823, Ibid., p. 41.

40. Ibid.

41. Contemporary reminiscence, ibid., p. 44.

42. Lt. Lewin's Diary, 11 December 1823, Mss. Eur F85/21, p. 211.

43. Revd G. Craufurd reminiscence, Edwardes & Merivale, 1, p. 47.

44. Private Diary of General Lindsay, ibid., p. 75 (note 15).

45. Edwardes & Merivale, 1, pp. 53-54.

46. Henry Lawrence's Arakan Journal, Mss. Eur. F85/21, pp. 82-83.

47. Ibid., pp. 85-88.

48. Edwardes & Merivale, 1, p. 60.

49. Ibid., p. 62.

50. Henry Lawrence's Arakan Journal, Mss. Eur. F85/21, p. 89.

51. Ibid., p. 109.

52. Ibid., p. 113.

53. Edwardes & Merivale, 1, p. 75.

54. Mrs Letitia Lawrence (senior) diary, May 1827, ibid., p. 84.

55. J. Lawrence to H. Edwardes, 4 April 1858, ibid., p. 21.

The 'confounded zeal' of Henry Lawrence, Revenue Surveyor 1833-38

1. Colonel Lawrence, Henry's father, died after a long illness, in May 1835, aged seventy-three.

2. H.L. to Letitia Lawrence, Autumn 1833, ibid., p. 127.

3. Cautley's greatest work would be the 350-mile stretch from Hardwar to Cawnpore of the Ganges Canal, which opened in 1854.

4. H.L. to Letitia Lawrence, 1 March 1831, Edwardes & Merivale, 1, p. 106-7.

5. H.L. to Letitia Lawrence, 25 March 1832, Mss. Eur. F85/21 p. 123.

6. H.L. to Letitia Lawrence, 16 November 1831, Edwardes & Merivale, 1, p. 108.

7. H.L. Lawrence to Letitia Lawrence, 25 March 1832, Mss. Eur. F85/21 p. 126.

8. Report of Examination Committee (Native Languages), 17 July 1832, Mss. Eur. F85/21, p. 220.

9. B. Crosbie, *Irish Imperial Networks*, pp. 106-117.

10. Probably General Sir George Brooke, see C.E. Buckland, *Dictionary of Indian Biography*, (London: Swan Sonnenschein & Co., 1906) p. 54

11. George Brooke to George Lawrence, 13 July 1832, Mss. Eur. F85/21, pp. 216-217.

12. George Lawrence, *Reminiscences*, pp. 2-3.

13. E. Morton to H.B. Edwardes, 26 July 1861, Mss. Eur F85/21, p. 135.

14. J.H. Simmonds to E. Morton, 15 July (1861?), ibid., p. 131.

15. R.H. Phillimore, ed., *Historical Records of Survey of India, 1830 to 1843*, Vol. 4, (Dehra Dun: Survey of India, 1958), p. 452.

16. Edwardes & Merivale, 1, p. 121.

17. Minute by the Governor-General dated 26th September 1832, *Selections from Revenue Records, North-West Provinces, 1822-1833* (Allahabad, 1872), pp. 385-418; Secretary to Governor-General Revenue Department, to Offg. Secretary to Government, with Vice-President in dated Council, 24th January, 1833, ibid., pp. 480-485.

18. J.W. Kaye, *Administration of the East India Company*, p. 698.

19. Minute by the Governor-General dated 26th September 1832, *Selections from Revenue Records, North-West Provinces, 1822-1833*, p. 416.

20. R.H. Phillimore, ed., *Historical Records of the Survey of India*, 1830-43, Vol. 4, pp. 213-4.

21. For a detailed explanation of this methodology, see Part 3, Chapters VI-X in H.L. Thuiller & R. Smyth, *A Manual of Surveying for India – Detailing the Mode of Operations on the Revenue Surveys in Bengal and the North-Western Provinces* (Calcutta: W. Thacker & Co., 1851).

22. R.H. Phillimore, ed., *Historical Records of Survey of India*, Vol. 4, Plate 12.

23. E.R. Neave (ed.), *Farrukhabad District Gazetteer* (Allahabad, 1911), p. 99.

24. See biographical notes on Saunders Alexius Abbott in R.H. Phillimore, ed., *Historical Records of Survey of India*, Vol. 4, pp. 417, 453.

25. Reminiscences of Saunders Abbott, in J.W. Kaye, *Lives of Indian Officers*, Vol. 2, p. 282.

26. Reminiscences of E.A. Reade, ibid., p. 281.

27. Reminiscences of Saunders Abbott, ibid., p. 282.

28. R.H. Phillimore, ed., *Historical Records of Survey of India*, Vol. 4, 417.

29. H.L. to Letitia Lawrence, 23 July 1833, Edwardes & Merivale, 1, p. 126.

30. Honoria Lawrence to Mrs Cameron, 11 February 1838, ibid., p. 154.

31. Ibid., p. 91.

32. Honoria Lawrence's Journal, November 1837, Mss. Eur. F85/80 p. 25.

33. J.L. to H.L., 10 June 1836, Mss. Eur. F85/21, p. 226.

34. Honoria Lawrence's Journal, November 1837, Mss. Eur. F85/78, p. 104.

35. Honoria Lawrence's Journal, Mss. Eur. F85/80, p. 30.

36. Honoria Lawrence's Journal, November 1837, Mss. Eur. F85/78, p. 102.

37. Ibid., p. 103.

38. 'Henry is continually on the lookout to prevent the servants and camp followers from plundering the people about us. They will levy firewood, earthen pots, eggs, in short everything they can get, and say that the sahib commands them.' 30 Dec 1837, Mss. Eur. F85/81, p. 43.

39. Honoria Lawrence's Journal, [no date] November 1837, Mss. Eur. F85/78, p. 103.

40. Honoria Lawrence's Journal, Mss. Eur. F85/81, p. 17.

41. Honoria Lawrence's Journal, 10 November 1837, Mss. Eur. F85/80, p. 28.

42. Honoria Lawrence's Journal, [no date] November 1837, Mss. Eur. F85/78, p. 104.

43. Honoria Lawrence's Journal, 15 December 1837, Mss. Eur. F85/81, p. 36.

44. Ibid., p. 38.

45. J.W. Kaye, *Lives of Indian Officers*, Vol. 2, p. 283.

46. Honoria Lawrence's Journal, 16 December, Mss. Eur. F85/81, p. 39.

47. Ibid., p. 40.

48. J.W. Kaye, *Lives of Indian Officers*, Vol. 2, p. 284.

49. General statement of work done by Revenue Surveys in the four years since scheme adopted at the survey meeting at Allahabad 1833. Superintendent of Revenue Survey's Office, Allahabad, 11th November 1837, Signed James Bedford, Deputy Surveyor-General. N.W.P. Proceedings (Revenue), IOR/P/217/67, no. 70; no. 74, Form 2 & 3.

50. James Abbott reminiscences, Edwardes & Merivale, 1, p. 119.

51. John Thornton, *Settlement of the Land Revenue in the North-Western Provinces*, The Calcutta Review, Jul-Dec 1849, Vol. 12, p. 433.

52. H.M. Elliot (Secy to Sudder Board of Revenue) to J. Thomason [Secy to Lieutenant-Governor of North-Western Provinces], 1 September 1837, N.W.P. Proceedings (Revenue), IOR/P/217/60, no. 111.

53. R.H. Phillimore, ed., *Historical Records of the Survey of India*, Vol. 4, p. 216.

54. H.M. Elliot to J. Thomason, 1 September 1837, N.W.P. Proceedings (Revenue), IOR/P/217/60, no. 111.

55. J. Thomason to H.M. Elliot, 14 November 1837, N.W.P. Proceedings (Revenue), IOR/P/217/62, no. 109.

56. Edwardes & Merivale, 1, p. 124.

57. J. Bedford to W.H. Macnaghten, secretary to the Governor-General of India, 11 November 1837, N.W.P. Proceedings (Revenue), IOR/P/217/63, no. 164.

58. Ibid.
59. J. Bedford to J. Thomason, 31 October 1837, N.W.P. Proceedings (Revenue), IOR/P/217/62, no. 202.
60. J. Bedford to W. Macnaghten, 11 November 1837, N.W.P. Proceedings (Revenue), IOR/P/217/63, no. 164.
61. J. Bedford to J. Thomason, 13 October 1837, N.W.P. Proceedings (Revenue), IOR/P/217/62, no. 106.
62. Ibid.
63. Ibid.
64. A reduction from '13 Rupees per square mile to 6 Rs', J. Thomason to H.M. Elliot, 14 November 1837, N.W.P. Proceedings (Revenue), IOR/P/217/62, no. 109.
65. Henry Morris, *Heroes of our Indian Empire*, (London: The Christian Literature Society for India, 1908), Vol. 1, p. 115.
66. Honoria Lawrence's Journal, 11 January 1838, Mss. Eur. F85/82, p. 2.
67. Ibid., 25 January 1838, p. 16.
68. Ibid., p. 20.
69. H. Lawrence to Letitia Hayes [nee Lawrence], 3 May 1838, Edwardes & Merivale, 1, p. 162.
70. R.H. Phillimore, ed., *Historical Records of Survey of India*, Vol. 4, pp. 417, 468.
71. Honoria Lawrence [Henry's note] to Mrs Cameron, 11 February 1838, Edwardes & Merivale, 1, p. 154.
72. Once the unsuspecting farmer had done so 'by a sly touch the needle was made to fly round to its pole.' Reminiscences of Saunders Abbott, J.W. Kaye, *Lives of Indian Officers*, Vol. 2, p. 283.
73. Ibid., p. 282.
74. Honoria Lawrence to Letitia Lawrence, 25 May 1838, Edwardes & Merivale, 1, p. 163; see also H.M. Elliot, Secretary to Sudder Board of Revenue to J. Thomason, Secretary to Lt. Gov. N.W.P., 27 April 1838, N.W.P. Proceedings (Revenue), IOR/P/217/68, no. 136.
75. H.L. to Miss M. Irwin, March 1838, Edwardes & Merivale, 1, p. 156.
76. H.L. to Letitia Hayes (nee Lawrence), 19 May 1838, ibid., pp. 161–162.
77. J. Thomason (Secy to Gov. Gen.) to H.M. Elliot (Secy to Sudder Board of Revenue) 12 September 1838, N.W.P. Proceedings (Revenue), IOR/P/217/71, no. 60.
78. F. Shore to H. Lawrence, 3 September 1836, Mss. Eur. F85/21, pp. 228-9.
79. R.G. MacGregor to H. Lawrence, 25 January 1835, Mss. Eur. F85/21, p. 224.
80. H. Lawrence to J.H. Simmonds, 5 January 1839? Mss. Eur. F85/21, p.133.
81. Superintendent of Revenue Survey's Office, Allahabad, 20 November 1838, IOR/P/217/76, No. 28, Table A.
82. H.M. Elliot, secy to Sudder Board of Revenue to F. Currie, offg. Secy. to the Gov. Gen., 4 January 1839, IOR/P/217/76, No. 27.
83. 'The Board have had no complaints indicative of the more frequent recurrence of errors in the Khushreh measurements of these two surveys than in others and there is therefore reason to suppose that the abolition of the interior professional survey has not been attended with results unfavourable to the accuracy of the Khusreh.' Ibid.
84. Clements R. Markham, *A Memoir of the Indian Surveys* (London: W.H. Allen & Co., 1878), p. 181.
85. Ibid., p. 98.
86. R.H. Phillimore, ed., *Historical Records of Survey of India*, Vol. 4, p. 8.

87. Ibid., p. 214.

88. Ibid., p. 230.

89. H.R. Neville ed., *Moradabad District Gazetteer*, Vol. XVI, (Allahabad, 1911) pp. 116-117.

90. E.A. Reade, Collector of Goruckpoor, to F. Currie, Commissioner of Revenue 5th Division, 29th July 1837, *Reports on the Revenue Settlement of the NW Provinces*, Vol. 2, Part 2 (Benares 1863) p. 444.

'Cutcherry on Horseback': John Lawrence and the Making of a Sahib-Zillah 1831-46

1. 21 January 1831 – appointed Assistant to the Chief Commissioner & Resident at Delhi; appointed 2 December 1833 – Officiating Magistrate and Collector of Delhi – Henry Thoby Prinsep & Rāmachandra Doss, *General Register of the Hon'ble East India Company's Civil Servants of the Bengal Establishment from 1790 to 1842* (Calcutta: Baptist Mission Press, 1844), p. 196.

2. See Chapter X: Ceremonial observed on the visit of Governor-General, Lord Amherst, to His Majesty the King of Delhi in 1827 in *Records of the Delhi Residency and Agency*, Punjab Government Records, Vol. 1 (Lahore, 1911), pp. 337-342.

3. See Chapters 3 & 4 in J. Holmes, *The Administration of the Delhi Territory, 1803-1832*.

4. Minute of Sir C.T. Metcalfe, dated 7th November 1830, in *Selections from the Revenue Records North-Western Provinces 1822-33*, pp. 218-9.

5. Charles Metcalfe to Lord Bentinck, 13 March 1831, in Edward Thompson, *The Life of Charles, Lord Metcalfe* (London: Faber & Faber, 1937), p. 134.

6. J.W. Kaye, ed., *Selections from the Papers of Lord Metcalfe* (London: Smith, Elder & Co., 1855), pp. 48-49.

7. C. Aitchison, *Lord Lawrence*, p, p. 36.

8. Percival Spear, *Twilight of the Mughals*, pp. 103-104 in Spear, Percival et al., *The Delhi Omnibus* (Oxford: Oxford University Press, 2002).

9. E. Stokes, *The Peasant and the Raj, Studies in Agrarian Society and Peasant Rebellion in Colonial India*, (Cambridge: Cambridge University Press, 1978), p. 58.

10. E. Stokes, *The English Utilitarians and India* (Oxford: Clarendon Press, 1959), pp. 21, 144.

11. C. Aitchison, *Lord Lawrence*, p. 24.

12. Narayani Gupta, *Delhi between Two Empires 1803-1931, Society, Government and Urban Growth* in Spear, Percival et al., *The Delhi Omnibus*, p. 4.

13. A. Shakespear, *Memoir on the statistics of the North-Western provinces of the Bengal Presidency*, (Calcutta, 1848), p. 27.

14. Sylvia Shorto, *British Houses in Late Mughal Delhi* (Woodbridge: The Boydell Press, 2018) p. 115.

15. Bosworth Smith, 1, p. 48.

16. Percival Spear, *Twilight of the Mughals*, p. 147.

17. Henry Yule's review of Bosworth Smith's Life of Lord Lawrence in *The Quarterly Review*, April 1883, p. 297.

18. William Dalrymple, *City of Djinns, A Year in Delhi* (London: HarperCollins Publishers, 1993), p. 99.

19. John Lawrence, *Murder of Commissioner Fraser – Delhi 1835, A Tale of Circumstantial Evidence* in Blackwood's Edinburgh Magazine, Vol. CXXIII, January – June 1878, p. 32.

20. Bosworth Smith, 1, p. 47.

21. Thomas R. Metcalf, *Ideologies of the Raj*, The New Cambridge History of India, III.4, (Cambridge University Press, 1994), p. 33.

22. J. Holmes, *Administration of the Delhi Territory 1803-1832*, p. 266.

23. Bosworth Smith, 1, p. 45.

24. Ibid., p. 47.

25. Charles Raikes, *Reminiscences of John Lawrence*, Mss. Eur. D1019/2 p. 342.

26. Bosworth Smith, 1, p. 63.

27. Ibid., p. 64.

28. Based on an 1840s census of the Panipat district, 186,194 persons were recorded as Hindus, while Muslims/non-Hindus numbered 97,226. A. Shakespear, *Memoir on the statistics of the North-Western Provinces of the Bengal Presidency*, p. 18.

29. Bosworth Smith, 1, p. 56.

30. Ibid., p. 59.

31. Ibid., p. 81.

32. Ibid., p. 61.

33. Ibid., p. 57.

34. Ibid., p. 58.

35. Ibid., p. 61.

36. Ibid., p. 58.

37. Ibid., p. 113.

38. Ibid., p. 61.

39. Later this Gujar chief would be implicated as a rebel during the 1857 Revolt. He was spared the death penalty due to the help he had given John Lawrence twenty years previous.

40. Bosworth Smith, 1, p. 63.

41. R. Temple, *Lord Lawrence*, p. 36.

42. C. Raikes, *The Englishman in India*, p. 334.

43. Bosworth Smith, 1, p. 55.

44. Ibid., 1, p. 57.

45. John Lawrence, *The Brothers*, 4 March 1845, Bosworth Smith, 1, p. 69.

46. Ibid., p. 71.

47. Ibid., p. 72.

48. Ibid.

49. Ibid., p. 74.

50. Ibid., pp. 79-80.

51. Ibid., p. 80.

52. This was situated on the Ridge, and later became known as Hindu Rao's house. It now forms part of the Hindu Rao Hospital.

53. John Lawrence, *Murder of Commissioner Fraser – Delhi 1835, A Tale of Circumstantial Evidence* in Blackwood's Edinburgh Magazine, Vol. CXXIII, January – June 1878, p. 32.

54. Ibid., p. 33.

55. John mistakes Wassil Khan for Kurreem Khan. Wassil Khan – Kurreem's brother-in-law, was another *sowar* in the Nawab's service. He was regarded as an accessory to the crime but not charged.

56. John Lawrence, *Murder of Commissioner Fraser – Delhi 1835*, p. 35.

57. The coded Persian note was not found in a bucket of water but under some logs of wood. See Assassination of Mr. William Fraser (Report of Mr. Colvin, the Commissioner), Board's Collections, IOR/F/4/1561/63983, Vol. 3, p. 12

58. John Lawrence, *Murder of Commissioner Fraser – Delhi 1835*, p. 35.

59. Ibid., p. 38.

60. W.H. Sleeman, *Ramblings and recollections of an Indian Official* (London: J. Hatchard and Sons, 1844) Vol. 2, pp. 209-231.

61. Assassination of Mr. William Fraser (Report of Mr. Colvin, the Commissioner), Board's Collections, IOR/F/4/1561/63983, Vol. 3, p. 63.

62. Ibid., pp. 38-39.

63. Henry Thoby Prinsep & Rāmachandra Doss, *General Register of the Hon'ble East India Company's Civil Servants of the Bengal Establishment from 1790 to 1842*, p. 196.

64. Based on an 1845 census of the Gurgaon District, Hindus accounted for 281,508 persons, while Muslims/non-Hindus numbered 178,818, See A. Shakespear, *Memoir on the statistics of the North-Western Provinces of the Bengal Presidency*, p. 39.

65. See Chapter 2 in K. Prior, *The British Administration of Hinduism in North India, 1780-1900*, (Unpublished PhD thesis, University of Cambridge, 1990).

66. John Lawrence, *Passive Resistance*, 1845, Bosworth Smith, 1, p. 90.

67. Ibid.

68. Ibid., p. 91.

69. Ibid., p. 92.

70. Ibid., p. 92.

71. Ibid.

72. Ibid., p. 93.

73. Ibid., p. 94.

74. Ibid., p. 95.

75. No details of John's Panipat revenue assessments appear to exist apart from a passing reference in the *Karnal District Gazetteer* to the third and fourth settlements undertaken during 1834-6. *Gazetteer of the Karnal District, 1883-84* (Lahore, 1884) p. 226.

76. E. Stokes, *English Utilitarians and India*, pp. 98-99.

77. Minute by the Governor-General dated 26th September 1832, *Selections from Revenue Records, North-West Provinces, 1822–1833*, p. 389.

78. *Circular Order by the Sudder Board of Revenue, North-Western Provinces, addressed to Commissioners of Revenue on the subject of settlements* (Calcutta: Baptist Mission Press, 1839); *Directions for Settlement Officers in the North-Western Provinces of the Bengal Presidency, Promulgated under the authority of the Honourable the Lieutenant Governor* (Calcutta, 1850).

79. J. M. Douie, *Punjab Settlement Manual*, (Lahore, 1930), p. 18.

80. *Circular Order by the Sudder Board of Revenue*, pp. 27-28.

81. *Settlement of Pergunnah Rewaree*, J. Lawrence, Officiating Collector, Goorgaon, to T.T. Metcalfe, Commissioner of Delhi, 22nd July 1838, A. Fraser, ed., *Statistical Report on the District of Goorgaon*, Appendix D, p. xxxix.

82. Ibid., Appendix D, p. xxxi.

83. Ibid., Appendix D, p. xxxii.

84. Ibid., Appendix D, p. xl.

85. Ibid., Appendix D, p. xxxix.

86. Ibid., Appendix D, p. xli.

87. Ibid., Appendix D, p. xlvi.

88. Ibid., Appendix D, p. xxxviii.

89. Ibid., Revenue rates value (Rs. 199540) as a percentage of Rent Rate value (Rs. 242930) = 82% (excluding *muqaddam* allowance), Appendix D, p. xl.

90. *Directions for Settlement Officers*, p. 41.

91. Douie mentions that the rule was lowered to two-thirds when Thomason's *Directions for Settlement Officers* was first published in 1844. J.M. Douie, *Punjab Settlement Manual*, p. 15.

92. *Circular Order by the Sudder Board of Revenue*, p. 29.

93. A. Fraser, ed., *Statistical Report on the District of Goorgaon*, pp. 85–86.

94. (Proposed assessment: Rs. 9287; Previous assessment: Rs. 8931 – an increase of Rs. 356 or 4% increase). Settlement of Pergunnah Shahjehanpoor, J. Lawrence, Officiating Collector, Gurgaon, to T.T. Metcalfe, Commissioner of Delhi, 25th July 1838, ibid., Appendix E, p. l.

95. Settlement of Purgunnah Borah – J. Lawrence, Officiating Collector, Gurgaon, to T.T. Metcalfe, Commissioner of Delhi, 4th August 1838, ibid., Appendix F, p. liv.

96. Ibid., Appendix F. p. lix.

97. Ibid., Appendix F, pp. liii – liv.

98. Ibid., Appendix B, p. xvi.

99. Ibid., Appendix B, p. xvi.

100. Ibid., Appendix B, p. xix.

101. *Gurgaon District Gazetteer*, p. 115.

102. A. Fraser, ed., *Statistical Report on the District of Goorgaon*, Appendix B, p. xviii.

103. The village statements contained all the details related to the assessment gathered by the settlement officer or in this case the tahsildar and recorded in the '*pargana* note-book'. See Baden-Powell, *The Land Systems of British India*, Vol. 2, p. 88.

104. C.C. Barnes, Settlement Officer, Gurgaon, to T.T. Metcalfe, Commissioner of Delhie, 26th September 1840, A. Fraser, ed., *Statistical Report on the District of Goorgaon*, Appendix I p. lxxxix.

105. C.C. Barnes, Settlement Officer, Gurgaon, to T.T. Metcalfe, Commissioner of Delhie, 13th February 1842, ibid., Appendix Q, p. cxxv.

106. Ibid.

107. *Settlement of Pergunnah Taroo*, – J. Lawrence, Officiating Collector, Gurgaon, to T.T. Metcalfe, Commissioner of Delhi, 30th November 1837, ibid., Appendix C, p. xxi.

108. Ibid., Appendix C, p. xxiv.

109. Ibid., Appendix C, p. xxvii.

110. G.C. Barnes, Settlement Officer, Gurgaon, to T.T. Metcalfe, Commissioner of Delhie, 21st December 1841, ibid., Appendix N, p. cxii. See also D. Ibbetson, ed., *Gazetteer of the Gurgaon District* (Lahore, 1884), p. 110.

111. *Directions for Settlement Officers*, p. 45; *Circular Order*, p. 30.

112. F.C. Channing, *Land Revenue Settlement of the Gurgaon District* (Lahore: Central Jail Press, 1882), p. 5.

113. A. Fraser, ed., *Statistical Report on the District of Goorgaon*, Appendix E, p. l; Appendix F, p. lvii.

114. Ibid., Appendix D, p. xxxi.

115. Bosworth Smith, 1, p. 59.

116. D.L. Drake-Brockman (ed.), *Etawah District Gazetteer*, (Allahabad, 1911) p. 101.

117. Bosworth Smith, 1, p. 112.

118. John Lawrence, *The Disputed Boundary*, ibid., p. 114.

119. Ibid., p. 120.

120. Ibid., p. 121.

121. Ibid., p. 122.

122. Ibid., p. 125.
123. Ibid., p. 111.
124. Ibid., p. 136.
125. Ibid., p. 137.
126. Ibid., p. 142.
127. Ibid., p. 143.
128. Ibid., p. 144.
129. Ibid., p. 146.
130. Ibid., p. 147.
131. Ibid., p. 161.
132. Ibid., p. 164.
133. Ibid., p. 166.
134. Ibid., p. 178.
135. Ibid., p. 179.
136. *Selected Reports on the Revision of settlement in the Delhi Territory*, No. 2. (Agra, 1846), J. Lawrence, *Pergunnah Delhie*, No. 261, 5 August 1844, p. 59.
137. Ibid., p. 60.
138. Ibid., p. 65.
139. Ibid., p. 65.
140. P. Spear, *Twilight of the Mughals*, p. 102.
141. *Selected Reports on the Revision of settlement in the Delhi Territory*, p. 68.
142. Percival Spear, *Twilight of the Mughals*, p. 102.
143. D.N. Panigrahi, *Charles Metcalfe in India, Ideas & Administration 1806–1835* (Delhi: Munshiram Manoharlal, 1968) p. 106.
144. C. Aitchison, *Lord Lawrence*, p. 29.
145. P. Spear, *Twilight of the Mughals*, pp. 108–109.
146. O. Wood and R. Maconachie, *Final Report on the Settlement of the Land Revenue in the Delhi District* completed in 1880 (Lahore: Victoria Press, 1882), p. 4.
147. *Selected Reports on the Revision of settlement in the Delhi Territory*, p. 66.

'The active and judicious measures' of Robert Montgomery, Collector and Magistrate 1829–49

1. For the background on the growth of 'colonial knowledge' in nineteenth century India, see chapters 4 & 6 of C.A. Bayly, *Empire and Information, Intelligence Gathering and Social Communication in India, 1780–1870*, (Cambridge: Cambridge University Press, 1996).
2. J. Thomason, collector of Azimgurh, dated Agra, December 16 1837, *Report on the Settlement of Chuklah Azimgurh* in *Selections from the Records of Government of North-Western Provinces*, Vol. 3 (Agra, 1855), p. 125.
3. 'In Memoriam – Henry Carre Tucker' in *The Church Missionary Intelligencer*, (January 1876), p. 17.
4. Ibid., p. 18.
5. R. Temple, *James Thomason* (Oxford: Clarendon Press, 1893), p. 54.
6. P. Penner, *The Patronage Bureaucracy in North India* (Delhi: Chanakya Publications,1986), p. 89.
7. *The Church Missionary Intelligencer*, p. 18.

8. Cheriakote, and Kurriat Mittoo in the 1834-5 season; Mahol in the 1835-6 season; Gopalpore, Kowreeah, Atrowleeah Tilhenee, Suggree in 1836-7; Ghosee and Nuthoopoor were settled in 1836-7 by both Thomason and Montgomery.

9. R. M. to F. Currie, Commissioner of Revenue, 9th Division. 30th July 1834, Settlement of Pergunnah Sugree, Mss. Eur. D1019/1, p. 60.

10. R.M. to F. Currie, March 1837, N.W.P. Proceedings (Revenue) IOR/P/217/64, No. 256, para. 7.

11. J. Thomason, *Report on the Settlement of Chuklah Azimgurh*, p. 139.

12. R. M. to F. Currie, 30 June 1836, N.W.P. Proceedings (Revenue) IOR/P/217/64, No. 254, para. 19.

13. R. M. to F. Currie, March 1837, N.W.P. Proceedings (Revenue) IOR/P/217/64, No. 256, para. 31.

14. J. Thomason, *Report on the Settlement of Chuklah Azimgurh*. p. 158.

15. R. M. to F. Currie, 30 June 1836, N.W.P. Proceedings (Revenue) IOR/P/217/64, No. 254, para. 18.

16. R. M. to F. Currie, 28 March 1837, N.W.P. Proceedings (Revenue) IOR/P/217/64, No. 257, para 14.

17. R. M. to F. Currie, March 1837, N.W.P. Proceedings (Revenue) IOR/P/217/64, No. 256, para. 34.

18. J. Thomason, *Report on the Settlement of Chuklah Azimgurh*, p. 159.

19. Ibid., p. 156.

20. R. M. to F. Currie, Commissioner of Revenue, 9th Division. 30th July 1834, Revenue Settlement of Pergunnah Sugree, Mss. Eur. D1019/1, p. 61.

21. J. Thomason, *Report on the Settlement of Chuklah Azimgurh*, p. 155.

22. R. M. to F. Currie, Commissioner of Revenue, 9th Division. 30th July 1834, Revenue Settlement of Pergunnah Sugree, Mss. Eur. D1019/1, pp. 56-62.

23. Ibid., p. 57.

24. Ibid., p. 58.

25. J. Thomason, *Report on the Settlement of Chuklah Azimgurh*, p.155.

26. R. M. to F. Currie, 28 March 1837, N.W.P. Proceedings (Revenue) IOR/P/217/64, No. 257, para. 9 & 10.

27. R. M. to F. Currie, 30 June 1836, N.W.P. Proceedings (Revenue) IOR/P/217/64, No. 254, para, 21.

28. J. Thomason, *Report on the Settlement of Chuklah Azimgurh*, p. 163.

29. F. Currie, Revenue Commissioner to Sudder Board of Revenue, 7th August 1837, N.W.P. Proceedings (Revenue) IOR/P/217/63, No. 250. para. 25.

30. J. Thomason, *Report on the Settlement of Chuklah Azimgurh*, p. 161.

31. Ibid., p. 164.

32. G. Campbell, Officiating Collector of Azimgurh, to H.C. Tucker, Commissioner, 5th Division, Benares; No. 393 of 1854, dated 29th November 1854 in Selections from the Records of Government, North-Western Provinces, Vol. 4 (Agra, 1856), p. 228.

33. J. Thomason, *Report on the Settlement of Chuklah Azimgarh*, p. 161.

34. F. Currie, Divisional Revenue Commissioner, no date, Mss. Eur. D1019/1, p. 83.

35. *The Church Missionary Intelligencer*, p. 18.

36. H. Tucker to R. M., 7 October 1840, Mss. Eur. D1019/1, p. 178.

37. Ibid., p. 19. See also H.C. Tucker, *The Bible in India* (1859) for his evangelical views.

38. H. Tucker to R. M., 4 December 1834, Mss. Eur. D1019/1, p. 75.

39. F.M. Thomason to Eliza Hutchinson, 4 December 1834, ibid., p. 63.

40. R.M. to Fanny, 8 December 1834, Ibid., p. 90.

41. The diary was destroyed by Robert's son, Bishop Montgomery, who felt that it was 'too simple and innocent'. The bishop, however, recorded some details of the diary in his notes in the Montgomery Papers. Ibid., pp. 66-67.

42. Ibid, Fanny to R.M., 21st March 1836, pp. 117-118.

43. Ibid., April 5th [no year], p. 108.

44. Ibid., p. 104.

45. Ibid., p. 106.

46. Ibid., p. 95.

47. Ibid., p. 111.

48. Ibid., p. 102.

49. Ibid., p. 96.

50. R.M. to Fanny, Camp Ghosee, 8 January 1837, Ibid., p. 92.

51. In 2018 the government of Uttar Pradesh renamed it Prayagraj.

52. Emma Roberts, *Scenes and Characteristics of Hindoostan*, Vol. 2, p. 1.

53. Ibid., p. 19.

54. Watercolour of Thomas Fortescue Esqr.'s House, Judge and Magistrate of Allahabad, painted by Sita Ram between 1814-15. J.W. Kaye, A History of the Sepoy War in India, 1857-58, (London, Longmans, Green & Co., 1870), Vol. 2, p. 257.

55. J. McCosh, *Medical Advice to the Indian Stranger*, (London: Wm. H. Allen & Co., 1841), pp. 124-5.

56. The revenue survey documents included the *shajra*, the *Khusrah*, the professional village map with tables and the *pargana* map.

57. *Report on the Settlement of the district of Allahabad*, R. M. to R. Lowther, Commissioner of Allahabad, 1st October 1839, in *Reports on the Revenue Settlement of the North-Western Provinces of the Bengal Presidency, under Regulation IX, 1833*, Vol. 2, Part 1 (Benares, 1863), p. 428.

58. Ibid., p. 429.

59. Ibid., p. 431.

60. Ibid.

61. Ibid., p. 432.

62. Ibid., p. 432.

63. Ibid., p. 437.

64. Ibid., p. 425.

65. Ibid., p. 442.

66. Robert Lowther, Revenue Commissioner of the Allahabad Division, to the Sudder Board of Revenue, [1839] Mss. Eur. D1019/1, p. 84.

67. F.W. Porter, *Final Settlement Report of the Allahabad District* (Allahabad, 1878), p. 89.

68. Ibid.

69. Ibid., p. 90.

70. Letter from the Secretary, Board of Revenue, North-Western Provinces, 23 April 1881. Ibid., p. 10.

71. *Report on the Settlement of the district of Allahabad*, p. 442.

72. F.W. Porter, *Final Settlement Report of the Allahabad District*, p. 89.

73. Lalita Panigrahi, *Social Policy and Female Infanticide* (New Delhi: Munshiram Manoharlal, 1972), p. 2.

74. Ibid., p. 18.

75. 'May not these efforts, prompted by the pure disinterested benevolence of his Christian rulers lead the Hindoo to recognise the presence of a higher spirit of morality, to which he is wholly a stranger, and tempt him onward to an examination into its origin and character, until he be led to embrace the purer faith,' wrote Revd John Cave-Browne, a chaplain in Bengal. John Cave-Browne, *Indian Infanticide – Its Origins, Progress and Suppression*, (London: Wm. H. Allen & Co.,1857), p. 203.

76. Lalita Panigrahi, *Social Policy and Female Infanticide*, p. 44.

77. John Cave Browne, *Indian Infanticide*, p.70.

78. Lalita Panigrahai, *Social Policy and Female Infanticide*, p. 90.

79. R. Montgomery, Magistrate Zillah Allahabad, to R. Lowther, Commissioner of Circuit, 4th Division, Allahabad, 28 January 1841. Accounts and Papers of the House of Commons, Vol. 35, p. 415.

80. See Selections from the Records of Government, North-Western Provinces, Vol. 3 (Agra 1855), p. 171; Lalita Panigrahai, Social Policy and Female Infanticide, pp. 93-4.

81. John Cave Browne, *Indian Infanticide – Its Origins, Progress and Suppression*, p. 73.

82. R. Montgomery, Esq. Magistrate Zillah Allahabad, to R. Lowther, Esq. Commissioner of Circuit, 4th Division, Allahabad, dated 28th January 1841. Accounts and Papers of the House of Commons, Vol. 35, p. 416.

83. Accounts and Papers of the House of Commons, Vol. 35, p. 61

84. R. Montgomery, Magistrate, Allahabad, to R. Lowther, Commissioner of Circuit, 4th Division, 7 February 1842. Accounts and Papers of the House of Commons, Vol. 35, p. 416.

85. John Cave Browne, *Indian Infanticide – Its Origins, Progress and Suppression*, p. 73.

86. The Court of Directors of the East India Company, 14 Dec 1842, Mss. Eur. D1019/1, p. 130.

87. John Cave Browne, *Indian Infanticide – Its Origins, Progress and Suppression*, p. 74.

88. Mss. Eur. D1019/1, p. 186.

89. R. M. memorandum on the death of his wife, 24 March 1842, ibid., p. 138.

90. R. M. to Mrs Hutchinson, [no date], ibid., p. 156.

91. Ibid., p. 156. All the children from this marriage had their lives cut short by disease. His eldest daughter, Frances Mary [10 October 1835 – 22 August 1855] died within a year of her marriage to Donald McLeod, aged nineteen years. Robby [17 December 1836 – 7 February 1853] died of pneumonia aged seventeen, while Robert's youngest daughter Mary Susan [8 November 1838 – 22 December 1860] died aged twenty-two.

92. R.M., Mss. Eur. D1019/1, p. 186.

93. Ibid., p. 190.

94. Ibid., p. 191.

95. Ibid., p. 204.

96. Henry Hutchinson Montgomery (1847-1932), later Bishop of Tasmania, was born on 3 September or 3 October 1847 at Cawnpore. His son Bernard Law Montgomery became first Viscount Montgomery of Alamein.

97. E. Edmond, *The Bengal Civil Service Gradation List, 1845-46* (Calcutta: W. Thacker & Co., 1845), p. 28.

98. F. Parkes, *Wanderings of a pilgrim in search of the Picturesque*, Vol. 1, p. 137.

99. Ibid., p. 136.

100. A brass plaque in the front veranda reads 'Fanny Parkes, Authoress of "Wanderings of a Pilgrim in search of the Picturesque" lived in this bungalow, April 1830 to February 1831.'

101. The Cawnpore Gazetteer mentions that during the Mutiny 'several bungalows escaped with the loss of their roofs, which had been burned.' H.R. Nevill, Cawnpore: A Gazetteer, being Volume XIX of the District Gazetteers of the United Provinces of Agra and Oudh (Allahabad, 1909) p. 264.

102. W. Muir, *The Honourable James Thomason: Late Lieutenant-Governor*, *The Calcutta Review*, XXI (1853), p. 507.

103. Ibid.

104. Ibid. Only three other officers did so: A. Fraser, *Statistical Report of the District of Gurgaon* (1849); C.W. Kinloch, *Statistical Report of the District of Futtehpore (1852)*; J.H. Batten, *Statistical Report of the Districts of Kemaon and Gurhwal (1851)*.

105. C.A. Bayly, Empire and Information, pp. 221-222; W. Muir, *The Honourable James Thomason,* p. 508.

106. R. Montgomery, *Statistical Report of the District of Cawnpoor* (Calcutta: J.C. Sherriff, Bengal Military Orphan Press, 1849).

107. Ibid., p. 4.

108. Ibid., p. 6.

109. *Statement Shewing the Mutations of Property since the Cession [i.e. 1802] up to 1846-47,* Appendix No. XII, Ibid, p. lxxxiv.

110. Ibid., p. 32.

111. Ibid., p. 32.

112. Ibid., p. 39.

113. Ibid., p. 16.

114. Ibid., p. 42.

115. Ibid., p. 44.

116. Ibid., p. 48.

117. Ibid., p. 48.

118. J. Thomason to R. M., 11 November 1847, Mss. Eur. D1019/1, p. 219.

119. Ibid., p. 221.

120. Sir Richard Temple, *James Thomason*, p. 174.

121. Memorandum on the Grand Trunk Road by R. Montgomery, Magistrate of Cawnpore, dated 17th April 1847 in *Selections from the Records of Government, North-Western Provinces*, (Agra, 1855), Vol. 1, p. 46.

122. Ibid., p. 47.

123. Ibid., p. 47.

124. Extract from a Report by Lieutenant Colonel J. Steel, Superintendent of Police and Supplies on the Grand Trunk Road, dated 28th March 1852, in *Selections from the Records of Government, North-Western Provinces*, Vol. 3, (Agra, 1855), p. 26.

125. The Agra Messenger, a regional newspaper, reported the phenomenon on 2nd December 1848, quoted in F. Parkes, *Wanderings of a Pilgrim*, Vol. 2, p. 452.

126. James Hutton, *A Popular Account of the Thugs and Dacoits, the Hereditary Garotters and Gang-Robbers of India* (London: WM. H. Allen & Co., 1857), p. 98.

127. Report on the Tusma-Baz Thugs by R. Montgomery, Magistrate of Cawnpore, 21st February 1848, in *Selections from the Records of Government, North-Western Provinces*, (Agra, 1855), Vol. 1, p. 54.

128. Letter from Major J. Graham, Assistant General Superintendent and Joint Magistrate, to Colonel W. H. Sleeman, General Superintendent, Jhansee, No. 137 of 1848, dated Agra, the 29th July 1848, in *Selections from the Records of Government, North-Western Provinces*, Vol. 1, p. 58.

129. Ibid., p. 58.

130. Ibid., p. 60.

131. Ibid., p. 60.

132. Ibid., p. 54.

133. Ibid., p. 61.

134. Hutton, James, *A Popular Account of the Thugs and Dacoits*, p. 100.

135. Wagner, K.A. *Thuggee: Banditry and the British in Early Nineteenth-Century India*, (Basingstoke: Palgrave, 2007), p. 121.

136. *Selections from the Records of Government, North-Western Provinces*, Vol. 1, p. 61.

The Great Game

1. J.D. Cunningham, *History of the Sikhs: From the Origins of the Nation to the Battles of the Sutlej*, (New Delhi: Rupa & Co., 2002), p. 406.

2. See Treaty of Turkmanchai between Russia and Persia (23 February 1828); Russian-Turkish Treaty of Adrianople (14 September 1829).

3. Colonel G. de Lacy Evans, *On the Practicability of an Invasion of British India*, (London: J.M. Richardson, 1829), pp. 86-87.

4. Edward Law, Lord Ellenborough, Lord Colchester ed., *A Political Diary 1828-1830*, (London: Richard Bentley & Son., 1881), Vol. 2, pp. 92- 93.

5. J.A. Norris, *The First Afghan War 1838-1842*, (Cambridge: Cambridge University Press, 1967), p. 42.

6. M.E. Yapp, *Strategies of British India – Britain, Iran and Afghanistan 1798-1850*, (Oxford: Clarendon Press, 1980), p. 202.

7. A. Burnes, *Travels Into Bokhara; being the account of A Journey from India to Cabool, Tartary, and Persia*, (London: John Murray, 1834), Vol. 2, p. 332.

8. M.E. Yapp, *Strategies of British India*, p. 228.

9. J.A. Norris, *The First Anglo-Afghan War*, p. 161.

10. M.E. Yapp, *Strategies of British India*, pp. 243-244.

11. H. Havelock, *Narrative of the War in Afghanistan in 1838-39*, (London: Henry Coburn, Publisher, 1840), Vol. 2, pp. 237-8.

12. Ibid., p. 240.

13. Ibid., p. 244.

14. Appointed second lieutenant on 5 May 1821, he was elevated to full lieutenant three year later. It took George a further twelve years to attain the rank of captain (5 May 1836) and then only a brevet one. Dodwell And Miles (ed.), *Alphabetical List of the Officers of the Bengal Army*, (London: Longman, Orme, Brown & Co., 1838) p. 166.

15. G. Lawrence, *Reminiscences*, p. 2.

16. Two hundred and twenty-three pages were devoted to his part in the 1st Anglo-Afghan War. His time spent as political agent at Peshawar over a similar time span in the mid to late 1840s covered only fifty pages, while his final Indian posting as the Governor-General's Agent to the Rajputana states covered a mere twenty-seven pages.

17. Linda Colley, *Captives: Britain, Empire and the World 1600-1850*, p. 363.

18. J.M. Kaye, *History of the War in Afghanistan*, (London: Wm. H. Allen & Co., 1874), Vol. 3, pp. 398-402.

19. G. Lawrence, *Reminiscences*, preface, pp. v-vi.

20. '…whether with my regiment or on the staff, I entreat that I may not be prevented going where my duty has clearly called me.' H. Lawrence to John Colvin, private sec. to Gov. General, 16 August 1838, Mss. Eur. F85/21, p. 139.

21. H. Lawrence to Col. Dunlop, Quarter-Master General of the Army, 16 Aug 1838, Mss. Eur. F85/21, p. 140.
22. Col. Dunlop to G. Lawrence, 11 Sept 1838, ibid., pp. 254-255.
23. See H.L. writings on the Adams incident, ibid., pp. 146-170.
24. See Honoria Lawrence to Henry Lawrence, 26 September 1838, Mss. Eur. F85/21, pp. 174-175.
25. 'In January 1838 my strength failed, I became subject to depression of spirits, faintings, dysentery, sickness and sleeplessness which never left me till the baby was born, and from April I scarcely took any exercise, or retained any food.' Honoria Lawrence Journal, Mss. Eur. F85/84, p. 1. See also Mss. Eur. F85/83, p. 10.
26. F. Currie to H.L., January 1839, Edwardes & Merivale, 1, p. 202.
27. J.L. to H.L. 21 January 1839, ibid., p. 202.
28. F. Currie to H.L., 28 January 1839, Mss. Eur. F85/22, pp. 7-8.

The Army of the Indus

1. Numbering some 30,000 men, the Army of the Indus consisted of a division each of the Company's Bengal and Bombay armies, a portion of Ranjit Singh's Punjabi soldiers and levies raised under the command of Shah Shuja.
2. J.A. Norris, *First Anglo-Afghan War*, p. 239.
3. J.M. Kaye, *History of the War in Afghanistan*, Vol. 1, p. 405.
4. G. Lawrence, *Reminiscences*, p. 5.
5. H. Havelock, *Narrative of the War in Afghanistan*, Vol. 1, p. 176.
6. G. Lawrence, *Reminiscences*, p. 6.
7. Major W. Hough, A Narrative of the March and Operations of the Army of the Indus, in the Expedition to Afghanistan in the Years 1838-1839 (London: Wm. H. Allen & Co., 1841), p. 39.
8. Ibid., p. 57.
9. G. Lawrence, *Reminiscences*, p. 7
10. Ibid., p. 11.
11. J.W. Kaye, *History of War in Afghanistan*, Vol. 1, p. 433.
12. Ibid., p. 438.
13. Ibid., pp. 440-1.
14. G. Lawrence, *Reminiscences*, p. 12.
15. W. Hough, *Narrative of the March and Operations of the Army of the Indus*, p. 105.
16. For a corrective to Kaye and Lawrence's interpretation, see J.A. Norris, *First Anglo-Afghan War*, p. 270.
17. Significantly Shah Shuja did not change the system of revenue assessment and left the same draconian revenue officers in charge. See J.W. Kaye, *History of the War in Afghanistan*, Vol. 1, p. 443.
18. G. Lawrence, *Reminiscences*, p. 13.
19. Ibid., pp. 16- 17.
20. G. Lawrence to H.L., 30 August 1839, Edwardes & Merivale, 1, p. 235.
21. Ibid., p. 236.
22. J.H. Stocqueler, *Memorials of Afghanistan: being State Papers, Official Documents, Dispatches, Authentic Narratives, etc., Illustrative of the British Expedition to, and Occupation of Afghanistan and Scinde, between the years 1838 and 1842* (Calcutta: Messrs. Ostell and Lepage, 1843), Appendix, No.1, The pursuit of Dost Mahommed Khan, by Major Outram of the Bombay Army, p. viii.

23. G. Lawrence to H.L., 30 August 1839, Edwardes & Merivale, 1, p. 237.

24. W. Hough, *Narrative of the March and Operations of the Army of the Indus*, p. 249.

25. G. Lawrence, *Reminiscences*, p. 25.

26. H. Havelock, *Narrative of the War in Afghanistan*, Vol. 2, p. 118.

27. W. Hough, *Narrative of the March and Operations of the Army of the Indus*, p. 251.

28. G. Lawrence, *Reminiscences*, pp. 26-27.

29. Ibid., p. 39.

30. J.A. Norris, *The First Afghan War*, p. 325.

31. G. Lawrence, *Reminiscences*, p. 42.

32. Ibid., p. 42.

33. Mohan Lal, *Life of the Amir Dost Mohammed Khan of Kabul*, (London: Longman, Brown, Green, and Longmans, 1846), Vol. 2, p. 344.

34. G. Lawrence, *Reminiscences*, p. 44.

35. Ibid., pp. 49-50.

36. Ibid., p. 52.

37. Ibid., p. 53.

38. Ibid., p. 54.

Political Agent at Ferozepur

1. The Cis-Sutlej states were a group of states located south of the River Sutlej in lower Punjab. After the Second Anglo-Maratha War of 1803-1805, and following an 1809 agreement with Maharaja Ranjit Singh, these states were brought under formal British protection. The Cis-Sutlej states included Ferozepur, Kaithal, Patiala, Jind, Thanesar, Maler Kotla, and Faridkot.

2. H.M. Lawrence, *Adventures of an Officer in the Service of Runjeet Singh*, (London: Henry Colburn, 1845), Vol. 2, p. 201.

3. Ibid., p. 199.

4. Honoria Lawrence to Mrs Irwin, 15 April 1839, Edwardes & Merivale, 1, p. 211.

5. H.L. to Capt. Woodward, 22 March 1839, Mss. Eur. F85/1, p. 4.

6. H.L. to A. Gordon, 7 June 1839, ibid., p. 6.

7. H.L. to Capt. Cooper, 19 February 1839, ibid., p. 4

8. H.L. to Capt. Woodward, 5 April 1839, ibid., p. 5.

9. H.L. to G. Clerk, [no date] June 1839, ibid., p. 8.

10. HL to Colonel C.M. Wade, 21 January 1840, Mss. Eur. F85/1, p. 17.

11. H.L. to the Accountant General, 13 April 1839, ibid., pp. 5-6.

12. J.L. Morison, *Lawrence of Lucknow*, p. 95.

13. J. Thomason to H.L., 20 March 1840, Mss. Eur. F85/23, p. 20.

14. Ibid., 8 June 1840, pp. 21-22.

15. Ibid., 20 June 1840, pp. 24-25.

16. G. Lawrence to Honoria Lawrence, 24 November 1839, Mss. Eur. F85/52, p. 1.

17. 'Today we heard from George all well and prospering. He has offered me his berth and were I a bachelor I would jump at it. My post has hitherto been very laborious and for a time will continue so, but I sigh for a little rest and a little time for self and domestic relations.' H.L. to Letitia Hayes, 22 December 1839, Mss. Eur. F85/69, p. 24.

18. H.M. Lawrence to J. Colvin, Private Sec. to Gov. Gen. 9th July 1840, Mss. Eur. F85/52, pp. 13-14.

19. J. Colvin, Private Sec. to Gov. Gen. to H.M. Lawrence 20th July 1840, Mss. Eur. F85/52, P. 15.
20. H.L. to T. Metcalfe, 1841, Mss. Eur. F85/1, pp. 27-29.
21. H.L. to G. Clerk, 1840, *Report on the Settlement of the Furreedkote Boundary*, Mss. Eur. F85/23, p. 52.
22. Ibid., p. 51.
23. Ibid., p. 52.
24. H.L. to G. Clerk, *Report on the Settlement of the Furreedkote Boundary*, pp. 54-55.
25. Ibid., p. 53.
26. H.L., *Report on the District of Ferozepore*, 1840, Mss. Eur. F85/19, p. 31.
27. H.L. to Letitia Hayes, 22nd December 1839, Mss. Eur. F85/69, p. 24.
28. H.L. to G. Clerk, *Report on the Settlement of the Furreedkote Boundary*, p. 57.
29. H.L., *Report on the District of Ferozepore*, p. 31.
30. Honoria Lawrence to Mrs Cameron, 26 May 1841, Edwardes & Merivale, 1, p. 216.
31. Edwardes & Merivale, 1, p. 225.
32. Ibid., p. 251.

The Rising

1. J.W. Kaye, *History of the War in Afghanistan*, Vol. 2, Appendix: Sources of Douranee Discontent from Major Rawlinson's Douranee Report, p. 395.
2. Macnaghten to Rawlinson, 13 June 1841, G. Rawlinson, *A Memoir of Maj-Gen Sir Henry Creswicke Rawlinson* (London: Longmans, Green & Co., 1898), p. 80.
3. G. Lawrence, *Reminiscences*, p. 54.
4. Ibid., p. 56.
5. Ibid., p. 57.
6. Ibid., p. 59.
7. Ibid., p. 61.
8. Ibid., p. 62.
9. Ibid., p. 63.
10. Ibid., p. 65.
11. Ibid., p. 67.
12. Ibid.
13. Ibid., p. 68.
14. Ibid., p. 69.
15. Ibid.
16. Vincent Eyre, The Military Operations at Caubul, which ended in the retreat and Destruction of the British Army, January 1842. With a Journal of Imprisonment in Afghanistan (London: John Murray, 1843), p. 29.
17. G. Lawrence, *Reminiscences*, p. 70.
18. Ibid., p. 71.
19. Ibid., p. 75.
20. Ibid., p. 79.
21. Ibid., p. 84.
22. Ibid., p. 85.
23. J.W. Kaye, *History of the War in Afghanistan*, Vol. 2, pp. 222-3.
24. G. Lawrence, *Reminiscences*, p. 85.
25. Honoria Lawrence to Mrs Cameron, 21 June 1842, Edwardes & Merivale, 1, p. 275.
26. G. Clerk to H. Lawrence, 5 Dec 1841, Mss. Eur. F85/24, p. 18.

27. Honoria Lawrence to Mrs Hayes, 12 December 1841, Edwardes & Merivale, 1, p. 271.
28. H.L. to G. Clerk, 29 October 1841, ibid., p. 216.
29. J.R. Becher, *Reminiscences*, Mss. Eur. F85/24, pp. 25-26.
30. G. Lawrence, *Reminiscences*, p. 90.
31. Ibid., p. 93.
32. Ibid., pp. 93-4.
33. Ibid., p. 96.
34. P. Macrory, *Signal Catastrophe* (London: Hodder and Stoughton, 1972), p. 180.
35. G. Lawrence, *Reminiscences*, p. 102.
36. P. Macrory, *Signal Catastrophe*, p. 189.
37. G. Lawrence, *Reminiscences*, p. 110.
38. Ibid., p. 112.
39. Ibid., p. 126.
40. C. Mackenzie, *Storms and Sunshine of a Soldier's Life 1825-1881*, (Edinburgh: David Douglas, 1884), Vol. 1, pp. 240-1.
41. Ibid., p. 241.
42. G. Lawrence, *Reminiscences*, p. 116.
43. Ibid., p. 117.
44. C. Mackenzie, *Storms and Sunshine of a Soldier's Life*, Vol. 1, p. 243.
45. G. Lawrence, *Reminiscences*, pp. 118-9.
46. Ibid., p. 122.
47. Ibid., p. 124.
48. Ibid., p. 127.
49. Ibid., p. 130.
50. Ibid., p. 133
51. This was later rejected by General Elphinstone on the grounds that it would prolong the troops' exposure to the freezing conditions.
52. Ibid., p. 137.
53. Ibid., p. 141.
54. M.E. Yapp, *Strategies of British India*, p. 425.
55. J.A. Norris, *The First Afghan War*, p. 384.
56. H.L. to Honoria Lawrence, 1 January 1842, Mss. Eur. F85/70c, p. 18.
57. H.L. to Honoria Lawrence, 5 January 1842, ibid., p. 20.
58. H.L. to Honoria Lawrence, 8 January 1842, ibid., p. 23.

Retreat from Kabul

1. G. Lawrence, *Reminiscences*, p. 143.
2. C. Mackenzie, *Storms and Sunshine of a Soldier's Life*, Vol. 1, p. 258.
3. G. Lawrence, *Reminiscences*, p. 144.
4. Ibid., p. 145.
5. Ibid., p. 146.
6. Ibid., p. 146.
7. Ibid., p. 149.
8. Ibid.
9. Ibid., p. 150.
10. Ibid., p. 152.
11. C. Mackenzie, *Storms and Sunshine of a Soldier's Life*, Vol. 1, p. 263.

12. G. Lawrence, *Reminiscences*, p. 154.
13. Ibid., p. 154.
14. Ibid., p. 158.
15. Ibid., p. 159.
16. Ibid., p. 161.
17. Ibid., pp. 161-2.
18. Ibid., pp. 162.
19. Ibid., p. 166.
20. Ibid., p. 167.

Captivity and Deliverance
1. G. Lawrence, *Reminiscences*, p. 170.
2. Ibid., p. 173.
3. Ibid., p. 184.
4. C. Mackenzie, *Storms and Sunshine*, Vol.1, p. 282.
5. V. Eyre, *Prison Sketches comprising portraits of the Cabul Prisoners* (London: Dickinson and Sons, 1843), p. 2.
6. V. Eyre, *The Military Operations at Caubul*, p. 243.
7. G. Lawrence, *Reminiscences*, p. 159.
8. Ibid., p. 200.
9. V. Eyre, *The Military Operations at Caubul*, p. 257.
10. G. Lawrence, *Reminiscences*, p. 184.
11. H.L. to Honoria Lawrence, 19 January 1842, Mss. Eur. F85/70c, p. 33.
12. H.L. to Honoria Lawrence, 25 January 1842, ibid., pp. 37-38.
13. H.L. to Honoria Lawrence, 1 January 1842 ibid., p. 18.
14. H.L. to Honoria Lawrence, 5 February 1842, ibid., p. 46.
15. H.L. to Honoria Lawrence, 10 March 1842, ibid., p. 74.
16. Edwardes & Merivale, 1, p. 347.
17. H.L. to G. Clerk, 5 April 1842, Mss. Eur. F85/2, p. 85.
18. See also B.J. Hasrat, *Anglo-Sikh Relations*, pp. 212-213.
19. General Pollock to Government of India, 6 April 1842, Edwardes & Merivale, 1, p. 354.
20. G. Clerk to H.L., 14 April 1842, ibid., p. 364.
21. Secy to Government to General Pollock, 24 February 1842, ibid., p. 365.
22. M.E. Yapp, *Strategies of British India*, p. 431.
23. G. Lawrence, *Reminiscences*, p. 186.
24. Ibid., p. 191.
25. Ibid., p. 197.
26. Ibid., p. 192.
27. Ibid., p. 190.
28. Ibid., p. 189.
29. Ibid., p. 187.
30. H.L. to G. Clerk, 27 April 1842, Mss. Eur. F85/2, p. 145.
31. H.L. to G. Clerk, May? 1842, Edwardes & Merivale, 1, p. 385.
32. H.L. to G. Clerk , 7 June 1842, Mss. Eur. F85/2, p. 262.
33. G. Clerk to H.L, 17 June 1842, Mss. Eur. F85/25, p. 29.
34. G. Lawrence, *Reminiscences*, p. 203.
35. Ibid., p. 206.

36. Ibid., p. 207.
37. Ibid., p. 210.
38. H.L. to Honoria Lawrence, 6 September 1842, Mss. Eur. F85/70c, p. 212.
39. G. Lawrence, *Reminiscences*, pp. 215-216.
40. General Pollock to Adjutant-General, 14 September 1842, Edwardes & Merivale, 1, p. 407.
41. G. Lawrence, *Reminiscences*, p. 222.
42. Ibid., p. 224.
43. H.L. to G. Clerk, 1 Nov 1842 [incorrectly dated 1843], Mss. Eur. F85/26, p. 91.
44. H.M. Lawrence, *Defence of Sir William Macnaghten*, Edwardes & Merivale, 1, p. 413.
45. G. Lawrence, *Reminiscences*, p. 226.
46. H.L. to G. Clerk, 1 Nov 1842 [incorrectly dated 1843], Mss. Eur. F85/26, p. 91.

Nepalese Sojourn

1. G. Clerk to H.L., 20 January 1843, Mss. Eur. F85/26, pp. 9-10.
2. H.L., to G. Clerk, [no date] January 1843, Mss. Eur. F85/26, p. 12.
3. H.L., to Letitia Hayes, 28 May 1843, Edwardes & Merivale, 1, p. 429.
4. J. Thomason to H.L., 1 May 1843, Mss. Eur. F85/26, pp. 19-20.
5. Bosworth Smith, 1, p. 168.
6. Edwardes & Merivale, 1, p. 432.
7. Bosworth Smith, 1, p. 168.
8. G. Clerk to H. Lawrence, 25 April 1843, Mss. Eur. F85/26, p. 15.
9. Major H.M. Lawrence, late Assistant Agent to Governor General, N.W.F. to Lieutt. Col. A.F. Richmond C.B., Agent to Governor General, N.W.F., Summary Settlement, Khytul Territory, 10 November 1843, Mss. Eur. F85/26, p. 93.
10. Ibid.
11. Ibid., p. 93.
12. Ibid., p. 94.
13. Ibid., p. 97.
14. Ibid., p. 95
15. Ibid., p. 98.
16. Ibid., p. 96.
17. Ibid.
18. Ibid., p. 96.
19. Gazetteer of the Karnal District, (Lahore, 1892) pp. 242-244.
20. H.L. to Pollock, 29 Aug 1843, Mss. Eur. F85/26, pp. 83-84.
21. 'Dear Major Lawrence, I really am very sorry that in error I addressed a letter to you as C.B. and there excited expectations which were disappointed. I have no power in the distribution of honours after the decision of the Queen Govt. has once been pronounced.' Lord Ellenborough to H.L, 24 September 1843, ibid., p. 29.
22. 'But now are you really going home? I hope not for methinks you can ill afford it. All I would say however – do not act hastily…' J. Thomason to H.L., 15 August 1843, Mss. Eur. F85/26, p. 23.
23. Lord Ellenborough to H.L, 14 September 1843, ibid., p. 27.
24. J. Thomason to H.L., 3 October 1843, ibid., p. 51.
25. Sir Henry Lawrence's Journal of Nepal, 3rd July 1845 entry, Mss. Eur. F85/95, p. 1.
26. Col. A.F. Richmond to H.L. 27 September 1843, , Mss. Eur. F85/26, pp. 40-41; H.L. to Col. A.F. Richmond, 1 October 1843, ibid., p. 88.
27. H.L. to a friend, 4 February 1844, Edwardes & Merivale, 2, p. 3.

28. H.L. to J. Marshman, 17 April 1844, Mss. Eur. F85/5A, p. 34.
29. J. Whelpton: Hodgson, Brian Houghton (1801–1894), ODNB
30. J. Thomason to H.L., 18 November 1843, Mss. Eur. F85/26 p. 67.
31. H.L. to Honoria Lawrence, 8 December 1843, Mss. Eur. F85/26, p. 106.
32. H.L. to Dr. Login, 11 December 1843, Mss. Eur. F85/26, p. 107.
33. H.L. to F. Currie, 26 October 1844, Mss. Eur.. F85, p. 80.
34. Ibid., p. 81.
35. H.L. to G. Clerk, 9 April 1845, Mss. Eur. F85/5A, p. 92
36. H.L. to Lord Auckland, 25 May 1845, Mss. Eur. F85/5A, p. 94.
37. Ibid.
38. Ibid., p. 95.
39. H.L. to George Clerk, 15 January 1845, Mss. Eur. F85/5A, p. 84.
40. Ibid.
41. H.L. to Honoria, 8 December 1843, Mss. Eur. F85/26, p. 106.
42. J. Lawrence & A. Woodiwiss, ed., *The Journals of Honoria Lawrence* (London: Hodder and Stoughton, 1980), 12 April 1844, pp. 150-151.
43. Capt. Smith was formally relieved of his post on 12th August 1844.
44. H.L. to Government, 13 July 1844, Mss. Eur. F85/5A, p. 61.
45. H.L. to Capt. Smith, 15 August 1844, ibid., p, 74.
46. H.L. to Capt. Ottley, 19 August 1844, ibid., p. 78.
47. H.L. to F. Currie, 28 October 1845, ibid., p. 115
48. Ibid., p. 116.
49. Henry Lawrence's Nepalese Journal, Mss. Eur. F85/95, p. 1.
50. Ibid.
51. H.M. Lawrence, *The Lawrence Military Asylum* (Sanawur: Lawrence Military Asylum Press, 1858), p. 3.
52. H.L. to Colonel Stuart, Secretary to Government Military Dept., 22 July 1845, Mss. Eur. F85/5A, p. 102.
53. H.L. to H. Vansittant, 9 March 1845, Mss. Eur. F85/5A, p.90.
54. Maharaja Gulab Singh to H.L., 6 January 1847, Mss. Eur. F85/30/2a, p. 227.
55. J.W. Kaye, *Lives of Indian Officers*, Vol. 2, p. 289.
56. Ibid., p. 290.
57. H.L. to George Clerk, 15 January 1845, Mss. Eur. F85/5A, p. 82.
58. H.M. Lawrence, *Recent History of the Punjab*, *The Calcutta Review*, May-June 1844, Vol. 1, p. 506.
59. Ibid., p. 507.
60. H.L., to an unnamed officer at HQ, 2 March 1844, Mss. Eur. F85/5A, p. 18.
61. H.L. to F. Currie, End of October 1845, Mss. Eur. F85/5A, pp. 117-118.
62. H.L. to J. Marshman, 29 November 1845, Mss. Eur. F85/5A, p. 125.
63. H.M. Lawrence, *Recent History of the Punjab*, *The Calcutta Review*, May-June 1844, Vol. 1, p. 507.
64. H.M. Lawrence, *Military Defence of our Empire in the East*, *The Calcutta Review*, Vol. 2, October-December 1844, pp. 39-40.
65. Ibid., p. 41.
66. Ibid., p. 45.
67. Ibid., p. 43.
68. Ibid., p. 52.
69. Ibid., p. 72.
70. E. Stokes, *English Utilitarians and India*, p. 10.

71. H.M. & H. Lawrence, *Romance and Reality in Indian Life, The Calcutta Review,* Vol. 2, Oct-Dec 1844, pp. 440-441.

72. Thomas R. Metcalf, *Ideologies of the Raj,* p. 25.

73. J. Malcolm, *The Political History of India from 1784 to 1832* (London, John Murray, 1826) Vol. 2, pp. 184-185.

74. *Romance and Reality,* pp. 377-78.

75. Ibid., p. 380.

76. Ibid., p. 443.

77. Ibid., p. 439.

78. Ibid., p. 439.

79. Ibid., p. 440.

80. Ibid., p. 441.

81. Henry based his historical information on the works of 'Forster, Malcolm, Prinsep and Burnes'. See George Forster, *A Journey from Bengal to England through the Northern part of India, Kashmire, Afghanistan, and Persia, and into Russia by the Caspian Sea* (London, 1798); John Malcolm, *Sketch of the Sikhs* (London, 1812); Henry T. Prinsep, *Origin of the Sikh Power in the Punjab and Political Life of Muha-Raja Runjeet Singh* (Calcutta, 1834); Alexander Burnes, *On the Political Power of the Sikhs beyond the Indus* (Calcutta, 1839). H.M. Lawrence, *Adventures of an Officer in the service of Runjeet Singh,* (London: Henry Colburn, 1845), Vol. 1, Preface, p. v.

82. H.M. Lawrence, *Adventures,* Vol. 1, p. 54

83. Ibid., Vol. 1, Preface, p. iv.

84. Ibid., Vol. 2, p. 261.

85. *The Calcutta Review,* Jan-Jun 1846, Vol. 5, pp. x-xiv.

86. See, for example, Baron Charles Hugel, *Travels in Kashmir and the Panjab,* (London: John Petheram, 1845); John Martin Honigberger, *Thirty-Five Years in the East* (London: H. Bailliere, 1852).

87. H.M. Lawrence, *Adventures,* Vol. 1, p. 29.

88. Ibid.

89. Ibid., p. 30.

90. Ibid., p. 29.

91. Ibid., p. 32. Although the 1809 treaty of 'perpetual friendship' confined the eastward limits of the Sikh kingdom to the River Sutlej, it also provided official British recognition of its sovereignty and allowed Ranjit to extend his rule in other directions.

92. Ibid., p. 53.

93. Ibid., p. 29.

94. Ibid., p. 40.

95. Ibid., pp. 34-35.

96. Ibid., p. 43.

97. Ibid., p. 222.

98. Ibid., Vol. 2, pp. 234-235.

99. Ibid., Vol. 1, p. 109.

100. Ibid., p. 112.

101. Ibid., Vol. 2, p. 233.

102. Ibid., Vol. 1, pp. 234-235.

103. Ibid., Vol. 2, p. 148.

104. Ibid., p. 101.

105. Ibid., p. 8.

106. Ibid., p. 142.
107. Ibid., p. 52.
108. See B.J. Hasrat, *Anglo-Sikh Relations*, pp. 205-206.
109. H.M. Lawrence, *Adventures*, Vol. 2, p. 37.
110. Ibid., pp. 135-136.
111. Ibid., pp. 232-233.
112. Ibid., p. 233.

Epilogue

1. A four-year old James Thomason travelling with his parents earlier in the century only narrowly escaped death from shipwreck in the Bay of Bengal. P. Penner, *The Patronage Bureaucracy in North India*, p. 83.
2. Bosworth Smith, 1, p. 62.
3. Mss. Eur. D1019/1, p. 36.
4. R. Temple, *James Thomason*, p. 101.
5. E. Stokes, *English Utilitarians and India*, p. 17.
6. Bosworth Smith, 1, p. 63.
7. F. Currie, Divisional Revenue Commissioner, no date, Mss. Eur. D1019/1, p. 83; The Court of Directors of the East India Company, 14 Dec 1842, Mss. Eur. D1019/1, p. 130.
8. J. Lunt: Lawrence, Sir George St Patrick (1804–1884), ODNB.

Abbreviations

EIC	East India Company
H.L.	Henry Lawrence
IOR	Indian Office Records
J.L.	John Lawrence
Mss. Eur.	Private Papers or 'European Manuscripts' of the Oriental and India Office Collections of the British Library
R.M.	Robert Montgomery
N.W.P.	North-Western Provinces

Bibliography

Asia, Pacific and Africa Collections (Indian Office Records), The British Library
Henry Lawrence Collection, Mss. Eur. F85
John Lawrence Collection, Mss. Eur. F90
Robert Montgomery Papers, Mss. Eur. D1019
N.W.P. Proceedings (Revenue), IOR/P/217
Records of the Board of Commissioners for the Affairs of India (1620–1879), IOR/F/4/1561

Foyle College Archives
Papers relating to John Lawrence's statue.

Published Government Records
Accounts and Papers of the House of Commons.
Circular Order by the Sudder Board of Revenue, North-Western Provinces, addressed to Commissioners of Revenue on the subject of settlements (Calcutta: Baptist Mission Press, 1839).
Final Settlement Report of the Allahabad District by F.W. Porter (Allahabad, 1878)
Final Report on the Settlement of Land Revenue in the Delhi District 1872–80, compiled by O. Wood & R. Maconachie (Lahore, 1882).
Land Revenue Settlement of the Gurgaon District by F.C. Channing (Lahore, 1882).
Memoir on the Statistics of the North-Western Provinces of the Bengal Presidency, compiled by A. Shakespear, (Calcutta, 1848).
Minutes of Evidence Taken Before the Select Committee into the affairs of the East India Company, House of Commons (16 August 1832), Vol. 5.
Parliamentary Papers on the Revenue Survey India (London, 1853).
Records of the Delhi Residency and Agency Punjab Govt Records (Lahore, 1911), Vol. 1 (Allahabad, 1915).
Report on the Settlement in the District of Kangra in the Trans-Sutlej States, by George Carnac Barnes (Lahore, 1862)
Reports on the Revenue Settlement of the North-Western Provinces of the Bengal Presidency, under Regulation IX, 1833, Vol. 1 (Benares, 1862).
Reports on the Revenue Settlement of the North-Western Provinces of the Bengal Presidency, under Regulation IX, 1833, Vol. 2 Part 1 (Benares, 1863).
Reports on the Revenue Settlement of the North-Western Provinces of the Bengal Presidency, under Regulation IX, 1833, Vol. 2 Part 2 (Benares, 1863).
Report on the Revision of Settlement of the Panipat Tahsil and Karnal Pargannah of the Karnal District, 1872–80, by D. C. J. Ibbetson (Allahabad, 1883).
Selected Reports on the Revision of Settlement under Regulation IX of 1833 in the Delhi Territory, 1838–39. No. 1, J. Lawrence, C. Gubbins, M.R. Gubbins (Agra, 1846).
Selected Reports on the Revision of Settlement under IX of 1833 in the Delhi Territory. No. 2., G. F. Edmonstone & J. Lawrence. (Agra, 1846).

Selections from the Records of Government, North-Western Provinces, Vol. 1 (Agra, 1855).
Selections from the Records of Government, North-Western Provinces, Vol. 2 (Allahabad, 1866).
Selections from the Records of Government, North-Western Provinces, Vol. 3 (Agra, 1855).
Selections from the Records of Government, North-Western Provinces, Vol. 4 (Agra, 1856).
Selections from Revenue Records, North-Western Provinces 1818–1820 (Calcutta, 1866)
Selections from Revenue Records, North-Western Provinces 1821 (Allahabad, 1873).
Selections from Revenue Records, North-Western Provinces 1822–33 (Allahabad, 1872).
Statistical Report of the District of Cawnpoor by Robert Montgomery (Calcutta, 1849).
Statistical Report on the District of Goorgaon compiled by Alexander Fraser (Agra, 1849).

Contemporary Journals, Serials, Newspapers, and Reference Works
Blackwood's Magazine
District Gazetteer
Foyle College Times
Dictionary of National Biography (ODNB)
The Asiatic Journal and Monthly Register for British and Foreign India, China, and Australasia
The Calcutta Review
The Church Missionary Intelligencer
The East-India Register and Army List
The Journal of the Asiatic Society of Bengal
The Journal of the Royal Asiatic Society of Great Britain and Ireland
The Imperial Gazetteer of India
The Indian Recorder
The Lahore Chronicle
The New York Times

Contemporary Works
Anon, *Life in the Mofussil or, The Civilian in Lower Bengal*, 2 Vols. (London: C. Kegan Paul & Co., 1878).
Alexander, R., *Account of the Family History of Rev. Robert Alexander and other Notes of the Families of Alexander and McClintock* (Londonderry, 1946).
Aitchison, Charles, *Sir, Lord Lawrence* (Oxford: Clarendon Press, 1892).
Baden-Powell, B.H., *The Land Systems of British India*, 3 Vols. (Oxford: Clarendon Press, 1892).
Bosworth Smith, R., *Life of Lord Lawrence*, 2 Vols. (London: Smith, Elder & Co., 1883).
Buckland, C.E., *Dictionary of Indian Biography*, (London: Swan Sonnenschein & Co., 1906).
Beames, John, *Memoirs of a Bengal Civilian* (London: Eland, 1984).
Burnes, Alexander, *Travels Into Bokhara; being the account of A Journey from India to Cabool, Tartary, and Persia*, 3 Vols. (London: John Murray, 1834).
Burnes, Alexander, *Cabool: A Personal Narrative of a Journey to, and Residence of that City, in the Years 1836, 7, and 8* (London: John Murray, 1843).
Buck, E.J., *Simla Past & Present*, (Calcutta: Thacker, Spink and Co., 1904).
Campbell, George, *Modern India: A Sketch of The System of Civil Government. To which is prefixed, some account of the natives and native institutions* (London: John Murray, 1852).
Campbell, George, *Memoirs of my Indian Career*, 2 Vols. (London, Macmillan & Co., 1893).
Carey, W.H., *A Guide to Simla*, (Calcutta: Wyman & Co., 1870).
Cave-Browne, Rev. John, *Indian Infanticide, its Origin, Progress and Suppression* (London: Wm. H. Allen & Co.,1857).

Cunningham, J.D., *History of the Sikhs: From the Origins of the Nation to the Battles of the Sutlej* (New Delhi, Rupa & Co., 2002).

Cust, R.N., *Pictures of Indian Life Sketched with the Pen from 1852 to 1881* (London: Trubner & Co., 1881).

Cust, R.N., *Memoirs of Past Years of a Septuagenarian* (Hertford: Stephen Austin & Sons, 1899).

Danvers, F.C. et al, *Memorials of old Haileybury College* (London, Archibald Constable & Co., 1894).

Dodwell, E., & Miles, J.S., (ed.), *Alphabetical List of the Officers of the Bengal Army, 1760–1837* (London: Longman, Orme, Brown & Co., 1838).

Doss, Ramchunder, *A General Register of the Hon'ble East India Company's Civil Servants of the Bengal Establishment from 1790 to 1842* (Calcutta: Baptist Mission Press, 1844).

Douie, James M., *Punjab Settlement Manual*, 4th edition (Lahore: Superintendent, Government Printing, 1930).

Eden, Emily, *Up the Country, Letters written to her sister from the Upper Provinces of India*, 2 Vols. (London: Richard Bentley, 1867).

Edmond, E., *The Bengal Civil Service Gradation List, 1845–46* (Calcutta: W. Thacker & Co., 1845).

Edwardes, H.B., & Merivale, H., *Life of Sir Henry Lawrence*, 2 Vols. (London: Smith, Elder & Co., 1872).

Edwardes, H.B. (Mrs), *Memorials of the Life & Letters of Major-General Sir Herbert B. Edwards*, 2 Vols. (London: Kegan Paul, Trench & Co., 1886).

Elsmie, G.R., *Thirty-five years in the Punjab* (Edinburgh: David Douglas, 1908).

Evans, Colonel G. de Lacy, *On the Practicability of an Invasion of British India* (London: J.M. Richardson, 1829).

Eyre, Lieut. V., *The Military Operations at Caubul, which ended in the retreat and Destruction of the British Army, January 1842. With a Journal of Imprisonment in Afghanistan* (London: John Murray, 1843).

Eyre, Lieut. V., *Prison Sketches, comprising portraits of the Cabul Prisoners, and other subjects* (London: Dickinson & Sons, 1843).

Fane, Henry Edward, *Five Years in India*, 2 Vols. (London: Henry Colburn, 1842).

Grant, Charles, *Observations on the State of Society among the Asiatic Subjects of Great Britain* (London, 1797).

Graham, Maria, *Journal of a Residence in India* (Edinburgh: Archibald Constable and Co., 1813).

Gibbon, Frederick. P., *The Lawrences of the Punjab* (London: J.M. Dent & Co., 1908).

Havelock, Capt. Henry, *Narrative of the War in Afghanistan in 1838–39*, 2 Vols. (London: Henry Coburn, Publisher, 1840).

Heber, Reginald, *Narrative of a Journey through the Upper Provinces of India*, 3 Vols. (London: John Murray, 1846).

Higginbotham, J.J., *Men whom India has Known* (Madras: Higginbotham & Co., 1874).

Honigberger, John Martin, *Thirty-five Years in the East* (London: H. Bailliere, 1852).

Hough, Major W., *A Narrative of the March and Operations of the Army of the Indus, in the Expedition to Afghanistan in the Years 1838–1839* (London: Wm. H. Allen & Co., 1841).

Hugel, Baron Charles, *Travels in Kashmir and the Panjab containing a particular account of the government and character of the Sikhs* (London: John Petheram, 1845).

Huggins, William, *Sketches in India* (London: John Letts, 1824).

Hutton, James, *A Popular Account of the Thugs and Dacoits, the Hereditary Garotters and Gang-Robbers of India* (London: WM. H. Allen & Co., 1857).

Innes, J. J. McLeod, *Sir Henry Lawrence: the Pacificator* (Oxford: Clarendon Press, 1898).

Johnson, James, *The influence of Tropical Climates* (London: J. Callow, 1815).

Kaye, John William, *A History of the Sepoy War in India, 1857–58*, 3 Vols. (London, Longmans, Green & Co., 1870).

Kaye, John William, *History of the War in Afghanistan*, 3 Vols. (London: Wm. H. Allen & Co., 1874).

Kaye, John William, *Lives of Indian Officers, Illustrative of the History of the Civil and Military Services of India*, 2 Vols. (London: A. Strahan & Co., Bell & Daldy, 1867).

Kaye, John William ed., *Selections from the Papers of Lord Metcalfe* (London: Smith, Elder, And Co., 1855).

Kaye, John William, *The Administration of the East India Company* (London: Richard Bentley, 1853).

Kaye, John William, *The life and correspondence of Charles, Lord Metcalfe*, 2 Vols. (London: Richard Bentley, 1854).

Kipling, Rudyard, *Kim* (London: Penguin, 2000).

Lal, Mohan, *Life of the Amir Dost Mohammed Khan of Kabul*, 2 Vols. (London: Longman, Brown, Green, and Longmans, 1846).

Laurie, W.F.B., *Sketches of Some Distinguished Anglo-Indians* (London: Wm. H. Allen & Co., 1887).

Law, Edward, Lord Ellenborough, *A Political Diary 1828–1830*, Lord Colchester ed., 2 Vols. (London: Richard Bentley & Son., 1881).

Lawrence, George, *Reminiscences of Forty-three Years in India* (London: John Murray, 1874).

Lawrence, H.M., *Adventures of an Officer in the Service of Runjeet Singh*, 2 Vols. (London: Henry Colburn, 1845).

Lawrence, H.M., *Essays, Military and Political, written in India* (London: Wm. H. Allen & Co., 1859).

Lawrence, H.M., *The Lawrence Military Asylum* (Sanawur: Lawrence Military Asylum Press, 1858).

Lawrence, H.M., Articles published in *The Calcutta Review*:
  The Recent History of the Punjab (1844, Vol. 1, pp. 449–507).
  Military Defence of our Indian Empire (1844, Vol. 2, pp. 32–72).
  The Sikhs and their Country (1844, Vol. 2, pp. 153–208).
  Romance and Reality of Indian Life [with Honoria] (1844, Vol. 2, pp. 377–443).
  Kashmir and the Countries around the Indus (1844, Vol. 2, pp. 469–535).
  The Kingdom of Oude (1845, Vol. 3, pp. 375–427).
  Mahratta History and Empire (1845, Vol. 4, pp. 178–239).

Lawrence Lowell, A. (ed.), *Colonial Civil Service* (London, Macmillan & Co., 1900).

Lind, James, *An Essay on Diseases Incidental to Europeans in Hot Climates* (Philadelphia, 1811).

Mackenzie, Lt. General Colin, *Storms and Sunshine of a Soldier's Life 1825–1881*, 2 Vols. (Edinburgh: David Douglas, 1884).

Malcolm, John, *The Political History of India from 1784 to 1832*, 2 Vols. (London: John Murray, 1826).

Malleson, G. B., *Recreations of an Indian official* (London: Longmans, Green and Co., 1872).

Markham, Clements R., *A Memoir on the India Surveys* (London: W.H. Allen & Co., 1878).

Martin, James Ranald, *Notes on the Medical Topography of Calcutta* (Calcutta: G.H. Huttman, 1837).

Martin, James Ranald, *The Influence of tropical Climates on European Constitutions* (London: John Churchill, 1856).

Martin, Robert Montgomery, *Statistics of the Colonies of the British Empire* (London: Wm. H. Allen & Co., 1839).

McCosh, John, *Medical Advice to the Indian Stranger*, (London: Wm. H. Allen & Co., 1841).

Morris, Henry, *Heroes of our Indian Empire*, Vol. 1, (London: The Christian Literature Society for India, 1908).

Muir, William, *The Honourable James Thomason, Lieutenant-Governor N.W.P. India 1843–1853 A.D.* (Edinburgh: T & T Clarke, 1897).

Parkes, F., *Wanderings of a Pilgrim in search of the Picturesque*, 2 Vols. (London: Pelham Richardson, 1850).

Peggs, J., *India's Cries to British Humanity* (London: Seely and Son, 1830).

Pelly, L., ed., *The Views and Opinions of Brigadier-General John Jacob, C.B.* (London, Smith, Elder & Co., 1858).

Prinsep, Henry Thoby & Doss, Rāmachandra, *General Register of the Hon'ble East India Company's Civil Servants of the Bengal Establishment from 1790 to 1842* (Calcutta: Baptist Mission Press, 1844).

Raikes, Charles, *Notes on the North-Western Provinces of India* (London: Chapman and Hall, 1852).

Raikes, Charles, *The Englishman in India* (London: Longmans, Green & Co., 1867).

Rawlinson, G., *A Memoir of Maj-Gen Sir Henry Creswicke Rawlinson* (London: Longmans, Green & Co., 1898).

Reece, Richard, *The Medical Companion for Visitors to the East and West Indies* (London: Longman, Hurst, Rees, Orme, and Brown, 1817).

Roberts, Emma, *Scenes and Characteristics of Hindoostan*, 3 Vols. (London: Wm. H. Allen & Co., 1835).

Roberts, Emma, *The East India Voyager* (London: J. Madden & Co., 1845).

Roebuck, Thomas, *The Annals of the College of Fort William* (Calcutta, 1819).

Sale, Lady Florentia Wynch, *A Journal of the Disasters in Afghanistan, 1841–2* (New York: Harper & Brothers, 1843).

Shore, Frederick John, *Notes on Indian Affairs*, 2 Vols. (London: John W. Parker, 1837).

Simpson, Robert, *The Annals of Derry* (Londonderry, 1847).

Sleeman, W.H., *Ramblings and recollections of an Indian Official* (London: J. Hatchard and Sons, 1844).

Smith, V.A., *The Settlement Officer's Manual for the North-Western Provinces* (Allahabad: North-Western Provinces and Oudh Government Press, 1881).

Spry, Henry, *Modern India with Illustrations of the Resources and Capabilities of Hindustan*, 2 Vols. (London: Whitaker & Co., 1837).

Stocqueler, J.H., *Memorials of Afghanistan: being State Papers, Official Documents, Dispatches, Authentic Narratives, etc., Illustrative of the British Expedition to, and Occupation of Afghanistan and Scinde, between the years 1838 and 1842* (Calcutta: Messrs. Ostell and Lepage, 1843).

Stocqueler, J.H., *The Handbook of India, A Guide to the Stranger and the Traveller and a Companion to the Resident* (London: Wm. H. Allen & Co., 1844).

Temple, Richard, *Lord Lawrence* (London: Macmillan and Co., 1893).

Temple, Richard, *Men and Events of my time in India* (London: John Murray, 1882). Temple, Richard, *James Thomason* (Oxford: Clarendon Press, 1893).

Thomason, James, *Directions for Revenue Officers in the North-Western Provinces of the Bengal Presidency regarding the Settlement and Collection of the Land Revenue, and other duties connected therewith* (Calcutta, Baptist Mission Press, 1850).

Thorburn, S.S., *The Punjab in Peace and War* (London: William Blackwood & Sons, 1904).

Thuillier, H. L., & Smyth, R., *A Manual of Surveying for India, Detailing the Mode of Operations on the Revenue Surveys in Bengal and the North-Western Provinces* (Calcutta: Thacker & Co., 1851).

Trevelyan, G., *The Competition Wallah* (London: Macmillan & Co., 1895).

Trotter, Lionel J., *Life of John Nicholson: soldier and administrator* (London: Thomas Nelson & Sons, 1897).

Trotter, Lionel J., *Life of the Marquis of Dalhousie* (London: W. H. Allen & Co., 1889)

Tucker, H.C., *The Bible in India* (London: W. H. Dalton, 1859)

Vibart, H.M., *Addiscombe its heroes and men of note* (London: Archibald Constable & Co., 1894).

Wallace, James, *A Voyage to India* (London: T. and G. Underwood, 1824).

Williamson, Thomas, *The East India Vade-Mecum*, 2 Vols. (London: Black, Parry and Kingsbury, 1810).

Yule, Henry & Burnell, A.C., Hobson-Jobson, *A Glossary of Anglo-Indian Words and Phrases, and of Kindred Terms* (London, John Murray, 1886).

Modern Secondary Works

Anon, *Introduction Caledon Papers* (Public Record Office of Northern Ireland, 2007).

Allen, Charles, *Soldier Sahibs: The Men who made the North-West Frontier* (London: John Murray, 2000).

Bandyopadhyay, Sekhar, *From Plassey to Partition, A History of Modern India* (Delhi: Orient Longmans, 2004).

Bayly, C.A., *Empire and Information, Intelligence Gathering and Social Communication in India, 1780–1870* (Cambridge: Cambridge University Press, 1996).

Bayly, C.A., *Imperial Meridian, The British Empire and the World 1780–1830* (London: Longman, 1989).

Bayly, C.A., *Indian Society and the Making of the British Empire* (The New Cambridge History of India, II.1; Cambridge: Cambridge University Press, 1988).

Bhattacharya, Neeladri, *The Great Agrarian Conquest: The Colonial Reshaping of a Rural World* (New York: State University of New York Press, 2019).

Bellenoit, Hayden J., *The Formation of the Colonial State in India: Scribes, Paper and Taxes, 1760–1860* (London: Routledge, 2017).

Colley, Linda, *Captives: Britain, Empire and the World, 1600–1850* (London: Jonathan Cape, 2002).

Cohn, Bernard S., *An Anthropologist among the Historians and Other Essays* (Delhi: Oxford University Press, 1990).

Cook, Scott B., *Imperial Affinities: Nineteenth century analogies and exchanges between India and Ireland* (Delhi: Sage Publications, 1993).

Collingham, E.M., *Imperial Bodies* (Cambridge: Polity Press, 2007).

Crosbie, Barry, *Irish Imperial Networks, Migration, Social Communication and Exchange in Nineteenth Century India* (Cambridge: Cambridge University Press, 2012).

Dalrymple, William, *City of Djinns: A Year in Delhi* (London: HarperCollins Publishers, 1993).

Dalrymple, William, *Return of a King, The Battle for Afghanistan* (London: Bloomsbury, 2013).

Devine, T.M., *Scotland's Empire, The origins of the Global Diaspora* (London: Penguin, 2004).

Diver, Maud, *Honoria Lawrence: A fragment of Indian History* (London: John Murray, 1936).

Edney, Matthew H., *Mapping an Empire: The Geographical Construction of British India, 1765–1843* (Chicago and London: The University of Chicago Press, 1997).

Foley, Tadhg and O'Connor, Maureen, eds., *Ireland and India – Colonies, Culture and Empire* (Dublin: Irish Academic Press, 2006).

Frykenberg, Robert Eric, ed., *Land Control and Social Structure in Indian History* (Wisconsin: University of Wisconsin Press, 1969).

Gilmartin, David, *Empire and Islam, Punjab and the Making of Pakistan* (London: I.B. Tauris & Co Ltd, 1989).

Harrison, A.T., ed., *The Graham Indian Mutiny Papers* (Belfast: Public Records Office of Northern Ireland, 1980).

Hasrat, Bikrama Jit, *Anglo-Sikh Relations 1799–1849: A Reappraisal of the Rise and Fall of the Sikhs* (Hoshiarpur: V.V. Research Institute Press, 1968).

Husain, Imtiaz, *Land Revenue Policy in North India: The Ceded & Conquered Provinces, 1801–33* (Calcutta: New Age Publishers, 1967).

Hutchins, Francis G., *The Illusion of Permanence, British Imperialism in India* (Princeton: Prince University Press, 1967).

Israel, Milton, *Communications and Power: Propaganda and the Press in the Indian National Struggle, 1920–1947* (Cambridge, Cambridge University Press, 1994).

James, Lawrence, *Raj: The Making and Unmaking of British India* (London: Abacus, 1997).

Jeffrey, Keith. ed., *'An Irish Empire'? Aspects of Ireland and the British Empire* (Manchester: Manchester University Press, 1996).

Jetley, M.M., *The Calm and the Storm – Delhi during 1803–57* (New Delhi: Himalaya Publishing House, 2015).

Keay, John, *India, a History* (London: Harper Collins, 2001).

Kenny, Kevin. ed., *Ireland and the British Empire* (The Oxford History of the British Empire, Companion Series; Oxford: Oxford University Press, 2004).

Khan, Manju & Parel, K.J., *Sanawar, A legacy* (Sanawar, 1997).

Khilnani, N.M., *British Power in the Punjab, 1839–1858* (Bombay: Asia Publishing House, 1972).

Kipling, Rudyard, *Kim* (London, Penguin, 1987).

Lawrence, John, *Lawrence of Lucknow* (London: Hodder and Stoughton, 1990).

Lawrence, John and Widdiwis, Audrey, ed., *The Journals of Honoria Lawrence* (London: Hodder and Stoughton, 1980).

Lee, Harold, *Brothers in the Raj, The Lives of Henry and John Lawrence* (Karachi: Oxford University Press, 2002).

Lee, Jonathan L., *Afghanistan, A History from 1260 to the Present* (London: Reaktion Books, 2018).

Linder, Leslie ed., *The Journal of Beatrix Potter from 1881 to 1897* (London: Frederick Warne, 1966).

Macrory, Patrick, *Signal Catastrophe* (London: Hodder and Stoughton, 1972).

Marshall, P.J., *East Indian Fortunes, The British in Bengal in the Eighteenth Century* (Oxford, Clarendon Press, 1976).

Metcalf, Thomas R., *Land, Landlords, and the British Raj* (Berkeley: University of California, 1979).

Metcalf, Thomas R., *Ideologies of the Raj* (The New Cambridge History of India, III.4; Cambridge, Cambridge University Press, 1994).

Montgomery, Brian, *Monty's Grandfather, A Life's Service for the Raj* (Poole: Blandford Press, 1984).

Moorhouse, Geoffrey, *Calcutta* (London: Weidenfeld and Nicolson, 1971).

Morison, J. L., *Lawrence of Lucknow, 1806–1857: being the life of Sir Henry Lawrence retold from his private and public papers* (London: G. Bell & Sons, 1934).

Nehru, Jawaharlal., *The Discovery of India* (New Delhi: Penguin, 2004).

Norris, J. A., *The First Afghan War 1838–1842* (Cambridge: Cambridge University Press, 1967).

Panigrahi, D.N. *Charles Metcalfe in India, Ideas and administration, 1806–1835* (New Delhi: Munshiram Manoharlal, 1968).

Panigrahi, Lalita, *British Social Policy and Female Infanticide in India* (New Delhi: Munshiram Manoharlal, 1972).

Penner, Peter, *The Patronage Bureaucracy in North India, The Robert M. Bird and James Thomason School 1820–1870* (Delhi: Chanakya Publications, 1986).

Phillimore, R.H., ed., *Historical Records of the Survey of India*, Vol. IV, 1830–1843, (Dehra Dun: Office of the Northern Circle, Survey of India, 1958).

Porter, Andrew, ed., Louis, Wm Roger, ed., *The Oxford History of the British Empire: Volume III: The Nineteenth Century*, (Oxford, Oxford University Press, 1999).

Pottinger, George, *The Afghan Connection: The Extraordinary Adventures of Major Eldred Pottinger* (Edinburgh: Scottish Academic Press, 1983).

Pottinger, George, *Sir Henry Pottinger, First Governor of Hong Kong* (Stroud: Sutton Publishing Ltd., 1997).

Reeves, Peter, *Landlords and Government in Uttar Pradesh, A Study of their relations until Zamindari Abolition* (Oxford: Oxford University Press, 1991).

Robins, N., *The Corporation that changed the World – How the East India Company shaped the Modern Multinational* (Hyderabad: Orient Longman, 2006).

Rosselli, John, *Lord William Bentinck, The Making of a Liberal Imperialist 1774–1839* (Berkeley & Los Angeles: University of California Press, 1974).

Scriver, P. & Prakash, V. ed., Colonial Modernities: Building, Dwelling and Architecture in British India and Ceylon (London: Routledge, 2007).

Sharma, Jai Bhagwan, *History and Problems of District Administration in India*, 3 Vols. (New Delhi: Sarup & Sons, 2003).

Shorto, Sylvia, *British Houses in Late Mughal Delhi* (Woodbridge: The Boydell Press, 2018).

Siddiqi, Asiya, *Agrarian Change in a Northern Indian State, Uttar Pradesh 1819–1833* (Oxford: Clarendon Press, 1973).

Silvestri, Michael, *Ireland and India: Nationalism, Empire and Memory* (Cambridge Imperial and Post-Colonial Studies Series), (New York: Palgrave Macmillan, 2009).

Spear, Percival et al., *The Delhi Omnibus* (Oxford: Oxford University Press, 2002).

Steggles, Mary Ann, *Statues of the Raj* (London: BACSA, 2000).

Stocker, Mark, *Royalist and Realist, The Life and Work of Sir Joseph Edgar Boehm* (New York & London: Garland Publishing, 1988).

Stokes, Eric, *The English Utilitarians and India* (Oxford: Clarendon Press: 1959).

Stokes, Eric, *The Peasant and the Raj: Studies in agrarian society and peasant rebellion in colonial India* (Cambridge: Cambridge University Press, 1978).

Subramanian, Lakshmi, *History of India, 1707–1857* (New Delhi: Orient Blackswan, 2010).

Thankappan Nair, P. (ed.,). *Calcutta in the 19th Century (Company's Days)*, (Calcutta: Firma KLM Private Limited, 19 v bnn 89).

Thompson, Edward, *The Life of Charles, Lord Metcalfe* (London, Faber and Faber, 1937).

Wagner, Kim A., *Thuggee. Banditry and the British in Early Nineteenth-Century India* (Basingstoke: Palgrave, 2007).

Woodruff, Philip, *The Men who Ruled India*, 2 Vols. (London: Jonathan Cape, 1963).

Wurgaft, Lewis D., *The Imperial Imagination – Magic and Myth in Kipling's India* (Wesleyan University Press: Connecticut, 1983).

Yapp, M.E., *Strategies of British India – Britain, Iran and Afghanistan 1798–1850* (Oxford: Clarendon Press, 1980).

Articles

Bayly, C.A., *Ireland, India and the Empire*: 1780–1914, Transactions of the Royal Historical Society 10 (December 2000).

Colley, Linda, *Britishness and Otherness: An Argument*, Journal of British Studies, Vol. 31, No. 4, (Oct. 1992).

Cook, Scott B., *The Irish Raj: Social Origins and Careers of Irishmen in the Indian Civil Service, 1855–1914*, Journal of Social History, Vol. 20, No.3 (Spring, 1987).

Naidis, Mark, *John Lawrence, Mutiny Hero*, Bengal Past and Present, LXXXII (1963) Vol. 82.

Morgan, Gerald, *Myth and Reality in the Great Game*, Asian Affairs, Vol. 4, 1973, Issue 1.

Vishwanath, L. S., *Efforts of Colonial State to Suppress Female Infanticide: Use of Sacred Texts, Generation of Knowledge*, Economic and Political Weekly, Vol. 33, No. 19 (May 9–15, 1998).

Yapp, M.E., *The Legend of the Great Game*, Proceedings of the British Library, Vol. 111, 2001.

Unpublished Theses

Bourne, John Michael, *Civil and Military Patronage of the East India Company, 1784–1858*, Ph.D. thesis, University of Leicester, 1977.

Harrington, Jack, *"No longer Merchants, but Sovereigns of a vast Empire": The writings of Sir John Malcolm and British India, 1810 to 1833*, Ph.D. thesis, University of Edinburgh, 2009.

Holmes, J., *Administration of the Delhi Territory 1803–1832*, Ph.D. thesis, University of London, 1955.

McLaren, M., *Writing and Making History – Thomas Munro, John Malcolm and Mountstuart Elphinstone: Three Scotsmen in History and Historiography of British India*, Ph.D. thesis, Simon Fraser University, 1992.

Penner, P., *The James Thomason School in Northern India, 1822-1853: A Biographical and Administrative Study*, Ph.D. thesis, McMaster University, 1970.

Prior, K., *The British Administration of Hinduism in North India, 1780–1900*, Ph.D. thesis, University of Cambridge, 1990.

Index

Abbott, James, 3, 4, 46
Abbott, Saunders, 46, 48, 51, 56, 57
Abdullah Khan Achakzai, 154
Addiscombe (EIC military seminary), 11, 13, 20–3
Adventures of an Officer, 203–9
Afghanistan
    First Anglo-Afghan War,
        Its origins, 129–32
        invasion route, 136–41
        'commercial diplomacy', 130–1
        Simla Manifesto of 1838, 131, 141
        George's appointment as military
            secy, 141–2
        surrender of Dost Mohammed, 143–4
        discontent in the provinces, 152
        subsidies to Ghilzai tribes
            slashed, 153
        Kabul uprising, 154
        inactivity of the military
            command, 157
        Bemaroo fiasco, 160
        negotiations & 11th December
            treaty, 161–2
        treaty of 22nd December, 163
        death of William Hay
            Macnaghten, 165
        the British predicament, 167–8
        retreat from Kabul, 169
        massacres at the Khord Kabul and the
            Tezin Passes, 172–3
        incarceration of the captives, 176–9,
            183, 186
        liberation, 186
Agra, 9, 63–4, 85, 89
Ahirs (Aheers), 81
Aitcheson, Sir Charles, 32, 63, 92
Alexander, James, 13–4
Alexander, Josias Dupre, 13
Alexander, Revd Mounsey, 14–5
Ali Masjid, 139, 179, 183

Allahabad, 8, 9, 44, 46, 52–9, 63, 87, 89, 94, 105–15
Amins, 45–6, 49, 53, 55, 60, 78, 84, 106, 149
Aminullah Khan Logari, 154, 163–6
Amritsar, ix, 129, 205, 216 n.1
Anticipatory Chapters of Indian History, 150–1
Arakan Campaign, 35–7
Attock, 151
Auckland, Lord (George Eden), 130–6, 153, 157, 159, 167, 181
Avitabile, General Paolo de, 168, 206
Azamgarh, 9, 55, 94–104, 112, 118, 212, 214
Aziz-ud-din, Fakir, 205

Badiabad Fort, 176–81
Bagramee, 169–70
Baha-ud-Din, Mirza, 178
Bala Hissar, 141, 154–7, 161–2, 165, 167, 169, 171, 185
Bamian, xvi, 140, 142, 186
Batten, J.H., 25–6, 220 n.52, 233 n.104
Bayly, Professor C.A., 9, 117
Beames, John, 24, 26
Bedford, Captain James, 53–55, 59
Bemaroo, 157–8, 160
Benares, xvi, 9, 95, 196
Bentinck, Lord William, 10, 43, 44, 62, 63, 77, 80, 209
Bhaiachara tenure, 91
Bird, Robert Merttins, 8, 44, 49, 52–5, 59, 77, 78, 84, 85, 119, 211
Bolan Pass, 136–7
Boehm, J. E., xix, xx
Bokhara, Emir of, 140
Bosworth Smith, R., 2, 4, 5, 17–8, 25, 66, 70, 72, 75, 85, 87
Brahmin, 76, 205
Bulandshahr, 123–4

Burmese War (1st Anglo-Burmese War/
    Arakan Campaign), 35–7
Burnes, Alexander, 130–1, 153–4, 156,
    158, 166
Butkhak, 170

Calcutta,
    description of, 28–34
Canoongoes, 78, 96, 98
Caroe, Sir Olaf, xxi
Cawnpore, 8–9, 42–43, 89, 94–5, 105,
    116–24, 196
Chandhi Chowk, 64, 66
Charikar, 158
Clerk, George, 134, 147–9, 159, 168,
    180–4, 187–90, 193–5, 199, 213
Conolly, Edward, 143
Cotton, Lieutenant-General Sir
    Willoughby, 141, 144
Court, General M.M., 206
Craufurd, Revd George, 34
Cumine, James, 25, 85–88
Currie, Frederick, 98, 100, 134, 195, 197,
    200, 214
Cust, Robert Needham, xx, 3

Dadur, 136
Dalhousie, Lord James Ramsay, 1
Dalrymple, William, 65
Delhi,
    description of, 64–6
    Delhi Gazette, 90, 150–1, 203
    Delhi Territory, 61–6
    'Delhi system', 62–3, 92,
    Settlement Report (1844), 90–3
    *Murder of Commissioner Fraser – Delhi
        1835*, 72–5
Dennie, Colonel William, 142
Dina Nath, Diwan, 205
Dost Mohammed, 130–2, 136, 139–44,
    162, 187, 209
Douie, J.M., 78, 80, 192

East India Company (EIC)
    finances, 9–10
    civil & military employment, 10–13
Education, see Foyle College, Addiscombe,
    Haileybury, Fort William College
Edwardes, Herbert, 4, 6, 17, 18, 43, 180
Ellenborough, Lord, 130, 181, 185, 192–4

Elphinstone, Mountstuart, 23
Elphinstone, General William, 144, 156
    Indecision, 154, 157
    opposition to military operations,
        161, 163–4
    retreat the only option, 167
    stops retreating column
        momentarily, 169
    rejects offer of terms, 174
    death, 182
Etawah, 9, 61, 87, 124, 150, 214
    The Disputed Boundary, 85–6
Evangelicalism, 34, 94–5, 101, 111,
    230 n.37
Eyre, Lieutenant Vincent, 156, 177–8,

Faridkot, 148–9
Female Infanticide, 94, 110–4, 212
Ferozepur, 134, 136, 145–50, 158–9, 167,
    188, 206, 208
Fort William College, 31–2, 43, 95, 211
Foyle College, xix, xxi, 1, 16, 17–8
Fraser, William, 65, 72
Fraser, Simon, 73–5

Gandamak, 175, 177, 185
Gandhi, Mahatma, xx
Ghazis, 165, 169–70
Ghazni, 138–40, 142, 158, 161, 186–7
Gibbon, F.P., 6
Gorakhpur, 9, 46–8, 51, 55–6, 59–60, 95,
    134, 210
Graham, Dr James, 14, 74
Grand Trunk Road (GTR), 32, 94,
    121–6
Gubbins, Charles, 74, 82
Gubbins, Martin, 25
Gujars, 81, 91
Gurgaon, 61, 66
    description of, 75
    Passive Resistance, 75–7
    Revenue Assessments, 77–84

Haileybury, East India College, 11–3,
    23–7, 31, 85, 95, 211
Haji Khan Kakar, 138, 140
Hamilton, Revd Richard, 16
Hardinge, Viscount Henry, 198
Hasrat, B.J., 6
Havelock, Captain Henry, 4, 136, 141

Heber, Bishop Reginald, 30–1
Herat, 131, 134
Heyland, Annie (R.M. sister), 114
Hodgson, Brian, 194–6
Hogg, Sir James Weir, 14
Hoshiarpur, xx, 3
Hough, Major William, 138, 141
Hudleston, John, 13, 22
Hutchinson, Eliza (R.M. Sister-in-law),
    102, 115
Hutton, James, 125

Innes, Lieutenant-General J.J. McLeod,
    4, 6,
Istumrardar, 78

Jagdalak, 173–7
Jagir, 66, 90, 206
Jagirdar, 61
Jalalabad, 139, 142, 153, 158, 161, 167–8,
    171–2, 176, 178, 182, 183–5
Jamabandi, 97–8, 101, 107
Jamrud, 168
Jats, 67, 81, 91
Jinnah, Mohammed Ali, xx

Kabul, 7, 62, 88, 130–2, 136, 138,
    140–3, 152–3, 158–62, 166–73, 178,
    181–88, 213
Kandahar, 137–9, 141–2, 152, 158, 161,
    181, 185
Kangra, (*Adventures of an Officer*), 206–9
Kathmandu, 193, 196–7
Kasauli, ix, 150, 199
Kaye, John William,
    on the Lawrences, 3, 19
    on Addiscombe, 20–22
    on Afghanistan, 132, 138, 158
    The Calcutta Review, 199, 204
Keane, Lieutenant-General Sir John,
    139, 141
Khojak Pass, 137, 181
Khusrah Survey, 44–6, 51, 55, 60
Khilnani, N.M., 6
Khord Kabul Pass, 153, 167, 171, 172, 182
Khyber Pass, 139, 141, 161, 168, 179,
    180–1, 183–4, 187
Knox, Revd George, 15
Knox, Revd James, 16, 18
Kohistan/Kohistanis, 139, 142, 167

Lahore, ix, xx, xxi, 1, 19, 62, 129–31, 150,
    168, 180, 186, 188, 198–9, 205–6, 208
Lake, General Gerald, 9, 61
Lawrence, Colonel Alexander Sr, 41
Lawrence, Aunt Angel, 18
Lawrence, George St. Patrick,
    character & reputation, 7–8
    EIC nomination, 13
    family background, 14–16
    Foyle College, 18
    Addiscombe Military Seminary, 20–1
    voyage to India, 28
    Calcutta, 33
    First Anglo-Afghan War,
        Army of the Indus, 136–7
        reception at Kandahar, 137–8
        fall of Ghazni, 139
        unsuccessful pursuit of Dost
            Mohammed, 140
        Shah Shuja's reception at Kabul, 141
        appointment as military sec., 141–2
        Afghan resistance, 142–3
        surrender of Dost Mohammed,
            143–4
        underestimation of discontent, 152–3
        Kabul rising & his response, 154–6
        his relations with Brigadier
            Sheldon, 155–6
        his defence of Macnaghten &
            Elphinstone, 156
        inactivity of the military
            command, 157
        pyrrhic British victories, 157–8
        Macnaghten opposed retreat, 160
        his support of the treaty of 22nd
            December, 163–4
        Macnaghten's death and George's
            incarceration, 165–6
        new treaty of 25th December, 166
        his return to the cantonments &
            discussion of options, 167
        retreat from Kabul, 169
        chosen as hostage, 171
        massacres at the Khord Kabul and the
            Tezin Passes, 172–3
        his response to the massacres, 174–5
        incarceration at Badiabad Fort, 176–9
        captives on the move again, 181–3
        his relations with Akbar Khan, 182–3
        incarceration at Shewaki Fort, 183

chosen as an intermediary & meets
   Henry, 184–5
his final incarceration at Bamian, 186
his liberation, 186–7
reasons for his survival, 187
Lawrence, Harriette (née Hamilton), 16,
   70, 87–9,
Lawrence, Henry,
character & reputation, 3–4, 6, 8
EIC nomination, 13
family background, 14–16
Foyle College, 17–19
Addiscombe Military Seminary, 20–3
voyage to India, 28
Calcutta, 33–5
Arakan Campaign, 35–7
Calcutta Review Articles, 20, 199,
   203–4, 209
   Recent History of the Punjab, 199
   The Seikhs and their Country, 199
   *Kashmir and the Countries around the
      Indus*, 199
   *Military Defence of our Empire in the
      East*, 200–1
   The Indian Army, 201
   Army Reform, 201
   Romance and Reality, 202–3
*Anticipatory Chapters of Indian
   History*, 150–1
Travels of a Topechee (Artilleryman), 41
Revenue Surveyor
   Surveying techniques/procedure, 44–46
   Moradabad survey, 43, 46
   Gorakhpur survey, 46–52
   survey reforms, 52–5
   Allahabad survey, 55–9
   criticism of survey, 59–60
political agent at Ferozepur, 145–51
   description of, 145
   military logistics, 145–7
   improvements at, 147–8
   Faridkot boundary settlement, 148–9
Anglo-Afghan War,
   appointment as liaison officer with
      Sikh troops, 159
   arrives at Peshawar on 28th
      December, 167
   efforts to garner Sikh support, 168
   failure to relieve garrison at Ali
      Masjid, 179
   views on General Pollock, 179

doubts over Sikh cooperation, 180
his involvement in taking the Khyber
   Pass, 180–1
his logistical support for Pollock's
   army, 183–4
his march towards Kabul, 185
reunited with George, 186
his achievements, 188
Kaithal,
   description of, 189–90
   revenue settlement, 190–2
Resident at Nepal,
   description of, 193
   type of work, 194–6
   relations with colleagues, 196–7
   origins of Lawrence Asylum, 197–9
   literary pursuits, 199–209
Lawrence, Honoria (née Marshall), ix, 16
description of Calcutta, 30–1
marriage, 47–8
opinion of Henry, 48
on Indian life, 48–57, 145, 210
health, 134, 150, 197
on British community in Nepal, 196
concern for barrack life, 197–8
literary interests, 199–203
Lawrence, John,
character & reputation, 2–6, 8
EIC nomination, 13
Family background, 14–16
Foyle College, 17–19
Haileybury College, 23–27
Voyage to India, 28
Calcutta, 32
assistant collector & magistrate at
   Delhi, 63–6
offg. magistrate & collector,
   Panipat, 67–75
offg. magistrate & collector,
   Gurgaon, 75–84
revenue settlements, 77–84, 90–3
settlement officer of Etawah, 85–7
furlough, 87–9
return to Delhi, 90–3
reminiscences,
   *Murder of Commissioner Fraser – Delhi
      1835*, 72–5
   Passive Resistance, 75–7
   The Brothers, 71–2
   The Disputed Boundary, 85–6
Lawrence, Sir John (biographer), 6

Lawrence, Letitia (sister), 13, 21, 33–4,
    41–2, 47, 88, 147, 149, 189
Lawrence, Letitia Catherine (Henry's
    daughter), 150
Lawrence, Letitia Catherine Sr (née
    Knox), 13, 21, 37, 41, 48, 87
Lee, Harold, 6–7
Lewin, Lt., 21, 34
Londonderry/Derry, xi, xix, 1, 13, 15,
    17–19, 26, 32
Lord, Perceval, 143
Lucknow, ix, 2, 4, 19, 216 n.1
Ludhiana, 130–1, 134, 145, 159, 162

Maafeedars, 99
Macaulay, Thomas Babington, 66
MacGregor, Robert Guthrie, 58
Macnaghten, Sir William Hay, 7, 54,
    130–2, 138, 141, 143–4, 152–7, 160–6,
    187, 213
Macnaghten, Lady, 170–1, 176, 178,
    181–3,
Mackenzie, Holt, 77, 80, 98, 118
Mackenzie, Captain Colin, 156–7, 162,
    164–71, 177–8, 183–4, 186
Mackeson, Major Frederick, 179–81, 184
Mahalwari settlement, 77
Marshall, Revd George, 16
McLeod, Donald, 25, 232 n.91
Malcolm, Sir John, 202–3, 207, 212
Malikana allowance, 108
Meerut, 9, 42, 66, 90, 95, 105, 134
Merivale, Herman, 6
Metcalfe, Sir Charles, 53, 55, 62–3, 65–6,
    68, 93, 202, 212
    his 'Delhi system', 62–3, 92
Metcalfe, Thomas, 73–4, 147–8
Mohammed Sharif Fort, 157
Montgomery, Bernard Law, 232 n.96
Montgomery, (née Lambert), Ellen
    Jane, 116
Montgomery (née Thomason), Frances
    (Fanny), 56, 101–104, 114–5, 212
Montgomery, Frances Mary (daughter),
    102, 232 n. 91
Montgomery, Bishop Henry Hutchinson
    (son), 231 n.41, 232 n.96
Montgomery, James (brother), 15, 218 n.26
Montgomery, Mary Susan (daughter), 102,
    232 n.91

Montgomery, Robert,
    character & reputation, 7–8
    EIC nomination, 13–4
    Family background, 15
    Foyle College, 17–19
    Addiscombe Military Seminary,
        20–1, 23
    voyage to India, 28–9
    Calcutta, 31–2
    Azamgarh,
        description of, 94–6
        revenue settlement, 96–101
        and James Thomason, 95–6, 101–2
        tours of the district, 102–4
    Allahabad,
        description of, 105
        revenue settlement, 106–10
        female infanticide, 110–4
        death of wife, 114
        furlough, 115–6
    Cawnpore,
        description of residence, 116–7
        Statistical Report of the District, 117–21
        crime reduction on the GTR, 121–2
        the Tashma-baz Thugs, 122–6
    early deaths of children, 232 n.91
Montgomery, Robby Thomason (son), 102,
    232 n. 91
Montgomery, Revd Samuel Law
    (father), 15
Montgomery, Samuel (brother), 15
Montgomery, Susan (mother - née
    McClintock), 15
Mootsuddy, 49
Moradabad, xi, 9, 43, 46, 53, 60
Munro, Sir Thomas, 23, 202–3, 207
Muqaddam, 62–3, 108
Musa Khan, 177
Mussoorie, 198

Nehru, Jawaharlal, xx
Nicholson, John, xxi, 4, 14, 186
Nott, General William, 142, 152, 181, 185–6

Ochterlony, David, 23, 64–5
Outram, Captain James, 4, 140

Panchayat, 62–3, 97, 107
Panipat, 61, 67–70
    The Brothers, 71–2

Parwan Darra, 143–4
Paternalism, 1, 3, 8, 41, 63, 103, 117,
    202–3, 206–7, 212
Patronage, 11–14, 22, 65, 116, 147
Pattidari tenure, 91, 96
Patwari, 98
Peshawar, 7, 121, 130, 159, 166–8, 178–9,
    184, 206
Peshkar, 106–7
Pollock, General George, 178–81,
    183–7, 192
Potter, Beatrix, xix, xx
Pottinger, Major Eldred, 158, 167, 171–3,
    179, 186,
Pottinger, Henry, 14

Qalat-i-Ghilzai, 142, 152, 158
Qizilbash, 157, 160, 167, 176, 186
Quetta, 137, 181

Raikes, Charles, 66–70
Rajputs, 81, 111–3, 205
Rangurs, 81, 91
Revenue Settlements,
    Allahabad District (1838–9), 105–10
    Azamgarh District (1833–37),
        Atrowleeah Tilhenee *pargana*, 96–100
        Mahol *pargana*, 96, 99–100
        Suggree *pargana*, 96, 98–9
        Kowreeah *pargana*, 96–7, 99
        Gopalpore *pargana*, 96–7, 99
        Nizamabad *pargana*, 97, 99, 100
    Delhi District (1844), 90–3
    Gurgaon District (1837–8)
        Borah *pargana*, 77, 80–1, 84
        Jharsa *pargana*, 66, 77, 81, 84
        Palwal *pargana*, 77, 82, 84
        Rewari *pargana*, 77–80, 84
        Shahjahanpur *pargana*, 77, 84
        Taoru *pargana*, 77, 83–4
    Kaithal District (1843–4), 190–92
Richmond, Colonel A.F., 193
Rikab Bashi Fort, 157
Romanticism, 41, 62, 201–4

Sabathu, 150, 199
Sale, Lady Florentia, 7, 182–4,
Sale, General Robert, 143, 153, 161, 168,
    171, 178, 181
Scott, Hercules, 3

Scott, Walter, 21, 87, 203
Seringapatam, 14–5
Shah Shuja, 131, 136, 138, 140–4, 152–5,
    160–3, 167, 180, 186, 187, 209, 213
Shajra map, 45, 231 n.56
Shakespeare, Sir Richmond, 186
Shelton, Brigadier-General John, 154–61,
    169, 174–7, 187
Sheikh, Lieutenant-General K.N., xxi
Shewaki, Fort of, 183–4, 186
Shikarpur, 136
Simla, 41, 43, 47, 52, 58, 131, 141, 150
Simla, Manifesto of 1838, 131, 141
Singh, Chattar, 7
Singh, Dhian, 205–6, 208–9
Singh, Gulab, 168, 199, 205–6
Singh, Ranjit, 129–31, 214
    his character (*Adventures of an
        Officer*), 203–9
Singh, Suchet, 205, 208
Siyah Sang, 154–5, 169
Skinner, Colonel James Sr, 75
Skinner, Captain James Jr, 163, 165,
    170, 173
Sleeman, W.H., 74, 122, 124
Sparrow, Miss, 115
Spear, Professor Percival, 64
Stewart, Robert (Lord Castlereagh), 14
Stokes, Professor Eric, 63, 92
Sturt, Lieutenant John, 155
Sudder Board of Revenue, 44, 52–5, 58–9,
    78, 80, 84, 96, 98–100, 110, 213
Sultan Jan Barakzai, 164, 166, 171, 177

Tahsildar, 76, 78, 82, 84, 99, 112–3, 119,
    122, 124, 228 n.103
Talukdars, 85, 91, 108, 212
Tashma-bazee Thugs, 122–6
Temple, Sir Richard, 4, 5, 8, 17–19, 69,
    212
Thanadar, 70, 113, 122
Thugee, xvi, 8, 122–6,
Thomason, James,
    background & early career, 28, 95
    revenue survey changes, 52, 54–55, 60
    Directions for Settlement Officers, 78,
        80, 84
    Azamgarh revenue settlements, 96–101
    and Robert Montgomery, 101–2, 116
    Female infanticide, 112

and the propagation of government
     information, 117, 121
and crime reduction, 121
and Henry Lawrence's career, 147, 189,
     193–4, 211
Tod, Lieutenant Colonel James, 203
Trevelyan, Charles, 66
Trevor, Captain Robert, 156–7, 162, 164–5
Trotter, J.L., 4
Troup, Captain Colin, 183–5
Tucker, Henry Carre, 96, 101–2
Utilitarianism, 66, 92, 94, 111, 201–2

Vitkevitch, Ivan, 131
voyage to India, 28–9
Yule, Henry, 190

Wellesley, General Arthur, 9
Wellesley, Governor-General Richard, 9
Wade, Major Claude, 130, 134, 139, 213
Wild, Brigadier, 159, 167, 179
Woodruff, Philip (aka Philip Mason), 5

Zuman Khan, 166

Dear Reader,

We hope you have enjoyed this book, but why not share your views on social media? You can also follow our pages to see more about our other products: facebook.com/penandswordbooks or follow us on X @penswordbooks

You can also view our products at www.pen-and-sword.co.uk (UK and ROW) or www.penandswordbooks.com (North America).

To keep up to date with our latest releases and online catalogues, please sign up to our newsletter at: www.pen-and-sword.co.uk/newsletter

If you would like a printed catalogue with our latest books, then please email: enquiries@pen-and-sword.co.uk or telephone: 01226 734555 (UK and ROW) or email: uspen-and-sword@casematepublishers.com or telephone: (610) 853-9131 (North America).

We respect your privacy and we will only use personal information to send you information about our products.

Thank you!